THE EUROPEAN UNION SERIES

General Editors: Neill Nugent, William E. Paterson, Vincent Wright

The European Union series is designed to provide an authoritative library on the European Union, ranging from general introductory texts to definitive assessments of key institutions and actors, policies and policy processes, and the role of member states.

Books in the series are written by leading scholars in their fields and reflect the most up-to-date research and debate. Particular attention is paid to accessibility and clear presentation for a wide audience of students, practitioners and interested general readers.

The series consists of four major strands:

- General textbooks
- The major institutions and actors

- The main areas of policy
- The member states and the Union

The series editors are **Neill Nugent**, Professor of Politics and Jean Monnet Professor of European Integration, Manchester Metropolitan University, and **William E. Paterson**, Director of the Institute of German Studies, University of Birmingham.

Their co-editor until his death in July 1999, **Vincent Wright**, was a Fellow of Nuffield College, Oxford University. He played an immensely valuable role in the founding and development of *The European Union Series* and is greatly missed.

Feedback on the series and book proposals are always welcome and should be sent to Steven Kennedy, Palgrave, Houndmills, Basingstoke, Hampshire RG21 6XS, UK or by e mail to s.kennedy@macmillan.co.uk

---

General textbooks

Published

Desmond Dinan **Ever Closer Union: An Introduction to European Integration** (2nd edn) (Rights: World excluding North and South America, Philippines and Japan)

Desmond Dinan **Encyclopedia of the European Union** (Rights: Europe only)

Simon Hix **The Political System of the European Union**

John McCormick **Understanding the European Union: A Concise Introduction**

Neill Nugent **The Government and Politics of the European Union** (4th edn) (Rights: World excluding North and South America, Philippines and Japan)

John Peterson and Elizabeth Bomberg **Decision-Making in the European Union**

Ben Rosamond **Theories of European Integration**

Forthcoming

Simon Bulmer and Andrew Scott **European Union: Economics, Policy and Politics**

Andrew Scott **The Political Economy of the European Union**

Richard Sinnott **Understanding European Integration**

Also planned

The History of the European Union
The European Union Source Book
The European Union Reader

The major institutions and actors

Published

Renaud Dehousse **The European Court of Justice**

Justin Greenwood **Representing Interests in the European Union**

(continued overleaf)

The main areas of policy

The member states and the Union

The European Commission

Neill Nugent

palgrave

First published 2001 by
PALGRAVE
Houndmills, Basingstoke, Hampshire RG21 6XS and
175 Fifth Avenue, New York, N.Y. 10010
Companies and representatives throughout the world

PALGRAVE is the new global academic imprint of St. Martin's Press I.I.C.
Scholarly and Reference Division and Palgrave Publishers Ltd (formerly
Macmillan Press Ltd).

ISBN 0–333–58742–1 hardback
ISBN 0–333–58743–X paperback

This book is printed on paper suitable for recycling and
made from fully managed and sustained forest sources.

A catalogue record for this book is available
from the British Library.

Library of Congress Cataloging-in-Publication Data
Nugent, Neill.
    The European Commission/Neill Nugent.
      p. cm – (European Union series)
    Includes bibliographical references and index.
    ISBN 0-333-58742-1 (cloth) – ISBN 0-333-58743-X (pbk.)
      1. European Commission. I. Title. II. Series.

JN33.5.N84 2000
341.242'2–dc21

                                              00-040436

10   9   8   7   6   5   4   3   2   1
10   09   08   07   06   05   04   03   02   01

Copy-edited and typeset by Povey–Edmondson
Tavistock and Rochdale, England

Printed in China

Contents

List of Tables, Figure and Boxes

Tables

Figure

Boxes

Acknowledgements

At an early stage of researching this book some of the work, especially on the history of the Commission, was undertaken in collaboration with Stephen George. I am grateful to him for the insights and assistance he provided.

My thanks go to the many people in the Commission who granted me interviews and responded to written and telephone queries. Christina Leb was very helpful in arranging some of the interviews.

Desmond Dinan, William Paterson and Luisa Perrotti read the first draft of the manuscript and Martin Westlake read parts of it. I am very grateful to them for the excellent feedback they provided. Naturally, any errors, omissions or misinterpretations that remain in the book are wholly my responsibility.

As ever, I owe a large debt to my publisher, Steven Kennedy, for his customary encouragement and support.

Finally, I would like to thank my wife, Maureen, for her continuing tolerance and excellent wordprocessing, and also my daughters, Helen and Rachael, for their understanding.

NEILL NUGENT

List of Abbreviations

ABB	activity-based budgeting
ACP	African, Caribbean, and Pacific Countries
APS	annual policy strategy
CAP	Common Agricultural Policy
CCP	Common Commercial Policy
CCT	Common Customs Tariff
CEEC	Central and Eastern European Country
CEN	*Comité Européen de Normalisation* (European Committee for Standardisation)
CENELEC	European Committee for Electrotechnical Standardisation
CET	Common External Tariff
CFI	Court of First Instance
CFP	Common Fisheries Policy
CFSP	Common Foreign and Security Policy
CIE	Committee of Independent Experts
COPA	Committee of Agricultural Organisations in the European Union
CoR	Committee of the Regions
COREPER	Committee of Permanent Representatives
CSF	Community Support Framework
DECODE	Designing the Commission of Tomorrow
DG	Directorate General
DRAMS	dynamic random access memory chips
EACEM	European Association of Consumer Electronics Manufacturers
EAGGF	European Agricultural Guidance and Guarantee Fund
EBCG	European Biotechnology Coordinating Group
EC	European Community
ECHO	Humanitarian Aid Office
ECJ	European Court of Justice
Ecofin	Council of Economic and Finance Ministers
ECSC	European Coal and Steel Community
ecu	European Currency Unit
EDA	Group of the European Democratic Alliance

EDC	European Defence Community
EEA	European Economic Area
EEC	European Economic Community
EFTA	European Free Trade Association
EIB	European Investment Bank
EMS	European Monetary System
EMU	European Monetary Union
EP	European Parliament
EPC	European Political Community; *also* European Political Cooperation
EPP/ED	European People's Party and European Democrats
EPROMS	erasable programmable read-only memory
ERDF	European Regional Development Fund
ERM	Exchange Rate Mechanism
ERT	European Round Table of Industrialists
ESC	Economic and Social Committee
ESF	European Social Fund
ESPRIT	European Strategic Programme for Research and Development in Information Technology
ETUC	European Trade Union Confederation
EU	European Union
Euratom	European Atomic Energy Community
EUREKA	European Research Coordinating Agency
FAO	Food Agricultural Organisation (UN)
FTC	Federal Trade Commission (US)
G7	Group of Seven
GAP	*Group des Affaires Parlementaires*
GATT	General Agreement on Tariffs and Trade
GDP	Gross Domestic Product
GNP	Gross National Product
IAEA	International Atomic Energy Agency
ICT	information and communications technologies
IEA	International Energy Agency
IGC	Intergovernmental Conference
IMF	International Monetary Fund
IRI	Institute for Industrial Reconstruction (Italy)
IT	information technology
ITF–ICFTU	Committee of Transport Unions in the Community
JHA	Justice and Home Affairs
JRC	Joint Research Centre

MAP 2000	Modernisation of Administration and Personnel Policy
MEP	Member of the European Parliament
MTF	Merger Task Force
NATO	North Atlantic Treaty Organisation
NGO	non-governmental organisation
NTB	non-tariff barrier (to trade)
OECD	Organisation for Economic Cooperation and Development
OJ	Official Journal of the European Communities
OLAF	European Anti-Fraud Office
PDB	Preliminary Draft Budget
PHARE	Programme of Community Aid for Central and Eastern European Countries
QMV	qualified majority voting
R&TD	Research and Technological Development
RELEX	External Relations (*relations extérieurs*)
SCA	Special Committee on Agriculture
SEA	Single European Act
SEM	Single European Market
SEM 2000	Sound and Efficient Management
SLIM	Simpler Legislation for the Internal Market
SME	small and medium-sized enterprises
SPP	Strategic Planning and Programming
TAO	Technical Assistance Office
TEC	Treaty Establishing the European Community
TEU	Treaty on European Union
UK	United Kingdom
UN	United Nations
UNICE	Union of Industrial and Employers' Confederations of Europe
US	United States of America
VAT	value-added tax
WTO	World Trade Organisation

Introduction

'Brussels has decided that . . .

'Brussels has decided that . . .' This phrase and phrases like it are commonly used in political and media circles in the member states of the European Union (EU) to suggest two things. First, that specified policy and legislative decisions have not been taken by national decision-makers but by 'European' decision-makers. Second, that those European decision-makers are unidentifiable, unrepresentative and unaccountable bureaucrats based in the European Commission.

The first of these suggestions, that many key decisions are now taken at EU level rather than at national level, is accurate. Since the European Community (EC), on which the EU is largely based, was constituted in the 1950s there has been a steady expansion of EC, now EU, policy interests and responsibilities, to such an extent that there are now very few policy spheres that are not touched by the EU in some way. Even policy issues that traditionally have been seen as embodying national sovereignty – such as defence and immigration – are now on the EU agenda as states find they do not have the capacity to deal with them satisfactorily when acting by themselves.

The second suggestion, that the EU is run by shadowy Commission officials – 'faceless Eurocrats', to use the pejorative jargon – is misleading. One reason why it is so is that the Commission is, as compared with most national bureaucracies, both open and identifiable. Significant interests which wish to make contact with the Commission can usually gain access to appropriate officials, whilst the Commission's most senior figures, Commissioners, are as visible in their respective spheres of orbit as are national politicians in theirs. Indeed, the President of the Commission is the very public embodiment of the EU. Another, and more important, reason why the suggestion is not true is that the Commission is but one component – albeit a central component – of a highly complicated EU decision-making framework. The Commission does not run the EU. Rather, it is a key player in a network of institutions and actors which combine to make up the EU's governing system.

The purpose and structure of the book

The purpose of this book is to provide an account and an analysis of the development, nature, operation and functions of the Commission. An essentially empirical approach is taken, though it is one that is informed by theory in that it draws on and makes eclectic use of a wide range of conceptual and theoretical approaches to assist both description and explanation.

The book opens with a chapter that introduces key features of the Commission. Chapter 2 provides a history of the Commission, using a largely chronological approach but also noting important themes. Chapters 3–7 examine the main parts of the Commission, with chapters on the President, the College of Commissioners, Commissioners' *cabinets* (private offices), and the structures and personnel of the Commission services. Attention then turns to the Commission in action, with Chapter 8 focusing on the Commission's relations with other EU actors, Chapter 9 on the Commission and the provision of leadership, and Chapters 10–12 on three of the Commission's main responsibilities – contributing to the making of legislation, undertaking executive functions, and participating in the European Union's external relations. Chapter 13, the Conclusion, reviews central themes of the book.

Central themes

There are four central themes running through the book.

The first is that the Commission has the ability to exercise firm and independent influence in the EU system of governance, but that the extent of this ability varies greatly according to circumstances. It is argued that whilst the Commission is subject to a range of external controls and limitations in much of what it does, it is very far from being, as some commentators have suggested, little more than an agent of others. Rather, the Commission is shown to have power resources that in some operating contexts – the nature of which vary over time and between policy areas – can be used to exercise considerable influence in an independent, or at least semi-independent, manner. This theme, which takes the book into territory that has been the subject of a vigorous and much-contested debate between scholars about the nature of the European integration process and the role and impact of supranational actors therein, features most particularly in Chapters 1, 9, 10 and 12.

The second theme is that the Commission is something of a hybrid, being partly political and partly administrative in character. This results in internal tensions and difficulties, but also provides the Commission with opportunities. The hybrid nature of the Commission is seen most obviously in it having political and administrative arms. The political arm consists of the Commissioners, who are appointed via a highly politicised process, who are almost invariably former national politicians of senior status, and who are expected to provide the Commission's political direction and take its major decisions. The administrative arm consists of the Commission's services, whose staff are appointed on a (mainly) meritocratic basis and whose tasks are, in theory at least, primarily of an executive and administrative character.

The mixed political and administrative character of the Commission is seen also in the nature of the roles the Commission exercises in the EU system. Some roles, such as initiating policy proposals and mobilising support behind initiatives, are commonly thought of as being the responsibility of politicians, whilst others, such as implementing policies and managing budgets, are normally thought of as being the responsibility of bureaucrats. The fact that the Commission undertakes both of these types of roles results in it being involved in most aspects of EU activity, but also makes for problems. For example, it imposes considerable strains on resources, with there being a need, if all roles are to be undertaken effectively and efficiently, for there to be a wide range of different types of skills amongst Commission staff. In recent years a series of internal reports have revealed that not all relevant skills have been present in sufficient quantities, with management skills being especially lacking. Another type of problem arising from the exercise of political and administrative roles is that external political actors and observers often have different expectations of the Commission and of what its priorities should be. This can result in criticisms of the Commission for being, at one and the same time, both over- and under-reaching in its actions. Where criticisms are made for over-reaching, they are often accompanied by assertions that an unelected body should not be acting in so political a manner.

The hybrid nature of the Commission is touched on in some form in all chapters of the book. However, the extent and nature of the touching naturally varies. Chapters 3–5 concentrate on the component parts of the political arm, Chapters 6 and 7 on the component parts of the administrative arm, Chapters 8, 9 and 10 on political roles, and Chapter 11 on administrative roles.

The third theme is that although the Commission has in important respects been a reasonably stable institution over the years, it has also been constantly adjusting and changing. This is so in respect of its organisational structures, its methods of operating, and the roles it exercises. To take, for example, the roles, they have not, in essence, changed greatly since the early 1950s when the Commission's forerunner, the High Authority of the European Coal and Steel Community (ECSC), was founded. Now, as then, the Commission is mainly concerned with initiating policies, formulating laws, implementing and overseeing the implementation of laws, acting as a broker and mediator between other policy participants, and exercising various external functions. However, if the essential nature of the roles has not changed greatly since the early days of the High Authority, the scope of the responsibilities related to the roles most certainly has. They have done so in response to both the deepening of the European integration process, which has produced a progressive increase in the range and volume of policy activity, and in response to the widening of the integration process, which has seen the EC/EU grow in size from six to fifteen member states. This third theme – of change within a framework of stability – features in all chapters.

The fourth theme is that the Commission has long been, and still is, an institution with significant internal organisational problems. For many years these problems were seen as being most acute at the level of the College of Commissioners, with questions being asked from the early 1970s about the ideal size of the College, the powers that should be assigned to the Commission President, and the ways in which policy portfolios should be assigned between Commissioners. In recent years organisational weaknesses have increasingly been seen as needing to be addressed at administrative levels too, with evidence mounting of the existence of inefficient administrative practices.

The enforced resignation in March 1999 of the College of Commissioners led by Jacques Santer brought the need to address organisational weaknesses to a head. It did so because the circumstances of the resignation highlighted organisational problems at both political and administrative levels that just could not be ignored. Santer's successor as Commission President, Romano Prodi, was accordingly appointed very much on the basis of a mandate to reform, and since he and the

College he leads assumed office in September 1999 a major reform programme has been under way. Because this programme is extensive in scope, leaving virtually no part of the Commission untouched, it is examined in most chapters, but especially in Chapters 2, 4, 6, 7 and 11.

Fuller observations on these four central themes of the book are made in the Conclusion.

An assumption

The EU's system of governance, within which the Commission exists and functions, is highly complex, embracing a wide range of actors and a diversity of formal and informal mechanisms and processes. The assumption is made here that readers will already have some familiarity with this system of governance. For those who do not, sources include the author's own text (Nugent, 1999) and Dinan (1999) and McCormick (1999).

Chapter 1

Introducing the Commission

The composition and structure of the Commission

In legal terms, the Commission is a single entity and when it formally acts it always does so collectively. However in practice the Commission has two distinct levels, or arms: the College and the services. Somewhat confusingly, the word 'Commission' is commonly used to refer both to the College and to the Commission as a whole.

The College of Commissioners

There are currently twenty members of the College of Commissioners: two from each of the five largest member states (France, Germany, Italy, Spain and the United Kingdom) and one from each of the other ten member states (Austria, Belgium, Denmark, Finland, Greece, Ireland, Luxembourg, Netherlands, Sweden and Portugal). The highly politicised and drawn-out processes by which members of the College are appointed are examined in Chapter 4, as are the characteristics of Commissioners.

Commissioners used to be appointed for four years, but this was lengthened to five years by the 1992 Maastricht Treaty so as to bring the College's term of office into close alignment with that of the European Parliament (EP). The first College to be appointed to a five-year term was that which assumed office under the presidency of Jacques Santer in January 1995. This College became, however, the first not to complete its term of office when, amidst allegations of general incompetence and inappropriate behaviour by some of its members, it was forced to resign in March 1999.

The post of Commission President, which is examined in detail in Chapter 3, has become increasingly important over the years. Although the President does not command the range of powers within the College that national leaders normally command within their Cabinets/Council of Ministers, he (there has not yet been a female President) does stand significantly 'above' his College colleagues. Indeed, it is common for Colleges, and more broadly the Commission, to be referred to by the President's name. So, for example, the 1985–88 College is referred to, after Jaques Delors, as the Delors 1 Commission (Delors led three Colleges), the 1995–99 College is known as the Santer Commission, and the College that replaced the Santer College is referred to, after its President, Romano Prodi, as the Prodi Commission.

The College sits at the apex of the Commission. The approval of the College is necessary for all major initiatives and decisions that are taken in the Commission's name. Nothing of significance can be decided without being referred up the Commission system to the Commissioners. There is a strong tendency in the College towards consensual decision-making, so voting, though permissible, is rare. The members of the College hold policy portfolios in a manner that is similar to the ways in which ministers at national level are responsible for particular areas of policy. Within their designated policy spheres, Commissioners are the most senior individual figures in the Commission.

Because of the nature of its membership – most Commissioners are former senior national politicians – and its responsibilities, the College is frequently described as the political arm of the Commission.

The services

The services, which constitute the Commission's administrative arm, are relatively small in size, totalling officially just over 21 000 full-time employees (see Table 7.1, pp. 164–5) – about the same as a reasonably important ministry in a medium-sized member state or a large city council. The most senior officials in the services have traditionally been appointed on the basis of national and political considerations, whilst other staff have been recruited through open competition. Promotion policies have been somewhat arbitrary and politicised, with an accompanying large measure of time-serving below the most senior levels. As is shown in Chapter 7, reforms being carried out under the Prodi Commission are seeking to place the whole of personnel policy on a more meritocratic basis, though with some regard for balance beween nationals of the member states.

Like national administrations, the Commission's administration is sub-divided. The main sub-units are called Directorates General (DGs). The number of these is subject to periodic change, but in recent years there have been between twenty and twenty-five. Prior to the Prodi Commission all DGs were assigned a Roman numeral and it was by these, rather than by their name, that they were normally known. So, for example, the DG for Industry was known as DG III, the DG for Development as DG VIII, and the DG for Energy as DG XVII. In the interest of making the Commission, and the EU as a whole, more transparent and understandable, Prodi decided to remove the numerals, so DGs are now referred to by their – in some cases streamlined – names.

Other sub-units are not constituted as DGs but rather as special services. Prominent amongst these are the Secretariat General, which has as its main task the promotion of effective internal coordination between the many different parts of the Commission, and the Joint Interpreting and Conference Service, which undertakes the heavy interpretation workload which follow upon the EU having eleven officially recognised languages.

The Commission's multi-dimensional nature

The Commission is often portrayed as being a homogeneous and monolithic institution, but in fact it is composed of many parts and contains within its ranks a wide range of different views and interests. As Cram (1994) has put it, the Commission is a complex 'multi-organisation'.

The most obvious distinction within the Commission is that between the political (College) and administrative (services) arms. Relations between the two are by no means always harmonious and have often been characterised by tension and friction. Commissioners and their personal staff – the latter of whom are located in *cabinets*, or private offices – at times feel that the services prefer to concentrate too much on their own agenda rather than giving full support to Commissioners' initiatives and policy preferences. For their part, the services sometimes feel that their work is undervalued by Commissioners and *cabinets*, and they frequently feel that *cabinet* officials interfere too much and too directly in the work of the services. Very soon after being nominated as Commission President-designate Prodi made it clear that one of his central organisational goals would be to bring the political and administrative arms of the Commission into a much closer and more harmonious working relationship (Prodi, 1999a, 1999b).

The political and administrative arms are themselves internally segmented, with Commissioners having to concentrate primarily on their portfolios rather than looking to the performance of the Commission as a whole and with services being obliged to focus on matters within their specified areas of responsibility. This segmentation can be a source of internal tension and friction within the Commission.

In the College, tensions and frictions sometimes arise, especially in cross-sectoral policy areas, over who is responsible for particular aspects of policy. This has, for example, long been a problem in the sphere of external policies, where Commissioners' portfolios are not wholly self-contained but rather overlap at the edges. With most Commissioners wanting to be responsible for as much as possible, 'turf disputes' can sometimes become decidedly sharp.

In the services, a common problem is differences between DGs over policy priorities and policy methods. One such persisting example is attitudes towards the management of the internal market, with the Competition DG long having adopted a strongly liberal/non-interventionist stance and DGs such as Transport and Regional Policy having been sympathetic to specific forms of public support and intervention in particular circumstances. Several commentators relate such policy content and policy style differences to cultural differences within the Commission, with the behaviour and actions of officials being seen to be at least partly influenced by identities officials have either assumed or brought with them. These identities are based along a number of lines, some of which are mutually reinforcing and others of which are cross-cutting. The most important identities are normally identified as being location within the Commission and nationality. Regarding location, studies have shown how some DGs virtually have their own sub-cultures, into which newcomers are usually quickly absorbed (see, for example, Abélèles, Bellier and McDonald, 1993; Cini,1996a, 1996b, 1997). Regarding nationality, studies reveal that whilst national practices and traditions are partly combined in a 'cultural compromise' (Abélès and Bellier, 1996), they are not totally extinguished and they do play a part in the everyday functioning of the Commission – especially where there are clusters of national officials (McDonald, 1997).

The functions of the Commission

The institutional structure of the EU positions the Commission at the very heart of the EU's system of governance. It has at least some involvement with every aspect of EU affairs and it is a direct participant at virtually every stage of EU policy and decision-making.

The central position occupied by the Commission in the EU system means that it undertakes a wide variety of functions. Most of these functions are provided for by the EU's treaties, though usually in only generally defined terms – as with Article 211 (ex-155*) of the Treaty Establishing the European Community (TEC) which, amongst other things, states that the Commission shall 'formulate recommendations or deliver opinions on matters dealt with in this treaty, if it expressly so provides or if the Commission considers it necessary'. A few functions have no explicit treaty base at all but are a consequence rather of practical necessities and/or of views within and outside the Commission as what it should be doing.

The nature of the functions

The Commission's functions are examined later in the book. Three functions – the legislative, executive and external – are given their own chapters, whilst others are examined at various places in Chapters 8–12. All, therefore, that will be attempted here will be an identification of and an introduction to the main functions. They are as follows:

Policy initiator   The Commission promotes and develops many of the policy initiatives that are launched at EU level. It is best known for launching proposals in respect of what may be thought of as grand and overarching policies, but in volume terms most of its initiatives are focused on detailed policies in particular sectors. Whether, however, grand or specific policies are concerned, the initiation and development process customarily involves activities ranging from floating ideas and promoting dialogue with interested parties to drawing up and issuing policy documents.

---

*The Treaty on European Union and the Treaty Establishing the European Community were renumbered following the 1997 Treaty of Amsterdam. This book uses the new numbering system, but on the first reference to well known and well used articles the former number is given in brackets.

A resource that is of considerable use to the Commission in enabling it to initiate policy debate and proposals is that it is generally recognised as being the main repository of 'the Union interest' – or, as it is still frequently referred to, 'the Community interest'. This is a very ill-defined and loose notion, but it helps the Commission to present itself as acting in the interests of the whole, as being 'the conscience of the Union' rather than, as is often the suspicion when initiatives stem from other sources, a particular interest. The notion also means that Commission proposals are not seen as representing, as Council proposals frequently are, the sum total or the lowest common denominator of national interests. The Commission is thus well placed to be, as it described itself in its submission to the 2000 Intergovernmental Conference (IGC), 'the driving force behind European integration' (Commission, 2000e: 11).

Legislative functions The Commission is, in several ways, crucial to the making of EU legislation. First, under the EC pillar of the EU it has the exclusive right to draft legislative proposals, save for a few exceptions in the justice and home affairs policy sphere. (Legislation is not made under the second and third pillars of the EU – the Common Foreign and Security Policy (CFSP) and Police and Judicial Cooperation in Criminal Matters pillars.) Second, alone of the EU institutions, the Commission is represented at, and can contribute to, all legislative stages – including those that are conducted in the Council of Ministers and the EP – which makes it ideally placed to be able to undertake the inter-institutional conciliation and brokeraging that EU legislative processes have come to require. Third, the Commission can employ useful power resources as proposals make their way through legislative processes – with, for instance, its subject expertise meaning that the Council and the EP may have to bow to it on technical/information grounds. Fourth, most administrative legislation is not subject to a full legislative examination but is made in the name of the Commission – usually via committees of national representatives which, though not rubber stamps, do not usually cause the Commission too many difficulties.

Executive functions The Commission undertakes executive responsibilities of a number of different kinds. For the most part these responsibilities are more concerned with setting out the ground rules and monitoring and coordinating the activities of others than they are with directly implementing policies and laws itself.

Responsibility for the implementation of EU policies and laws can be thought of as being stretched along a spectrum, with the Commission carrying the main responsibility at one end and agencies of various sorts doing so at the other. The only major policy area where the Commission carries extensive direct implementation responsibilities is competition policy, although there are parts of several other policies – usually the funding parts – where there is also direct implementation. Where the Commission is not the direct implementer it still has executive responsibilities to perform. Two of these responsibilities are especially important. First, the Commission draws up and issues administrative legislation: that is, the detailed rules that it is not possible to incorporate in treaties or primary legislation but which are vital in policy areas where circumstances change quickly and where highly specific, often very technical, regulation is required. Second, so as to ensure that policies are applied in a reasonably consistent manner throughout the EU, the Commission attempts to supervise, or at least keep a watching brief on, the outside agencies that are responsible for most direct implementation.

Legal guardian   Closely related to, and overlapping with, its supervisory responsibilities, the Commission has a legal guardianship function. This function, which is exercised in association with the European Courts – the Court of Justice (ECJ) and the Court of First Instance (CFI) – involves ensuring that the EU's treaties and legislation are respected. As is shown in Chapter 11, it is an extremely difficult function to perform since infringements of EU law can be very difficult to detect, and when they are so there are often reasons – economic, social and political – which make it questionable as to whether they should be pursued.

Infringements can take many different forms, but whoever the suspected infringer may be, and whatever the suspected nature of the infringement, the Commission is obliged to deal with each case it chooses to investigate with great care and according to procedures that are specified in the treaties. All parties who are investigated are given a full opportunity to explain themselves and to refute any allegations made against them. If the Commission finds that an infringement has occurred it has the power to impose financial penalties, which can be subject to judicial appeal.

External representative and negotiator   The Commission undertakes many external responsibilities on behalf of the EU. These have grown in importance as the EU has become an increasingly significant international actor. The nature of the responsibilites are described in Chapter 12, so comment here will be limited to making the general point that the responsibilities are far from confined to the sphere of external activity with which the EU and the Commission are most commonly associated, namely trade. Amongst responsibilities that are non-trade or non-exclusively trade in character are the management of development aid, association with the work carried out under the EU's CFSP pillar, and numerous tasks in regard to the process of EU enlargement.

Mediator and broker   In the EU's multi-actor, multi-interest, multi-view system, in which policy processes are many, varied and often complex, there is frequently a need for mediation and brokerage functions to be performed so as to allow policy participants to have confidence in the system and to enable decisions to be made and be applied. The Commission is by far the best-placed actor to perform these functions. It is so for three main reasons. First, it is obliged by treaty to be non-partisan in its behaviour and actions. Under Article 213 (ex-157) of the TEC, Commissioners are charged to act in 'the general interest' and to be 'completely independent in the performance of their duties'. They 'shall neither seek nor take instructions from any government or from any other body'. These stipulations are generally respected, with the result that the Commission is generally regarded as an honest broker when, for example, it advances suggestions and proposals for tackling difficulties and resolving problems. Second, the Commission is often in the best position to judge how a concerned or aggrieved policy actor can be assuaged, how a problem may be resolved, and what approach is likely to command support amongst decision-makers. This is because of the Commission's knowledge of the nature and functioning of the EU, which is derived in no small part from the fact that in most policy sectors the Commission is usually present at every stage of the policy cycle, from initiation to evaluation. Third, embedded in the internal culture and thinking of the Commission are attitudes that help to underpin the exercise of these functions. For example, officials recognise almost as a matter of course the difficulties that can arise if an important policy actor, especially a member state, becomes dissatisfied over a matter, which naturally results in them encouraging and assisting actors to find solutions to problems when that seems to be desirable or necessary.

The Commission is thus well placed to undertake much of the mediation and brokering that is necessary if the EU system is to operate in a harmonious and efficient manner. The mediating and brokering functions are undertaken in many contexts and vary considerably in nature. They range from trying to reach accommodations with governments of member states on problems they may be experiencing in implementing existing EU laws to identifying ways in which differences within and between the Council of Ministers and the EP in the framework of legislative and budgetary decision-making procedures can be reconciled.

Mobiliser   If an initiative is to advance at EU level it must achieve wide support. Preferably, it should be supported by all the main policy actors who have a direct interest, be they institutional, governmental, or non-governmental. At a minimum it must command the support of the principal decision-makers.

The diversity of interests existing in the EU means that sufficient support is usually not automatically forthcoming for initiatives, wherever they may come from and whatever form they take. Rather, support usually has to be mobilised. The Commission frequently exercises such a mobilising role. Amongst the ways it does so are the following: Commissioners and their representatives meet with decision-makers, opinion formers and the leaders of important interests; Commission members and officials address gatherings of interested and affected parties in the member states; the merits and advantages of initiatives are explained by Commission representatives when opportunities arise in the many forums in which they engage with other policy actors on a regular basis – such as in Commission advisory committes, in Council meetings at their different levels, and in EP committees; and policy documents of an explanatory and consultative nature are issued regularly.

This mobilising function is closely related to the mediating and brokering functions that were identified above. It is, however, perhaps a rather more pro-active function in that it tends to involve more in the way of initiating and pressing on the part of the Commission. Sometimes, indeed, what happens is that the Commission spots favourable circumstances for the development of an initiative and, acting as a 'purposeful opportunist' (Cram, 1993, 1997), seeks to take advantage of the circumstances by bringing key actors together to help develop policy and/or persuade them that a particular course of action is desirable.

Tensions between functions

There are tensions between some of the Commission's functions, with the skills and resources that are necessary for the effective and efficient undertaking of some functions not necessarily being the same as those that are required for others.

Over thirty years ago David Coombes, in a study of the early Commission, noted the emergence of what has subsequently been the main tension between roles, namely that between being a promoter of integration on the one hand and a policy administrator on the other (Coombes, 1970). The former role requires dynamic and innovative leadership whilst the latter is dependent on more routine and bureaucratic capacities. Until recently, insufficient attention was given to ensuring that the routine and bureaucratic capacities were in good order. Under the presidency of Jacques Delors in particular they were neglected with, as Anand Menon has observed 'the Commission's workload, rather than how well the work was done, [being] taken as the measure of its standing' (Menon, 1999: 14).

Another example of tension between roles concerns mediating and mobilising. It can be difficult for the Commission to appear to be neutral and to successfully broker a compromise on, say, a policy proposal when it has previously been attempting to convince policy actors that the proposal should take a particular form.

A central (and independent?) policy actor

The Commission is not the formal and final EU decision-maker on major issues – the European Council, the Council of Ministers and the EP have greater powers in that regard – but on most matters that concern the EU it is an extremely important policy actor. Even in spheres of activity where its treaty powers are weak, its influence usually looms large.

As the EU has extended its policy reach over the years, so has the extent of Commission influence grown. This is no more clearly seen than in regard to the creation of the Single European Market (SEM), which has been at the heart of much policy activity since the 'relaunch' of the European integration project in the mid-1980s. Although the SEM programme is usually thought of as being deregulatory in character, much of it in fact has consisted of transferring regulation from the national to the European level. The transfers have covered not just narrowly defined market-related matters such as product specifications and trading conditions but also a wide range of social measures such as working conditions and consumer protection. As Majone (1994) has pointed out, regulatory activity normally requires a high degree of administrative and technical discretion and an expertise that tends to privilege administrative power over political power – which in the EU context means that the Commission is privileged more than any other EU actor.

Fitzmaurice has described the Commission as being 'animateur, impressario and manager . . . the "player manager" of the EU system' (1994: 181). This very much captures the diversity of the Commission's roles, some of which are political in nature in that they involve providing leadership, drive and mediation between the many participants in EU's policy processes, and others of which are more managerial and administrative in character in that they are concerned with the execution of policies, laws and budgets. The Commission has been assigned and assumed functions and responsibilities that have resulted in it taking on some of the characteristics of a government and some of the characteristics of a secretariat cum civil service. In power terms, it is perhaps best thought of as being somewhere between the two – a hybrid, with powers which are less than those exercised by governments in national settings but which are much greater than those exercised by secretariats of other international organisations.

The role of the Commission in the EU system, and more particularly the extent to which the Commission can act independently and autonomously when using its powers and undertaking its functions, has been the subject of an extensive and lively debate amongst scholars. At one end of a wide spectrum of views is the intergovernmentalist position, which sees the Commission essentially as an agent of the member states, facilitating their ability to take decisions and implementing the decisions they take, but not itself acting in a manner that does anything much more than reflecting and applying the will of the member states as expressed via the European Council and Council of Ministers. The best known proponent of this position is Andrew Moravcsik (1991, 1993, 1995, 1998). At the other end of the spectrum is the supranational position, which acknowledges that the member states are the EU's main formal decision-takers but suggests that they are frequently guided and led in what they do by a Commission that is, in important respects, relatively independent. Amongst those who, broadly speaking, subscribe to this position are Daniel Wincott

(1995), Janne Matláry (1997a, 1997b) and Sandholtz and Stone Sweet (1998).

Scholarly perspectives on the autonomy/dependence of the Commission are explored at some length in Chapter 9. Let it be made clear here, however, that the working assumption of this book is that although it is certainly true that the governments of the member states have been reluctant to allow the Commission too much latitude – as is witnessed by their creation and maintenance of various control mechanisms on Commission decision-making – the evidence nonetheless indicates that in some policy areas and in some circumstances the Commission does enjoy a considerable amount of independence and does exercise a significant degree of autonomy. To take, for example, agenda-setting in the EC pillar, numerous case studies have shown the Commission to be the main instigator of ideas, initiatives, and proposals that have worked their way through decision-making processes to become established policy. The Commission is able to exercise such agenda-setting influence because it is in possession of a range of appropriate power resources: it has, for example, the formal power to table policy and legislative proposals; it has access to privileged information of a technical nature; it is well placed to be able to judge the political climate – not least because it is usually aware of the likely reactions of national governments to initiatives; and it is at the centre of a host of useful and potentially influential policy networks.

But whatever viewpoint is taken regarding the independence and autonomy of the Commission, the fact is that it is a central EU policy actor. In undertaking its numerous duties and functions it is required to use and display a wide range of skills and qualities. It must, for example, be innovative and proactive, especially in relation to policy development. It must be responsive to the needs and preferences of others, especially the member states and the other main EU institutions. And it must be vigilant and efficient, especially in respect of financial management and the implementation of sensitive policies and laws.

Concluding remarks

The Commission is a unique institution in terms of its membership, organisation and functions. Taking functions to illustrate this point, the Commission exercises not only administrative functions of the kind that are normally undertaken by bureaucracies but also political functions that are normally the responsibility of political executives. The exercise of its political functions results in the Commission exerting a considerable influence not only on day-to-day events and on specific policy issues, but on the European integration process as a whole.

The various aspects of the Commission's uniqueness that have been introduced in this chapter are examined at length later in the book.

Chapter 2

The History of the Commission

Introduction

Until 1967 each of the three Communities that were founded in the 1950s had its own executive authority. These authorities were the High Authority of the European Coal and Steel Community (ECSC), the Commission of the European Atomic Energy Community (Euratom), and the Commission of the European Economic Community (EEC). The 1965 Treaty Establishing a Single Council and a Single Commission of the European Communities, which came into effect in July 1967, merged the High Authority and the two Commissions into one Commission of the European Communities. This single Commission was re-named the European Commission following the creation of the European Union (EU) in the Maastricht Treaty.

This chapter examines the history of the Commission in its various guises. An important theme of the chapter is that whilst the Commission has been constantly developing, a surprisingly large number of its core features emerged in its very early years.

The High Authority of the European Coal and Steel Community, 1952–67

The creation of the High Authority

In May 1950 Robert Schuman, the French Foreign Minister, proposed, in what became known as the Schuman Declaration, that France and Germany pool their markets for coal and steel, that the pool be managed by a High Authority with independent powers to act, and that any democratic European country which accepted these principles join France and Germany in negotiations. (The Schuman Declaration is reproduced in Salmon and Nicoll, 1997: 44–6.)

Much of the planning behind the Schuman Declaration had been undertaken by Jean Monnet, the former head of the post-war French Planning Commission and 'one of those people who are best described as "entrepreneurs in the public interest"' (Duchêne, 1994: 61). Underlying Monnet's thinking was the view that the creation of a commonly administered common market for coal and steel could provide the foundations for Franco–German, and more broadly Western European, reconciliation. It could do so both economically and politically: economically by demonstrating the shared advantages that could accrue from the dismantling of economic barriers and the pooling of resources; politically by requiring political elites to work together in a common organisational framework.

Monnet's preference was for the organisational framework of the ECSC to be highly supranational in character, with the executive High Authority being given extensive powers over the coal and steel industries and not being subject to institutional control by the governments of the member states. This view was, however, challenged during the negotiations between France, Germany, Italy and the three Benelux countries that led to the 1951 Treaty of Paris which created the ECSC. The Benelux countries, which in later years were to strongly support supranational developments, were particularly suspicious, believing that the High Authority might be dominated by Franco–German interests. As a result, during the course of the negotiations a Common Assembly and, more significantly, a Council of Ministers were added to the institutional framework. The Assembly was to be drawn from national parliaments and was given only limited powers but the Council of Ministers, whose members were to be national ministers, was given a wide range of important powers.

The decision to create the Council meant the High Authority would not be as independent or as powerful as Monnet has hoped, though the duties of its members were described in the Treaty as being supranational in character. Nonetheless, the High Authority was still assigned significant powers. Some matters it could decide on its own – including the imposition of levies and the contracting of loans to carry out its tasks, the guaranteeing or the granting of investment loans to undertakings, and the authorisation and prohibition of practices effecting competition in the market. Some matters it could decide only after consulting the Council – including the initiation and facilitation of research and the definition of unfair pricing practices.

And some matters it could not take decisions on, but it could bring forward initiatives and proposals for approval by the Council – including the setting of minimum and maximum customs duties and, in the event of a decline in demand, the declaration of a period of 'manifest crisis' and the establishment of a system of production quotas.

Virtually no attention was given by either Monnet or the national governments to the question of whether the High Authority should be given some sort of direct democratic base. Insofar as the legitimacy of the High Authority was considered it was assumed to stem from its establishment by democratic governments, the controls that would be placed on it by the Council and its position as a non-partisan, technocratic, expert body.

The composition of the High Authority was the subject of considerable debate during the treaty-making negotiations. France and Germany, prompted in no small degree by Monnet, wanted there to be just five members so as to emphasise that the High Authority was not to be a body of national representatives. This, however, was not acceptable to the Benelux countries which, largely because of their concerns about Franco–German domination, insisted that the membership should include a national from each member state. It was eventually agreed that there should be nine members: two from each of France and Germany; one from each of Belgium, the Netherlands, Luxembourg and Italy; and a ninth member to be coopted by the other eight members. All members were to be chosen 'on the grounds of their general competence' and their independence was to be 'beyond doubt'.

The seat of the High Authority was to be in Luxembourg.

Organisational features of the High Authority

Drawing on the model of the French Planning Commission, which he himself had largely created, Monnet wanted the High Authority to be an innovative organisation that was adventurous in spirit and open to new ideas. Routine and detailed work should be left, as far as possible, to national authorities.

In line with his vision of what its role should be, Monnet wanted the High Authority to be small, non-hierarchical, and informal (Conrad, 1989: 21). As he said shortly after being appointed the first President of the High Authority, 'If one day there are more than two hundred of us, we shall have failed' (Monnet, 1978: 405). Rather than a structured framework being imposed, it should be recognised that the High Authority was a new type of institution which must be able to evolve in a manner appropriate to the tasks it had to perform.

In the event, Monnet's hopes were quickly dashed. A heavier than anticipated workload, stemming largely from an increasing involvement in the management and administration of policies, resulted in the size of the ECSC's staff numbering approximately 550 employees within two years of the organisation beginning its operations in July 1952 (Merry, 1955: 169). This increasing workload and size, coupled with evidence that the non-hierarchical structure was creating delays in decision-making, duplications of effort, overlapping competences, and inadequate internal coordination, resulted in a movement towards a more bureaucratic structure and hierarchical mode of operation. According to Mazey (1992: 43), between 1952 and 1956 'the administrative services of the High Authority . . . were transformed from an informal grouping of sympathetic individuals into a professional bureaucracy which, in terms of its structure and "technocratic" character, resembled the French administration'. Spierenburg and Poidevin (1994: 246–51) date the bureaucratisation of the Higher Authority a little later than Mazey, suggesting that it did not get fully under way until René Mayer – a former French Prime Minister and senior civil servant who took a much greater interest in the administrative functioning of the High Authority than had Monnet – succeeded Monnet as President in June 1955. Though, however, Spierenburg and Poideven are not wholly in accord with Mazey on dates, they fully agree with her on key essentials: the initial open organisational style was unsuccessful and within a few years it had been replaced by a more traditional bureaucratic model that incorporated many features of the French administrative system.

The model that was established from the mid-1950s thus saw a movement away from Monnet's preferences on the organisational character of the High Authority. In particular: hierarchical and formal structural lines supplanted horizontal and informal lines; recruitment procedures, which initially also had been informal, were standardised and placed on a more openly meritocratic basis; the notion of informal national quotas at senior administrative levels was introduced, thus undermining Monnet's principle of always choosing 'the best'; and a larger gap than Monnet had wanted opened between the High Authority's members and officials.

The record of the High Authority

The record of the High Authority over its fifteen year lifespan was mixed.

On the credit side, it certainly played an important part, especially in its early years, in helping to remove many – though by no means all – trading restrictions within its spheres of sectoral competence. The more open trading environment that was thereby created appears to have been an important factor, along with generally favourable economic circumstances, in promoting increased volumes of production and trade. Also on the credit side, the High Authority helped to promote, as Urwin (1995: 55) puts it, 'a European ambience and presence': both member and non-member states were obliged to recognise its existence and its influence.

On the debit side, the High Authority was not able to establish itself as the dynamic and forceful institution for which Monnet had hoped. Rather, it tended to operate in a cautious manner. The main reason for this was that the governments of the member states did not take easily to having their sovereignty circumscribed by a supranational body when important national interests were at stake. As early as 1954 Merry was commenting that 'In political, and perhaps in economic matters, there is little doubt but that the Council of Ministers constitutes a strong check upon the High Authority' (1955: 181). Knowing that the governments of the member states were paying very close attention to its activities resulted in the High Authority tending to consult with, and pay close attention to the wishes of, the Council even it was not required to do so by the Treaty. It also resulted in relations between the High Authority and national governments frequently being uneasy. As Spierenburg and Poidevin (1994: 649–50) have noted: 'Governments had conflicting interests, and they had no intention of giving the High Authority *carte blanche*. In the Council they were keen to defend their national interests and regularly dismissed High Authority proposals whenever those interests were under threat.'

These High Authority–national government difficulties and tensions came to a head in 1959 when the Council did not support High Authority proposals for tackling a crisis in the coal industry. When the ECSC had been launched coal had been in short supply, but by the beginning of 1959 it was clear that there was overproduction and surplus stocks. These had come about mainly as a result of the increasing use of oil, a slowing down of economic growth, and two successive mild winters. The High Authority responded to the situation by asking the Council for emergency powers to impose import controls and production quotas through the declaration of a manifest crisis. The request was refused. It was so for a variety of different national reasons, not least that France and Germany were wary of giving the High Authority too many powers. Thereafter, the High Authority's prestige and standing was seriously undermined, as was demonstrated in the 1960s when its efforts to progress the development of a common energy policy made little headway.

The Commission of the European Economic Community, 1958–67

The creation of the EEC Commission

In October 1950, only a few months after the Schuman Declaration, the French Prime Minister, René Pleven, proposed that a European Defence Community (EDC) be established. Shortly after the signing of the ECSC Treaty in April 1951 the six ECSC countries duly opened negotiations on the EDC and in May 1952 an EDC Treaty was signed in Paris. There was, however, stiff resistance in France to the ratification of the EDC and the European Political Community (EPC) that came to be associated with it, most particularly from the Gaullists who objected to any notion of supranationalism in a policy area so central to national sovereignty, and from the Communists who were closely allied with the Soviet Union. Aware that a ratification motion was likely to be defeated in the National Assembly, the French Government prevaricated, but eventually called a procedural motion in August 1954 on whether the Treaty ought to be discussed. The motion was heavily defeated and the EDC project thereby collapsed.

The collapse of the EDC was a major setback for the cause of European integration. However, it did not bring an end to, or even much of a pause in, efforts to advance the integration process. Rather, it led to many leaders and prominent political figures in the six ECSC countries looking for alternative, and less politically sensitive, ways and approaches. Many different ideas were advanced as to how best to proceed, but there was a general acceptance that the EDC experience had demonstrated that overt political integration implying significant extensions in supranationalism was too sensitive and that attention ought to be concentrated more on economic integration. In this context, the debate increasingly focused around two broad sets of ideas. On the one hand, there were those who championed the merits of a general economic customs union and beyond that of a common market. The governments of the Benelux countries and of West Germany increasingly inclined to this position. On the other hand there were those who were more cautious and who argued that the next integration stage should build on the ECSC sectoral approach by widening it to such key policy areas as transport and energy. This tended to be the preference of the French Government, but not on a wholly consistent basis since the composition of the Government kept changing.

In June 1955 at Messina the Foreign Ministers of the ECSC states met to discuss further integration. Their deliberations resulted in the establishment of a committee under the chairmanship of the Belgian Foreign Minister, Paul-Henri Spaak, to study ways in which a fresh advance towards the building of a new Europe could be achieved. The Spaak Committee reported in April 1956 and recommended that attention should be focused on the establishment of a common market and a nuclear energy community. The Committee's deliberations on these two topics were then developed into formal negotiations in the framework of an intergovernmental conference, which led to the signing in March 1957 of two Treaties of Rome: one establishing the EEC and the other establishing Euratom.

Of the three Communities that were created in the 1950s, the EEC was given by far the broadest remit. In the words of Article 2 of the EEC Treaty:

> The Community shall have as its task, by establishing a common market and progressively approximating the economic policies of Member States, to promote throughout the Community a harmonious development of economic activities, a continuous and balanced expansion, an increase in stability, an accelerated raising of the standard of living and closer relations between the States belonging to it.

To pursue this general task and a range of more specific tasks that were set out in other Treaty articles, an institutional structure based on the ECSC model was created. Two of the ECSC's four main institutions – the Assembly and the Court – were to be expanded in size and their remit extended to the three Communities, whilst the

High Authority and the Council of Ministers were given their own counterparts in the two new Communities.

Reflecting the mood that followed upon the collapse of the EDC, and a feeling that the name 'High Authority' was over-grand, 'High Authority' was replaced with 'Commission' for both the EEC and Euratom. In the same spirit, the word 'supranational' did not appear in the 1957 treaties to describe the duties of Commissioners. (The word was subsequently deleted from the ECSC Treaty when it was amended by the 1965 Merger Treaty.)

Both Commissions were to be more subject to control by the Council than was – in formal treaty terms at least – the High Authority. This was partly because of the prevailing mood in respect of supranationalism, but was also partly because both of the two new Communities were perceived as being potentially more important than the ECSC – the EEC because of its wide remit and Euratom because of the sensitivity of its subject matter.

The main duties explicitly assigned to the Commission in the EEC Treaty were proposing legislative measures (an exclusive right), overseeing the implementation of EEC policies and laws, and representing the Community in trade negotiations with third parties. A less explicit duty was that it should take initiatives and bring forward proposals which furthered the general aims and interests of the Community as specified in the Treaty. Given that the Treaty defined some of those aims and interests in only the most general of terms, this duty allowed for the possibility of the Commission being a highly pro-active agenda-setter and being a key player in the future development of the European integration process.

Like the High Authority, but unlike the Euratom Commission (see below), the EEC Commission was to have nine members. They were to be appointed 'by common accord of the Governments of the Member States', with no more than two members of the nationality of the same state. The duty of these members was to serve the interests of the Community as a whole rather than those of member states, as several provisions of Article 157 of the Treaty made clear: the independence of Commissioners was to be 'beyond doubt'; Commissioners should, 'in the general interest of the Community, be completely independent in the performance of their duties'; and '[i]n the performance of these duties, [Commissioners] shall neither seek nor take instructions from any Government or any other body'. During the nine years of the EEC Commission, there was a total of only 14 Commissioners. Seven were former national politicians, all of whom had been either senior or junior ministers, and seven were former civil servants, academics, or 'technicians'.

Virtually as soon as the EEC Commission was established it was decided to make use of a support system for Commissioners that had been employed, but not much developed, for members of the High Authority: *cabinets*. Based largely on the French *cabinet* system, Commissioners' *cabinets* were to be small private offices personally appointed by, and accountable to, the Commissioner. They were to undertake a wide range of political and administrative tasks, some of which – such as acting as unofficial and innovative think tanks, offering tactical advice, and acting as antennae for Commissioners – were thought to be not suitable for, or to be not the *forte* of, 'regular' Commission officials. The size of *cabinets* was limited initially to four officials for the Commission President and two for other Commissioners, but this grew as the tasks being undertaken by *cabinets* grew. By the end of the 1960s *cabinets* were not only providing key services for their individual Commissioners but were undertaking vital services for the Commission and the Community as a whole – most particularly by acting as intermediaries and brokers between Commissioners, between Commissioners and the services, and between the Commission and the member states.

The important role that was quickly assumed by *cabinets* is but one of many ways in which French practices strongly influenced the construction and development of the EEC Commission. Other ways included the designing of the Commission's structure along the lines of the High Authority (which, as was shown above, was itself modelled on the French Planning Commissariat), an acceptance from the outset that a certain politicisation of administrative organisation and functioning was normal, and the systems established for staff recruitment and grading which, according to Page (1997: 7), were similar to those long used by France. However, other influences were also important, and became more so as the Commission developed. As Berlin (1988: 38–9), Cassese (1988a: 12–13), and Stevens (2000) show, the Commission was established and built on the foundations of a mixture of administrative structures, patterns and styles. Initially, the most important of these patterns and styles unquestionably derived from the French administrative system, but as the EEC acquired more functions and duties German influences in particular became apparent. This was partly because the President of the EEC Commission throughout its nine-year existence was a German, Walter Hallstein, and partly because from the early 1960s Germany became less reticent about pressing its views and preference in international settings. The German influence on the character of the Commission was not, and never has been, commensurate with the influence that might have been expected from such a large state, but it certainly helped to shape, for example, the more hierarchical decision-making structures and the greater internal compartmentalisation between services that became features of the Commission in the 1960s. Cassese (1988a: 12) perhaps goes too far in claiming that within a few years the organisation and working rules of the Commission were 'halfway between a French ministry and the German *Bundeswirtschaftminis- terium* [Economics Ministry]', but his description does nonetheless indicate how German influence was increasingly felt.

The record of the EEC Commission

Before becoming Commission President Walter Hallstein had been State Secretary in the West German Foreign Office – in effect Chancellor Adenauer's foreign policy chief – and had led the German team during the negotiations on the EEC. He had thus been a key player on the European stage for some time. Hallstein was in no doubt about the leading role the Commission should play in advancing the European integration process, or about the political nature of that process. During a series of lectures he delivered in 1962 explaining and advocating the integration cause he stated:

> Our Commission [the EEC Commission] . . . is at once a motor, a watchdog, and a kind of honest broker; the word 'executive', in fact, only vaguely describes it.
>
> 'Political Integration' is not too bold and too grandiose a term to describe this [integration] process; in the long run, as I have suggested, its starting point, its goal, its methods, and its subject matter all lie within the political domain. (Hallstein, 1962: 21, 67)

So as to give effect to his desire and determination that the Commission should be exercising a dynamic role in helping to drive the integration process forward, Hallstein sought to ensure that the Commission as an organisation was enthused with a pioneering spirit and that its services were adequately staffed and structured. He was largely successful in achieving these aims.

In respect of the first aim, several participants and commentators have referred to the strong sense of unity and of idealism that existed in the Commission, at both College and services levels, in its early years (see, for example: Coombes, 1970; Groeben, 1987; Marjolin, 1989). Virtually all Commissioners and a high proportion of senior staff (most of whom were seconded from national administrations in the very early years) were attracted to the Commission in large part because they were 'good Europeans' who wished to play a part in 'the building of Europe'.

In respect of the second aim, the size of the Commission's staff was gradually increased and an organisational structure was established. Regarding the size of staff, Hallstein, like Monnet with the High Authority, wanted the Commission to concentrate primarily on development and planning work, rather than routine implementing work, so he did not wish to see staff numbers become excessively large. However, he recognised the need for adequate staffing resources and saw the Commission grow from less than a hundred employees in its early months to over 2000 by the end of 1963. Believing strongly that only people of the highest quality should be appointed but also that the Commission should recruit on a broadly proportional national basis, Hallstein took a close personal interest in both overall personnel policy and in individual appointments to senior positions.

Regarding the organisational structure, lines of responsibility and of control were established: Commissioners assumed policy responsibilities, which were called portfolios, at the 'political' level; Directorates General – of which there were originally nine – and an Executive Secretariat were created to undertake policy and other tasks at the 'administrative' level; and an overall hierarchical system was established, with the College responsible for all final Commission decision-making, with Commissioners being responsible for policy development within their portfolio, and with relationships between Commissioners and DGs (which were normally on a one-to-one basis in the early years) and within DGs being primarily vertical in character.

The organisational base of the Commission was further consolidated by the entry into force in January 1962 of Staff Regulations for the EEC and Euratom. Based on the equivalent Staff Regulations of the ECSC which had been adopted in 1956, these Regulations incorporated many of the classical organisational principles customarily used in national civil services – such as open competition on the principle of merit, higher posts to be filled by internal recruitment, and recruitment and promotion to be non-discriminatory – but in modified forms. The most important modifications provided for:

(1) recruitment not only to be on the basis of merit but also to be 'on the broadest possible geographical basis from among nationals of Member States of the Communities' (Article 27); and (2) 'A procedure other than the competition procedure may be adopted by the appointing authority for the recruitment of Grade A1 or A2 officials and, in exceptional cases, also for recruitment to posts which require special qualifications' (Article 29). The main intent of these modifications was to ensure that there was a reasonable representation of nationals from all member states amongst Commission staff, and that at senior levels the representation was approximately proportionate to size. The Staff Regulations have continued to be important over the years, as Stevens (2000: 43–47) shows.

Turning to policy, the Commission made considerable progress in its early years. It persuaded the Council to accelerate the timetable for the establishment of the customs union and engineered and brokered agreements on technically complex matters concerning the dismantling of internal tariffs and quotas and the establishment of common external tariffs. It laid the foundations of the Common Agricultural Policy (CAP) framework. And in the Kennedy Round of the General Agreement on Tariffs and Trade (GATT) negotiations it represented the Community's interests and was able to demonstrate keen leadership and mediating skills in so doing. There were policy areas where the Commission was less successful, notably transport and energy where policy documents were produced but the Council was largely unresponsive, but overall the first few years were characterised by vigour, enterprise and success. As Cini has put it, there was an emphasis on 'strategic goal setting [and] the construction of ambitious new policies', with many officials approaching their tasks in a visionary manner and as 'a once-in-a-lifetime opportunity to start from scratch, to create policies afresh rather than relying on incremental change' (Cini, 1996b: 43).

However, the situation changed in the mid-1960s when the French President, Charles de Gaulle, concerned at what he saw to be the increasingly supranational direction in which the EEC was moving and annoyed by Hallstein's activist presidential style – he was infuriated when Hallstein claimed that as Commission President he could be regarded as a kind of European prime minister (Urwin, 1995: 103) – created a crisis by withdrawing France in 1965 from participation in all but the most routine work of the Council of Ministers. The origins of what came to be known as the 'empty chair' crisis lay in a proposal from the Commission that the establishment of the CAP should be accompanied by a change in the funding of the Community from national contributions to a system of 'own resources' based on external tariff revenues and agricultural import levies. The Commission then linked this idea of own resources to a proposal that the EP should – in the interests of democratic accountability – be given the power to scrutinise and vote on the budget. De Gaulle objected vigorously to this proposed increase in the power of the Parliament and took advantage of the situation to stiffen his already well known opposition to what he saw to be two other supranational threats: the boldness of the Commission and its inclination to present itself as being in some respects an embryo European government; and the increased use of qualified majority voting (QMV) in the Council that was scheduled from 1966.

The crisis dragged on for seven months until it was eventually resolved at a special Council meeting in Luxembourg in January 1966. The terms of the agreement represented a considerable blow for the Commission, which saw its prestige and power considerably undermined. There were three main elements to the agreement. First, the Commission's funding proposals were put to one side and the existing system of national contributions was retained. (The proposals were, however, reactivated and given effect in 1970, by which time de Gaulle had been replaced as French President by Georges Pompidou.) Second, in what came to be known as the 'Luxembourg Compromise', a political understanding was reached whereby even where there was treaty provision for QMV, decisions would be taken by unanimity when one or more member states declared they had very important national interests at stake. This was unfavourable for the Commission because it meant a single country would be able to veto proposals it brought to the Council. Third, a number of specific restrictions and obligations were placed on the Commission. In particular: the Commission was not, as it had in the own resources case, to make public proposals addressed to the Council and the member states before the latter had received them; the Commission was to work more closely with the Council when developing important initiatives; and the Commission President was no longer to receive the credentials of foreign 'ambassadors' to the EEC, but was to do so alongside the Council President.

The 1965–66 crisis showed that the Commission was not as powerful as Hallstein and others had assumed it to be. More particularly, it showed that its power and authority were severely limited if its actions were opposed by the government of a member state, especially a large member state. Appeals to 'the Community interest' could not be utilised successfully against a government invoking a national interest. As Robert Marjolin, a Commissioner who opposed the College's approach to the crisis, later wrote, 'The truth of the matter is that, inevitably, the members of the Commission, however dedicated to the European idea, had to take the positions of national governments into account or else risk losing all effectiveness . . . [The 1965 crisis erupted] because the majority of the Commission strayed from this golden rule' (Marjolin, 1989: 314) In the years following the crisis the Commission was much more careful to test the likely reactions of national governments to new proposals before formally launching them.

As well as damaging the authority of the Commission, the crisis was also damaging to the personal reputations and positions of Hallstein and his strongest supporter within the College, the Dutch Commissioner Sicco Mansholt. This was because they were known to have been the main proponents of the Commission's strategy in the events leading up to and during the crisis and to have been instrumental in ensuring that Commissioners who had warned against confronting de Gaulle were overruled: six of the nine Commissioners broadly backed the strategy (Loth, 1998: 141). Neither Hallstein nor Mansholt was to fully recover from the Commission's resounding defeat. After the German Chancellor, Kurt-Georg Kiesinger, acceded in the spring of 1967 to de Gaulle's insistence that Hallstein be permitted to serve for no more than six months as President of the new combined Commission, Hallstein asked not to be renominated. Mansholt stayed on as a Commissioner, but did not seek the presidency.

The Commission of the European Atomic Energy Community, 1958–67

The establishment of the Euratom Commission

Euratom was established with the aim of 'creating the conditions necessary for the speedy establishment and growth of nuclear industries' (Article 1, Euratom Treaty). This aim, and the functions that were associated with it, were modelled largely on the French Atomic Energy Commission, largely because France was a strong supporter of Euratom's establishment and had the most advanced domestic nuclear sector.

Euratom's structures and powers were, with appropriate modifications for the Community's narrower and more specialised policy focus, much the same as those of the EEC. The Euratom Commission was thus modelled, in the same fashion as the EEC Commission, on the High Authority, though like the EEC Commission it was less independent of the Council than the High Authority.

Unlike the High Authority and the EEC Commission, the Euratom Commission did not consist of nine members, but rather of five: one from each member state except Luxembourg, which had no national nuclear programme.

The record of the Euratom Commission

The Euratom Commission got off to a bad start when its first President, Louis Armand, resigned for health reasons only a few months after assuming office. Etienne Hirsch, a former associate of Monnet at the French Planning Commissariat, replaced Armand in February 1959, but it was not until the end of that year that the basic start-up tasks of recruiting staff and setting priorities had been completed. So it was 1960 before the Euratom Commission really began work, and by that time the circumstances within which it had to work had changed considerably.

Euratom had been devised in the context of a shortage of coal and a concern about dependence on oil from the Middle East which had been heightened by the Suez crisis in 1956. However, as was noted above in relation to the ECSC, by 1959 coal supply was in surplus. This meant that some of the urgency went out of the project to develop nuclear energy.

At the same time, the delay in getting Euratom under way allowed time for national rivalries to become embedded. The last coalition governments of the French Fourth Republic had seen Euratom as part of the price it could exact from West Germany for agreeing to the common market in industrial goods. As the only member state with a large-scale nuclear research programme, France expected to attract the bulk of the research funding that was available through Euratom. However, West Germany and also Italy were developing research programmes of their own, and these were accelerated following the agreement on Euratom in order to put them in a position to attract a share of the funding. Moreover, the technology that was being developed in these two states was different from that on which the French programme was based. By the time that the Euratom Commission had sorted out its internal position, what interest remained in nuclear energy was thus competitive rather than cooperative.

Hirsch tried to exercise strong leadership on behalf of Euratom, but this brought him into conflict with France, which under de Gaulle's leadership became much less sympathetic to the Euratom project. Two issues in particular led to clashes between Hirsch and the French Government. The first was over the right of the High Authority to inspect French plutonium facilities. France maintained that these were directly related to its nuclear weapons programme and had therefore to be protected for reasons of national security. When Hirsch tried to press this in the Council of Ministers he did not get the backing of the other member states, which weakened the authority of the Commission. The second issue was over the right of the Commission to divert funds away from other uses to invest in a joint programme of reactor development, which had been agreed provisionally between the Commission and the United States. France objected to the agreement in principle because it implied subsidisation of 'foreign' nuclear technology. As in other areas, the French view of the purpose of technological research was that it should make Europe independent of the United States. However, Germany was developing its nuclear research programme on the basis of the same technology as that of the United States, and Italy was more interested in securing the cheapest source of energy as rapidly as possible than in long-term research to develop an independent nuclear base that would in any case favour French research projects. Hirsch gained majority support in the Council of Ministers for his position on this issue, but it proved to be a pyrrhic victory because France subsequently insisted that decisions on budgetary matters be taken by unanimity.

Michel Chatenet, who replaced Hirsch in 1962 after de Gaulle refused to nominate the latter for a second term of office, did not attempt to assert a strong role for the Euratom Commission. It is doubtful if he could have succeeded even if he had tried because, as has been indicated, Euratom was by now in a very difficult operating environment. In addition to the unfavourable factors that have already been noted, Euratom was badly affected by: the trend to intergovernmentalism that affected all the Communities following the election of de Gaulle to office in France; it dealt with an issue that in the case of France touched on an area of high politics – the development of a nuclear-weapons capability, the research for which was closely bound up with the research for the development of a nuclear-energy capability; there was an absence of agreement between technical experts about which of the competing nuclear technologies ought to be supported and developed; and the existence and success of the EEC meant there was no great 'integrationist pressure' on governments to make a success of Euratom in the sense that a failure for Euratom did not signal a failure for the overall integration process.

National interests thus prevailed during the years of the Euratom Commission's existence. Little progress was made in breaking down national barriers, in promoting cooperative activities, or in developing direction – let alone control – from the centre.

The post-merger Commission, 1967–

The Commission of the European Communities that was created by the 1965 Merger Treaty began functioning in July 1967. Its first President was the Belgian Jean Rey, who had been a member of the EEC Commission since its establishment in 1958. Fourteen members were appointed to the new College, but only on an interim basis and when its term of office ended in 1970 the size of the College was reduced to nine: that is, to what had been the size of both the High Authority and the EEC College. Since 1970, the size of the College, and indeed also of the administrative services, has increased every time there has been an EC/EU enlargement (see Table 3.1, p. 64).

The first decade, 1967–77

The first decade of the single Commission is often thought of as having been a period when there was a general malaise, even stagnation, in the European integration process. This impression is not wholly correct, for there were integrationist advances. Deepening occurred in a number of ways, such as with the development of new policies in the environmental and regional spheres. Widening occurred via the 1973 accessions of Denmark, Ireland and the U.K.

These advances notwithstanding, however, it is the case that the overall integrationist record for the period can be described as being, at best, only modest. The Commission was far from wholly responsible for this state of affairs, but it did play its part in that it was less innovative and driving than it might have been expected to be. For much of the time it appeared to be an excessively cautious, even defensive institution, concerned primarily to avoid any further erosion of its position and to ensure it did not get drawn into another damaging clash with a national government. It seemed to generally lack collective self-confidence.

Two factors are especially important in explaining these characteristics of the Commission during this period.

The context   Although the Hallstein Commission has been given great credit for its achievements, it should be recognised that most of them took the form of directly applying, or filling out the details of, commitments set out in the EEC Treaty. The two most obvious achievements – the creation of the customs union and the CAP – were the policy bedrocks of the Treaty and their establishment was required over the course of a twelve-year transitional period. (In the event, they were established ahead of schedule.) The Hallstein Commission made very little progress in policy areas where the Treaty was vague and no timetable was attached, such as with the coordination of national economic policies and the development of a common transport policy.

The Hallstein Commission may thus be said to have been successful in dealing with the 'easy' policy issues. That is to say, it played a central role in assisting the EEC to achieve those policy goals that were clear and that were scheduled in the EEC Treaty. It was, however, less successful in moving the EEC onto more difficult ground, where the precise nature of goals was unspecified and where no timetable was attached. This more difficult ground was inherited by the Hallstein Commission's successors. When these successors were assigned what amounted to a clear and fully supported mandate by the member states – such as the decisions of the 1969 Hague summit to change the financing arrangements for the budget and to explore the possibility of EC enlargement to the UK and other applicant states, or the decision of the 1974 Paris summit to establish a European Regional Development Fund (ERDF) – then the Commission was able to act with considerable effectiveness. When, however, there was no mandate, or the mandate was vague and not based on solid political foundations – such as with the Hague summit's declaration that the Community should establish economic and monetary union by 1980 – then the Commission was less effective.

Not only were issues less defined and more problematical for the post-Hallstein Commissions, but the decision-making context within which the Commission operated was unfavourable to it exercising a strong political role. The Luxembourg Compromise effectively meant that virtually all decisions had to be taken by consensus in the Council. The impact of this was no more clearly demonstrated than in the fate of the 1968 Mansholt Plan to tackle the structural problems of Community agriculture (Sicco Mansholt had become Agriculture Commissioner): a combination of differing national interests and the unanimity requirement resulted in the Commission's plans for reform becoming bogged down, and eventually being greatly watered down, in the Council. Similar resistance by member states resulted in many of the Commission's attempts to open up the internal market through measures designed to remove non-tariff barriers (NTBs) to trade being blocked or weakened.

The unfavourable decision-making context was made worse by two further factors in the 1970s. First, the 1973 enlargement to Denmark, Ireland, and the UK was not conducive to Commission pioneering or activism. This was partly because Danish and British attitudes towards further integration hovered between suspicion and hostility. It was partly also because the enlargement created considerable disruption within the Commission, with over 300 officials leaving the Commission services so as to enable officials from the acceding states to be accommodated. Second, the international economic recession that began in 1971, and really began to bite after the 1973 rise in the price of oil, made the governments of the member states less inclined to agree to integrative measures that would weaken their ability to preserve domestic markets for domestic producers.

Lack of leadership   The Commission lacked strong and forceful leadership during this period. Part of the reason for this was the contextual factors that have just been outlined. There were, however, also other reasons.

First, the tenure of office of the President was short. Hallstein had been EEC Commission President for over nine years, but the governments of the member states restricted the tenure of Hallstein's immediate successors, which inevitably limited what they could achieve. The first President of the combined merged Commission, Jean Rey, who had been the Belgian Commissioner in the EEC Commission since 1958, was given a fixed three-year term. Thereafter, the tenure of the President was set at two years, which could be renewed. As events turned out, Rey's successor, Franco Maria Malfatti, did not even serve two years, but left during his second year so as to be able to take part in a general election in Italy. Sicco Mansholt served out the remaining months of Malfatti's term. Mansholt was followed by the Frenchman, François-Xavier Ortoli, whose term was renewed.

Second, of the four Presidents in this period, only Mansholt had sufficient strength of character, political stature and vision to be able to offer real leadership, but he was strictly an interim appointment. Rey was in many ways a typical Belgian politician: that is, he was a conciliator, well practised in bringing together different interests. This was an admirable quality for the President of the first single Commission since an important part of the job was forging a unified functioning institution out of the staffs of the three previously separate institutions, but it was not a quality that leant itself to creating a crusading spirit for and within the Commission. Malfatti was visibly ill at ease in Brussels. He spoke only Italian and clearly saw the position of Commission President as a way of enhancing his domestic political career. Ortoli was a highly intelligent, efficient and well respected President, but he was a technocrat rather than a politician and he had no great wish to expand the scope of the Commission or for it to assume a vigorous campaigning role.

Third, the Colleges of Commissioners were less enthusiastic than had been Hallstein's about the causes of European integration and a leading role for the Commission. There were individual Commissioners who were strong advocates of European integration and of a pioneering role for the Commission, most notably Mansholt in the Rey and Malfatti Commissions and the Italian federalist Altiero Spinelli in the Malfatti/Mansholt/Ortoli Commissions, but they were in a minority. Most Commissioners took a more temperate view of what the Commission should be doing, which meant that the Colleges of which they were members were not collectively committed or partisan.

The Jenkins Commission, 1977–81

The appointment of Roy Jenkins as Commission President from January 1977 raised high hopes for a revival in both the influence and status of the Commission. These hopes were based on Jenkins' well known pro-integration views and on the fact that, unlike his predecessor, he was not a technocrat but rather was a politician of some standing. He had held very senior ministerial posts in British

Labour governments of the 1960s and 1970s and possessed a good international reputation.

An important priority for Jenkins was to enhance the profile and standing of the Commission presidency. This he achieved, largely through developing – after a difficult start – good working relationships with most national heads of government. These relationship led to him being treated as a valued participant at meetings of the European Council and enabled him to persuade the national leaders, despite French reservations, that the President of the Commission should represent the Community as a whole at the annual Group of Seven (G7) summits.

Another priority was to improve the efficiency of the Commission and to this end one of Jenkins' first acts as President was to establish a committee under the chairmanship of the former ECSC High Commissioner, Dirk Spierenburg, to draw up a report on the internal workings of the Commission. The report, which was presented in 1979, identified problems and made recommendations that were similar to those of a report drawn up under the Belgian Prime Minister, Leo Tindemans, for the European Council in 1976 (Tindemans Report, 1976). Amongst the problems identified in the Spierenburg Report were: a lack of cohesion within the College; an imbalance between Commissioners' portfolios; an over-fragmented organisational structure at both College and administrative levels (at administrative level 247 divisions and 92 specialised services were identified); an inefficient distribution of staff; and problems in the career structure. Amongst the recommendations that were made were: a reduction in the number of Commissioners to one per member state; a reduction in the number of portfolios and a re-balancing of the contents of portfolios to make them more equal; a re-grouping of DGs so that they corresponded more closely to Commissioner portfolios; a reduction in the number of divisions and specialised services; and a strengthened presidency, with the President becoming actively responsible for overseeing the coordination of Commission activities (Spierenburg, 1979). In the event, virtually all of the proposals ran into opposition from some quarter: the large member states did not wish to lose one of 'their' two Commissioners; some Commissioners were uneasy about the position of the presidency being over-elevated; Jenkins – who did not have a high regard for some of his fellow Commissioners – did not favour 'equalising' Commissioners' portfolios; and senior Commission officials did not want to see their bureaucratic empires and interests undermined. Unsurprisingly in the face of this opposition, the Spierenburg Report was left largely unimplemented, though many of its contents have echoed over the years in subsequent investigations and reports on the Commission.

Jenkins' desires to enhance the position of the Commission presidency and improve the Commission's organisational efficiency were part of a wider aim: to help the Community break out of the *immobilisme* into which it had fallen. The greatest contribution that he made in this regard during his presidency – and it was largely down to his own efforts rather than those of the Commission as a whole – was to promote and help broker the European Monetary System (EMS) that was established in 1979. The key political decisions on EMS were made, as Jenkins has acknowledged (Jenkins, 1989), by the French President, Valéry Giscard d'Estaing, and the West German Chancellor, Helmut Schmidt, but Jenkins' prompting role in public speeches and mediating role in behind-the-scenes meetings were vital.

The record of the Jenkins' presidency is mixed. On the one hand there were disappointments and failures, with some problems – including a need for CAP and budgetary reform – becoming ever more pressing but remaining unresolved at the end of the presidency. On the other hand, the period witnessed a modest upturn in the integration process, a revival of the institutional position of the Commission, and a higher status for the office of Commission President.

The Thorn Commission, 1981–85

Gaston Thorn was the Luxembourg Foreign Minister at the time of his appointment as Commission President. He had previously been his country's Prime Minister and Finance Minister.

Thorn's Commission is usually portrayed in an unfavourable light, especially when compared with the dynamism of the Delors period that succeeded it. The Commission is seen as being insufficiently innovative under Thorn, doing little more than reacting to events and being sidelined on most important issues by national leaders. According to Cini (1996b: 66), 'Where there were achievements, they were often based on deals done at national level, rather than on initiatives taken at the centre. The Commission's position within the European policy process seemed at an all-time low.'

But though negative interpretations of the Thorn Commission certainly have some validity, the case should not be exaggerated.

Significant progress was made with a number of extremely awkward problems during its 'watch'. For example, the most difficult round of enlargement negotiations to date, with Portugal and Spain, which had begun in 1978 and 1979 respectively, and which absorbed much of the Commission's time and energy, were largely completed by the end of the College's period of office. A Common Fisheries Policy (CFP), which had been under negotiation for many years, was established. And agreements were successfully promoted between the member states on such contentious issues as CAP reform, budgetary reform, and the size and national allocations of the Structural Funds.

Arguably, however, the most important achievement of the Thorn Commission was to promote a recognition and an acceptance that Europe's poor economic performance in comparison with the US and Japan needed to be tackled by policies at the European level. Thorn and the Commissioner for the Internal Market, Karl-Heinz Narjes, did much to highlight the problems faced by industrialists in trading across national borders within the EC. Etienne Davignon, the Commissioner for Industrial Policy, was also highly active in pointing to the damaging effects on Europe of its still segmented markets. His efforts were more narrowly focused than those of Thorn and Narjes, but they were arguably more influential in persuading governments to accept change. Davignon assembled a network of leading industrialists involved in the European electrical and electronics industries to discuss their common problems in the face of US and Japanese competition. Out of these discussions came the ESPRIT programmes of collaborative research in information technologies and also the European Round Table of Industrialists (ERT), which was to become a base from which important multi-national and European business firms worked with the Commission to persuade governments to liberalise the EC's internal market.

The efforts of Thorn, Narjes and Davignon laid some of the foundations on which Delors was able to build the main achievements of his presidency.

The Delors Commissions, 1985–95

Jacques Delors is by far the best known and, in the post-Hallstein period, longest serving, person to be President of the Commission. He headed three Colleges: 1985–89, 1989–93 and 1993–95 (the last College being, for reasons that are explained below, transitional).

Delors' background and appointment   Prior to his appointment as Commission President, Delors was Minister of Finance in the French Socialist Government between 1981 and 1984. In this post he was instrumental in persuading his colleagues to abandon an economic policy based on reflation, which was weakening the French franc within the EMS, and to adopt a programme of austerity so as to put the economy back on a sound footing. Although he was not to know it at the time, this policy stance was to prove crucial in persuading two national leaders who might not have been expected to support his candidacy for the Commission presidency to do so. One of these leaders was the British Prime Minister, Margaret Thatcher, who ordinarily would not have approved the appointment of a Socialist to any position of importance. The other leader was the German Chancellor, Helmut Kohl, whose support for Delors was even more crucial since it had tacitly been understood by the national leaders that the presidency would be given to a German if the Federal Government chose to put forward a candidate.

The internal market programme and the Single European Act   As is shown in Chapter 3, before taking up the Commission presidency in January 1985 Delors gave much thought to how the process of European integration, to which he was personally strongly committed, could be relaunched (Grant, 1994: 66). He settled on the idea of reinvigorating the EC's goal of creating an internal market. Accordingly, within just six months of the new College assuming office, the Commission produced a White Paper, *Completing the Internal Market* (Commission, 1985). Compiled under the auspices of the Internal Market Commissioner, Lord Cockfield – who worked very closely with Delors – the Paper recommended that a target date of December 1992 be set for agreement on some 300 measures that it identified as being necessary for the internal market to be completed. The contents of the White Paper were duly approved by the European Council at its June 1985 Milan meeting.

The Milan summit also decided to convene an Intergovernmental Conference (IGC) to review the institutional functioning of the EC, and more particularly to examine the treaty reforms that would be necessary if the internal market programme was to be achieved. Much of the thinking behind the convening of the IGC was based on the fact that it would not be possible for the Commission's proposed measures to be approved by the Council unless decisions could be taken by

QMV, and although QMV had begun to be used in the Council on a limited basis in the 1980s where the EEC Treaty so permitted, most of the internal market measures envisaged would be subject to a unanimity requirement. The IGC culminated at the December 1995 Luxembourg summit, where the member states agreed to what became the Single European Act (SEA). The contents of the SEA were generally welcomed by the Commission since they contained much for which it had been pressing: the 1992 objective was incorporated into the EEC Treaty; the powers of the EP were increased; there was an expansion of the EEC's policy competences; and, above all, the policy areas in which QMV applied were extended, most notably to most of the measures that would need to be adopted for the establishment of the internal market.

The decision to extend the QMV treaty base meant that it became legally more difficult for a single member state to block a Commission proposal. But the SEA reform on voting in the Council was given full effect only because it was accompanied by two other, closely related, developments. First, it came to be increasingly accepted that votes would indeed be taken if, after full deliberations and after having taken note of particular difficulties faced by member states, no consensus could be reached in the Council on issues that needed to be resolved. Second, the Luxembourg Compromise virtually died in the 1980s.

These developments – the extensions to the legal base for QMV, the changing attitudes in the Council to QMV and the virtual expiration of the Luxembourg Compromise – greatly strengthened the Commission's position in respect of policy development and also brought about a significant change in its policy role. Its position was strengthened because its proposals were now much less subject to being vetoed or severely watered down by a single member state. Its role was changed in that it was obliged to start thinking about majorities and blocking minorities in the Council, and how proposals could be shaped to achieve the former and avoid the latter. Such thinking inevitably led it to assume increasingly important brokerage functions in its relations with member states.

The internal market programme, or Single European (SEM) programme as it was increasingly called, imposed a considerable workload on the Commission. For the most part, however, schedules for producing the 300 measures were met, and the Council was able to convert the vast majority of these into legislation by the end of 1992.

Broadening the agenda   The establishment of the SEM was not the end of the integration project for Delors. Rather, as was noted above, he saw it as a launching pad for other developments. In particular, he argued that the market ought to be given a social dimension and ought to be accompanied by monetary union. On both of these issues he was supported by most of the governments of the member states.

The social dimension idea was given formal expression when in 1989 the Commission issued the *Community Charter of the Fundamental Social Rights of Workers*, which came to be commonly referred to as the Social Charter. This was not so much concerned with making specific legislative proposals – they were contained in a separate action programme – but rather was intended to serve as a reference point for the development of the social dimension. The Charter was duly endorsed by eleven votes to one (Margaret Thatcher voting against) at the December 1989 Strasbourg European Council meeting, and much of it was used as a basis for what became the Social Chapter of the Maastricht Treaty.

As for monetary union, Delors persuaded the June 1988 Hanover summit to establish a high-level committee, made up mainly of central bank governors and under his chairmanship, to study the subject. When it reported, in April 1989, the committee provided a plan for a three-stage movement to Economic and Monetary Union (EMU). The June 1989 Madrid summit agreed that the 'Delors Report' provided a basis for further work, that stage one should begin on 1 July 1990, and that an IGC would be needed to provide a basis for developments beyond stage one.

The IGCs and the Maastricht Treaty   The December 1989 Strasbourg summit formally agreed – with Thatcher voting against – to convene an IGC on EMU.

At the same time, however, as the national governments and the Commission were deliberating about EMU and were moving forward to the holding of an IGC on the issue, the collapse of communism in Central and Eastern Europe, and then in the Soviet Union itself, brought political union very much onto the agenda. It did so in three main ways. First, the reunification of Germany – which Delors had helped to facilitate by supporting Chancellor Kohl's policy of pressing ahead with a rapid reunification when most of the leaders of the governments of the member states counselled caution – meant that the EC's institutional arrangements needed to be reviewed. This was because Germany now became by far the largest member state and could therefore lay claim to more representation in the EC's institutions. Second, some member states were concerned that Germany would now switch much of its attention to its neighbours in the East, so efforts must be made to tie it in more tightly to the EC. Third, there was a widely held feeling that the collapse of communism and of the East–West division was likely to produce a more unpredictable and uncertain world and in that world the EC might well need more structured arrangements for conducting its external political relations.

These problems resulted in a decision being taken at the European Council meeting in Dublin in June 1990 to establish on IGC on Political Union that would parallel the IGC on EMU. The two ICGs were formally opened at the December 1990 Rome summit and met throughout 1991. They reported to the December 1991 Maastricht summit, where final agreement was reached on the contents of what became the Maastricht Treaty on European Union (TEU).

The EMU provisions of the TEU were broadly acceptable to the Commission. There were aspects of them which it did not like, but the general shape and schedule of the plan to move towards the establishment of a single currency by the end of the decade were recognisably based on the principles of the 1989 Delors Report and subsequent Commission proposals.

The Political Union provisions were, however, much less satisfactory from the Commission's viewpoint. As it had done in 1985, the Commission urged various treaty changes on the IGC, including extensions in QMV, in the legislative role of the EP, in policy competences, and in its own authority and powers. The IGC did in fact agree to significant developments in respect of all of these matters. Amongst the developments was a boost to the legitimacy of the Commission through two important changes in the procedures for appointing the President and the College: in nominating a person to be President, the governments of the member states would henceforth be required to consult with the EP; and incoming Colleges would be subject as a body to a vote of approval by the EP. So as to strengthen the force of these new requirements the terms of office of the College and the EP were brought into close alignment by: (a) extending the terms of office of the College from four to five years (EP elections are held on a fixed five-yearly basis); (b) deciding that there would be an interim two-year College from January 1993 to January 1995. This alignment of the terms of office of the College and the EP would enable the national governments' consultation with the

EP on the President-designate to occur shortly after EP elections and the vote of approval on the whole College to be held about six months later.

These measures did not, it has to be said, fully address a growing 'legitimacy problem' for the Commission. As Drake (1996) has noted, the Commission was now operating in an environment in which legitimacy could not, as it could with the High Authority in the 1950s, be justified as deriving from its status as a competent body of experts authorised by member states to act independently in the interests of Europe. In an era when the tasks and responsibilities of the Commission had become very far-reaching in terms of the implications for national policies, sovereignties and identities, and at a time when the Commission was acting in a highly pro-active manner, 'the legitimacy of an unelected, expert institution . . . to propose and manage the [integration] process was not as self-evident' (Drake, 1996: 53). A more full-blooded attempt to tackle the legitimacy problem could have taken a number of forms, including ensuring that there would be a direct relationship between the composition of the College and the preferences of voters as expressed at EP elections. Nonetheless, the reforms did mark a modest 'democratic advance' for the Commission and as such helped to underpin its position in the EU system.

Given that the IGC on Political Union produced changes that the Commission supported, why was its overall outcome viewed as being unsatisfactory? It was so mainly because Commission attempts to protect the organisational unity of the Community – by ensuring that all policy areas were placed within the framework of the EEC, or EC as it was now re-named – failed. Two strengthened policy areas were located in new and separate intergovernmental pillars – one covering Common Foreign and Security Policy (CFSP) and the other Justice and Home Affairs Policy (JHA) – where the Commission's role and powers would be much weaker than in the EC pillar.

Further setbacks and increasing difficulties   The Commission was widely perceived as having suffered a serious setback by the decision of the IGC to base the EU on a pillar rather than on a unitary structure. The Commission's standing was further undermined in 1992 when Delors was seen as being at least partly responsible for the decision of the Danish people to reject ratification of the Maastricht Treaty in June 1992. Blame was attached to Delors partly because of his close association with monetary union, about which there were considerable doubts in Denmark, and partly because shortly before the referendum he had cast doubts on whether small states would be able to continue exercising their current levels of influence in a future enlarged Community.

Delors' remarks on the future of small states were made within the context of increasing signs that the Community would soon have to embark on accession negotiations with several member states of the European Free Trade Association (EFTA). That this was so marked a retreat by the Commission from the strategy it had developed in 1989–90, which was to head off membership applications from EFTA states which were being stimulated by the success of the SEM and the ending of the Cold War. Delors did not wish to initiate an enlargement round, fearing that another widening of the Community would endanger the deepening process to which he was so committed. He therefore proposed, as an alternative to enlargement, the creation of a European Economic Area (EEA) which would, in effect, extend the SEM programme to the EFTA states, but which would stop short of full EC membership. The EFTA states duly negotiated the EEA with the EC and it came into operation in January 1994, but it was never likely to be enough for most of the EFTA members because it meant they became subject to EC market legislation without having a direct say in determining it. As a result, before the EEA was even formally established applications to join the EC were lodged by Austria, Sweden, Finland, Switzerland and Norway.

At the same time as the Commission's reputation was being damaged by the problems associated with the Maastricht Treaty and enlargement, its position was also being weakened by internal problems at College level. The second and third Colleges over which Delors presided were not as cohesive as had been the first. This was partly because of personality clashes, partly because of differences over policy responsibilities and priorities, and partly because of growing dissatisfaction with Delors' extremely high profile and personalised leadership style – he worked very much through his *cabinet* and did not always consult other Commissioners even when he dealt with matters that touched on their policy portfolio. On occasions, differences within the Colleges even spilt over into the public domain, as for example in 1990 when Agriculture Commissioner, Ray MacSharry, and Trade Commissioner, Frans Andriessen, openly disputed over who was responsible for agricultural negotiations in the GATT Uruguay Round negotiations.

Miscalculations and internal problems thus made it more difficult for the Commission to be as effective in the later years of the Delors' presidency as it had been in the early years. But a factor that was largely beyond its control also weakened its ability to make the case for further integration and to prod the member states into action. This factor was the general mood of caution towards the nature and pace of the integration process that came to infect the governments of most member states after the June 1992 Danish referendum and the later referendum in France in September 1992 when there was only a very narrow majority in favour of ratifying the Maastricht Treaty. Governments became sensitive to the charge that they had moved too far ahead of public opinion and, in consequence, they shifted their attention away from further expansion towards consolidation.

The balance sheet   As has just been shown, the Commission lost some of its effectiveness in the later stages of the Delors presidency. But that should not obscure how much was achieved, especially in the early years. Integrationist measures in which the Commission was a key player – most notably as an agenda-setter, a facilitator of decision-making, and an implementer of policies and laws – include: the SEM programme; the plan and schedule for EMU; institutional reforms, especially those contained in the SEA; the social dimension; important budgetary reforms providing for medium-term budgetary planning and for increases in the size of the budget and of the Structural Funds; and the development, in the Delors III College, of a major initiative designed to promote growth, competitiveness and employment.

These achievements were in no small measure due to Delors. His personal qualities counted for much: vision, intelligence, enthusiasm, forcefulness, and sheer hard work. He did not concern himself with the principle of collegiality, but rather worked with and through a few Commissioners who he respected, a highly effective team of personal advisers and assistants led by his forceful *chef de cabinet*, Pascal Lamy, and sympathisers holding influential positions in the Commission administration. Perhaps most importantly of all, he was advantaged by establishing a position that allowed him to work closely with, and to be generally admired and respected by, important national leaders. So much so that there was, as Dinan (1997a: 257) has noted, a period in the late 1980s and very early 1990s when 'the decisive Franco–German driving force of European integration had seemingly turned into a Franco–German–Commission partnership, personified by Mitterrand, Kohl, and Delors'.

The Santer Commission, 1995–99

Jacques Santer was the Luxembourg Prime Minister at the time of his nomination to be Commission President. His College was the first to be subject to the revised procedures for the appointment of the President and the College as a whole that were included in the Maastricht Treaty. Both procedures proved to be lengthier and more problematical than had been foreseen. Accounts of how events unfurled are given in Chapters 3 and 4.

The challenges and achievements Santer made it clear from the beginning of his presidency that he was not greatly interested in expanding the responsibilities of the EU or the powers of the Commission. As he told the EP in January 1995, on the eve of the Parliament's confirmatory vote on his College, 'We should take as our motto: "Less action, but better action"' (Santer, 1995a: 11).

   In the spirit of 'better action', there were important initiatives designed to make the operation and working practices of the Commission more effective and efficient. Internal Commission reform had been largely neglected by Delors, who had little personal interest in the issue, but it unquestionably needed addressing. It did so because many of the Commission's internal structures, mechanisms and working practices were dated, having evolved in an essentially gradualistic rather than rational decision-making manner. So, for example, DGs had been created (and occasionally disbanded) in a somewhat *ad hoc* way, whilst staff were caught up in an outmoded and rigid personnel policy framework that was not capable of placing people where they were most needed to respond to the Commission's expanding and changing responsibilities.

   Under Santer's presidency, three internal reform projects were set in motion: Sound and Efficient Management (SEM 2000), which was launched in 1995, was designed to ensure that the Commission used sound financial management practices; Modernisation of Administration and Personnel Policy (MAP 2000), which began in 1997, was aimed at simplifying, and where possible decentralising, administrative and personnel procedures; and Designing the Commission of Tomorrow (DECODE) was a screening exercise undertaken in 1998 of the Commission's tasks, organisation and resources that was intended to provide a basis for decisions to be taken in 1999 on such matters as the reorganisation of the Commission's services and the possible delegation of administrative tasks to specialist agencies. (See Cram, 1999; Stevens, 2000, for fuller accounts of these reform projects.) The Santer Commission thus gave internal reform a high priority. By early 1999 much of the SEM 2000 and MAP 2000 reform projects had been, or were in the process of being, implemented, whilst the DECODE screening had been completed and recommendations were being considered. Given this record, it is thus highly ironic that, as is shown below, the College found itself under very strong attack from late 1998, and in March 1999 was forced to resign, largely because it was perceived as not having properly tackled, let alone having taken control of, inefficient administrative practices within the Commission. The fact is that although many Commission administrative practices in 1998–99 continued to be unsatisfactory, the Santer Commission gave the issue of internal Commission reform much more attention than had any of its predecessors.

As for 'less action', Santer intended that the Commission he led would not be so expansionist as had been the Delors' Commissions. In particular, legislative activity would be guided by the principles of proportionality and subsidiarity, whereby EU legislation would be proposed only when it was necessary to achieve treaty objectives and in respect of matters where legislation at EU level was likely to be more effective than legislation at national levels.

But though the commitment to less legislative activity was realisable, and indeed in a numerical sense was inevitable given that virtually all of the SEM legislative programme was now in place, it was less easy to reduce activity on other fronts. Quite the contrary in fact, for the Santer College knew even before it assumed office that in some respects the workload of the Commission was likely to increase. This was because a number of major challenges facing the EU were already on the table, and the incoming Commission would be deeply involved in them all. Four of these challenges loomed especially large.

The first was an impending IGC. Whereas the 1985 and 1991 IGCs had been called at relatively short notice, it had been specified in the Maastricht Treaty that an IGC would be held in 1996. All interested parties thus had ample time to prepare their positions. Indeed, a preparatory stage was even built into the IGC process via the creation of a pre-IGC Reflection Group composed of a senior representative from each of the national governments and the Commission.

Santer's approach to the IGC was, as it was to prove to be on many other issues, more collegial and less personal than had been that of

Delors. Whereas the latter had exercised a tight control over the Commission's input into the 1985 and 1991 IGCs, Santer involved other Commissioners and Commission officials and asked one of his fellow Commissioners, Marcelino Oreja, to coordinate the Commission's approach to the IGC (Dinan, 1997a: 255).

The more consolidationist outlook of the Santer College, coupled with the more restrained outlook in EU circles towards the integration process, meant that the Commission's inputs into the IGC were less ambitious and involved lower expectations than had been the case in the 1985 and 1991 IGCs. In both its submission to the Reflection Group (Commission, 1995c) and in its opinion to the IGC (Commission, 1996b) the Commission was cautious. It was not, however, as cautious as it was presented by many observers as being. In its opinion to the IGC it argued that a number of treaty reforms were necessary to make the Union closer to its citizens, to enable the Union to make its presence felt in the world, and to provide the Union with an institutional system that would work in a future expanded EU. Amongst the reforms it called for, most were familiar: more QMV in the Council; more powers for the EP; simplified decision-making procedures; the transfer of most JHA policy responsibilities to the EC pillar; and a much firmer and more supranational CFSP pillar. Most of these proposals were also advocated, in some degree, by all member states apart from the UK. That obstacle, however, was removed when the Conservative Government lost to Labour in the May 1997 General Election. The way was thus cleared at the end of the IGC process for agreement at the June 1997 Amsterdam summit on a treaty which, if it did not go as far as the Commission would have liked, was more acceptable than had been its Maastricht predecessor, not least in that it strengthened the position of the Commission President (see Chapter 3).

The second major challenge facing the Santer Commission was EMU, the third and final stage of which was scheduled to begin before the end of the College's term of office. Although the European Council, the Ecofin Council (Economic and Finance Ministers), and European and national bankers occupied more high-profile positions than the Commission in the movement towards the third stage of EMU, the articles of the post-Maastricht EC Treaty covering economic and monetary policy were littered with references to the Commission: 'The Council shall, acting on a recommendation from the Commission . . .', 'The Commission shall monitor the development of . . .', 'The Commission shall prepare a report on . . .' and 'Where a

Member State is in difficulties . . . the Commission shall immediately investigate the position of the State in question . . . and state what measures it recommends the State concerned to take'. The Commission was thus not itself to take key final decisions on the process of transition towards EMU, but it was to exercise a variety of important guiding, advisory, and monitoring tasks. The successful completion of these tasks played an important part in enabling decisions on the nature and composition of the third stage of EMU to be taken in 1997–98 and the single currency to be launched in January 1999.

In addition to the EMU tasks it was formally allocated in the Maastricht Treaty, the Commission was also expected to be at the forefront in explaining and advocating EMU to the world outside the EU's inner circles. This public relations responsibility is one that all Commissioners and many senior Commission officials undertake, but EMU imposed a particularly heavy workload in this respect. In 1997 alone, the Economic and Financial Affairs Commissioner, Yves-Thibault de Silguy, made 120 speeches on the euro-currency (*European Voice*, 29 January–4 February 1998: 32).

Enlargement was the third major challenge. The Santer Commission's management of enlargement is considered at length in Chapter 12, so let it just be noted here that it involved processing and advancing applications from ten Central and Easten European countries (CEECs) that were submitted from 1994, developing and implementing programmes to assist the applicants to meet the conditions of membership, submitting opinions on the applications to the European Council in 1997, and beginning negotiations with six states (five CEECs and Cyprus) in 1998.

The fourth major challenge involved developing plans for future EU expenditure and the major expenditure policy areas. Since 1988 the EC/EU has set its annual budgets within the framework of multi-annual financial perspectives which establish targets and limits for overall expenditure and for categories of expenditure. The first financial perspective covered 1988–92 and the second 1993–99. A third financial perspective would thus need to be agreed by 1999 so as to enable it to come into operation by 2000.

Agreement on the final contents of financial perspectives is a matter for the Ecofin Council and ultimately the European Council, but the detailed preparation is the responsibility of the Commission. It is a responsibility that involves extensive work, since all EU policy areas are affected by the financial provisions that are made for them. In consequence, the preparation of draft financial perspectives involves all parts of the Commission and is accompanied by extensive politicking and lobbying both from within and without.

The drafting of the third financial perspective was an extremely difficult exercise since it was necessary for the perspective to include provisions allowing for enlargement to CEECs – all of which would be net beneficiaries from the budget if existing EU policies, especially the CAP and the Structural Funds, remained in their present form. The Commission's recommendations were issued in a major document it issued in July 1997 under the title *Agenda 2000 – For a Stronger and Wider Union* (Commission, 1997b). Amongst the policy proposals made in *Agenda 2000* were: a range of measures to make agriculture more competitive in world markets (to be attained primarily by lowering domestic prices), more consumer-friendly, and more environmentally sensitive; reforms to the Structural Funds to make them more efficient and visible; and the completion, refining, and in a few cases more vigorous development, of a number of internal policies concerned with growth, employment, and quality of life. To the surprise of many observers, the Commission indicated that if its proposed reforms were implemented, the overall budgetary ceiling of the 1993–99 financial perspective (equivalent to 1.27 per cent of member states' gross national product) could also apply in the post-2000 perspective. After almost two years of deliberations and negotiations involving, amongst other things, the production by the Commission of follow-up legislative proposals, the member states agreed at a special European Council meeting in Berlin in March 1999 on an *Agenda 2000* package and a financial framework for 2000–06. Though containing modifications and amendments to the Commission's original proposals, especially on CAP, the package broadly reflected the thinking and direction of the Commission's 1997 document.

The resignation of the College   As the above paragraphs show, the Santer Commission achieved much. In particular, it initiated and carried through internal administrative changes, it facilitated the creation of the single currency, it managed the preparations and early negotiations for the largest and most difficult enlargement round in the EU's history, and it set the agenda and direction of the *Agenda 2000* budgetary and policy reform package.

However, it is likely that it will not be for its achievements that the Santer College will be remembered most, but rather for the circumstances in which it left office. This is because in March 1999, amidst allegations that some of its members had acted disreputably and that collectively it had been neglectful of some of its duties, the Santer College resigned. In so doing, it became the first College not to complete its term of office.

The circumstances that led to the resignation of the Santer College can be traced back to a growing dissatisfaction on the part of MEPs that Santer himself, and some of his colleagues in the College, were not up to the job. Notwithstanding the achievements of the College, there was seen to be too much complacency and, in some cases, incompetence. The College would, however, have ridden out such feelings had not a number of factors combined from late 1998 to produce a growing groundswell of dissatisfaction with the College in the EP. Amongst the factors producing the groundswell were: a Court of Auditors report that revealed (not for the first time) evidence of 'missing' EU funds and that was strongly critical of aspects of Commission management practices; circulating heresay that some Commissioners – most particularly the Commissioner for Research, Edith Cresson – were favouring relatives and friends in appointments and the awarding of contracts; and a rather dismissive response by Jacques Santer to the criticisms that were being made of himself and some of his colleagues. It was probably only because Santer agreed to the creation of a special committee to investigate the allegations of fraud, nepotism and mismanagement that the Commission avoided being censured. A censure motion was put but, because many MEPs preferred to await the committee's verdict before condemning the Commission, it did not command majority support: 232 voted in favour and 293 against. (Under the EC Treaty the EP can dismiss the College only by a two-thirds majority of the votes cast, including a majority of all MEPs. However, political realities mean that it is very unlikely that a College defeated by a nominal majority could stay in office.)

The special committee's report was issued two months later, in March, and was highly critical of aspects of the College's work and behaviour (Committee of Independent Experts, 1999a). Particular criticisms were made of: Santer in his capacity as the Commissioner responsible for the Commission's Security Office for taking 'no meaningful interest in its functioning' and allowing it to develop as 'a state within a state' (point 6.5.7); Cresson, for showing favouritism to someone known to her when issuing contracts (points 8.1.1–8.1.38); and Commissioners as a whole for being reluctant to assume responsibility for their actions – 'The studies carried out by the

Committee have too often revealed a growing reluctance among the members of the hierarchy to acknowledge their responsibility. It is becoming difficult to find anyone who has even the slightest sense of responsibility' (point 9.4.25). Meeting on the day the report was published and aware that MEPs were preparing for a motion of censure that almost certainly would have been passed with a large majority, the Santer College collectively resigned – nine months before the scheduled end of its term of office. The resignation and a censure vote could possibly have been avoided had Santer and Cresson stepped down, but neither was willing to do so. The resignation of the Commission was widely interpreted as a triumph for the EP and as a highly significant step forward in its long campaign to exercise greater control over Commission activities. (For fuller accounts of the resignation of the College, see MacMullen, 1999; Tomkins, 1999)

Almost immediately after resigning the Santer College announced that it would stay in office in a caretaker capacity until a replacement College was appointed. During this period it would not launch any significant new initiatives or take any major policy decisions. To emphasise the transitional nature of the situation, Commissioners were now referred to as Acting Commissioners. A delay in the appointment of the new College until September – occasioned largely by the July 1999 EP elections and the customary EU 'shutdown' in August – resulted in the Santer College not finally leaving office until almost six months after its resignation (though Santer himself resigned in July after being elected to the EP).

The Prodi Commission, 1999–

Aftermath of the resignation   The decision of the Santer College to stay in office on an interim basis gave the governments of the member states time to consider what they should do in the unprecedented situation that had arisen. In addition to having to consider who they wished to nominate to the new College there were two collective decisions to be made. First, who should replace Jacques Santer as Commission President? Extraordinarily, Santer initially considered trying to stay on himself, but MEPs quickly made it clear that they would not support him. Second, should the replacement College be appointed on an interim basis to see out the remaining months of the Santer College's term or should the process of appointing a new full-term College be brought forward? If the former option was chosen, a consequence would probably be that most of the current Commissioners would seek to stay in office for another few months (although MEPs made it clear that Santer and Cresson would have to go). If the latter option was chosen, most of the current Commissioners would probably resign or be replaced by their national governments.

A special summit to consider these questions did not have to be called since one was already scheduled for ten days after the College's resignation. This was the March 1999 Berlin summit, which had been arranged by the German Council Presidency to enable final decisions to be taken on the *Agenda 2000* package of budgetary and policy reforms. At the summit, the national leaders decided, for reasons that are set out in Chapter 3, to nominate the former Italian Prime Minister, Romano Prodi, to be the new Commission President. They further decided that they did not wish for an interim College, but rather for a full-term one (European Council, 1999a, Part II).

As is shown in Chapter 3, Prodi announced soon after being nominated that fundamental reform of the Commission would be a prime objective of his presidency. This helped to pave the way for a relatively easy endorsement of him by the EP in June. The nomination of the Commission's other members then followed over the summer months, in time for EP confirmatory hearings to be held in September. The ways in which the members of the new College were nominated – with a more influential role than hitherto for the President-designate – are described in Chapter 4, as is the outcome of what proved to be a relatively comfortable EP confirmation.

Priorities and objectives   Colleges do not start *ab initio* when they consider their priorities and objectives. Like policy actors everywhere, their options are shaped and conditioned by existing circumstances.

The circumstances that brought the Prodi College to office were such that comprehensive reform of the functioning of the Commission had to be at the very top of its agenda. Prodi quickly initiated action on this. He did so in three main ways. First, new codes of conduct for Commissioners and for the relations between Commissioners and the services were drawn up, as also were new rules of procedure for the operation of the Commission (Commission 1999b–1999g). Second, one of the (only four) returning Commissioners, Neil Kinnock, was given the portfolio of Administrative Reform and a brief to present a report by early 2000 on the reform of the Commission. Third, each of the Commissioners-designate was required to give Prodi an undertaking that they would resign if the President required them to do so.

This undertaking was designed to enable the President to avoid the sort of situation that had arisen with Edith Cresson in the closing months of the Santer Commission, when her refusal to resign had been an important factor in the crisis that eventually enveloped the whole College.

Kinnock's reform proposals were made public in early 2000 with the issuing of a consultation paper in January (Commission, 2000a) followed by a White Paper in March (Commission, 2000b). With the reform strategy having as its objective . . . 'to make changes which will ensure that efficiency, accountability, transparency, responsibility and service are applied as working conventions everywhere in this unique multinational administration' (Commission 2000a: iii), a range of reforms were announced that would transform aspects of the functioning of the Commission. Amongst the reforms were to be an overhaul of staffing policy, the introduction of more efficient and performance-oriented working methods, the creation of a new system of financial management, and the establishment of a planning system that would relate priorities more closely to resources and would prevent the Commission from becoming overloaded by taking on tasks it was not equipped to undertake. Box 2.1 provides a summary of the major reforms.

Other priorities and objectives identified by Prodi at the beginning of his presidency were more traditional, but in some cases were given a sharper edge by prevailing circumstances. He told the EP in May 1999 that priority areas would include: strengthening the CFSP and Europe's profile on the international stage (widely judged to be urgent following the EU's disjointed response to the crisis in Kosovo); developing policies to create an area of freedom, security and justice within the EU (already mandated by the Amsterdam Treaty, signalled by the European Council at its December 1998 Vienna meeting as a priority area, and at that stage scheduled to be the subject of a special European Council at Tampere in October 1999); and pursuing policies that would stimulate economic growth in Europe and combat unemployment (hardly a controversial priority, but one that was seen by many EU decision-makers as more important than ever as the euro struggled to establish itself as a strong currency) (Prodi, 1999a).

In September, on the day the EP voted to approve his College, Prodi particularly emphasised the importance that must be attached to not letting the enlargement process drift: firm dates should be set for the accession of the leading applicants, whilst the more backward applicants should be offered 'virtual membership' as soon as possible

Box 2.1 Reforming the Commission: Summary of the Contents of the 2000 White Paper

The reform strategy is built on three related themes: reform of the way political priorities are set and resources are allocated; comprehensive reform of human resources policy; and a thorough overhaul and modernisation of financial management and control.

The programme of reform is arranged under five headings:

1   *A culture based on service*
    This heading emphasises that the following principles underpin the whole reform process: independence, responsibility, accountability, efficiency and transparency.

    Some specific actions had already been taken under this heading with the adoption in September 1999 of a Code of Conduct for Commissioners and a Code of Conduct Governing Relations Between Commissioners and Departments. New actions proposed include a Code of Good Administrative Behaviour for Commission Officials, a Committee on Standards in Public Life covering all EU institutions, new rules to improve public access to EU documents, and the speeding up of payments of monies owed by the Commission.

2   *Priority setting, allocation and efficient use of resources*
    Under this heading a more effective method for setting priorities and allocating resources is laid out. The intention is to move away from: (1) a system in which priorities have generally not been linked to resources; (2) a management culture that has emphasised control rather than objectives.

    There are three strands to this aspect of the reform programme:

    1   *The introduction of 'activity-based' management* 'This system aims at taking decisions about policy priorities and the corresponding resources together, at every level in the organisation. This allows the resources to be allocated to policy priorities and, conversely, decisions about policy priorities to be fully informed by the related requirements.'

        As part of this process, the planning of Commission activities and the use of resources is to become more policy-driven. To this end, a new Strategic Planning and Programming (SPP) function to be established in the Secretariat General 'to assist the College in taking decisions on policy priorities and the allocation of resources as well as to promote performance management throughout the Commission'. An annual policy strategy (APS) to be produced setting out policy objectives, proposed policies, and the matching of resources to tasks. The APS to form the basis of the annual work programme and to be the main driver of the budgetary process.

    $\longrightarrow$

2 *Developing an externalisation policy* The Commission is to continue to make use of outside resources in the public and private sectors but to develop a clearer policy on externalisation 'to bring order to what already occurs and, notably, to devise more efficient and accountable methods for handling financial programmes'. Externalisation should not be used to cover for shortfalls in internal resources but 'should only be chosen when it is a more efficient and more cost effective means of delivering the service or goods concerned'.

3 *Performance-oriented working methods* Working procedures need to be simplified, modernised and made more performance-oriented. Areas for attention to include better inter-service coordination, the greater use of quality-management techniques, and better use of modern technologies.

3 *Human resources development*

A modernised and integrated human resources policy 'from recruitment to retirement' is to be established. Key elements of this to include:

1 *Greater weight to be given to management abilities* This is to apply to appointments, staff training and assessment performance.

2 *Career development* The main changes here are to be:
- new recruits to be initially appointed on a probationary basis only;
- improved career guidance to be provided for all staff and internal mobility to be encouraged;
- staff training to be extended and improved;
- a new and more linear career structure to be developed – with more grades than under the existing system – in which merit will determine promotion from grade to grade;
- the performance appraisal system to be adapted to ensure it is fair, transparent and objective.

3 *Non-permanent staff* The reliance on contract staff to be reduced, though not eliminated. A proposal to be made to convert part of the Commission's budget for contract staff into permanent posts.

4 *Equal opportunities to be more actively promoted* This includes a minimum target of doubling the number of women in top management within five years.

4 *Audit, financial management and control*

The existing systems for financial management and control are no longer suitable to deal with the enormously increased volume and range of projects and transactions with which the Commission deals.

Box 2.1 continued

Procedures 'need to be made simpler and faster, more transparent and decentralised'. To this end:

1   *The responsibilities of authorising officers and line managers are to be clearly defined*   As part of this: (a) clearer rules are to be drawn up defining the responsibilities of all financial actors; (b) these rules are to include such principles as competitive procedures for allocating funding, equal treatment of all tenderers, and transparent selection procedures; (c) as far as possible, the person taking the decision to approve an operation should also be the one authorising the expenditure.

2   *Overhauling financial management, control and audit*   The existing system under which the Financial Control DG is responsible for both vetting proposed projects and evaluating results is unsatisfactory and should be abandoned. Controls to be devolved to the DGs, the Financial Control DG to be abolished and a Central Financial Service and an Internal Audit Service to be established with such responsibilities as defining financial roles and procedures, specifying standards, and monitoring controls and advising on their application. An Audit Progress Committee also to be established to exercise an overall monitoring of auditing processes.

3   *Protecting the Community's financial* interests   A series of measures to be taken to 'maximise the prevention of irregularities and the fraud-proofing of legislation and financial management rules and procedures'. The measures to include: better coordination between the Anti-Fraud Office (OLAF) and other Commission departments; closer involvement of OLAF in the fraud-proofing of legislation and systems for tender and contract management; more effective management of the recovery of unduly paid funds.

5   *Delivering and sustaining reform*
Implementation of the reform programme to begin immediately, but some of it – including changes to Staff Regulations and the Financial Regulation, and an increase in resources – is dependent on Council and EP approval.

   A detailed Action Plan constitutes Part II of the White Paper. Several Commission structures are charged with seeing to its delivery – notably a Reform Group of Commissioners, a Reform Task Force, and Planning and Coordination Groups chaired by Directors General. A second Deputy Secretary General to be appointed with the specific remit of improving working practices and associated tasks.

Source: Commission (2000b).

(Prodi, 1999c). This ambitious approach to enlargement was confirmed when, in November, the Commission recommended to the European Council that accession negotiations should be opened in 2000 with the applicant states not currently negotiating, except for the special case of Turkey – though Turkey should be given candidate status and preparations for the eventual opening of negotiations with Turkey should begin (Commission, 1999j).

With the December 1999 Helsinki summit accepting most of the Commission's recommendations on enlargement, it seems likely that enlargement and internal reform will be the central themes of the Prodi College.

Concluding remarks

This chapter has traced the evolution of the Commission, from the tiny and experimental High Authority of the early ECSC to the major European institution that it is today.

Perhaps the single most striking feature of the history of the Commission is its consistent position as a key policy actor in the European integration process and in the functioning of the EC/EU. It is a position, however, that has varied considerably in its effectiveness, both as regards time periods and policy areas. This has been partly because of variations in the Commission's own performance – as seen, for example, in the way the leadership offered by the President has almost alternated between strong (Monnet, Hallstein, Delors, and arguably Jenkins) and weak (in varying degrees and different ways, Thorn, Santer, and the Presidents of the early and mid-1970s). It has been partly also because the Commission's ability to guide and shape policy development has been much affected by the operating contexts in which it has found itself. The most important feature of these contexts has been the views of the governments of the member states. At some times and in some policy areas governments have been supportive of the Commission, as with the establishment of the customs union and the CAP in the 1960s and the development of the SEM from the mid-1980s. At other times, however, governments have contested and resisted Commission initiatives, as with the attempt to develop a nuclear-energy policy after 1958 and the efforts to remove non-tariff barriers to trade in the 1970s.

Later chapters will return to this issue of the Commission's policy impact and effectiveness.

Chapter 3

The President

Appointment

The Maastricht changes

Prior to the entry into force of the Maastricht Treaty there were no special treaty provisions for the appointment of the President of the Commission. He or she was to be appointed on the same basis as the other Commissioners: namely for a four-year term, which could be renewed, and by 'common accord of the Governments of the Member States' (Article 158, EEC Treaty). In practice, however, because of the importance of the post, special provisions did apply. Whereas other Commissioners were appointed on the basis of national nominations which were automatically confirmed by the Council of Ministers, the President was appointed only after extensive soundings and consultations between the governments of the member states at the highest levels.

The Maastricht Treaty changed the procedures by which the President and the other members of the Commission were to be appointed. The key provisions were set out in Article 158: 2 TEC:

> The governments of the Member States shall nominate by common accord, after consulting the European Parliament, the person they intend to appoint as President of the Commission.
>
> The governments of the Member States shall, in consultation with the nominee for President, nominate the other persons whom they intend to appoint as members of the Commission.
>
> The President and the other members of the Commission thus nominated shall be subject as a body to a vote of approval by the European Parliament. After approval by the European Parliament, the President and the other members of the Commission shall be appointed by common accord of the governments of the Member States.

These provisions incorporated two changes from the previous treaty provisions in respect of how Presidents were to be appointed. First, the President was to be nominated before other Commissioners. In practice, this is what had happened since Roy Jenkins was nominated in 1976, with Presidents normally being nominated at the June European Council meeting in the year prior to the January when new Colleges are scheduled to take up office. Second, the EP was given a consultative role in the nomination for President and a confirmatory role in regard to the whole Commission. This latter power of confirmation was, rather like the appointment of the President before the appointment of other Commissioners, putting into treaty form what had become an established practice. However, so as to give the confirmatory power greater credibility and meaning, the term of office of Colleges was extended from four years to five so as to bring them into close alignment with the term of the EP: Colleges were now scheduled to assume office in the January after the fixed five-yearly June EP elections, thus ensuring that the confirmatory vote should normally be held six months or so into the life of a new Parliament. (The tenures of office of Colleges and the EP were brought into alignment by appointing the College that assumed duties in January 1993 for a two-year period only, see Table 3.1.)

The appointment of Santer

The Maastricht provisions did, of course, provide only a skeletal outline of how Presidents were to be chosen. Much remained to be fleshed out by political action. In 1994, when the provisions were used for the first time, that political action was intense. There were three main reasons for this. First, Jacques Delors had used his ten-year period of office to increase the importance and the status of the position. The President had always enjoyed more standing than his fellow Commissioners, but not usually by much – and barely at all during the Thorn Presidency. By 1994, when the deliberations on Delors' successor began in earnest, it was clear that the President had considerable potential to impose a very real stamp on the nature and direction of Commission activities. Second, there were real differences between the governments of member states over what sort of President they wanted. The spectrum spread from those who, like the Germans, would ideally have preferred a dynamic and forceful President in the Delors mould, through the majority of governments who judged the prevailing mood as requiring a less adventurist and rather more consolidating figure, to the British Government which wanted the most cautious figure they could get. Third, the EP decided

Table 3.1   *Presidents and size of the Commission since 1967*

Dates of office of Colleges	President/nationality	Number of members of Colleges
July 1967–July 1970[a]	Jean Rey (Belgium)	14
July 1970–March 1972	Franco Maria Malfatti (Italy) (resigned)	9
March 1972–January 1973	Sicco Mansholt (Netherlands) (interim President)	9
January 1973–January 1977	François–Xavier Ortoli (France)	13
January 1977–January 1981	Roy Jenkins (United Kingdom)	13
January 1981–January 1985	Gaston Thorn (Luxembourg)	14
January 1985–January 1989	Jacques Delors (France)	14[b]
January 1989–January 1993	Jacques Delors (France)	17
January 1993–January 1995	Jacques Delors (France)	17
January 1995–July 1999	Jacques Santer (Luxembourg) (resigned)	20
July 1999–September 1999	Manuel Marin (Spain) (interim President)	20
September 1999–	Romano Prodi (Italy)	20

Notes:
a First Commission following the merger of the High Authority of the ECSC and the Euratom and EEC Commissions.
b 17 from January 1986.

to take as much advantage as it could of the right given to it by the Maastricht Treaty to be consulted on the nomination. Crucially in this regard, when the EP revised its Rules of Procedure in 1993 it included a new Rule 32 on the Nomination of the President of the Commission that provided for it to hold a debate and vote on the President-designate (European Parliament, 1993). The Rule was designed to establish a right of veto for the EP over the European Council's nominee.

In the event, the selection of the new President proved to be even more fraught and tortuous than had been anticipated. Names were bandied around for months before the June 1994 Corfu European Council meeting, which was supposed to agree on who would be the nominee, but there were problems associated with all of those who could be regarded as serious runners. With the summit fast approaching, Chancellor Kohl and President Mitterrand, after only minimal consultations with the other member states, let it be known that they favoured the appointment of the Belgian Prime Minister, Jean-Luc Dehaene. At the time, it was thought this initiative was likely to be successful. One reason for anticipating success was that there was a widely held feeling that, following Delors, it was the turn of someone from a small member state to be President. Another reason was that Dehaene was essentially a centrist and pragmatic figure who was unlikely to upset any government by being adventurist or over-bold. And yet another reason was the political weight of France and Germany behind the proposal. Far, however, from the Kohl–Mitterrand initiative being successful, it was contested and subsequently withdrawn. The reason for this was that the British Prime Minister, John Major, refused to back Dehaene, even when, at Corfu, the two remaining alternative figures with their hats still in the ring, the Dutch Prime Minister, Ruud Lubbers, and the UK Commissioner, Leon Brittan, withdrew their candidatures – Lubbers having been supported only by the Netherlands, Italy, and Spain and Brittan only by the UK. Despite being subject to intense pressure from the other national leaders to accept Dehaene, Major refused to do so and the summit broke up without agreement. With Germany about to assume the Council Presidency, Chancellor Kohl announced that a special meeting of the European Council would be convened in the near future to resolve the matter.

There then followed a short period of intense diplomatic activity, in which the Germans took the lead. Following widespread consultations, a new name emerged – that of the Luxembourg Prime Minister,

Jacques Santer. Although little different from Dehaene in his political outlook and views, the British raised no objections to Santer, thus confirming the suspicions of many that the resistance to Dehaene was based not on the publicly stated reasons – he was said to be too integrationist and federalist – but rather on irritation at what was seen to be yet another demonstration of attempted Franco–German domination of the EU and a need to satisfy backbench supporters in the House of Commons that Major's Government would stand up for the UK's interests in Europe. With Santer's name proving to be acceptable to all – with his placatory manner and exudance of bonhomie he had made few political enemies – a specially convened half-day summit in Brussels in early July approved his nomination after only twenty minutes' discussion.

The problems at European Council level had repercussions when the EP came to look at the nomination a few days later. There were always likely to be difficulties in the EP given that, as noted above, the Parliament was determined to assert that it had the right of confirmation and not just of consultation, and given too that the confirmation/consultation was scheduled for the first plenary session after the June 1994 elections – when MEPs would be eager to assert that they were not to be taken for granted. Santer's position was made more awkward by the rushed and rather secretive way in which his name had emerged, and the almost total lack of any prior meaningful discussions about his nomination with EP officers. Extensive political manoeuvring occurred in the days before Parliament took its decision, with some governments lobbying their MEPs to back Santer and with Santer himself both addressing the larger EP political groups and attending and responding to the plenary debate on his nomination. Chancellor Kohl, speaking on behalf of the Council, accepted that Santer would be obliged to withdraw if he was not endorsed by the EP – thus granting the EP its much-sought-after power of confirmation. When the EP vote was held there was a narrow majority in favour of endorsement, with 260 votes for, 238 against, and 23 abstentions.

The subsequent events leading to the endorsement of the whole College in January 1995 are described in Chapter 4.

The appointment of Prodi

The nomination of Santer's successor, Romano Prodi, was relatively smooth. This is highly ironical given that it occurred in the wake of the extraordinary events of March 1999, when the Santer College resigned nine months before the end of its term of office. The fact is, however, that within a fortnight of the resignation, the governments of the member states, at the special Berlin summit that had been called to finalise decisions on the *Agenda 2000* reform package, unanimously agreed to nominate Prodi. The main factors leading to them doing so were: his Centre-Left political background (eleven of the fifteen national leaders were, broadly speaking, from the Centre-Left); his known attachment to the virtues of the market (important for Centre-Right national leaders, and also for most of those from the Centre-Left); his political experience (he had been Italian Minister for Industry as long ago as 1978–79 and had been Prime Minister from 1996 to 1998); his leading role in championing and overseeing the restructuring of Italian industry when chairman of the Institute for Industrial Reconstruction (IRI) in 1982–89 and 1993–94; and his nationality – there was a feeling that it was desirable for the Commission President to come from a large member state and from a southern member state.

Before officially becoming President-designate Prodi needed the backing of the EP. As was shown above, in 1994 the EP had won for itself a *de facto* confirmatory power on the European Council's nominee for Commission President. The Amsterdam Treaty had upgraded this into a *de jure* right, by amending the first paragraph of Article 158: 2 – now re-numbered Article 214: 2 – to read: 'The governments of the Member States shall nominate by common accord the person they intend to appoint as President of the Commission; the nomination shall be approved by the European Parliament.' Helped by firm assurances that he was wholeheartedly committed to tackling Commission malpractices, Prodi's nomination was approved at the last plenary session of the 1994–99 Parliament, in May, when MEPs voted in favour by 392 votes to 72, with 41 abstentions.

The European Council had made it clear at the Berlin summit that it wished to see Prodi and his College appointed quickly, and not just to serve out the remaining months of the Santer College's term but those months plus a full five-year term. The EP elections and the summer holiday period prevented the wish for a quick appointment process being realised and it was not until the end of August that the EP confirmation hearings on the members of the new College began. When they did the issue of whether the appointment was for the four remaining months of the Santer College's term or for five years and four months was raised, with leaders of the European People's Party and European Democrats (EPP/ED) – the largest group in the EP following the June elections – indicating that they wished for a four-month appointment and for another round of confirmation hearings and a vote to be held in December or January. Prodi rejected this suggestion that he and his College should be put on probation and threatened to resign if the EP insisted upon it. With the exception of British Conservatives (who were also complaining about four members of the Santer College returning), EPP/ED leaders quickly backed down and, as is shown in Chapter 4, the College was endorsed at the September plenary without much difficulty.

Powers and influence

The Commission President used to be thought of as *primus inter pares* in the College. Now, however, he is very much *primus*. His powers and influence, over and above those which he exercises as a member of the College, stem from and are dependent on five main factors.

First, there are the *treaties*. Prior to the Amsterdam Treaty this was the least important of the factors since there were only a handful of specific references to the President in the treaties and only two of these were of much significance in terms of having direct implications for power and influence: Article D of the Common Provisions of the TEU (like Article 2 of the SEA before it) gave the President membership of the European Council and, as was noted above, Article 158(2) of the EC Treaty post-Maastricht required that he be consulted by the member states on the persons they intended to nominate as members of the Commission. Beyond these two treaty articles, it could be argued that the post-Maastricht requirement that the President be nominated by a special procedure also had implications in that it rather separated him out from, and in some respects elevated him above, his fellow Commissioners.

The Amsterdam Treaty considerably strengthened these treaty provisions. One way in which it did so was by amending Article 158 (now re-numbered 214) so that the governments of the member states 'shall by common accord with the nominee for President, nominate the other persons whom they intend to support as Members of the Commission'. In other words, the President was now not just to be consulted on the other members of the College but was to be positively involved in the nomination process and could veto national nominees. Another way in which the Amsterdam Treaty strengthened the President's position was via a new provision of the TEC stating that 'The Commission shall work under the political guidance of its President' (Article 219). That is to say, the President was authorised, indeed was now expected, to take the lead in setting the Commission's aims and objectives and guiding its activities. And yet another way in which the Amsterdam Treaty strengthened the position of the President was in a Declaration on the Organisation and Functioning of the Commission which stated that 'the President of the Commission must enjoy broad discretion in the allocation of tasks within the College, as well as in any reshuffling of those tasks during a Commission's term of office' (Declaration 32). Hitherto, the distribution of portfolios within the College had largely been on the basis of negotiation between the President and Commissioners and had been more or less fixed for the whole term of office except when EU enlargements necessitated some re-arranging. Now, portfolios were to be allocated by the President and he could change them during a College's term.

Second, there is *custom and practice*. Evolving expectations and norms, which have been shaped by the ways in which incumbents have interpreted the presidential role and by what has been seen to work and not work, have resulted in changing assumptions and anticipations about what the presidency can and should be doing. It had, for example, come to be generally accepted even before the Amsterdam changes that he would seek to set the overall 'tone' for his Commission, that he might sometimes seek to offer a lead in important or controversial issue areas, and that he had overall responsibility for seeing to the effective and efficient running of the Commission system.

Third, there are a series of *operating procedures* and *support mechanisms* which assist the President in undertaking the duties and living up to the expectations which are attached to the office. These procedures and mechanisms take many different forms. They include:

- Presidents can, within reason, assign whatever responsibilities they choose to themselves. All Presidents incorporate in their portfolio responsibility for some of the key central services, including most especially the Secretariat General, the Legal Service, and the Press and Communications Service (of which the Spokesman's Service is part under Prodi). (The responsibilities and importance of these services is described in Chapter 6.) In addition, policy responsibilities can be assumed if desired. So Delors, for reasons of personal interest, took much of the responsibility for providing the policy lead on EMU, whilst Santer assumed a general and coordinating – though not day-to-day – policy responsibility for monetary matters, the common foreign and security policy, and institutional reform. Prodi did not assign himself a specific policy brief.

- Under the Commission's Rules of Procedure (Commission, 1999d) the President convenes and approves the agenda of College meetings. He also chairs these meetings. He is thus in a strong position to influence, if not quite to fully control, what issues the College considers, when it considers them, and what form the consideration takes. In acting as College chair, the President must, of course, not over-press his own preferences, or difficulties may arise. A balance needs to be struck between 'effective chairmanship of the Commission and the maintenance of a collegiate consensus, while at the same time attempting to imprint a policy direction on the Commission' (Donnelly and Ritchie, 1997: 42).
- The President can, in effect, require other Commissioners to see him on request and to brief him as necessary, but this requirement does not work the other way around.
- The President's *cabinet* is larger than the *cabinets* of other Commissioners. It is so primarily because, as is shown in Chapter 5, it undertakes a very wide range of coordinating, liaising, chivvying, and information-gathering tasks on behalf of the President. In performing these tasks the *cabinet* is in almost constant contact with key people across the Commission and in other EU institutions, which helps the President to normally have a better overall knowledge of EU developments than the EU's other main political players.
- The President attends many influential meetings and gatherings which are not open to other Commissioners. These include weekly meetings with the chairpersons of COREPER I and COREPER II, monthly meetings with the Permanent Representatives of the member states, and regular periodic meetings with the Presidents of the Council and of the EP. In addition, there are many *ad hoc* and informal meetings with Heads of Government of the Member States.

Fourth, there are the *personal qualities and goals of the incumbent*. As was shown in Chapter 2, these qualities and goals have been highly variable in nature, with some Presidents having been strong in character and ambitious in aim and others having been less robust in fighting the Commission's corner and less desirous of advancing ideas and proposals of their own. In general terms it is clear that Monnet (in the ECSC High Authority), Hallstein (in the EEC Commission), and Jenkins and Delors (in the EC Commission) have been the strongest and most activist Presidents, with each having been closely associated with the launching of a number of initiatives and with the subsequent attempts to drive these initiatives through decision-making mechanisms. Significantly, none of these Presidents worried too much about developing collegiality or team spirit, preferring to work through trustees who could be relied upon. Significantly, too, and this says much for what an ambitious President can seek to do, the initiatives which are probably most associated with Jenkins and Delors – proclaiming the need of a European Monetary System (EMS) in the case of the former and laying the foundations (via the Delors Committee of bankers and financiers) of EMU in the case of the latter – were both conducted on an almost personal basis and with little reference, except for the imparting of information, to the rest of the Commission.

Fifth, and finally, the *climate of the times* has important consequences for what the President of the Commission can achieve. This point was touched on in Chapter 2 where it was noted that Thorn, whose Presidency is frequently presented in unfavourable terms when compared with his successor, Delors, was operating in difficult circumstances. The possibilities for progress on key issues were limited in the early 1980s by a number of factors, including ill feelings that existed between some national governments because of recurring disagreements on budgetary-related issues. When these disagreements were eventually resolved (temporarily, as it turned out) at the June 1984 Fontainebleau summit, the way was eased for the incoming Delors Commission to move on to other matters, most notably the opening up of the internal market. The importance of the climate of the times was demonstrated again in the early to mid-1990s when it came to be widely felt, especially after June 1992 when the Danish people rejected the TEU in a referendum, that the integration momentum was being rushed – not least by Delors in his public pronouncements on the subject. In consequence, Delors was obliged to become less bold, and many governments began to form the view that his successor would need to be a rather different sort of figure: more of a consolidator and less of an adventurer.

* * *

To explore a little further the powers and influence of the President of the Commission, it will be useful to have a close look at some of the key features of the Delors and Santer presidencies.

The Delors presidencies

Preparing for office

Before assuming office in January 1985 Delors resolved that the Commission over which he would preside would make its mark. With this in mind he spent much of the autumn of 1984 casting around for 'a big idea' which would provide a focus and an impetus for the incoming Commission (Grant, 1994: 70). Institutional reform, monetary union, and defence cooperation were all considered as possibilities for particular targeting, but eventually the completion of the internal market was settled on as the issue to be singled out and emphasised. There were two main reasons for this decision. First, extensive consultations undertaken by Delors and his advisers revealed that whereas all the other possible issues would be strongly resisted by at least some governments of the member states, the opening up of the European market would command general support. Indeed, there was already a momentum under way, stimulated in no small part by business interests, to dismantle the barriers which were fracturing the market and hindering economic development. Second, Delors saw, in a way in which few others did, that market integration would inevitably bring other important issues onto the agenda: it would, for example, be possible to pass all the laws that would be required for the market barriers to be removed only if there was a reform of decision-making processes, whilst movement towards a more integrated market would raise the question of whether there could ever be a fully integrated market without economic and monetary integration.

Different roles

Delors was thus instrumental in giving the internal market objective a high priority. He was also instrumental in the objective being given a high profile in that he did much to promote it in the early months of his presidency. He was, however, willing to leave most of the detailed drafting of what came increasingly to be referred to as the Single European Market (SEM) programme, or '1992' programme (1992 being set as the year for completion of the programme), to the relevant Commissioner – Lord Cockfield – and Commission officials. This division of labour, with Delors being prominent in offering political leadership and momentum and Cockfield concentrating more on giving the general principles of the initiative practical effect through the formulation of specific proposals, worked because: (1) there was a broad consensus in the College on the prioritisation of the SEM programme; (2) Delors and Cockfield developed a high regard for each other's capacities; (3) Delors and Cockfield were broadly content with their own roles. In most of the other major issue areas that arose and were pursued during the ten years of Delors' presidency, such a neat relationship between Delors and his fellow Commissioners did not usually exist. An important reason for this was that there was frequently a tension between, on the one hand, Delors wanting to be associated not only with general issues but also sometimes with the specifics of issues and, on the other, Commissioners being unwilling to assume a secondary role and wishing to be permitted a considerable measure of independence in their respective spheres of responsibility. Largely as a result of such tensions, Delors' role in respect of major Commission initiatives varied. Five examples of the sort of role he played may be cited.

First, in some issue areas which he regarded as being especially important or as falling within his own spheres of interest and expertise, Delors sought to keep tight control over Commission policy and activities. He was not able to evade the principle of collegiality – whereby the College must give (by majority vote if necessary) its approval to the general lines of Commission policy and to proposals and documents issued in the Commission's name – but beyond this requirement other Commissioners were not much involved in these issue areas. Institutional matters and EMU were such issue areas.

Second, in some important issue areas with which Delors wished to be closely involved but where other Commissioners had clear portfolio interests and responsibilities, Delors took the public lead and undertook much of the detailed work but did so in collaboration with the relevant Commissioners. The Commission's proposals in 1987–88 and 1992 on the future financing of the EC/EU were drawn up on such a basis, with significant inputs being made by several Commissioners and many parts of the services, but with Delors and his personal staff doing much of the work to pull the pieces together and put them into a coherent shape: hence the common description of the two sets of proposals as the Delors I and Delors II financial packages.

Third, Delors occasionally personally involved himself in issue areas that fell within the portfolio remits of other Commissioners because he felt the individuals concerned were just not up to the job. Naturally, intervention by Delors on these grounds was fraught with difficulties and was a recipe for tensions, not least since he was not inclined to hide his feelings when he saw, or thought he saw, incompetence and poor work. Such was the case in his second Commission when the member of his *cabinet* responsible for social policy, Patrick Venturini, virtually took over the portfolio of the ineffectual Commissioner for Social Policy, Vasso Papandreou, and was ironically referred to as her *chef de cabinet* (Endo, 1999: 54).

Fourth, on a few occasions, Delors became directly involved in an issue area because he disagreed with what the Commissioner responsible was doing. As with intervention on the grounds of incompetence, this did not make for good relations between Delors and the Commissioner concerned. An instance of Delors becoming involved for such reasons occurred in May–June 1992 when the Commissioner for the Environment, Carlo Ripa di Meana, announced that he would not attend the United Nations Conference on the Environment and Development – the so-called 'Earth Summit' – because the EC's positions on most of the key issues to be considered at the Summit were too weak to be of much value. Delors quickly made it clear that he thought the Commission should be represented at the Summit and arranged for Commissioner Matutes (whose portfolio covered energy and transport) to replace di Meana and for himself to be present at the Summit's most important, or at least most high-profile, stages. Di Meana resigned shortly after the Summit to become Minister of the Environment in the Italian Government.

Fifth, Delors was quick and adept at taking a policy lead when unexpected and/or unprecedented issues arose. The best example of this is the Commission's response to German reunification and its support for the rapid incorporation of the former East Germany into the EC. At the strategic level, this issue was handled mainly by Delors, who dealt directly with Chancellor Kohl and largely succeeded in keeping those Commissioners who wished to be involved in deliberations – notably Leon Brittan, who queried Delors' position – on the sidelines.

Relations with other policy actors

The President of the Commission is, and was even more so pre-Amsterdam, in possession of only limited formal powers of his own. If he is to be effective, as opposed to simply being visible, it is important that he is able to carry other key policy actors with him when he involves himself in issues and/or offers strategic or tactical leads. Delors' ways of working with other actors were variable, and his record of success in persuading them to his viewpoint was mixed.

With national political leaders, of which Heads of Government are the most important followed by Foreign Ministers and Ecofin Ministers, Delors enjoyed respect and was generally recognised as doing a good job. His enthusiasm, dynamism, forcefulness and intellect were all widely admired. Even Margaret Thatcher, who became very antagonistic towards him because of what she regarded as his over-enthusiasm for integration and his over-reaching interpretation of what she kept emphasising was an appointed and essentially administrative post, did not deny his capabilities. Rather, indeed, her objections to Delors were based precisely on his capabilities and the fact that he put them to full use in seeking to further the integration process.

The high esteem in which Delors was held by most national decision-makers did not mean that they ceded to him, or to the Commission, decision-making powers which were properly theirs. Nor did it mean that Delors and the Commission did not suffer defeats and have to make unwanted concessions in the European Council and the Council of Ministers. What, however, it did mean was that there was normally a predisposition to allow Delors considerable room for manoeuvre in charting the future of the integration process and a predisposition also to give proposals with which he was personally associated very serious consideration.

When necessary, Delors was prepared to argue his and the Commission's case very forcefully with national political leaders. Usually, however, he would not strike out on a course of action without having reason to believe that there was likely to be a considerable measure of support for at least the principles of such action at senior governmental levels. This information could be attained by engaging in soundings of various kinds, many of them in the form of face-to-face contacts in national capitals between

Delors and Heads of Government. The possibilities for, and the usefulness of, such face-to-face contacts were facilitated by several national leaders with similar centrist and pro-integrationist views to those of Delors holding office for much of the period of his presidency: Kohl in Germany, Mitterrand in France, Lubbers in the Netherlands, Santer in Luxembourg, Martens in Belgium, and Gonzales in Spain. Regular contacts with these and other national leaders led to good personal relations in some instances, which further helped Delors to prepare the ground and build support for ideas, initiatives, and proposals which he had in mind or was seeking to carry through.

With his fellow Commissioners, Delors did not go out of his way to establish close personal relations or to encourage a shared identity in the College. A distant manner of this sort perhaps does not matter too much if the President conceives of his role as being limited in scope and if he does not wish to involve himself directly in policy areas which are the responsibility of other Commissioners. However, neither of these conditions applied to Delors. Frictions and tensions thus inevitably arose, all the more so since Delors was quite open in his preference for doing much of his work not through the appropriate Commissioner(s) but through networks of 'loyalists' made up of advisers and officials who were found at different levels and different places in the Commission system. Particularly important amongst the loyalists were his *cabinet* staff, who were extremely hard-working, very competent, and committed to ensuring that the 'Delors line' was followed (see Ross, 1993, 1994, 1995).

An example of the way in which Delors' personal style and inclination to sometimes interfere in policy areas which were the responsibility of other Commissioners could lead to sharp disputes was given above, with the case of di Meana and the Rio Earth Summit. An even more public overflowing of tensions between Delors and another member of the College occurred in November 1992 in connection with the difficulties which were then being experienced by the EC and the US in resolving differences on agricultural issues within the context of the GATT Uruguay Round. Feeling that the Commissioner for Agriculture, Ray MacSharry, who was leading the Commission's negotiating team, was being unduly inflexible and was preventing a deal being struck, Delors sought to play an active role himself and use the weight of his office to facilitate progress. This 'interference' proved to be ill-judged, for MacSharry, a forceful figure himself, announced that he was withdrawing from the negotiating team because of Delors' interference, though he was not resigning from his post of Commissioner. MacSharry's action had the effect of exposing Delors as having overreached himself. Within days Delors backed down, MacSharry was reinstated as the Commission's chief external negotiator on agricultural issues, and Delors' standing within the Commission was damaged.

But though Delors' style and working methods did create problems with and for other Commissioners, the situation should not be exaggerated. With most Commissioners most of the time Delors established an acceptable working relationship which enabled them, within the framework of overall Commission policy, to get on with their responsibilities in a reasonably free and unhampered manner.

With the Commission administration, Delors sought to keep himself in touch with, and to influence, what was going on via a number of means. These means involved a mixture of the traditional and the new.

Foremost amongst the traditional means was making use of established Commission structures and mechanisms. So, for example, like other Presidents, Delors worked closely with the Secretary General, who is the Commission's senior administrative official. There were two Secretary Generals during Delors' tenure as President – Emile Noël until 1987, followed by David Williamson. Relations with both were a little difficult at first, but they gradually settled down into the customary Commission President–Secretary General relationship of 'partnership' (Endo, 1999: 41–4).

Another traditional means used by Presidents to make their influence felt within the Commission administration is effective use of their *cabinets*. Delors' *cabinet,* headed by the driving and remorseless Pascal Lamy, undertook all the customary functions of presidential *cabinets* with regard to the Commission administration, and more besides. Prominent amongst the functions it undertook were: it sought to extract information from the administration so as to keep Delors fully informed about what was going on; it sought advice from the appropriate parts of the administration if a presidential initiative was being considered or prepared; it sought to encourage the administration to come forward with proposals which the President favoured; it sought to move the administration along if it felt progress on a matter was too slow; and it sought to enhance the promotion prospects of those who were sympathetic to what Delors was doing. In approaching and undertaking these various tasks Delors' *cabinet* was much more vigorous, pro-active and interventionist than any of the preceding presidential *cabinets*. It also acted in a more confident and demanding manner than had been seen hitherto. This all gave rise to considerable resentments amongst officials, with particular sources of grievance being the way in which Delors' *cabinet* staff frequently assumed that officials should fall in line with their thinking, and the way too in which Commission hierarchical structures would often be by-passed by *cabinet* staff 'reaching down' into the administration to deal directly with officials who had a responsibility or expertise in a matter in which they were interested.

An innovatory means used by Delors to assist him in his dealings with the Commission administration was to make use of loyalists who held important and influential, though not by any means always the most senior, positions in the administrative system. For the most part these loyalists were French and had links of some sort with Delors' past, if only by having an affinity with the French Socialist Party. Much has been made by commentators of whether these people can be described as having constituted a 'Delors' network' within the Commission. If 'Delors network' is taken to imply that there was a clearly identifiable group of people who met regularly to exchange ideas and to discuss tactics, then no such network existed. If, however, 'Delors network' is taken to imply something looser – a body of people who were mostly known to each other personally and who could be relied on to provide support for the President when the need arose – then indeed a network did exist.

In sum, Delors created a very strong power base of his own within the Commission's administration. As Peterson has noted (1995b: 475): 'Delors' reliance on his parallel government made lines of authority and communication within the Commission even more complicated than they appeared on paper.'

The Santer presidency

By contrast with the dynamism and activism of Delors, Santer is usually thought of as having been a weak President. Unquestionably there is something in this characterisation. Santer did not have Delors' personal drive and leadership and he did not offer anything in policy terms to match Delors' 'big ideas' of the completion of the internal market and the creation of EMU. Santer's call to 'do less, but do it better', in many ways captures the differences in ambition and spirit between the two Presidents.

But the contrast between the Delors and Santer presidencies should not be overstated. One reason why it should not be so is that Delors was not so influential when the 'policy window' that had opened in the mid-1980s began to close from 1990–91. The later years of his presidency were framed by a much less favourable environment for policy expansionism and this resulted in these years being more 'normal' in terms of the impact he and his Commission were able to exert on EU affairs. Santer inherited this less favourable environment, so it would seem only reasonable to compare his policy impact with the post-1990 Delors years rather than the dynamic 1985–90 years.

Another reason why the contrast between the policy achievements of the Delors and Santer presidencies ought not to be overstated is that, as was shown in Chapter 2, much was in fact accomplished on Santer's 'watch'. The single currency was launched, the largest and most difficult enlargement round in EC/EU history was progressed, the *Agenda 2000* reform programme was developed and approved, the opening and liberalisation of the internal market was extended into difficult and hitherto protected sectoral areas, and significant reforms designed to improve policy coordination and managerial efficiency within the Commission were carried through. Though Santer and his College ended their time in office in near-disgrace, their achievements were considerable.

But though the contrast between the Delors and Santer Commissions is not quite so great in terms of policy accomplishments as it might at first appear, the contrast between them in terms of style is very marked. In summary, Santer operated on a much more 'correct' basis. He did not rely so much on his *cabinet* to drive issues through or on a network of adherents and sympathisers to get things done. He was much less inclined to circumvent the Commission's rules of procedure if they were inconvenient or presented barriers. And he was much more collegial in his method of working, though this is not to say his College was necessarily more cohesive – as Peterson (1999a: 53) notes, there was more voting in the Santer College than there ever was under Delors.

Santer's greater collegiality was a manifestation of his general approach, which was to emphasise conciliation and consensus-building much more than had Delors. Santer was an incrementalist and a consolidator rather than a pioneer, which meant that whilst he was less daring than had been Delors he was much less prone to get himself into difficulties by being 'ahead of the game'. That is not to say, however, that he did not attempt to press the pace on anything. He was, for example, an open campaigner for significant institutional reform at the 1996–97 IGC, using his 1996 'State of the Union' address to the EP (an occasion he initiated in 1995) to criticise the member states for approaching the Conference with a 'lack of dynamism' and with 'ambitions pitched too low'. He warned that the European agenda would not remain intact 'if the outcome of the IGC does not match the scale of the institutional challenge represented by enlargement' (*European Report*, 21 September 1996). Rather ironically, it might be thought, given that his style was so much less presidential than that of Delors, one of the issues on which Santer pressed the IGC most strongly was the powers of the Commission President: he saw to it that the Commission submission to the IGC included calls for the President to be approved by the Parliament and to be empowered 'to play a decisive part in the choice of the Commission's Members, the better to ensure collegiality' (Commission, 1996b: 20). As was noted above, these calls were accepted by the member states and were incorporated in the Amsterdam Treaty.

Concluding remarks

This chapter has had much to say about the presidency of Jacques Delors. This has been partly because his presidency is still relatively recent, it has been partly because of the length of his term of office, but it has been mainly because the nature of the presidency changed very considerably during Delors' tenure. As has been shown, he built the Commission presidency into a high-profile and potentially very powerful position both within the Commission system itself and also, more broadly, in the EU system as a whole.

The Maastricht and Amsterdam treaties have further consolidated and institutionalised this elevation of the Commission presidency, with the increased powers given to the President in the appointment of the other Commissioners, in the allocation of Commissioners' portfolios, and in guiding the political direction of the Commission. But it should not be thought that these increased powers will necessarily enable Romano Prodi or his successors to impose themselves as much as Delors did in the early years of his presidency. Those years were the exception rather than the norm, made possible by the occupancy in office of a strong and visionary personality at a time when the contextual circumstances for integrationist advance were exceptionally favourable. The norm is that Commission Presidents do not have such strong personalities and do not enjoy such favourable operating environments. As such, whilst Presidents can certainly make a considerable impact both inside the Commission and in the EU more generally, their role and influence should not be exaggerated.

Chapter 4

The College

Appointment

Leaving aside the special case of the President of the Commission, the TEC provides for a three-stage process in the appointment of Commissioners. As was shown in Chapter 3, these stages are provided for in Article 214 of the TEC. As with many treaty articles, the formal provisions tell only part of the story of what actually happens in practice.

The *first stage*. This involves the governments of the member states, 'by common accord with the nominee for President', making nominations. This nomination process must meet the requirements of Article 213: 1 (ex-157: 1) which specifies 'The Commission must include at least one national of each of the Member States, but may not include more than two members having the nationality of the same State'.

The requirements of Article 213: 1 have come to be accepted as having two specific implications. First, the five larger member states – France, Germany, Italy, Spain and the UK – each have two Commissioners and all other states have one. Since the 1995 enlargement of the EU, this has meant that there have been twenty Commissioners. Second, member states do not make nominations in excess of their own 'national entitlement', and they do not query or challenge each other's nominee(s).

Until the Maastricht Treaty the President-designate had no formal involvement in the nomination process, but the Treaty changed the TEC to give him a consultative role. In fact, the possibility for consultation had long existed – the custom of nominating the President six months or so before he assumed office and in advance of nominations for the other Commissioners having been established with Roy Jenkins' nomination in 1976. However, not much use was made of this consultation possibility in practice, and not much changed in 1994 when the Maastricht consultation requirement was given its first outing. Jacques Santer, whose nomination as President-designate was announced in July 1994, was informed by member states about their nominations but was not in any real sense consulted about them. Indeed, the names of some nominees for the new Commission were leaking out within days of Santer's nomination: that is to say, before consultation was even possible, let alone meaningful.

The Amsterdam Treaty strengthened the President's hand by upgrading the right to consultation to the above-noted system of nominations being made by 'common accord' between the national governments and the President. Romano Prodi sought to take advantage of this by spending considerable time visiting national capitals to discuss with national leaders the sort of College he wanted. However, this did not prevent governments from having the upper hand over 'their' nomination(s) and did not have much noticeable effect in encouraging them to look at the overall composition of the College. Certainly there were people who Prodi is thought to have attempted to persuade governments to nominate – including one of the serving French Commissioners, Yves-Thibault de Silguy, and the French Justice Minister, Elisabeth Guigou – who were not appointed. It may be that discouraging noises from Prodi resulted in a few governments thinking again about a nominee, and it is probable that the decision of both Sweden and Luxembourg to nominate a woman was influenced by pressure from Prodi – who was anxious that women be well represented in the College. But there is not one nominee that can definitely be attributed to intervention by Prodi. It has been suggested that, concerned that there was too narrow a range of collective experience amongst the nominations, Prodi succeeded in persuading the Irish Government at a late stage in the nomination process to alter their first choice – the former Justice Minister, Maire Geoghegan-Quinn – to someone who had a wider experience outside the world of professional politics. However, Irish sources indicate that the decision to nominate David Byrne, the country's Attorney General, rather than Quinn was determined more by domestic political factors.

The *second stage*. The nominees for Commission posts, including the President, must be subject as a body to a vote of approval by the EP.

This requirement, like the consultative role given to the President in regard to nominations, was formally established by the Maastricht Treaty. It built on evolving practice: in February 1981, just after the new Thorn-led Commission had assumed office, the EP, on its own initiative, voted on the investiture and programme of the new Commission; and in 1985, 1989 and 1993, Jacques Delors voluntarily submitted the three Colleges over which he presided to votes of confidence in the EP before they formally took up office.

In typical fashion, the EP in 1994–95 sought to use its new Maastricht Treaty power to the maximum possible extent. This it did by not just contenting itself with a plenary debate on the new College followed by a vote, but by 'requiring' all Commissioners to appear before 'examining' EP committees in US Senate-type public 'hearings'. There was no obligation on the twenty members of the new Commission to submit themselves to this process, but all agreed to do so. Had any Commissioner-designate refused to appear before the appropriate hearing, Parliament's only way of retaliating would have been to refuse to endorse the College as a whole since, unlike the US Senate, the EP has no power to withhold approval from individual nominees.

The hearings should have been held in November 1994 but were delayed until early January so as to enable representatives from the three new member states (Austria, Finland and Sweden) to participate. Two or three hearings were held each working day over the period of one week, with most hearings being conducted before around 60–70 MEPs and lasting for between two and three hours. Following the hearings, the EP's Conference of Presidents (which is composed of the Parliament's President and the chairpersons of the political groups) met with Santer and put to him views which had emerged during the hearings process. It was made clear that the process had raised doubts about the competence of some of the nominees to handle the portfolios they had been allocated, with five nominees being singled out: Pádraig Flynn, Ritt Bjerregaard, Erkki Liikanen, Anita Gradin and Yves-Thibault de Silguy. The Conference of Presidents did not call for these Commissioners-designate to be replaced (which would have been beyond Santer's control) but rather for the remit of their portfolios to be altered. Flynn, for example, was deemed to be competent to retain the social and employment portfolio but not to be competent to retain the equal opportunities portfolio (he had been strongly criticised by members of the Women Right's Committee for being too male chauvinistic). Bjerregaard came in for the strongest criticism, not least since she had rather insensitively responded to stiff questioning by MEPs by declaring that they were 'not a real parliament'. Santer told the Conference of Presidents that he was not prepared to adjust the allocation of Commission portfolios, which drew the response that if he had not changed his mind in one week's time – when MEPs were due to hold their confirmatory vote after Santer had addressed them in plenary session – then the EP might delay or block the Commission's appointment. The week's interlude allowed time for reflection, for politicking, and for gatherings and meetings of various kinds. By the end of the week no Commissioners-designate had withdrawn their nominations and no portfolios had been re-assigned, but four 'concessions' had been made to try and persuade MEPs to support the new College. First, pacifying statements were put out by some of the Commissioners-designate who had been under attack. Pádraig Flynn, for example, emphasised that he was wholly supportive of equal opportunities issues, while Ritt Bjerregaard claimed that she had been misquoted over the remarks that the EP was not a real parliament. Second, modest changes in arrangements for meetings of groups of Commissioners were announced, including that Santer himself would chair a group to monitor the high priority that would be given by the Commission to equal treatment for men and women. Third, Santer told MEPs when he addressed them that he supported fuller powers for the EP, that the Commission would be taking the views and opinions of the EP very seriously, and that he would be proposing that the 1990 Code of Conduct governing relations between the EP, the Council, and the Commission be reviewed. Fourth, throughout his plenary address Santer adopted the strongly pro-integrationist stance that most MEPs wanted to hear. Amidst considerable reservations that not much had really been achieved, the EP voted to confirm the Santer Commission by 418 votes to 103, with 59 abstentions.

The EP arranged their approach to the confirmation vote on the Prodi Commission in a similar manner to that of the Santer Commission, though with some refinements and adjustments. One refinement was that Commissioners were obliged to complete long questionnaires a month or so before their hearings. These questionnaires – which covered a range of issues relating to Commissioners' portfolios and also to the aims and operation of the Commission as a whole – were used as a basis for much of the questioning in the investigatory committees. For the most part, the hearings – which were held over a period of one and a half weeks in late August/early September – proceeded more smoothly than they had done in 1995. A few Commissioners-designate were put under particular pressure, such as Loyola de Palacio for why she had not been more robust in investigating alleged CAP frauds when she was Spanish Agriculture Minister, but none saw their position seriously threatened by their hearing.

After the hearings Prodi met with the leaders of the political groups in the Committee of Presidents to discuss general issues and to address some matters that were his personal responsibility. Foremost amongst the points on which the EP leaders wanted clarification was whether there would be more consultation with Parliament on Commission proposals before their submission, and what Prodi would do if the Parliament passed a motion of no confidence in an individual Commissioner – something for which there is no treaty provision, just as there is no treaty provision for the President to dismiss a Commissioner. On the first of these points Prodi offered full consultation in the framework of 'a new culture of openness and mutual cooperation'. On the second point he stated 'where the Parliament expresses a lack of confidence in a member of the Commission – subject to the substantive and representative nature of the political support for such a view – I as President of the Commission will examine seriously whether I should request that member to resign' (*Guardian*, 8 September 1999).

A week after the committee hearings were completed there was a debate in plenary session followed by a vote in which the Prodi Commission was endorsed by 414 votes to 142, with 35 abstentions.

Clearly this second stage of the appointment process can be a fraught time for Commissioners-designate. It is, however, also a stage that can be of considerable value to an incoming College: it obliges Commissioners to be well informed about their responsibilities before assuming office; it helps to publicise the policy priorities of Commissioners; and it bolsters the Commission's claim to legitimacy and to have some democratic underpinning.

The *third stage*. Shortly after being approved by the EP, the nominees are formally appointed by unanimous approval of the governments of the member states. Assuming no special circumstances apply, Commissioners are appointed for five years and take up office in the January after the June in which the fixed five-yearly EP elections are held. Special circumstances did, of course, apply in 1999 following the resignation of the Santer College, which resulted in the Prodi College assuming office in the September for a period of five years and three and a half months.

The treaty requirement that the final appointment be by the unanimous approval of the governments of the member states has always suggested more than actually happens. It amounts to no more than rubber stamping approval by the Council of Ministers.

*   *   *

If a vacancy arises during a College's term of office, the TEC states that a replacement is appointed by unanimous agreement of the national governments. Somewhat anomalously given the provisions for nominations at the beginning of a College's term, no role is assigned to the Commission President, though in practice it is likely that he will be at least consulted. The last time a replacement Commissioner was appointed was in April 1994 (that is, pre-Amsterdam), when one of the Spanish Commissioners, Abel Matutes, resigned so as to be able to stand in the June 1994 EP elections. He was replaced by Marcelino Orejo.

When a vacancy arises towards the end of a College's term of office, it is usually decided not to make a replacement at all but rather to re-assign the departing Commissioner's duties. This happened, for example, when one of the Italian Commissioners, Carlo Ripa de Meana, resigned in the early summer of 1992. It also happened when three 'acting' Commissioners resigned in the months after the College's resignation in March 1999: Martin Bangemann left to take up a corporate appointment, whilst Santer and Emma Bonino stepped down to become MEPs.

Removal from office

Having been appointed, the assumption is that a College will serve its full term. The only formal way in which a College may be removed against its will is under Article 201 (ex-144) TEC, which specifies that the members of the Commission must resign as a body if the EP passes a motion of censure by a two-thirds majority of the votes cast, representing an absolute majority of its members. Several such motions have been put to the vote over the years, but until the events of early 1999 – which were described in Chapter 2 – none came within striking distance of success.

There are a number of reasons why there have been few votes of censure and why there has been, the 1999 case apart, only limited support for those that have been tabled. Three of these reasons are especially important. First, the Commission is often virtually an ally of the EP on major policy issues, with resistance to EP views usually being more common amongst the governments of the member states in the European Council and the Council of Ministers. Second, in so far as there is EP dissatisfaction with the Commission it is normally on matters of detail and of tactics rather than on matters of fundamental substance. Third, if the EP should dismiss the Commission it cannot designate its successor – although, of course, post-Maastricht it can reject a replacement College it judges to be unacceptable.

The events that led to the resignation of the Santer College in March 1999 occurred because the first two of the reasons that have just been identified did not apply. Regarding relations between the two institutions, they deteriorated sharply as the crisis deepened, with a strong personal edge being introduced when Jacques Santer challenged the EP in December 1998 to 'back me or sack me' and when Edith Cresson was seen to be arrogantly dismissive of the charges of corruption made against her. Regarding the nature of the issues involved, both the criticisms made of certain Commissioners on an individual basis and of the Commission as a body for mismanagement and incompetence were deemed to be extremely serious.

An important lesson of the 1999 crisis is that it showed a College can be forced from office without the stipulations of Article 201 necessarily being applied. One way in which it showed this was through the January vote of censure, which although lost (by 232 votes to 293) was accompanied by widespread comment from practitioners and observers to the effect that political realities would have forced the College to resign even if had suffered just a nominal majority defeat. Another way in which the crisis showed that the full application of Article 201 is not necessarily required for a College to be forced out is that the resignation occurred largely because, following the publication of the damning report by the Committee of Independent Experts, the Santer College *anticipated* that the requirements of Article 201 would be met if it did not resign.

Composition

There are no rules specifying what sort of people, with what sort of background and experience, should be Commissioners. It is entirely up to national governments who they nominate, and entirely up to the EP (since the Maastricht Treaty) and the President-designate (since the Amsterdam Treaty) whether the nominations are accepted.

Andrew MacMullen (1996, 1997) has undertaken detailed studies of the composition of the fifteen Colleges that assumed office between August 1952 (the ECSC High Authority) and January 1995 (the Santer Commission). In total, 120 people served in these Colleges, with half serving more than one term. MacMullen's overall conclusions are as follows:

> The College has been predominantly male and late middle aged. The majority have been university educated, mostly with qualifications in law or economics. The dominant occupational experiences have been as State officials, managers in private or public business, and lawyers. Political affiliations have been largely centrist and increasingly within the partisan boundaries of the main national governing parties. A national political career at the parliamentary and ministerial level is becoming almost the norm. Active experience in European and international organisations is a very frequent characteristic. (MacMullen, 1997: 46)

The Prodi College continued very much in this tradition, as will now be shown.

- Regarding *age*, the average at the time of initial appointment to the Prodi College in September 1999 was 52, which is what it was when the Santer College was appointed in January 1995. Ten Commissioners were in their 50s, two in their 60s, and eight in their 40s. The oldest, at 66, was the Dutch Commissioner, Frits Bolkestein, whilst the youngest, at 40, was the Greek Commissioner, Anna Diamantopoulou.
- Regarding *gender balance*, male domination continued. There were no female Commissioners until 1989, when two were appointed to the Delors II College. This number dropped to one in the Delors III College, and then increased to five in the Santer College. Under Prodi the number stayed at five, despite his hope that it would increase.
- Regarding *party political background*, the College has long been highly politicised in the sense that national nominations are strongly coloured by domestic party political affiliations. The nominations to the Prodi College displayed the customary pattern of smaller member states mostly nominating someone from their largest party and the five large member states 'splitting' their representations. A furious domestic political row broke out in Germany, which spilled over into the EP plenary hearings, when the coalition partners of the SPD/Green Government did not make a nomination from the main opposition CDU Party – which had comfortably won the June EP elections – but rather took one post each themselves.

The fact that eleven of the fifteen EU governments were, at the time of the nomination process, broadly Centre-Left in their political make-up, meant that the Prodi College was naturally given an overall Centre-Left tilt, even though the June 1999 EP elections, which were held just before governments began submitting their nominations, produced a Centre-Right majority. Whilst precise labels cannot be attached in all cases, in broad terms the College consisted of eleven Commissioners with a Socialist/Social Democrat political affiliation, six with a Christian Democrat/ Conservative affiliation, two with a Liberal affiliation, and one with a Green affiliation. Crucially, all governments continued with the long-established custom of nominating broadly mainstream people who were not associated with political extremes or with anti-Europeanism. So whilst the Prodi College, like its predecessors, contained people from different political traditions, the range of political opinion was such as to make for the likelihood of manageable working relationships.

- Regarding *ministerial experience*, there has been a marked strengthening of the College over the years, from an average of around one-quarter of Commissioners in the pre-merged 1967 Colleges having previous national ministerial experience, to two-fifths in the Rey–Thorn period, to over one half in the Delors 1– Santer period (MacMullen, 1997: 42–3). Furthermore, not only has there been a growing proportion of the College with ministerial experience, but there has been a growing proportion with senior ministerial experience.

Three-quarters – fifteen members – of the Prodi College had ministerial experience, but this relatively high figure was partly offset by a slight dip in the number with senior ministerial experience: only one (Prodi himself) was a former Prime Minister; one (Antonio Vitorino of Portugal) was a former Deputy Prime Minister; there were no former Foreign Ministers; and there were two former Economic/Finance Ministers (Erkki Liikanen of Finland and Pedro Solbes Mira of Spain). Having ministerial experience can be of considerable value to Commissioners, partly because of the political and administrative skills acquired (including the experience of having negotiated in the Council) and partly because having been a minister – and especially if it has been as a senior minister – adds political weight, and perhaps an extra element of legitimacy, when dealing with other EU actors.

- Regarding *European and international experience*, there was less experience of other EU institutions and international organisations in the Prodi College than had been the case in the Delors and Santer Colleges. For example, just three had been elected to the EP and one of these – the Belgian Commissioner, Phillippe Busquin – only as recently as the June 1999 election. However, most of Prodi's Commissioners had extensive European knowledge of some kind, acquired in many cases in their national ministerial posts and/or in membership of European committees in national parliaments.

  The most striking feature of the Prodi Commission in terms of its European experience, and indeed its most striking feature of all, was that only one four members of the outgoing College – one-quarter as compared with the more normal half – were returning: Frans Fischler, Erkki Liikanen, Mario Monti and Neil Kinnock. Most members of the Santer College left for what are the traditional reasons: a wish to move elsewhere (former Commissioners often assume business and/or academic positions, usually on a part-time, but sometimes on a full-time, basis); voluntary retirement on personal grounds; and – almost invariably the most common reason for not returning – changes in the political complexion of national governments and corresponding changes in the exercise of political patronage. Some Commissioners were, however, mindful that the EP hearings could be stormy for former members of the Santer College, especially if they were thought to be particularly responsible for the Commission's problems or if too many members of the College sought to return.

Collegiality

An important principle associated with the College of Commissioners is *collegiality*. The principle has four main dimensions.

First, Commissioners are not appointed on an individual basis, but collectively as a body. Neither the EP nor the Council of Ministers can, during the appointment process, pick and choose which nominees they are prepared to accept.

Second, there is no rolling or gradually unfolding process of personnel turnover during the lifetime of a College. Having been appointed, the assumption is that all Commissioners will serve their full term unless there is a death or a resignation. Usually no more than one or two Commissioners fail to complete their term. A partial undermining of this principle may be said to have occurred with all Commissioners of the Prodi College having promised to resign if the President requested their individual resignation and with Prodi having promised EP leaders that he would give due weight to Parliament's views if it requested him to ask a Commissioner to resign. However, both of these sets of circumstances were envisaged as being used only if very serious reasons applied – and these reasons were generally assumed not to include weak performance in office.

Third, linked to the assumption – it is not a formal requirement – that Commissioners will serve their full term, is the fact that there is no formal provision for the dismissal of individual Commissioners, except under the rather unlikely circumstances of Article 216 TEC applying whereby if 'any member of the Commission no longer fulfils the conditions required for the performance of his duties or if he has been guilty of serious misconduct, the Court of Justice may, on application by the Council or the Commission, compulsory retire him'. No Commissioner has ever been removed for misconduct, although one (Borschette) was retired in 1976 by the Court after suffering a stroke. Clearly, the promises given in 1999 by Commissioners-designate to Prodi and by Prodi to the EP, mean that there are now informal mechanisms by which, in extreme circumstances, Commissioners could be dismissed.

Fourth, the College is collectively responsible for decisions and actions taken in the name of the Commission. For this reason, all important and controversial issues are channelled through meetings of the College and no Commissioner can, without risk of being rebuked and possibly publicly humiliated by colleagues, attempt to be too independent in public, especially after the College has taken a decision on a matter. Commissioners are assigned individual policy responsibilities and are delegated certain decision-making powers, but these are within carefully demarcated parameters. Within the parameters, Commissioners must still always formally act under the name of the Commission rather than in an individual capacity.

In practice, there is not quite so much collegiality as there might appear to be on the surface. Collegiality is perhaps best thought of as an ideal, which came closest to being achieved under the EEC presidency of Walter Hallstein but which has subsequently been only partially realised. Certainly as the College has grown in size, as the power and status of the presidency has increased, and as some portfolios have come to be seen as more important than others, then so has collegiality become less fully attainable. The fact is, as is noted at several points in this book, the Commission is far from being a wholly cohesive and united institution. Rather, plurality and heterogeneity characterise much of its nature and activities.

An important aspect of how collegiality is weakened in practice is in the appointments process. Commissioners are not appointed on the basis of a shared programme or a common outlook. The College may be formally appointed as a body, but the governments of the member states are influenced primarily by national considerations when they decide who they wish to nominate. Very little thought is given at nomination stage, except by the President, to the needs of the College as a body. Even when such thought is given it cannot easily be acted upon, since governments do not consult with one another about their nominees. When all the names are known, the EP and the Council do not assess the proposed composition of the College-designate with a view to its overall potential coherence or seeming balance.

As a result of the nature of the nomination process, the membership of the College is always highly diffuse, most obviously in terms of nationality but also in terms of political orientation. Fifteen nationalities and up to twenty political parties have been represented at the Commission table since 1995. Although Commissioners can usually develop reasonable working relationships – helped by the broadly pro-European and Centre Left/Centre Right views they almost invariably hold – differences on particular issues naturally frequently arise. In such circumstances consensus may not be possible, with the consequence that decisions may have to be taken by majority vote.

Sometimes differences between Commissioners bubble to the surface, as is perhaps to be expected given the pressures on them to 'defend portfolio interests', their natural inclination to keep an eye on the implications of EU policies for their country, and their habit – built on years of domestic political activity – of publicly opposing decisions and views with which they disagree. Examples of publicly expressed differences in the Delors Colleges were given in Chapter 3. Under Santer, examples of differences included Pádraig Flynn (the Social Affairs Commissioner) and Franz Fischler (the Agriculture Commissioner) openly disagreeing in 1996 over plans by the former to phase out subsidies to EU tobacco growers, and Leon Brittan (the UK Trade Commissioner) and Franz Fischler clashing in the same year over the Commission's handling of the UK's BSE crisis.

The College in operation

The College deals with its business in one of three main ways.

The delegation procedure

The delegation procedure or, as it is more commonly referred to within the Commission, the *habilitation* procedure, allows for certain types of measures to be dealt with by individual Commissioners acting under powers that have been delegated to them by the College. Confined essentially to administrative and technical matters, and excluding all measures that are concerned with financial and personnel issues, the procedure means that College meetings are not taken up dealing with straightforward and routine business. It also means that the Commission is able to act quickly when technical adjustments to existing legislation are necessary – as, for example, is almost continually the case with aspects of the CAP.

The written procedure

The written procedure is commonly used for proposals where no delegation procedure applies but where discussions or deliberations in College meetings do not seem to be necessary because all points have been agreed by the relevant DGs and approval has been given by the Legal Service. Any member of the College can request the Secretariat General to initiate proceedings to deal with a measure via written procedure. Under the procedure, all *cabinets* are sent copies of the draft proposal and if no objection is made within a specified period – which is normally a few days but can be as little as one day in the case of 'expedited' written procedures – the decision is made. However, any member can raise objections and request that the measure be referred to a College meeting. The procedure is used for routine and minor issues, such as customs and agricultural regulations, and also for non-controversial urgent matters, such as the granting of emergency food aid following disasters. Like the delegation procedure, the main purpose of the written procedure is to enhance the efficiency of the Commission by ensuring that the agendas of College meetings are not weighed down with routine and uncontroversial items.

College meetings

All matters not dealt with by either delegation or written procedure are referred to a full College meeting. Outside holiday periods there is usually a College meeting every week, on Wednesdays. Additional meetings are called as and when business requires them. Normally the College meets in Brussels, except in EP plenary weeks when it meets in Strasbourg.

Attendance at College meetings   Article 5 of the Commission's Rules of Procedure states 'Members shall be required to attend all meetings. The President shall rule which situation will allow Members to depart from this requirement' (Commission, 1999d). Under Santer, the attendance record of all Commissioners was over 75 per cent and in most cases was around 90 per cent. The Commissioners with the lowest attendance records were, as would be expected, mainly those with external relations portfolios.

Unlike Council of Ministers meetings, where teams of advisory officials support ministers and 100 or more people can be present, College meetings are much more restricted affairs. The only people who regularly attend are the Commissioners themselves, the Secretary General and his Deputy, the Director General of the Legal Service, the *chef de cabinet* of the President, the Spokesman (from the Press and Communication Service), and the Director of the *Greffe* (the Commission's Registry which is based in the Secretariat General) who assists the Secretary General in providing secretarial services for the meeting. If a Commissioner is unavailable, he/she can be represented by his *chef de cabinet*, who can speak, but not vote, on his/her behalf. Where particularly complex or technical matters are being considered, a Commissioner with direct responsibilities can be supported by his/her *chef de cabinet* and the appropriate director general. On very sensitive matters the College can decide to meet in restricted session, which normally means just the Commissioners and the Secretary General.

Preparation of College meetings   Apart from matters of urgency, all issues on the College's agenda have always been extensively discussed at pre-meetings of the Commissioners' staff. These pre-meetings take various forms, but they basically involve members of the Commissioners' *cabinets* coming together in various combinations to keep each other, and where appropriate their Commissioners, informed about what is going on in their respective spheres, and to try and resolve any differences which may exist well before they get to the Commissioners' meeting. The most important of these pre-meetings is that of the *chefs de cabinet,* which is held two days before the College meeting. The *chefs* meeting is chaired by the Secretary General and has as its main purpose a review and examination of the proposed agenda of the College meeting so as to try and ensure that it proceeds as smoothly and efficiently as possible. Where a proposed agenda item requires a decision by the College, preparation at the Monday meeting can involve the *chefs* doing one of a number of things: they may be able to reach preliminary agreement themselves on the item, with reference then being made to the College for (anticipated) confirmation only; they may decide that whilst differences still exist between DGs and/or between *cabinets,* they probably are resolvable if the item is held back for further deliberations; or they may conclude that whilst differences still exist on important points, the item must be resolved and should be referred to the Commissioners for that purpose.

In addition to preliminary work undertaken at *cabinet* level, items on College meeting agendas are sometimes also prepared by Commissioners' groups. The purpose of these groups is to 'contribute to a better preparation and co-ordination of the activities of the Commission and of its services'. As part of this contribution, 'The Commission may invite a standing or ad hoc Commissioners' group to prepare the discussion of any item likely to be discussed at a future meeting of the Commission' (Commission, 1999e). Six standing Commissioners' groups were established at the beginning of the Santer College – on growth, competitiveness and employment, equal opportunities, external relations, the information society, cohesion, and trans-European networks. Five were established at the beginning of the Prodi College – with those on growth, competitiveness and employment, equal opportunities, and external relations being retained, those on the information society, cohesion, and trans-European networks not being reconstituted, and new groups on reform and on interinstitutional relations being established.

Agendas of College meetings   The agendas and papers for College meetings are prepared by the Secretary General and his staff in consultation with the President and his staff.

All sorts of items can be on the agenda of College meetings, ranging from matters that require an immediate decision to matters that are the subject of an ongoing debate. By way of illustration of just how diverse College agendas can be, a listing of recurring items now follows.

- Proposals for the development of policies need to be discussed or formally adopted. After adoption they may need to be reviewed. Such proposals may be drawn up on the Commission's own initiative or at the request of an outside body – most commonly the European Council or the Council of Ministers. They appear in several different forms, including Green Papers, White Papers, strategic programmes, action programmes, communications, and reports. The demarcation lines between these different forms of policy proposal are blurred and overlapping, but they each have as their general purpose providing a framework for EU activities in the policy spheres they cover. Usually this framework includes a range of measures, including legislative measures, which it is indicated should be taken if specified goals are to be achieved. On adoption by the Commission, these policy frameworks are referred to the Council of Ministers, or perhaps to the European Council in the case of White Papers, for approval and action.
- Approval is required for some types of proposed Commission executive action and/or legislation. Most Commission executive decisions and legislation are concerned with the routine and straightforward and are dealt with by delegated or written procedure. Sometimes, however, there is a need for referral to a College meeting, perhaps because the issue in question is disputed at sub-College levels and/or because it is deemed to have a political edge. An example of the sort of issue that may be referred on either or both of these counts is the distribution of financial assistance under the Structural Funds – with national governments carefully monitoring Commission decisions and with the Competition DG sometimes claiming that particular grants and subsidies are undermining its policies to increase market competitiveness.
- Proposals for Council or for EP and Council legislation often require the approval of a College meeting.
- The Preliminary Draft Budget (PDB) must be placed on the agenda of a College meeting early each year. The PDB is the first draft of the EU budget which applies from the January of the following year and is drawn up in the Budget DG under the general direction

of the Commissioner who holds the budget portfolio and in close liaison with other DGs.

- In a similar manner to the PDB, proposals for the agricultural Annual Price Review must also be referred to a College meeting early in the year for its approval. The Review is concerned mainly, although not exclusively, with price proposals for the forthcoming agricultural year. (For most products the agricultural year begins in April or May.)
- The Commission's annual work programme has to be approved by a College meeting. This normally occurs in October, thus enabling discussions on its contents to be held with the Council and the EP before the beginning of the year to which it applies. The work programme sets out the Commission's general aims and priorities for the year, including listing the legislative proposals it intends to bring forward. The programme invariably consists of a mixture of ongoing commitments and intended new initiatives and developments.
- Under new rules on the internal coordination of Commission activities drawn up under Prodi's guidance, the College must hold a single policy debate each year to set policy and budgetary priorities that are to serve as parameters for the PDB and the work programme.

The conduct of College meetings   The manner in which agenda items are dealt with at College meetings depends on their nature and on whether points of disagreement remain after the *chefs de cabinet* meeting. Matters which the *chefs* have agreed do not require discussion by the College are designated as 'A' points and are normally approved without comment, whilst matters that are high-profile, controversial, sensitive, or unresolved are discussed.

Where matters are discussed, the relevant Commissioner – that is to say, the Commissioner whose portfolio includes responsibility for the matter under consideration – takes the lead. This is usually done by providing an introductory summary of key points, explaining what course of action is being proposed, and providing clarification when it is requested. Where the portfolios of other Commissioners also cover or touch on aspects of the matter under consideration, as is often the case, then these Commissioners, too, are likely to have something to say. Beyond the Commissioners who have a portfolio interest in the matter, other Commissioners can contribute to the discussion if they wish.

In theory, all Commissioners are of the same standing, and the role they can play and the influence they can exercise in College meetings is potentially equal. In practice, some Commissioners are more important and some are more influential than others. A number of factors account for this. First, there is, as was shown in Chapter 3, the special position of the President. He has considerable influence over the content of agendas and, as the chairperson of all College meetings, can do much to steer the course of debate. Furthermore, the status and power of his office is now such that if he comes down strongly in support of a particular position other Commissioners may feel uncomfortable about not falling into line. Second, as is shown later in this chapter, the portfolios of some Commissioners carry more weight and are more concerned with central EU interests than are the portfolios of others. This inevitably means that some Commissioners have a close and direct involvement with many of the major issues which come before the College, while others are more on the margins of discussions and deliberations. Third, some Commissioners come to College meetings much better prepared than others. With Commission business covering such a broad range of affairs, and with individual Commissioner responsibilities being very heavy and very complex in many cases, Commissioners cannot be expected to master policy areas that are not part of their own portfolios. However, if a Commissioner does wish to exercise an influence in the College beyond his/her own brief, either at a general level or on a particular matter, then he/she does need to familiarise himself/herself with relevant material. This involves hard work and good briefing by his/her *cabinet*. Commissioners do not display the quality of hard work and the attribute of good briefing in equal measure. Fourth, Commissioners vary in how bright they are intellectually and how persuasive and forceful they are in debate. Leon Brittan, for example, who was a Commissioner in the Delors II, Delors III and Santer Colleges is generally recognised as an example of a Commissioner whose high intelligence enabled him 'to punch beyond his (portfolio) weight'.

Taking decisions   As regards what happens when the College needs to take decisions, the rounds of meetings that prepare College business ensure that there is likely to be a consensus by the time an item appears on the College agenda. Certainly the College, like the Council of Ministers, always prefers to operate on the basis of consensus. If, in the event, no consensus does exist, the item is likely to be referred back to the *chefs* and/or to the services for further consideration. If, however, it is clear, perhaps after referral back, that no consensus is possible, and if it is agreed that a decision should be, or needs to be, taken, then the Commission can proceed by majority vote if a quorum of Commissioners – which means a majority of Commissioners – is present. Figures on the use of voting in the College are not available, since votes are not minuted and in any event the minutes themselves are not published. Interview and hearsay evidence, however, indicates that votes are rare – usually no more than three or four a year. That there should be so few votes is testimony to the College's inbuilt preference for proceeding by unanimity since, technically, votes are very easy to call: 'A vote shall be taken if any Member so requests' (Commission, 1999d: Article 8).

An example of a vote occurred in July 1999 when the (Acting) Competition Commissioner, Karel van Miert, brought a proposal to the College that a book price-fixing agreement in Germany and Austria preventing retailers from discounting be declared unlawful because it did not have an exemption from EU rules on restrictive practices. Van Miert's proposal failed to obtain majority support by one vote, with dissenting Commissioners being sympathetic to the cultural protection argument of German publishers and the German government that the agreement ensured a wide range of German-language books was published and/or believing that such a contentious proposal ought not to be taken by the Acting College but should be left to its successor. Mario Monti, the Acting Commissioner for the Internal Market and the Commissioner-designate for Competition, described the system as a cartel masquerading as the promotion of culture and vowed to bring the matter back to the College (*Financial Times*, 15 July 1999).

Of course, decisions may sometimes be taken with less than unanimous support without a vote actually being held. This occurs when Commissioners, though dissatisfied with a decision, do not press for a vote – most likely because they do not wish to be thought of as being overly awkward or to be seen as being in a minority. Both of these considerations led to Prodi backing down in September 1999, only days after his College had been appointed, on the issue of whether Commissioners should have, as was established practice, their own spokespersons or whether, as Prodi preferred, spokespersons should represent only the Commission as a whole. Faced with opposition to his proposals from other Commissioners – which was motivated partly by the domestic political value 'dedicated' spokespersons can provide – and the near-certainty of defeat if a vote was taken, Prodi did not press the issue, with the consequence that Commissioners were able to continue to have their own spokespersons.

The allocation of portfolios

All Commissioners have a specific responsibility for a particular area or areas of Commission and EU business. These responsibilities make up what is known as a Commissioner's portfolio. Table 4.1 gives a listing of Commissioners' portfolios at the beginning of the Prodi Commission.

Portfolios are assigned at the beginning of a College's term of office and the expectation is that a Commissioner will stay with the same portfolio for the full five years. Up to the Prodi College, the only circumstances which resulted in a rearrangement of portfolios during a term of office were when there was a need to fit in new Commissioners following an enlargement of the EU – as when Spain and Portugal became members of the EC one year into the life of the Delors I Commission in January 1986 – and when there was a change in Commission personnel – as when Commissioner di Meana resigned in 1992 and Commissioner van Miert assumed the environment portfolio for the remaining few months of the Delors II Commission. It is possible that under Prodi and his successors changes in portfolios will also be made if Commissioners are seen by the President to be unsuitable or ineffective in their post. One reason for anticipating such a development is the greater scrutiny to which the Commission is to be subject following the resignation of the Santer College. Another reason is that the Declaration on the Organisation and Functioning of the Commission that was attached to the Amsterdam Treaty referred to the possibility of the President 'reshuffling' the allocation of tasks in the College 'during a Commission's term of office' (Treaty of Amsterdam, 1997: Declaration 32).

The number, the scope, and the remit of portfolios is not constant. Variations have occurred over the years in response to a number of factors, five of which have been especially important. First, portfolios have had to reflect and cover the increasing and changing nature of EU interests and policy involvement. So, for example, there were no portfolios in the early years of the EEC in such spheres as the environment, research, or justice and home affairs, because these

Table 4.1   *Commissioners' portfolios and services responsibilities at the beginning of the Prodi Commission*

Name	Country	Portfolio	Services responsibilities
Romano Prodi	Italy	President	Secretariat General, Legal Service, Press and Communication Service
Neil Kinnock	UK	Vice-President for Institutional Reform	Personnel and Administration DG
Loyola de Palacio	Spain	Vice-President for Relations with the Parliament, Transport and Energy	Transport and Energy DG
Michel Barnier	France	Regional Policy	Regional Policy DG
Frits Bolkestein	Germany	Internal Market	Internal Market DG, Taxation and Customs Union DG
Philippe Busquin	Belgium	Research	Research DG Joint Research Centre
David Byrne	Ireland	Health and Consumer Protection	Health and Consumer Protection DG
Anna Diamantopoulou	Greece	Employment and Social Affairs	Employment and Social Affairs DG
Franz Fischler	Austria	Agriculture	Agriculture DG Fisheries DG
Pascal Lamy	France	Trade	Trade DG

Name	Country	Portfolio	Services responsibilities
Erkki Liikanen	Finland	Enterprise and Information Society	Information Society DG, Enterprise DG
Mario Monti	Italy	Competition	Competition DG
Poul Nielson	Denmark	Development and Humanitarian Aid	Development DG, European Community Humanitarian Aid office
Chris Patten	UK	External Relations	External Relations DG, Common Service for External Relations
Viviane Reding	Luxembourg	Education and Culture	Education and Culture DG, Publications Office
Michaele Schreyer	France	Budget	Budget DG, Financial Control DG, European Anti-Fraud Office
Pedro Solbes Mira	Spain	Economic and Financial Affairs	Economic and Financial Affairs DG
Günther Verheugen	Germany	Enlargement	Enlargement DG
Antonio Vitorino	Portugal	Justice and Home Affairs	Justice and Home Affairs DG
Margot Wallström	Sweden	Environment	Environment DG

did not fall within the EEC's, and therefore within the Commission's, remit. Second, the four enlargement rounds of the EC/EU (in 1973, 1981, 1986 and 1995) have meant that there have been periodic needs to increase the numbers of portfolios so as to find things for the increasing numbers of Commissioners to do. This has been managed by creating new (and sometimes rather marginal) portfolios and by splitting established portfolios between Commissioners. Third, Commissioners-designate have sometimes pressed for a particular portfolio to be created, or at least shaped, for them. Fourth, Commission Presidents have had their own views as to how portfolios are best arranged in the interests of efficiency. Santer, for example, was of the view that the division in the Delors III Commission between external political and external trade portfolios had not been wholly satisfactory and he sought to rectify this by introducing a more markedly regional dimension into the portfolios of Commissioners with external responsibilities. Prodi reversed this decision. Fifth, Commission Presidents have had different ideas about what responsibilities they themselves have wished to undertake, and this has had implications not just for their own portfolio but also for the portfolios of others. It used to be the case that because Presidents were seen as having a general coordinating role and also had specific responsibilities for certain Commission services (notably the Secretariat General) they did not formally assume policy portfolios. As was shown in Chapter 3, Delors and Santer did assume policy responsibilities, but Prodi returned to the pre-Delors arrangements and did not assign himself a specific policy portfolio.

Some Commission responsibilities are generally regarded as being more important than others. Amongst the most important are, on the one hand, some of the long-established and 'core' areas of EU activity such as external trade, competition and agriculture, and, on the other hand, some of the newer and growing areas of EU activity such as economic and monetary affairs and external political relations. There are also responsibilities which are very important for a period because of prevailing circumstances. At the time of allocation of portfolios in the Prodi College these areas included the reform of the Commission and enlargement. Beyond areas that are commonly accepted as being extremely important, are areas that are regarded by most as being of second-order importance, but which are of critical importance to particular member states and their governments: fisheries, for example, is of very great importance to Spain, whilst cohesion policies are important to Ireland and the poorer southern states.

Considerations of what are and what are not important policy areas play a very significant role in respect of the distribution of portfolios between Commissioners-designate. With virtually all Commissioners-designate being people who at some time have held significant political positions in their own country, it is natural that they should want something important to do within the Commission. Inevitably, therefore, the process of distributing portfolios is somewhat charged.

Prior to the Prodi College there were no prescribed procedures for how the allocation of portfolios should be made, other than a general statement in the Commission's Manual of Operational Procedures stating that it was up to the Commission itself to decide upon its divisions of competences. In practice, it came to be gradually accepted that the President-designate took the lead role in the process, but his position was not like that of a national Prime Minister who can offer posts on a take it or leave it basis. Rather, the President-designate was informed by the governments of the member states as to who his fellow Commissioners were to be and it was then his job to find them appropriate and acceptable responsibilities as best he could.

Presidents-designate went about this allocation process in slightly different ways, but the essence of what happened was as follows:

- As the names of Commissioners-designate become known over the summer and autumn of the year before the new Commission was to assume office (in the January), the President-designate began, in private, to attach names to responsibilities. This involved taking soundings with the Commissioners-designate and usually also involved lobbying of the President-designate by the governments of some member states. In considering the allocation of portfolios the President-designate had to seek to strike a balance between a number of pressures and constraints to which he was subject: (1) the five member states with two Commissioners normally expected at least the more senior of 'their' Commissioners to be given one of the key portfolios (the notion of 'the senior' French/German/Italian/Spanish/UK Commissioner is ill-defined, but it exists); (2) re-nominated Commissioners were often seeking advancement to a more important portfolio; (3) some governments were anxious that a portfolio of particular importance to their country was allocated to (one of) their Commissioner(s); (4) for both job interest and status reasons, no Commissioner-designate wanted to be given a portfolio which carried only minor and marginal responsibilities;

and (5) most of the returning Commissioners and some of the new Commissioners indicated strong preferences for specific portfolios – for example, in the summer of 1994 the returning UK Commissioner, Leon Brittan, informed Santer that he wished to retain responsibility for external trade (which, in the end, he did) and relations with Eastern Europe (which he did not), whilst the new UK Commissioner, Neil Kinnock, let Santer know that he hoped to be allocated transport (which he was).

• At some stage before the new College assumed office, the President-designate drew up what he hoped was a near final distribution of portfolios. Most of the more important responsibilities would be, or would be close to being, single-issue area portfolios, whilst many of the less important responsibilities would be combined together to make up what was hoped would be seen as being an important 'package' portfolio. Commissioners-designate would be informed as to what the President-designate had in mind for them.

• The distribution of portfolios was formally confirmed at a meeting of all the Commissioners-designate. Prior to Delors being nominated President-designate, this meeting was usually the occasion for prolonged haggling and bargaining, but Delors managed to make it more of a rubber-stamping occasion for decisions that had already been taken. Santer built on the Delors formula, by presenting the meeting as the occasion when Commissioners-designate were to be informed as to what they would be doing.

The process of distributing portfolios that has just been described has become more presidential-driven over the years. This was formalised in the Amsterdam Treaty, with the Declaration on the Organisation and Functioning of the Commission stating that 'the President of the Commission must enjoy broad discretion in the allocation of tasks within the College' (Treaty of Amsterdam, 1997: Declaration 32). But though this meant that the President in theory had virtually a free hand in assigning portfolio allocations, in practice he was not released from all of the problems and constraints that had applied to his predecessors. Or, at least, he was not released from them if he wished to preside over a good-spirited College that enjoyed harmonious relations with the governments of the member states.

It is sometimes suggested that the main problem for Presidents in allocating portfolios is finding sufficient worthwhile jobs for all Commissioners. However, Prodi told the June 1999 Cologne

European Council meeting that this was not his experience: 'the notion that it is not possible to carve out substantial jobs for all 19 Commissioners needs to be dispelled . . . Indeed the main challenge I am facing is to find a way of squeezing all of the work of the Commission into 19 portfolios' (Prodi, 1999b: 1). Prodi's remarks chime with what would be expected, for though the size of the College has increased over the years as a result of enlargements (see Table 3.1, p. 64), there has been a parallel increase in the range of EU policy involvement and interests. Of course, the increased EU policy activity has not resulted in the creation of College jobs of comparable weight and importance, and this is where the problem lies: jobs covering important policy areas where the EU is a key decision-maker, such as external trade and competition, are of first-rank importance; jobs covering reasonably significant areas of EU activity such as regional policy and relations with the Third World, are of middle-rank importance; and jobs, covering rather rather marginal areas of EU activity or areas where national policies are still dominant, such as tourism and culture, are of limited importance. There are various ways in which Presidents can arrange and combine the jobs so as to ensure that each portfolio contains at least something of significance, interest and challenge. Santer used several of these ways when assigning responsibilities in his College: some existing portfolios were divided – for example, social affairs and employment policy, and immigration, justice and home affairs policy, which had been combined in the Delors III Commission in the portfolio of the Irish Commissioner, Pádraig Flynn, were separated; new responsibilities were created, most notably through the creation of new external regional responsibilities; and middling and minor responsibilities were combined to produce weighty, if often somewhat bizarre, 'packages' – Marcelino Oreja's portfolio, for example, consisted of relations with the EP, relations with the member states on transparency and information, culture and audiovisual policy, the Office for Official Publications, and institutional matters and the 1996 IGC.

As part of his determination to improve the effectiveness and efficiency of the Commission, Prodi was resolved to be less inclined than his predecessors to use 'tricks' when deciding on the composition and allocation of portfolios. Whilst he was well aware of the need to ensure nobody was given a portfolio that covered only peripheral issues and/or was clearly less substantial in content than their reasonable expectations, he was determined there should be a streamlining in the content of portfolios and that as far as possible portfolio allocations should be on the basis of individual suitability. As he told the Cologne European Council, 'There will be a rational, well balanced, coherent spread of portfolios. This will send the right messages in terms of policy and avoid grey zones between the different Commissioners . . . There will be no horse trading' (Prodi, 1999b: 5). In practice there was some horse trading and manoeuvring, partly as a consequence of Commissioners-designate indicating preferences and a few hinting that they would not allow their name to go forward unless they were given a big job. Prodi bent to such pressures up to a point and did display flexibility – changing, for example, his intention to assign relations with the EP to Neil Kinnock, who lobbied hard for something more substantial. However, Prodi refused to accommodate one of the two people France proposed to nominate, former Culture Minister Jack Lang, who rejected the external relations portfolio he was offered and pressed to be given a 'super-intelligence' portfolio combining media, culture, youth, training, education, and information technology. Prodi did not bow to the pressure, which resulted in Lang deciding not to be a nominee. So as to avoid any possible last-minute or collective attempts to question or untangle the arrangements he had made, Prodi did not convene a meeting of the Commissioners-designate before announcing the remits and allocations of portfolios at a press conference in early July.

Regarding the promised streamling of the content of portfolios, some related policy areas, such as agriculture and fishing, that had been separated under Santer were brought together in one portfolio by Prodi. There were still a few instances of rather mixed packages – most notably with Loyala de Palacio, one of the Commission's two Vice Presidents, being given responsibility for relations with the EP and other EU institutions, transport policy, and energy policy – but nothing on such a scale as in the Santer College. Much of the 'room' that was required to make the streamlining possible was found via Prodi not assuming any direct policy responsibilities himself and by the creation of new portfolios – for administrative reform, enlargement, and the enterprise and information society.

Regarding Prodi's intention to allocate portfolios on the basis of individual suitability, this certainly did determine many of his decisions – with, for example, Pedro Solbes Mira becoming Commissioner for Economic and Financial Affairs (he had been Spanish Minister for Economics and Finance in 1993–96), Neil Kinnock becoming Commissioner for Administrative Reform (he had championed and pushed through internal reforms in the UK Labour Party when he was its leader from 1983–92), and Poul Nielsen becoming Commissioner for Development and Humanitarian Aid (he had been Danish Minister for Development Cooperation in 1994–99). At the same time, however, it was noticeable that Prodi maintained tradition by allocating all of the less important portfolios to Commissioners who displayed at least one, and in most cases two, of the following characteristics: they were newly appointed, as opposed to being re-appointed; they had not held senior ministerial office in their member state; they came from a small member state or were the junior Commissioner from one of the five member states with two Commissioners.

The exercise of portfolios

The position of Commissioners in relation to their policy portfolios is sometimes compared to that of national ministers and sometimes to that of the most senior national civil servants. In fact, neither comparison is very satisfactory.

As for the comparison with national ministers, Commissioners have neither the political responsibility for their portfolios, nor the clear lines of control and communication to the appropriate sections of the services, that is normally associated with ministers in national governments. Taking the political responsibility aspect of this first, most final decisions about policy in the EU are not taken by the Commission or by individual Commissioners but by, in some combination, the European Council, the Council of Ministers and the EP. As a result, though the Commission and Commissioners may legitimately be criticised for proposals they make and for tactics they use, notions of responsibility, whether collective or individual, can hardly be applied to them with the same conviction that they can be to national ministers. As for the lines of control and communication to the services, these have been clarified and tightened under Prodi (Commission, 1999c), but Commissioners do not sit at the top of DGs in the way that national ministers sit at the top of ministries. The formal heads of DGs are directors general, not Commissioners.

As for the comparison with the most senior national civil servants, Commissioners are, for the most part, much more politicised, much more high-profile, and much more involved in policy formation. Senior national civil servants are not normally expected to offer policy leads in the way that Commissioners are, and are not expected to appear in decision-making forums and argue for and defend policy initiatives in the way that Commissioners must do in the Council of Ministers and the EP.

Commissioners thus find themselves in a rather curious position, being placed in some respects between the EU's 'pure' politicians and civil servants, and being themselves both partly politicians and partly civil servants. From this curious position they take responsibility for the policy areas and issues that are included in their portfolios. 'Take responsibility' can involve a number of things, and individual Commissioners do not always interpret their roles in quite the same way. In general, however, Commissioners do the following in regard to their portfolios.

- *They carry a general responsibility for the work of those parts of the services that fall within their remit.* This is not a responsibility for day-to-day affairs, for that lies with directors general. Rather, it is a responsibility of a general overseeing kind, which has as its purpose ensuring the Commission services are working well and are fulfilling their various obligations. It is a difficult task to undertake, and in some cases is made more difficult by Commissioners responsibilities covering more than one DG (see Table 4.1, p. 102–3). There used to be some instances, most notably in the sphere of external relations, where different parts of the same DG reported to different Commissioners, but this practice has now ceased.

- Linked to and overlapping with the responsibilities they have for keeping an eye on the work of the services, *Commissioners involve themselves in policy development and do much to set the pace in their respective policy spheres.* This they do by playing a leading role in establishing priorities, by being actively involved in developing and monitoring work programmes, and by directly involving themselves in the preparation of policy and legislative proposals which they judge to be of particular interest or importance.

  As part of their policy activity work, Commissioners must act as a channel for work coming up from the services which needs the approval of the College. If the matter in hand is judged to be particularly important, controversial, or sensitive, this may involve the Commissioner and his/her *cabinet* staff engaging in protracted discussions and deliberations with the services before the matter is referred to the College, and then the Commissioner having to be active in the College explaining, and perhaps defending, what is being proposed. If the matter is more routine in character and is relatively uncontroversial, the Commissioner's role may be more that of an intermediary between the services and the College, with the matter going through the College meeting fairly quickly or, more likely, not being referred to the College meeting at all but being dealt with by delegated or written procedure.

Whichever procedure applies when an initiative is to be launched or a decision is to be taken – reference to a College meeting, delegated procedure, or written procedure – the principle of collective responsibility, which was explored earlier in the chapter, always applies. This imposes restrictions on Commissioners. One way in which it does so is that there is an expectation that Commissioners will work within the framework of the College-approved annual work programme. Another way in which it does so is to set specific limitations on what Commissioners do, for though they can, in an individual capacity, do much to float ideas, initiate proposals, formulate policies, and prepare decisions, they must always be aware that nothing can assume authoritative and official Commission status unless it is approved by the College.

- *Commissioners are the Commission's main external representatives, spokesmen, negotiators, and apologists for the policy areas which fall within their portfolios.* Commissioners exercise this function in relation to other EU institutions, the member states, non-member states, and the vast range of outside interests which wish to have contact with the Commission. So, to take relations with other EU institutions: two Commissioners, including the President, attend European Council meetings; the Commissioners responsible for policy areas attend Council of Ministers meetings – in the case of an important General Affairs or Ecofin Council this may mean as many as four Commissioners attending, whilst in the case of a Transport or Fisheries Council it is unlikely to mean more than one; the Commissioners responsible represent the Commission in EP policy debates, answer questions from MEPs and attend EP committee meetings when requested to do so; the Commissioner for Employment and Social Affairs includes in his/her portfolio responsibility for Commission relations with the Economic and Social Committee; and the Commissioner for Regional Policy includes in his/her portfolio responsibility for relations with the Committee of the Regions.

As regards non EU institutional actors with which Commissioners have to deal, the many forms of activity include: acting often not only as the Commission's representative but also as the EU's representative in negotiations with non-member states – most particularly on trade issues, but often also in such policy spheres as fisheries, the environment and transport; meeting with government ministers from member states (or having telephone conversations with them) – perhaps to try and resolve points of difference on a Commission proposal, perhaps to consider difficulties which are being experienced in implementing a policy programme, or perhaps to see if an understanding can be reached on a matter where the Commission has taken, or is intending to take, action which the member state judges to be damaging to its interests; meeting with leaders of important companies and sectional interests; and addressing gatherings and conferences in member and non-member states.

The summary of Commissioners' portfolio responsibilities that has just been given is necessarily couched in rather general terms. Inevitably, there are, in practice, many variations from 'the standard model' as to just what precisely Commissioners do and how they do it. Five factors are especially important in accounting for variations.

First, and most obviously, there is the composition of portfolios. All sorts of variations come in here. For example: some responsibilities – notably those covering external relations, trade, enlargement and development and humanitarian aid – involve extensive travel and dealings with representatives of non-member states, whilst others – such as those for research, for the budget and for employment and social affairs – are much more EU-based; some responsibilities – such as trade and agriculture – are largely concerned with managing and adjusting existing policies, whilst others – such as transport and judicial and home affairs – offer considerable opportunities for developing new policies; and some responsibilities, notably those which are exercised in policy spheres where institutional and sectional interests abound – such as the environment, agriculture and regional policy – involve extensive dealings with external lobbying bodies of various kinds, whilst others – especially those that do not touch too directly on specific interest groupings, such as economic and financial affairs, or those that are concerned with internal institutional matters, such as administration and personnel – are not so subject to targeting and pressurising from outside interests.

Second, there are variations in the extent to which Commissioners must work with other Commissioners. No portfolios are wholly self-standing and completely insulated, but there are degrees of overlap and spillover. Where the overlap and spillover is considerable, then a shared responsibility between Commissioners may be formalised – as it was by Santer who designated Monika Wulf-Mathies (the Regional Policy Commissioner) as the Commissioner responsible for the Cohesion Fund, but specified that this responsibility was to be exercised with Neil Kinnock (Transport) and Ritt Bjerregaard (Environment). More commonly, overlap and spillover between Commissioners is managed through intervention by the President (see Chapter 3), Commissioners' groups (see above), meetings of members of Commissioners' *cabinets* (see Chapter 5), and informal contacts of various kinds.

Third, Commissioners vary in how they perceive and interpret their roles. Some wish to be very much 'hands on' and to be closely involved with all significant activities that fall within their area(s) of responsibility. This usually results in such Commissioners having highly active *cabinets* that work closely with the appropriate sections of the services, and usually results also in such Commissioners establishing direct and close working relationships with senior figures in the services. By contrast, other Commissioners distance themselves somewhat from day-to-day affairs and focus rather more on general policy issues – including sometimes policy issues that are not strictly part of their portfolio brief. Working in this 'hands off' way may be a matter of personal style and preference, or it may be because of a lack of interest in the details of the subject matter of the portfolio. Whatever the explanation, it is likely to result in fewer demands being made on the *cabinets* of Commissioners operating in such a manner and the Commissioners themselves having only limited direct contacts with the services. (The 'Brussels circuit' abounds with gossip about Commissioners who keep their distance from the services, and sometimes also keep their distance from Brussels!)

Fourth, Commissioners differ in the notice they take of, and the emphasis they give to, the interests of their own member states. In theory, of course, nationality should not be an issue since one of the first things Commissioners do on assuming office is to give a 'solemn undertaking' before the Court of Justice that in the performance of their duties they will 'neither seek nor take instructions from any government or from any other body' (Article 213 (2) TEC). In practice, complete impartiality is neither achieved nor attempted. There are three main reasons for this:

(1)   It is unrealistic. Commissioners are, after all, national nominees who have usually been deeply embedded in national public life for many years. Clearly they cannot be expected, on appointment to the Commission, suddenly to divest themselves of all loyalties and attachments to their member states. Indeed, a consideration of most national governments when making their nomination(s) to the Commission is precisely that the individual(s) concerned will keep an eye on the national interest (as defined by the government of the day). To try and ensure that such an eye is duly kept on the national interest, Permanent Representations may 'brief' their Commissioner(s) on issues that are of particular relevance to the member state, governments keep in close touch with members of 'their' Commissioner(s)' *cabinet(s)*, and national ministers may communicate directly with 'their' Commissioner(s) when a perceived need arises. On this last type of Commissioner–home member state linkage, a fuss blew up in November 1996 when the UK Chancellor of the Exchequer, Kenneth Clarke, admitted he had sent a briefing document about the UK Government's position on EMU to the two UK Commissioners prior to the Commission finalising a paper on the subject. He informed Parliament:

> The first [of several government papers that had 'leaked'] is a briefing note that was prepared at the request of the European Union Commissioners, Sir Leon Brittan and Neil Kinnock. It was designed to help them be aware of British views at an early stage of the negotiations [on the EMU stability pact] before the Commission's thinking on the stability pact was finalised. The note was requested by them and sent to both of them in confidence. The reason why it was in confidence is that European Commissioners are constitutionally independent, although I am quite sure that other Commissioners regularly receive briefings from other Governments. (House of Commons Debates, vol. 288, col. 25, 25 November 1996)

Clarke was doing nothing that was much out of the ordinary and his last comment is doubtless true. In any event, as former

Commissioner Lord Cockfield has observed, 'as with all
lobbying activities the dividing line between "information"
and "influence" can be a very narrow one' (1994: 110). For
governments, however, attempts by Commissioners to maintain
this dividing line have not always been welcomed and have led
on occasions to Commissioners who have wished to be re-
appointed not being so because they have been seen as not
defending national interests with sufficient vigour in the
Commission. A particularly notable example of such a refusal
to re-appoint concerned the aforementioned Lord Cockfield, the
Internal Market Commissioner in the Delors I Commission,
whom Mrs. Thatcher replaced with Leon Brittan in the Delors II
Commission on the grounds that Cockfield had 'gone native'
and had not looked after British interests sufficiently well.
(Ironically, Brittan also soon began to distance himself from the
UK Conservative Government on certain key policy issues.)

(2) In certain circumstances the work of the Commission can be
assisted by Commissioners making 'national inputs'. Commissioners must not press the interests of their member states too
hard, but it can be helpful for the Commission if Commissioners
can use national contacts to help resolve difficulties or if they can
use their knowledge of their own states to warn of proposals or
actions that will be resisted from national capitals.

(3) In respect of senior posts in the Commission's administration –
particularly in the A1–A3 grades – Commissioners have a widely
acknowledged, though unofficial, responsibility to ensure that
their country has its 'entitlement'. (Unofficial national quotas
exist at the most senior administrative levels, though under Prodi
they are being diluted – see Chapter 7.) They also have a
responsibility to keep a general eye on fellow nationals amongst
the A-grades to try and ensure that the best are promoted.
Commissioners go about these personnel tasks in various ways,
but the very existence of the tasks gives a specific national
dimension to Commissioners' responsibilities.

None of these reasons for lack of complete Commission impartiality
is to suggest that Commissioners are, in effect, national representatives in Brussels. On the contrary, Commissioners do, for the most
part, approach and undertake their duties and tasks in an impartial
manner (apart from the special case of their personnel responsibilities). Were this not to be so, Commissioners would very quickly be

criticised and lose credibility, whilst the College would come to resemble and duplicate the Council of Ministers. Nonetheless, variations do occur in just *how* impartial *some* Commissioners are at *some* times. There is, in effect, a gradation of positions. At one end of the spectrum are Commissioners who do not worry too much about the views of their governments back home. Such independence may be based on any one of, or on a mixture of, several reasons: there may be no ambition to be re-appointed to the Commission, and therefore no need to bow to the national government's wishes; there may be no intention of returning to national political life, and therefore no requirement to maintain good relations with the appropriate political authorities at home; there may be a fundamental disagreement with the position being adopted by the national government on a particular matter or matters; and several Commissioners are usually from national political parties which are not in the national government. (This latter situation is most likely with Commissioners from those member states which have two Commissioners and with Commissioners from states where national elections have brought about a change in the composition of the government.) At the other end of the spectrum are Commissioners who are, or are thought to be, just a little bit too sympathetic to 'their' national interests. This trait is not displayed by such individuals across the policy spectrum, but surfaces rather on specific issues that are judged to be of particular importance to the Commissioner's member state. Occasionally, the adoption by a Commissioner of a sympathetic attitude to his/her member state's interests on an issue results in considerable friction, and can spill into the public domain. Such an occasion occurred in 1997 when one of the Italian Commissioners, Emma Bonino, was sharply critical of a Commission report that cast doubt on whether Italy would meet the Maastricht conditions for joining the single currency in 1999.

Fifth, and finally, Commissioners naturally vary in their personal capacities and qualities. Just as the brightest, the sharpest and the more forceful Commissioners are advantaged in their potential to make an impact in the context of the College, so it is the case in respect of the exercise of portfolios. This applies to Commissioners' dealings with both Commission and non-Commission actors: with Commission actors, be they other Commissioners or officials, weak Commissioners are normally quickly exposed and find it difficult to impose themselves; with non-Commission actors, such as representatives of foreign governments or EP committees, a Commissioner who struggles in verbal exchanges or who is not fully in charge of his/her brief is unlikely to be a very effective representative of the Commission. Weaker Commissioners can protect themselves up to a point by having high quality *cabinets*, but complete protection is obviously not possible, and in any event it tends, in practice, to be the highest-quality Commissioners who have the highest-quality *cabinets* – the two tending to go together because high-quality Commissioners tend to be less concerned when making appointments to their *cabinets* with whom they feel comfortable and more concerned with who can be of greatest assistance to them.

Concluding remarks: prospects for reform

In the almost continual debates that have occurred since the 1970s on the institutional make-up of the EU, considerable attention has focused on the nature of the College, and more particularly on its size. Many have argued that the College has become, as a result of being automatically expanded with each wave of EC/EU enlargement, far too large. With the EU likely to increase its membership to twenty and more states in the foreseeable future, the suggestion has increasingly been made that it is time to engage in a radical pruning of the College's membership and to tie the pruning to revisions in the distribution of responsibilities in the College. Prominent amongst the reforms that have been advocated are removing the right of the large member states to have two Commissioners, removing the 'entitlement' of small member states to have a Commissioner, capping the size of the College, and differentiating between 'senior' Commissioners who would be responsible for policy planning and 'junior' Commissioners who would be responsible for day-to-day policy implementation. (For a review of the arguments associated with these and related reform proposals, see Spence, 2000.)

Only the first of these reforms is likely to be acted upon, with the Amsterdam Treaty having signalled the willingness of the large states to give up their second Commissioner provided they are 'compensated' by being given increased voting weight in the Council of Ministers. The 2000 IGC is likely to provide this 'compensation' and a 'one Commissioner per member state' rule will probably be in place well in time for the appointment of the College that is scheduled to assume office in early 2005.

Arguably member states should grasp the nettle by favouring some of the more radical proposals that have been made for reforming the College. For example, adoption of the most radical proposal – removing the national 'entitlement' to a Commissioner, perhaps as part of a capping exercise – could facilitate internal collegiality, consensus, cohesion and coordination. However, as matters stand, this proposal, like other radical reform proposals, is both politically unacceptable and potentially dysfunctional. It is politically unacceptable because member states find comfort in having 'one of their own' in the College, even though Commissioners are supposed to be independent and not in any sense national representatives. It is potentially dysfunctional in that it could weaken member states' confidence in both the College and the Commission as a whole.

Cautious and incremental reform is thus likely to continue to be the order of the day.

Chapter 5

Commissioners' *Cabinets*

A key role in the Commission system, but one that is somewhat underexplored in the academic literature, is exercised by Commissioners' *cabinets*. In essence *cabinets* are Commissioners' private offices, charged to exercise whatever duties Commissioners require of them.

Originating in the Continental, and more especially in the French, model of ministerial *cabinets*, the idea behind the *cabinet* system in the Commission is that Commissioners carry such important responsibilities on both an individual and collective basis that they need to be supported by teams of high-level personal assistants. (On the origins and development of the Commission *cabinet* system, see Mazey, 1992; Ritchie, 1992; Donnelly and Ritchie, 1997.) These teams are not part of the Commission services but rather work directly for, and are answerable directly to, Commissioners.

The examination of *cabinets* that is undertaken in this chapter is organised into three main sections: appointment and membership, organisation, and functions and functioning.

Appointment and membership

Although they are formally appointed by the Commission President, *cabinet* members are in practice appointed by the Commissioner to whom they are attached and they hold office at his/her discretion. When a Commissioner's term of office ends his/her *cabinet* dissolves.

Prior to the Prodi College, *cabinets* consisted of six or seven A-grade officials (see Chapter 7 for an explanation of the grading system) plus a similar number of support staff. The only exception to this was the President's *cabinet*, which was about twice the size of the other *cabinets*. In total, over 300 *cabinet* staff were salaried from the EU budget, whilst a small number were financed from other sources – most commonly secondment from national civil services.

Believing that *cabinets* had come to assume too powerful a position in the Commission system, Prodi announced shortly after his nomination as President-designate that he wished to see the size of *cabinets* reduced. Under his guidance new rules governing the formation of *cabinets* were drawn up and were subsequently approved by the incoming College. Under the new rules: the President has nine A-grade staff in his office and the other Commissioners have six; Commissioners other than the President have an administrative and secretarial support staff of ten B- and/or C-grades, of whom no more than two may be B-grades; the President has a support staff of fifteen, of whom no more than three may be B-grades (Commission, 1999b: Part 1.3).

The great majority of *cabinet* members were, before the Prodi Commission, fellow nationals of the Commissioner, though at least one of the A-grade officials was required to be a non-national. This 'national packing' had certain benefits. For the *cabinets* themselves it helped to foster teamwork. For the governments of the member states it provided an *entrée* into the Commission at senior level, with *cabinet* members in close and regular touch with 'their' governments in the national capitals and in the Permanent Representations in Brussels. This *entrée* could be used for both policy purposes and appointments purposes: regarding the former, governments could seek to channel their preferences into the upper reaches of decision-making via 'their' *cabinet(s)*; regarding the latter, *cabinets* were expected to work with 'their' government in monitoring the placement and performance of fellow nationals in the Commission and to assist 'their' Commissioner(s) in promoting the appointment and promotion claims of fellow nationals to key posts. For the Commission, national 'packing' enabled *cabinets* to be used as an important source of information about when an initiative or a proposal was likely to create difficulties arising from national preferences and circumstances.

However, the national make-up of *cabinets* also had disadvantages. It promoted national competitiveness in policy promotion and development with, for example, *cabinets* sometimes pressurising for favoured national policies to be incorporated in the Commission's annual programme. It also fostered national protectiveness in policy implementation with, for example, *cabinets* sometimes 'lobbying' for a particular outcome in a competition policy case. The effect of this national competitiveness and protectiveness was to weaken Commission collegiality.

As part of the fundamental reform of the functioning of the Commission that he was resolved to oversee, Prodi made clear soon after his nomination that he had the national composition of *cabinets* firmly in his sights (see, for example, his address to the Cologne

European Council in June 1999, Prodi, 1999b). He wanted *cabinets* to become more multi-national and to ensure that they would become so he saw to it that the new rules governing the formation of *cabinets* included provisions specifying that each *cabinet* should include at least three nationalities and that the *chef de cabinet* or the *deputy chef de cabinet* should preferably be of a different nationality from that of the Commissioner (Commission, 1999b: Part 1.3).

Prodi quickly set an example for the practice he was promoting by appointing an Irishman, David O'Sullivan, as his *chef de cabinet*. O'Sullivan's career path to the most senior and important of *cabinet* positions (*chef* of the President's *cabinet*) is worth outlining since it displays many of the characteristics that are typical of the careers of *cabinet* members. Born in Dublin in 1953, he was awarded a degree in economics and sociology at Trinity College Dublin and a *diploma des hautes études européenes* from the College of Europe at Bruges before joining the Irish Foreign Ministry. Having passed the *concours* (entry exam) in 1978 he entered the Commission at A7-level in 1979 and worked in DG I (External Relations) until 1985, including spending four years at the Tokyo delegation. Between 1985 and 1989 he was a member of the *cabinet* of the Irish Commissioner, Peter Sutherland, (who held the competition policy portfolio) and from 1989 to 1992 was head of unit in the Commission's Task Force for Human Resources, Education, Youth and Training. From 1993 to 1996 he was in the *cabinet* of Sutherland's successor as Irish Commissioner, Pádraig Flynn, and then moved to DG V (Employment, Industrial Relations and Social Affairs). In February 1999, only three months before being approached by Prodi, he was appointed Director General of DG XXII (Education, Training and Youth). (This outline of O'Sullivan's career draws on the profile of him in *European Voice*, 20–26 May 1999.) In May 2000 O'Sullivan was appointed Secretary General of the Commission and was succeeded as Prodi's *chef de cabinet* by an existing cabinet member, the Frenchman Michel Petite. (For a career profile of Petite see *European Voice*, 25–30 May 2000.)

Like O'Sullivan, *cabinet* members often have had a 'European' education, usually are in their 30s or 40s at the time of their appointment, and generally have been working in the public sector – with at least half recruited from within the Commission services. Prodi has institutionalised the 'in-house' recruitment trait by incorporating the following in the new rules for the formation of *cabinets*: in the President's *cabinet* no less than five of the nine members must be existing Commission staff and no more than four may be 'outsiders'; in other Commissioners' *cabinets* no less than three of the members must be existing staff and no more than three may be 'outsiders'; with the exception of a Commissioner's personal assistant/secretary, all support staff at both B- and C-grades must be serving Commission staff; the secondment of officials from outside is not allowed (Commission, 1999b, Part 1.3).

Other characteristics of *cabinet* members are that they are normally very bright (with intellectually self-confident Commissioners tending to have the sharpest *cabinets),* hold views that do not jar sharply with those of the Commissioner and are very hard-working (hours are long and demands are constant). It can also be helpful to have a skill or an expertise required by the Commissioner, previous working collaboration with the Commissioner, and a party political attachment that is shared with the Commissioner.

A striking feature of both O'Sullivan's and Petite's careers is movement between *cabinets* and the Commission's services. But though they have made such movements unusually frequently, the practice of movement between the two is well established. This is because Commissioners need staff who have a good understanding of how the Commission works, whilst when Commissioners leave the Commission their *cabinet* staff frequently wish to transfer back into the services or, if they came from elsewhere, be appointed to the services. A source of resentment on the part of Commission officials who have never served in a *cabinet* (the overwhelming majority) is the way in which as a College comes to the end of its term of office the *cabinet* staff of retiring Commissioners seek not only 'a safe landing' in the services but a landing at a senior level. Widely resented, however, though the practice of 'elevated transfers' is, it has been common – as is witnessed by the large numbers of Commission staff at A3-grade and above who have served at some time in a *cabinet*. In line with the spirit of the reforms he introduced on *cabinet* recruitment, Prodi saw to it that the new rules governing the formation of *cabinets* state that no guarantee may be given to temporary staff ('outsiders') concerning recruitment to the services, since the ordinary rules for recruitment will apply to them (Commission, 1999b, Part 1.3).

Organisation

The organisation of a *cabinet* depends very much on the preferences of the Commissioner and the *chef de cabinet*. Some *cabinets* operate on a fairly hierarchical basis, with the *chef* closely directing the work of other *cabinet* members and with most communications between *cabinet* members and the Commissioner being channelled through the *chef* and perhaps also the *deputy chef*. Other *cabinets*, by contrast, are more open in their structure in that the position of the *chef* is not so overbearing and there are frequent meetings – on an individual and collective basis – between the Commissioner and his/her staff.

An organisational feature that all *cabinets* share is an internal division of labour, with each *cabinet* member being expected to provide general support for the Commissioner and also to assume responsibilities for particular aspects of the Commissioner's work. As part of the general support, a task falling to all *cabinet* members, but especially *chefs*, is to represent their Commissioner in all sorts of forums both inside and outside the Commission where the Commissioner cannot be, or does not choose to be, present. Most *cabinet* members, but again especially *chefs*, are likely to have a good knowledge of their Commissioner's mind and policy preferences so when representing him/her can assume a considerable degree of responsibility on his/her behalf. Box 5.1 shows how responsibilities were organised in two typical *cabinets* at the beginning of the Prodi Commission.

Functions and functioning

Phrases such as 'the eyes and ears of the Commissioner' and 'the promoter and protector of the Commissioner's interests' are commonly used to describe the role of a Commissioner's *cabinet*. Useful, however, though such phrases are for giving a general indication of the role of *cabinets*, they need to be given greater precision. The Code of Conduct for Commissioners that was adopted by the College at the very beginning of the Prodi presidency gave such greater precision:

The role of the Commissioners' Offices is:

- firstly to contribute to proper operation of the principle of collective responsibility by keeping the Commissioners informed about matters not falling within their specific areas;
- to assist Commissioners with the content and the prioritising of their policy area, implementation of the policy being the responsibility of Directorates-General;

Box 5.1 Responsibilities in Commissioners' Cabinets[a]

(This box takes two typical *cabinets* at the beginning of the Prodi Commission)

Commissioner	**Mario Monti (Italian)**
Portfolio	Competition
Head of Cabinet	Enzo Moavero Milanesi (Italian) Management of *cabinet*, personnel, reform, institutional questions, Intergovernmental Conference, prospective task force
Deputy Head of Cabinet	Marc Van Hoof (Belgian) Competition, state aid, telecommunications liberalisation, enterprise information society, Economic and Social Committee, Court of Justice
Members of Cabinet	Stefano Manservisi (Italian) Competition, international aspects, Council, Court of Auditors, external relations, trade, customs, enlargement, development, European Community Humanitarian Office, anti-fraud, financial control, mediator, security bureau
	Angelo Marcello Cardani (Italian) Competition, economic analysis, liberalisation (except telecommunications), European Parliament, Economic and Social Committee, Committee of the Regions, taxation, research, economic and monetary affairs, budget, Statistical Office, transport, energy, Euratom
	Carles Esteva Mosso (Spanish) Competition, mergers, joint ventures and dominant positions
	Elisabetta Olivi (Italian) Competition, state monopoly of a commercial character, infractions, information, Press and Communication Service, internal markets, Justice and Home Affairs, education, culture, employment and social affairs, health and consumer protection, environment

$\longrightarrow$

Commissioner	Anna Diamantopoulou
Portfolio	Employment and Social Affairs
Head of Cabinet	Giorgios Glynos (Greek) General coordination, Secretariat General, security and protocol, personnel, administrative reform
Deputy Head of Cabinet	Kirsty Hughes (British) Employment strategy, European Social Fund policy, development and coordination, adaptation to industrial changes, work organisation and the information society, research and analysis of demography and the social situation, Commission Group on Growth, Competitiveness and Employment, enterprise and the information society, research, economic and monetary affairs, trade, Forward Studies
Members of Cabinet	Themistoklis Galeros (Greek) National employment monitoring and European Social Fund operations including Community initiatives, budget financial coordination and accounts, contracts and subsidies, audit and control, monitoring and evaluation, agriculture, fisheries, regional policy, budget
	Barbara Hellerich (German) Equal opportunities for women and men and matters regarding families and children, social protection, social inclusion and civil society, integration of people with disabilities, social economy, Commission Group on Equal Opportunities, environment, education, culture
	Gerassimos Zorbas (Belgian) Relations with social partners and organisation of the social dialogue, labour law, industrial relations, fundamental social rights and anti-discrimination, free movement of workers, coordination of social security schemes, health, safety and hygiene at work, health and consumer protection, internal market, competition, state aids and infringements, International Labour Organisation
	Natalia Kokoni (Greek) Relations with the European Parliament, enlargement, external relations, development and humanitarian aid, Intergovernmental Conference, Justice and Home Affairs, transport, energy, information and publications, liaison with press and communication

[a] Situation in early 2000.
Source: Hill & Knowlton (1999).

- to act where necessary as the interface between Commissioners and the departments they are responsible for, but without interfering in departmental management;
- to perform administrative support, representation and political contact duties connected with the Commissioners' functions. (Commission, 1999b: Part 1.3)

Prodi saw to the drawing up of these rules because he believed, as many in the Commission believed, that *cabinets* had become too involved in activities that were not properly theirs, and more particularly had become too interfering and too intrusive in the daily work of the services. How effective the new rules will actually prove to be in 'reining in' *cabinets* remains to be seen, but it is likely that the functions that *cabinets* have long performed will continue to be so, albeit perhaps in modified form in some cases. There are four main such functions.

Supporting and assisting the day-to-day work of Commissioners

The most obvious function of *cabinets* is to provide support and assistance for the day-to-day work of Commissioners. Commissioners have very heavy demands made upon them so they are necessarily extremely reliant on their *cabinets* if they are to perform their duties efficiently and in a manner that will enable them to maximise their potential influence.

A key component element of the support function is providing information and advice. This naturally applies particularly in respect of matters falling within the Commissioners' portfolios. To ensure appropriate information and advice is given *cabinet* members are expected to have both a good overall understanding of matters falling within their Commissioner's portfolio and also to have, or to quickly acquire after appointment, specialist knowledge.

Information and advice to the Commissioner must be provided not only on matters within his/her portfolio but also on other matters where the Commissioner wishes to make a contribution to debate and/or to be an active participant in Commission decision-making. Although Commissioners do not normally seek to interfere in routine decision-making outside their portfolio, they may take an interest in non-portfolio issues that are of particular interest to them (such as when there are potential implications for their area of responsibility or when there are particular consequences for their member state) and they are likely to want to contribute when decisions are being taken on such general matters as the annual work programme, the composition of the preliminary draft budget, and major cross-sectoral policy initiatives. Given that Commissioners must spend most of their working time focusing on portfolio-related issues, they are inevitably heavily reliant on sound briefings from their *cabinets* if they are to exercise a significant influence on non-portfolio or cross-sectoral issues.

Another important component of the support function of *cabinets* is acting as a buffer and a filter for Commissioners in relation to lobbyists. A host of policy actors and would-be policy actors seek access to the upper reaches of the Commission for such purposes as explaining difficulties they are having with existing EU laws, being given early indications of likely policy developments, and influencing upcoming decisions. *Cabinets* manage much of this lobbying activity, and in so doing shield their Commissioners, by dealing with many lobbyists themselves, by referring lobbyists to the services where appropriate, and by deciding if and in what form direct access to Commissioners should be granted.

Closely related to this 'shielding' and 'protecting' role, *cabinet* members must also exercise a representative role on behalf of their Commissioner. This role is undertaken via the numerous contacts *cabinet* members have with Commission-based and non-Commission-based individuals, representatives, groups, and organisations.

A link between Commissioners and the services

Following on from their supporting function, *cabinets* are a key link between Commissioners and the services. More particularly, *cabinets* are key links between Commissioners and the DG(s) and special services for which they have responsibility. Commissioners do, of course, have direct dealings with senior officials in their areas of policy responsibility, but most day-to-day and routine contacts between the political and administrative arms of the Commission are channelled via *cabinets*.

There are considerable variations in the relations between *cabinets* and services. Relations are usually at their most harmonious and productive when *cabinets* are in frequent and close touch with 'their' DG(s). Leon Brittan (a Commissioner between 1989–99), for example, encouraged his *cabinet* to establish such relations by engaging in extensive consultations with senior service officials and by providing them with *cabinet* policy and briefing papers. When good relations are established, *cabinets* and services become familiar with what the other is prioritising, doing and thinking and so are well positioned to resolve possible problems at an early stage. There should, for example, be little question of a *cabinet* blocking a dossier from a DG with which it has been working closely, although there may be some reference back for re-drafting.

But the relationship between *cabinets* and services 'bristles with ambivalence' (McDonald, 1997: 51) and it has long been recognised that it is a source of tensions and resentment (see, for example, the 1979 Spierenburg Report). Part of the problem is that some *cabinet* members regard themselves as being rather special and 'a cut above' regular Commission staff. The main problem, however, is that *cabinets* sometimes act in ways that are perceived as being insensitive to, or dismissive of, the work and practices of the services. For example: *cabinets* may seek to put what is seen by a DG to be undue pressure on it to prepare or advance a particular dossier; *cabinets* may be highly critical of dossiers on which a DG has been working for many months; a *cabinet* member, who is likely to be of middle-ranking A4- or A5-grade, may seek to use the authority of his/her Commissioner to lean on a senior service official, who may be of A3 or higher grade; and a *cabinet* may attempt to circumvent the normal chain of command within the services by dealing directly with officials who are handling particular matters.

Such practices were especially prevalent during Jacques Delors' period as Commission President. His *cabinet*, under the drive and example of its *chef*, Pascal Lamy, and united in its commitment to Delors' vision of a dynamic Europe led by a vanguard Commission, became notorious for 'using what worked' when formal procedures and channels were seen to create difficulties or to be inefficient. The Delors *cabinet* frequently bypassed official hierarchical lines and 'reached into' the DGs to deal directly with people who they knew, or who they thought, could do a job for them. This method of operating created a certain amount of tension and resentment amongst services staff – not least since the Delors' *cabinet* tended to work predominantly through French networks. The practice resulted in many service managers attempting to maintain control by discouraging their officials from dealing directly with *cabinets* and resulted also in officials who were approached by *cabinets* usually seeking cover by ensuring superiors were informed. (On the functioning of the Delors *cabinet*, see Ross 1993, 1994, 1995; Cini, 1996b; Endo, 1999.)

By focusing on ends and not worrying too much about means, *cabinets* have unquestionably sometimes been able to cut through traditional and bureaucratic channels to create a momentum behind initiatives. For example, Ross (1993) has described how under Delors' presidency *cabinets*, especially Delors' own *cabinet*, acted in this way to promote and advance a Commission document on industrial policy that was published in 1990, followed by a more specific document on the electronics industry that was published in 1991. But though the practice of vigorous intervention by *cabinets* has sometimes produced policy benefits, it has also created problems. The damage to morale in the services has already been alluded to. Another problem has been that some policy papers – including, many observers believe, a number in recent years that have been aimed at tackling unemployment – have been overrushed and underprepared because of pressure from *cabinets*.

Aware of the problems pro-activist and 'interfering' *cabinets* were creating, Jacques Santer and his *chef de cabinet,* Jim Cloos, sought to encourage a climate in which *cabinets* meddled less with the detailed work of the services and were more respectful of the Commission's Rules of Procedure. They had some success, as is evidenced by the fact that, as Peterson (1999a: 56) has noted, 'fewer charges of "terrorism", or sabotage of the work of the services by headstrong members of *cabinets*, were heard during the Santer era'.

But though there was a toning down of *cabinet* interference in the work of the services under Santer, Romano Prodi let it be known soon after becoming President-designate that he believed *cabinet*-service relations were still unsatisfactory. The main problem, in his view, was that the roles and responsibilities of *cabinets* and services had become blurred. There should be 'a clearer definition of the relationship between politics and administration in the workings of the Commission' (Prodi, 1999a). He emphasised 'the need to clarify the respective roles of *cabinets* and services and to ensure that there is a genuine shift in the balance of power from the *cabinets* towards the Commission's services. The role of *cabinets* should be to support their Commissioners in the development of policy. Directorates General should be responsible for the implementation of policy' (Prodi, 1999b). As part of this re-definition of the respective roles of *cabinets* and services, Prodi indicated that he believed *cabinets* had become too involved in refining legislative texts when their role should be confined to negotiating over political aspects of law making (*European Voice*, 10–16 June 1999: 2). The new listing of the roles of *cabinets* (see pp. 123 and 126) was partly designed to restrain *cabinets* from such 'over-reaching'.

In practice, it doubtless will not be wholly possible to make the clear distinctions called for by Prodi between policy development and policy implementation and between the functions of *cabinets* and those of the services. The fact is that in any public sector system policy development and policy implementation invariably shade into one another, while in the Commission system *cabinets* and the services are highly dependent on one another and so inevitably overlap in what they do. That said, however, sharper lines of responsibility are certainly possible, and if they emerge they may, amongst other things, boost morale amongst services' staff who will have less cause for complaint about 'interference and meddling' by *cabinets*.

A change required by Prodi that is more straightforward is that insofar as it is practicable Commissioners and their *cabinets* are to be based in the same buildings as 'their' DGs and special services rather than, as has been the previous practice, being separately located in Commission 'headquarters'. This should, by bringing the political and administrative arms of the Commission into greater physical proximity with one another, improve relations and communications between the two.

Promoter of the coordination of Commission activities

Achieving satisfactory internal coordination of its many and varied activities is a major problem for the Commission. The problem arises from the combination of a number of factors: the array of the Commission's policy responsibilities; the cross-sectoral nature of many of these responsibilities; the existence of so many DGs and special services; and the lack of political direction from above such as is normally provided in nation states by governments.

There are mechanisms for promoting coordination at services level, and Prodi has made it clear that he wishes to see these enhanced. Coordinating mechanisms at services level cannot, however, deal with or resolve all coordination issues, especially when they involve 'turf disputes' between different parts of the Commission, when they raise questions about the Commission's priorities, and when they contain a clear political dimension. Ultimately such disputes may be resolvable only at College level. Before, however, being considered by a College meeting they are examined, discussed, and negotiated at *cabinet* level. One way in which coordination is attempted at *cabinet* level is simply via informal exchanges between members of relevant *cabinets*. *Cabinet* members tend to know their counterparts in other *cabinets* reasonably well (though familiarity may decline under the Prodi system of *cabinet* members now being based in different buildings) and so can sometimes reach understandings in *ad hoc* conversations and meetings. A second way in which *cabinet*-level activity can promote coordination is via meetings of all *cabinet* members who are responsible for particular policy areas. In the past there were normally at least half a dozen of these meetings – called *special chefs'* meetings – each week, but under Prodi they have been cut back, which may create problems given the role they have played in promoting different types of coordination. On the one hand, they have assisted horizontal coordination on specific policy and legislative proposals by injecting a political dynamic into issues that have not been resolvable at services level and also by providing an opportunity for Commissioners other than the sponsoring Commissioner to make (through their *cabinet* representatives) an input into the policy-making process. On the other hand, they have promoted the general coordination of Commission activities by ensuring that proposals are evaluated in the context of the Commission's overall policy priorities. *Special chefs'* meetings are convened and chaired by the relevant policy specialist in the President's *cabinet*, which highlights the position of the President's *cabinet* as a third way in which coordination is promoted at *cabinet* level. The President's *cabinet* attempts to monitor the activities of all the services and of all Commissioners' portfolios and intervenes with relevant policy actors as and when it deems it to be appropriate. In so doing, the President's *cabinet* often attempts to broker between different views and interests so as to try and ensure that the Commission is as coherent and cohesive in its behaviour and actions as possible. A fourth and final way in which *cabinets* can promote coordination is at *chef de cabinet* level, with relevant *chefs* sometimes dealing directly with one another on an informal basis on particular issues and with all *chefs* gathering together for the weekly *chefs de cabinet* meeting. The nature and purpose of the *chefs'* weekly meeting was considered in Chapter 4, so let it just be said here that it is, because of the status of its membership and because it is the last decision-making stage before College meetings, sometimes able to settle issues that previous actors in the decision-making process have not been able to resolve.

Preparer of College meetings

All Commission decisions are formally taken collectively by the College. In practice, most routine decisions are actually delegated to individual Commissioners, but even so the collegiate principle means that a considerable volume of business is referred to the College's weekly meeting.

So as to ensure that they proceed in an efficient and effective manner, College meetings are carefully prepared. Most of the administrative preparations – including circulating agendas and papers and checking that all internal requirements for the taking of decisions have been met – are undertaken by the Secretariat General. What may be thought of as the political and policy preparation is undertaken largely via *cabinets*.

This preparation by *cabinets* is focused mainly on trying to ensure that as far as possible the contents of College agenda items – be they policy papers, legislative proposals, or actions such as the initiation of ECJ cases or the imposition of fines against business firms – are agreed in advance. If they can be, the items are listed as A-points on the College agenda and are, unless a Commissioner wishes to raise a late point or objection, approved without discussion. College efficiency is thereby promoted and potentially damaging direct confrontations between Commissioners are avoided.

The preparation takes three main forms. First, the *cabinets* of lead Commissioners liaise with their counterparts in other *cabinets*, and where appropriate with the services, to try to reach agreement on the contents of dossiers. This process involves *cabinet* members seeking to have as much as possible of their Commissioner's views incorporated into dossiers, but having to be prepared to make concessions except on points that the Commissioner is prepared to take to the College. Second, the President's *cabinet* liaises closely with other *cabinets* to see that items are brought before the College in good order, on schedule, and with as much support as possible. Third, in the manner that was described in Chapter 4, the weekly *chefs de cabinet* meeting works with the Secretariat General to finalise and streamline the agenda of College meetings.

Concluding remarks

Cabinets occupy an extremely important position in the Commission's organisational system. From their position they undertake a number of vital functions.

The precise nature of these functions, and the ways in which they are undertaken, will be affected by the changes to the size, composition and roles of *cabinets* that have been introduced by President Prodi. They may not, however, be affected as much as has been anticipated in some quarters, for the fact is that policy roles (supposedly to be the responsibility of Commissioners and their staff) and executive roles (supposedly to be the responsibility of the services) are not in practice easily disentangled.

Commissioners cannot do their jobs properly or exercise as much influence as they are potentially capable of doing unless they have strong *cabinet* back-up. The relationship between Commissioners and *cabinets* is, however, two-way in the sense that not only are Commissioners dependent on their *cabinets* if they are to be effective and successful but so also are *cabinets* dependent on their Commissioner. Good advice and strong support are of limited value if they are not, or are not capable of being, used properly.

Chapter 6

The Services

The services of the Commission are organised into departments, much as national civil services are organised into ministries. Most of these departments are called Directorates General (DGs), with the remainder being variously called special, general and internal services. (In the interest of brevity, only the term 'special services' will be used here.)

The distinction between DGs on the one hand and special services on the other used to be sharply drawn. In terms of public perception the most obvious distinction between the two was that whereas special services 'only' had titles, DGs had numbers and titles. Moreover, it was by the numbers that they were most commonly known. So, for example, the DG for Competition was DG IV, the DG for Agriculture was DG VI, and the DG for Energy was DG VIII. At a more fundamental level DGs were generally viewed as being more important than special services in that they were seen as being where most policy issues were handled, whilst special services were seen as essentially providing support to the DGs or, in a few cases, dealing with temporary or fledgling policy issues. It was indicative of this perception of DGs as being more important that when, as occasionally happened, special services were converted into DGs it was common to describe them as having been 'upgraded'.

In reality the significance of the distinction between DGs and special services has never been as great as it has seemed. One reason for this is that although it is certainly true that special services tend to be more concerned with providing support for Commission policy activities rather than directly handling policies themselves, there is a broad and grey area where policy activity and support activity intertwines and overlaps. A second reason is that most of the work undertaken by special services is by no means of secondary importance. On the contrary, tasks undertaken by, for example, the Secretariat General and the Legal Service are absolutely central to the effective and efficient functioning of the Commission and placement in these services is much sought after by serving and aspirant Commission officials. And a third reason is that not all DGs are directly policy-focused. Rather, some – notably Personnel and Administration and Budget – are engaged largely in 'in-house' horizontal tasks.

As an almost symbolic recognition of the limited importance of the distinction between DGs and special services, the numbering system for DGs was removed in September 1999. The removal was not, however, done for that reason but rather as part of Romano Prodi's efforts to make the Commission more publicly accessible and transparent. Proudly proclaiming soon after his nomination as President-designate that he had no intention of learning the numbers of DGs, Prodi made it clear that he thought the numbering system served only the convenience of insiders. Accordingly, the numbers were abolished as soon as the Prodi Commission assumed office. At the same time, DG titles, which in some cases had become very long and cumbersome, were shortened and made more 'user-friendly', as a comparison of Tables 6.1 and 6.2 shows.

This chapter is structured around examinations of the DGs, the Secretariat General (the most important of the special services), other special services, conflicts between services, and mechanisms for inter-service coordination.

The Directorates General

Number and focus

Shortly after the EEC came into being in 1958 there were nine DGs. In recent years the number has consistently been in the low-to-mid twenties. At the time of writing (March 2000) there are twenty-three.

The increased number of DGs as compared with the early days of the Community is primarily a consequence of the EC/EU having extended its policy interests. So, for example, the creation of the Justice and Home Affairs DG in 1999, out of a department previously located in the Secretariat General, was a response to the Commission's developing role in this policy sphere since Maastricht and the increasing responsibilities it was assigned under the Amsterdam Treaty. The single most important factor in explaining the establishment and focus of DGs is thus that they reflect what the EU does. Because the EU has well developed responsibilities in such policy spheres as competition, agriculture and the environment, so DGs are found in these spheres. By the same token, because the EU, unlike

Table 6.1   *Directorates General before the Prodi reorganisation*[a]

DG I	External Relations: Commercial Policy and Relations with North America, the Far East, Australia and New Zealand
DG IA	External Relations: Europe and the New Independent States, Common Foreign and Security Policy and External Missions
DG IB	External Relations: Southern Mediterranean, Middle and Near East, Latin America, South and South–East Asia and North–South Cooperation
DG II	Economic and Financial Affairs
DG III	Industry
DG IV	Competition
DG V	Employment, Industrial Relations and Social Affairs
DG VI	Agriculture
DG VII	Transport
DG VIII	Development
DG IX	Personnel and Administration
DG X	Information, Communication, Culture, Audiovisual
DG XI	Environment, Nuclear Safety and Civil Protection
DG XII	Science, Research and Development
DG XIII	Telecommunications, Information Market and Exploitation of Research
DG XIV	Fisheries
DG XV	Internal Market and Financial Services
DG XVI	Regional Policies and Cohesion
DG XVII	Energy
DG XIX	Budgets
DG XX	Financial Control
DG XXI	Taxation and Customs Union
DG XXII	Education, Training and Youth
DG XXIII	Enterprise Policy, Distributive Trades, Tourism and Cooperatives
DG XXIV	Consumer Policy and Consumer Health Protection

Note: [a] Situation in July 1999.

Table 6.2 *Directorates General after the Prodi reorganisation*[a]

Agriculture
Budget
Competition
Development
Economic and Financial Affairs
Education and Culture
Employment and Social Affairs
Energy and Transport
Enlargement
Enterprise
Environment
External Relations
Financial Control
Fisheries
Health and Consumer Protection
Information Society
Internal Market
Justice and Home Affairs
Personnel and Administration
Regional Policy
Research
Taxation and Customs Union
Trade

Note: [a] Situation in March 2000.

nation states, has only very limited policy responsibilities in such policy spheres as defence, domestic law and order, and social security, self-standing and established DGs are not found in these spheres and the policies are dealt with by other means: sometimes via task forces but more usually as part of the work of DGs whose main responsibilities lie elsewhere – as in the way that the DG for Employment and Social Affairs deals with social security policy. In addition to the EU's varying involvement in spheres of activity, other factors that help to explain the existence – and non-existence – of DGs are: bureaucratic pressures, either for the creation of new DGs or for the continuing existence of established DGs; whether a service is thought to be best designated as a DG or as a special service; and what is deemed to be in the interests of organisational efficiency.

All of these factors, but especially the organisational efficiency factor, played a part in the radical overhaul of DGs that occurred at the beginning of the Prodi Presidency. Amongst the more important changes that were made were:

- A new DG for Enterprise – with a mission to promote innovation – was created out of the previous DG III, DG XIII, and DG XXIII (see Table 6.1 for the titles of 'pre-Prodi' DGs).
- DG IB was disbanded as part of a streamlining of the external policy DGs.
- In recognition of the increased importance and workload of the enlargement process, a new Enlargement DG was established – largely from the previous Task Force for Enlargement and from country desks in the previous DG IA.
- A new Health and Consumer Protection DG was created, largely out of the previous DG XXIV and relevant parts of DG V, DG VI and DG XI.
- A new Education and Culture DG was created, mainly from the previous DG X and DG XXII.

Size

DGs naturally vary in size according to their responsibilities, their workloads and their needs for technical and specialised expertise. Most DGs have a total full-time and permanent staff of between about 150 and 500. These numbers include usually between around 70 and 120 policy making A-grade officials. The largest DGs are Personnel and Administration, which has a staff of just over 2000, and Agriculture, which has just over 850. The reason why these are the largest DGs is that they are more involved in day-to-day administration of policy than are other DGs.

In addition to full-time and permanent staff many temporary staff are also employed by DGs (see Chapter 7). In some DGs as many as one-quarter of staff are of this type.

Structure

Figure 6.1 provides a diagrammatic representation of the organisational structure of the Internal Market DG, which is a medium-sized DG. Large DGs naturally have more internal organisational sections and small DGs have fewer. However, whatever their size and however many internal sections they have, all DGs conform to the same type of organisational structure as that set out in Figure 6.1.

The key components of the structures of DGs are as follows:

- DGs are headed by directors general, who are employed at the Commission's, and the EU's, most senior administrative grade – A1. The principal responsibilities of directors general are to see to the good running of their DGs, to represent their DGs in dealings with outside agencies (both inside and outside the Commission), and to be the main channels of communication between their DGs and 'their' Commissioner. In addition to these general responsibilities, most directors general also have particular responsibilities, with sections of their DGs reporting directly to them. For example, in the Environment DG three units report directly to the director general: one covering legal affairs and the application of EU law, one covering relations with other institutions and the European Environment Agency, and one covering finance and contracts.

  But though all directors general have broadly similar responsibilities, differences do exist regarding how they do their jobs. To some extent differences are explained by differing role interpretations. So, for instance, in seeking to champion their DG's interests, some directors general are more sensitive than others to the need to look also to wider Commission interests. To some extent differences are explained by personal preferences, with, for example, some directors general wishing to involve themselves in specific policy matters and others preferring to concentrate on overall policy coordination. And to some extent differences are explained by the circumstances in which directors general find themselves. For example, directors general of large DGs with diverse responsibilities have little option but to spend much of their time dealing with internal coordination and, perhaps, internal arbitration, whilst directors general of DGs that do not see eye to eye with their Commissioner on important policy matters may have to engage in protracted exchanges with the Commissioner and his/her *cabinet*.

  All directors general have senior staff to support and assist them. These staff come in various forms and combinations, but in large and important DGs they typically consist of up to three or four deputy directors general, two or three assistants, and a couple of advisers. External Relations is an example of a DG where such support is provided: there are four deputy directors general, two

Figure 6.1 *The organisational structure of a DG*

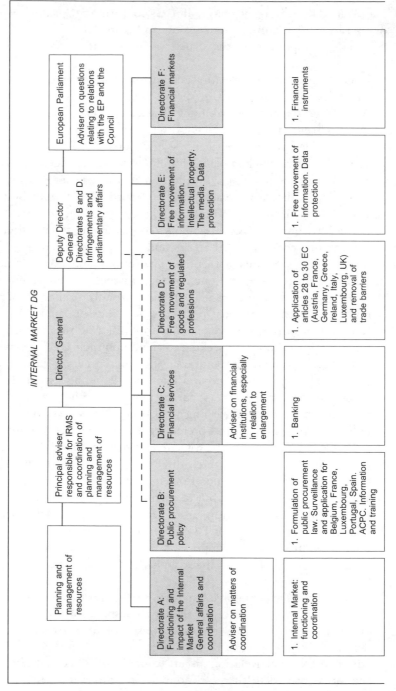

2. Internal market: monitoring of market integration and reform	2. Formulation of public procurement law. Surveillance and application for: Denmark, Greece, Ireland, Italy, UK. Public procurement advisory committees	2. Insurance	2. Application of Articles 28 to 30 EC (Belgium, Denmark, Finland, the Netherlands, Portugal, Spain and Sweden). Application of safeguard clauses	2. Industrial property	2. Securities and organised markets
3. Internal market: external dimension	3. Formulation of public procurement law. Surveillance and application for Austria, Finland, Germany, the Netherlands, Sweden. Relations with other Community policies	3. Stock exchanges and securities	3. Postal services	3. Copyright and neighbouring rights	3. Investment service providers
4. Internal Market: dialogue and promotion	4. Public procurement: international relations. Economic aspects. Electronic procedures. SIMAP	4. Financial transactions and payment systems	4. Regulated professions (qualifications)	4. The media, commercial communications and unfair competition	4. Financial reporting

Source: Based on *Internal Market DG homepage (Europa website)*, May 2000.

assistants to the director general, one chief adviser reporting to one of the deputy directors general, and six senior officials reporting to the chief adviser.

- DGs are divided into directorates, which are headed by directors who are usually at A2-grade. Most DGs contain between three and six directorates, though there are variations from this norm. The Agriculture DG, for example, has eleven directorates. Figure 6.1 illustrates the sort of division of labour which exists between directorates.

- Directorates are divided into units or, as they are sometimes known, divisions. A typical directorate contains between three and six units. Units are headed by heads of unit, who are usually at A3-grade but can be at A4 or even A5, and normally contain between three and seven A-grade officials plus three or four administrative and clerical staff. One of the A-grade officials may be designated deputy head of unit. Typically, there are at least three or four nationalities in a unit. An illustration of the type of work undertaken by units is provided in Figure 6.1.

There is thus a clear hierarchical structure within DGs, with a pyramid formation in which levels report upwards to the next highest level. So:

- the basic organisational entity is the unit
- staff within units report to the head of unit, or perhaps to the deputy head of unit if there is one
- units are grouped into directorates, which are headed by directors, and it is to directors that heads of unit report
- directors report to directors general or, in the case of larger DGs, often to deputy directors general who are responsible for coordinating areas of a DG's work.

To avoid the possibility of DGs or sections of DGs being 'captured' by nationals of a particular member state, it is customary – especially at senior levels – for officials to be of a different nationality to those to whom they report.

There are a few departures from the pyramidical formation, but they do not seriously undermine the essence of the hierarchical structure. One departure concerns the position of advisers, who are scattered around DGs at all levels and who sometimes report not to their apparent head – be it a head of unit or a director – but to their next but one head. Another departure concerns the task forces that are located in some DGs. As with advisers, task forces – which can be either temporary or semi-permanent in nature – sometimes skip a level when reporting, including, in a few cases, skipping even the director general and reporting directly to the relevant Commissioner.

Relations with Commissioners

Mention of 'the relevant Commissioner' leads to the issue of the relationships between DGs and the Commissioners to whom they report. Commissioners are not formally heads of DGs – that position belongs to directors general – but they do carry a general, if rather ill-defined, responsibility for those parts of the services whose work corresponds to their portfolios (see Table 4.1, pp. 102–3). Ideally the relationship between Commissioners and DGs is one to one, but this is by no means always the case, for the portfolios of some Commissioners cover the work of more than one DG.

As was shown in Chapter 4, the relationships Commissioners have with 'their' DG(s) vary considerably. In terms of policy priorities and objectives most Commissioners work easily and well with their DGs, though occasionally Commissioners do become involved in confrontational, even stormy, exchanges and disputes. Much depends on whether or not the views of Commissioners and DGs naturally coincide, whether there is give and take on both sides, and whether or not Commissioners have particular agendas of their own. In terms of day-to-day working relationships, some Commissioners establish direct, close and regular contacts with senior DG officials, especially directors general, whilst other Commissioners keep a distance between themselves and their DGs and rely heavily on their *cabinets* to channel communications. The practice established at the beginning of the Prodi Commission whereby, insofar as it is possible, Commissioners are now based in the same building as 'their' DG(s) means that it is more important than ever that Commissioners and senior officials strike good working relationships. When such relationships have not been possible, directors general have occasionally resigned 'in the interests of the service' – as, for example, in 1995 when Peter Wilmott, the Director General of DG XXI, left office largely because of his poor relations with Mario Monti (the Internal Market Commissioner), in 1996 when José Almeida Serra, the Director General of DG XIV, left largely because of his poor relations with Emma Bonino (the Fisheries Commissioner), and in 2000 when Allan Larsson, the Director General of the Employment and Social Affairs DG, left largely because of his poor relations with Anna Diamontopoulou (the Employment and Social Affairs Commissioner).

But whatever the precise nature of Commissioner–DG relationships, if a Commissioner decides to press a matter – such as a request for a new policy document or for revisions to a draft legislative proposal – then the DG concerned has little choice but to comply, even if it has reservations. An example of a Commissioner so pressing a matter despite DG reservations occurred as the Delors III Commission approached its end in late 1994, when the outgoing Research Commissioner, Antonio Ruberti, insisted that all the specific programmes making up the Fourth Framework Research Programme be completed, be published, and be ready to call for proposals by 15 December. Ruberti's insistence was passed down the line of command in DG XII even though many officials within the DG felt too much was being asked because some programmes were unlikely to be finally agreed by the EP and the Council before early December and also because much linguistic/jurist work still needed to be done on the programmes.

Significant differences between Commissioners and DGs of the kind just cited are not, it should be emphasised, common. This is partly because Commissioners and DGs come to know each other and learn what is wanted and expected of them by the other, and partly because both are working within the same broad frameworks – namely, the frameworks of the Commission's and the DG's annual work programmes. Where differences do arise between Commissioners and DGs they tend, therefore, to be on specifics rather than on matters of substance. Such differences can normally be resolved at a fairly early stage of policy- and decision-making processes, with Commissioners themselves perhaps not even being directly involved but having their views transmitted to relevant DG officials via members of their *cabinets*.

Responsibilities

The type of work undertaken in DGs is enormously wide ranging. Tasks officials can find themselves involved with include:

- preparing policy papers
- drafting legislative proposals
- drawing up action and work programmes
- implementing EU legislation

- overseeing the implementation of EU legislation undertaken by national agencies
- assessing the impact of EU policies and legislation
- gathering information and writing reports.

These tasks, and others, are examined in later chapters of this book. Suffice it here, therefore, for attention to be restricted to noting the principal differences between DGs in respect of their responsibilities.

Perhaps the most obvious differences is in the extent to which DGs are focused on a particular policy sector. As with most attempts to distinguish between DGs, it is not possible to erect hard and fast categories in respect of this distinction, but clearly some DGs are much more focused on particular policy sectors than are others. Regional Policy, Fisheries, and Agriculture are examples of DGs that are focused on policy sectors. By contrast, Personnel and Administration, Budget, and Financial Control are examples of DGs whose foci are not directed towards particular policy sectors but are cross-sectoral in nature and/or are concerned with 'in-house' management or policy processes. In the language of organisational theory, the former type of DGs have responsibilities which are largely vertical in character, whilst the responsibilities of the latter type are more horizontal.

A second difference is the extent to which DGs are dealing with policy areas where there have been significant transfers of power from the member states to the EU. Examples of DGs dealing with policy areas where there have been significant transfers include Trade, Competition, Agriculture, and Fisheries. Examples of DGs where transfers have been more modest include External Relations, Employment and Social Affairs, and Energy and Transport.

The extent to which there have been transfers of power links to a third difference between DGs, namely the extent to which they have executive responsibilities. Naturally there is a close relationship between the extent of the policy transfers and the extent of executive responsibilities. Executive responsibilities take many different forms, including whether the Commission is itself a direct administrator (as with much of competition law) or is more of an overseer of administration undertaken by agencies in the member states (as with much of agricultural and environmental law). Specific examples of executive responsibilities of DGs include: drawing up anti-dumping duties against the imports of a third country (a responsibility of the Trade DG); investigating whether certain types of proposed mergers between companies should be authorised (a responsibility of the Competition DG); and making marginal adjustments to CAP prices to reflect changes in world market conditions (a responsibility of the Agriculture DG).

Closely related to executive responsibility differences is a fourth difference: the involvement of DGs in policy and legislative development on the one hand and routine administration on the other. As with all of the differences between DGs that are being outlined here, this difference is one of degree rather than one of fundamental type, for all DGs are involved in both development and administrative activities. Nonetheless, the difference certainly does exist, as is seen, for instance, by comparing the balance of the work responsibilities of the Budget and Personnel and Administration DGs on the one hand with the Information Society and Education and Culture DGs on the other. The work of the first two involves policy and legislative development (though precious little legislative development in the case of Personnel and Administration), but most of their work is concerned with maintaining and adjusting existing policies and in consequence much of it is of a routine and administrative kind. By contrast, the existence of only limited policy and legislative development in the spheres covered by the Information Society and Education and Culture DGs gives them rather less to do in the way of managing existing policies and potentially more to do in the way of developing new policies.

The Secretariat General

Responsibilities

The Secretariat General is, essentially, the secretariat of the Commission and, more particularly, the secretariat of the College of Commissioners. In this capacity it is charged with ensuring that the Commission as an institution is working efficiently and effectively. It does this by utilising the overview it has of what is going on in the different parts of the Commission and of the deep knowledge it has of EU politics and procedures.

In more specific terms, the Secretariat General has five main tasks: memory bank, watchdog and facilitator of coordination, procedural monitor, promoter of organisational efficiency, and manager of relations with other EU institutions.

Memory bank The Secretariat General acts as a sort of memory bank and information agency for the Commission. It does this by closely monitoring and keeping abreast of activities and developments throughout the services, in the College, and in the other EU institutions as they affect the Commission. Information acquired and stored is then made available to those parts of the Commission that need it and/or can benefit from it. So, for example, the College is kept informed about matters such as the extent to which work programmes are on target, why a particular policy or legislative proposal has been delayed, and whether problems can be expected in the EP on a forthcoming matter. The services are informed about College approved priorities, programmes, and decisions, are 're-minded' of what is expected of them if they seem to be failing to deliver on time – as, for example, with a dossier that is behind schedule – and are generally kept in touch with what is deemed to be relevant information stemming from elsewhere in the EU and Commission systems.

Watchdog and facilitator of coordination The Secretariat General seeks to ensure that the many different facets of Commission activities are properly coordinated and are pulling in the same direction. This responsibility to act as a force for cohesion was boosted when David Williamson became Secretary General in 1987 and established as one of his main priorities ensuring that the enormous range of activities in which the Commission is involved are harnessed within an agreed framework and are properly linked with one another. The responsibility has grown further under the presidency of Romano Prodi, who soon after being nominated as President-designate established as one of his internal reform goals a reduction in the involvement of Commissioners' *cabinets* in policy coordination and an increase in coordination by the services. As part of this shift of responsibility to the services, the Secretariat General was given a key role under new rules on closer cooperation:

> The Secretariat-General will help develop a culture of cooperation within the institution. It will support coordination at all levels, by encouraging it, facilitating it and participating in it, ensuring that all tools are properly structured. It will develop internal coordination activities in the areas of advice, identifying/spreading good practice and reporting.

Inter alia, the Secretariat-General will:

- check whether appropriate mechanisms are necessary to ensure coordination between departments in particularly difficult or strategically important cases;
- automatically inform the weekly meeting of Directors-General and heads of department of any matters likely to be appearing on the agendas of forthcoming Commission meetings so that their substance can be examined and so as to report on progress so far as regards their preparations;
- regularly inform the weekly meeting of Directors-General on medium-term programming of future initiatives in the context of the implementation of the Commission's work programme;
- if necessary and depending on the nature of the problem, refer cases to the weekly meeting of Directors-General, the GCOM, or any other appropriate coordination body;
- consider whether meetings of interdepartmental working parties might under certain circumstances replace written interdepartmental consultations; and
- revise the current list and structure of the interdepartmental working parties and look at creating a website on their activities and setting up an electronic letter box for the use of departments so that the list of working parties can be updated on a regular basis. (Commission, 1999f)

At a general level, the Secretariat General undertakes its coordinating responsibility by attempting to keep an overall eye on what is going on in the many different parts of the Commission and, more particularly, by playing a major role in planning the work of the Commission. This latter task includes, most crucially: (1) drawing up, on the basis of information provided to it by the services, the Commission's annual work programme, which is published in October and provides a general framework for the Commission's priorities and objectives for the forthcoming year; and (2) on the basis of the annual work programme and of the priorities of the Council and the EP, agreeing – if possible by January – an inter-institutional legislative programme for the forthcoming year.

At more issue-specific levels, coordination involves the Secretariat General in many different types of activities. For example, it checks that all services with a potential interest in a matter are consulted when proposals for the EU to do something are brought forward. It ensures that different parts of the Commission that are undertaking related work liaise closely with each other – as, for example, with anti-fraud activity. And it liaises with the services to better enable the Commission to be able to present a common front – 'to respect collegiality' to use the official description – in its dealings with other institutions and agencies.

Procedural monitor The Secretariat General sees that internal Commission procedures are observed. Whenever the Commission takes a decision – be it on the launching of an important White Paper, on the issuing of a legislative proposal, or on making a minor technical adjustment to existing legislation – the relevant procedures laid down in the Commission's Rules of Procedure must be followed. The purposes of such procedures are various, of which the principal ones are to ensure that: (1) no decisions are taken without all possible interested parts of the Commission having had the opportunity to make an input; (2) all possible information relating to decisions is considered; (3) decisions are not referred to the College without being properly prepared and considered; (4) decisions are not taken at too low a level within the Commission; (5) decisions are well drafted; (6) decisions are within the Commission's competence. Different procedures apply to different types of decisions, with the Secretariat General acting as a clearing house to see that the correct procedures have been used and that all stages within the procedures have been respected.

Promoter of organisational efficiency The Secretariat General concerns itself with whether the structure and operating practices of the Commission services could be improved. This responsibility has increased in importance as the steady expansion of EU policy involvement has meant that the Commission has had more to do, as EU institutions have had to be sensitive to the growing interest in administrative efficiency that has been apparent in western countries since the 1980s, as budgetary restraints have made it difficult to increase the numbers of administrative staff, and as reform of the Commission has assumed a prominent place on the EU agenda.

Questions that the Secretariat General has to consider in exercising this organisational efficiency responsibility include whether changes in procedures and mechanisms could improve effectiveness and whether a particular part of the services – a directorate, perhaps – would be better located elsewhere. In considering such questions, the Secretariat General works particularly closely with, on the services side, the DG for Personnel and Administration and the Legal Service, and, on the College side, the President and the Commissioner for Personnel and Administration.

Manager of relations with other EU institutions   The Secretariat General has important responsibilities regarding the management of the Commission's responsibilities with other EU institutions.

Within the Commission these responsibilities require the Secretariat General to not so much concern itself with the details of policy content – which is essentially for the DGs – but rather to monitor developments, to coordinate activities, and to provide a range of administrative services (for example, the Secretariat General officially notifies other institutions of Commission decisions).

Outside the Commission the responsibilities require the Secretariat General to be in regular direct contact with officials of other institutions and to be represented at many of the key forums of these institutions. Prominent amongst these forums are:

- *The European Council*   The President of the Commission, one other Commissioner, and the Secretary General of the Commission, are the only Commission representatives who can attend formal summit sessions.
- *Ministerial-level meetings of the Council of Ministers*   Relevant Commissioners plus officials from both the Secretariat General and relevant DGs are usually present.
- *The Committee of Permanent Representatives* (COREPER)   Very senior officials from the Secretariat General and relevant DGs attend meetings of COREPER and its associated bodies. So, for example, COREPER II (the Permanent Representatives themselves) is normally attended by the Deputy Secretary General plus the director general(s) responsible. (Occasionally, when very important dossiers are being discussed, relevant Commissioners may also attend.) The Antici Group (which prepares much of the business of the European Council and of ministerial and COREPER II meetings) is normally attended by the head of the unit in the Secretariat General which is responsible for relations with the Council and also often by a deputy director general or chief adviser from the DG(s) responsible.
- *EP plenary sessions*   Officials from both the directorate in the Secretariat General responsible for relations with the EP and from relevant DGs are always present in Strasbourg during plenary week.

- *Council working parties and EP committees* Officials from the responsible DGs are always present and officials from the Secretariat General usually attempt to be present. If, as commonly happens, many meetings are held on the same day, the Secretariat General – which is generally understaffed – may not have enough A-grade personnel available for all meetings to be attended, in which case judgements have to be made as to which meetings are likely to be the most important. It may then be decided that an A-grade official will attend an EP committee at which a legislative proposal is to be discussed, but that a *stagiare* (trainee on temporary placement with the Commission) will be sent along to an EP committee where there is no legislative proposal on the agenda. When the Secretariat General is not represented at all at meetings, information about what happened is usually obtained from DG officials who attended.

The seemingly remorseless increase in EU business, coupled with the greater complexity and greater inter-institutional interdependence that treaty reforms have brought to decision-making procedures, have necessitated improved communications between the main EU institutions. One way in which these improved communications have been achieved has been in a mushrooming of informal direct contacts – on the telephone, through the internet, and in *ad hoc* meetings – between officials in the services of the institutions. The Secretariat General, and especially the directorates with responsibility for relations with the Council and with the EP, has been much involved in this activity. Another way in which communications have been improved has been through the establishment of standing inter-institutional meetings and groups. The best known of these meetings and groups is that between the Presidents of the Council, the EP and the Commission, but another one that is of considerable significance, and one in which the Secretariat General plays a very important role, is the Interinstitutional Coordination Group – which is better known as the Neunreither Group after the director general in the EP who founded it. The Group, which usually meets on the Thursday before EP plenary weeks, is attended by, amongst others, representatives from the secretariats of the Council, the EP, the Commission, and the Economic and Social Committee. The main functions of the Group are to deal with matters on the plenary agenda, to review progress on the agreed annual legislative programme, to plan future agendas, and to tackle interinstitutional problems relating, for example, to different interpretations of procedural requirements (for more information on the Group see Westlake, 1994: 21).

An important aspect of the Secretariat General's management of relations with other institutions is the role it exercises as a filtering agency for approaches to the Commission for action of some kind. For example, requests from the Council for a Commission report or proposal are not sent directly to DGs or to special services but are sent to the Secretariat General, which circulates them throughout the services whilst, at the same time, indicating where the main responsibility would appear to lie. (Normally this is fairly obvious.) Written EP questions are dealt with in much the same way, with the Secretariat General distributing them throughout the services and suggesting, and later finalising, an attribution.

In addition to the Secretariat General's horizontal responsibilities relating to the efficiency and effectiveness of the Commission, it also has limited direct policy responsibilities.

From time to time policy areas that are new or are in the process of being developed are located in the Secretariat General. As these policy areas become established as part of 'normal' Commission business, they are given a 'proper' base in the Commission structure, either within an existing DG or as a DG in their own right. This is what happened, for example, with justice and home affairs after it was established as a separate EU pillar by the Maastricht Treaty: its initial organisational base was as a task force within the Secretariat General, but in 1999 it became a DG in its own right.

Until mid-2000 a rather special policy role was played by the Forward Studies Unit, or *Cellule de Prospective* to give it its more commonly used French title, which was a directorate within the Secretariat General. Established in 1989 on the initiative of Jacques Delors, the Unit was essentially a think tank engaged in innovative research and forward planning. The Unit was responsible for many research programmes, though limited resources – there were normally no more than twenty A-grade staff located in the Unit – meant that it could not undertake much original research itself. Rather, it concentrated on putting together and coordinating the work of research teams. In May 2000 Prodi announced that the Unit would be strengthened, would shift the focus of its work from distant scenarios to more immediate practices, would have as its main role assisting the President in developing and implementing policies, and would be renamed the Economic and Political Council (Prodi, 2000).

Size and structure

There are some 200 A-grade officials in the Secretariat General plus support staff.

The structure of the Secretariat General is similar to DGs with, below the Secretary General, the work grouped mainly into directorates, which are themselves divided into units. In early 2000 there were, as Table 6.3 shows, six directorates. Most of these directorates contain between two and four units. For illustrative purposes, the units in three of the Secretariat's General's directorates are listed in Table 6.4.

The Secretary General

The Secretary General is the Commission's most senior official. He is of director general rank, but several factors combine to place him at a level that is, in practice, significantly above the Commission's other directors general: he is the head not of a policy department but of the Commission's main coordinating department; he reports directly to the President of the Commission; he chairs the weekly Monday meeting of the *chefs de cabinet*; he also chairs the weekly Thursday meeting of the directors general; and he is recognised as having a general responsibility for seeing that the Commission services are well organised and function efficiently The Secretary General thus occupies a position from which he can do much to help set the tone for the way in which the Commission operates and is run.

The Secretary General also carries responsibilities for the relations of the Commission services with other EU institutions. He is, for example, the only Commission official allowed to attend meetings of the European Council. He plays an important part in the Commission's relations with the Council of Ministers: by attending some important ministerial meetings – especially of the General Affairs Council; by meeting members of the Antici Group on a weekly basis so as to inform them (and, therefore, also their Permanent Representations) of developments within the Commission; by regularly attending working lunches with the Permanent Representatives, at which information flows both ways and attempts are made to clarify and sort out looming problems; and by frequently meeting his counterpart in the Council – either on a bilateral basis or in a three-way meeting with the EP Secretary General. As for relations with the EP, there are bilateral meetings with its Secretary General, too; there are occasional appearances before EP committees; and there

Table 6.3 *Directorates in the Secretariat General*[a]

Directorate A	Registry
Directorate B	Horizontal questions: institutional aspects, Community law, information
Directorate C	Coordination
Directorate D	Relations with the Council
Directorate E	Relations with the European Parliament, the European Ombudsman, the Economic and Social Committee and the Committee of the Regions
Directorate F	Forward Studies Unit

Note: [a] Situation in March 2000.

Table 6.4 *Units within selected directorates of the Secretariat General*[a]

Directorate A – Registry
1 Meetings of the Commission and of *chefs de cabinet*, oral procedures, follow-up of Commission decisions, dissemination of documents
2 Written procedures and delegation of powers, publications in the *Official Journal* and notification of Commission official instruments
3 Secretariat of ECSC Consultative Committee

Directorate C – Coordination
1 Coordination and programming of Commission work
2 Europe and the citizen
3 Organisation and management

Directorate E – Relations with the European Parliament, the European Ombudsman, the Economic and Social Committee and the Committee of the Regions
1 Relations with Parliament I (part-sessions, horizontal committees, follow-up to opinions and resolutions, Parliamentary Affairs Group)
2 Relations with Parliament II (sectoral committees, petitions and transmission of documents) and with the European Ombudsman
3 Written and oral questions
4 Relations with the Economic and Social Committee and the Committee of the Regions

Note: [a] Situation in March 2000.

is extensive parliamentary correspondence to deal with and sometimes parliamentary delegations to receive – mostly on administrative-related matters.

Only four people have been Secretary General since the Commission was constituted in 1958: the Frenchman, Emile Noël, from 1958 to 1987; the Briton, David Williamson, from 1987 to 1997; the Dutchman (with an Italian background), Carlo Trojan, from 1997 to May 2000; and the Irishman, David O'Sullivan, from June 2000. The first three (O'Sullivan was assuming office as the book was going to press) all contributed significantly to the integration process, and more particularly to the development of the Commission. Noël played a leading part in helping to get the basic Commission structure established, whilst Williamson, and more especially Trojan, did much to drive internal reform. Of course, no Secretary General has had the power to push through desired courses of action by themselves, and to exercise influence they have had to work closely with Commission Presidents. For the most part satisfactory working relationships have been established, though both Noël in his last two years and Williamson in his early years had difficulties with Delors – not least because Delors was prone to use his *chef de cabinet*, Pascal Lamy, for tasks that Noël and Williamson thought were properly theirs. Even Delors, however, recognised, as other Presidents have done, that a supportive Secretary General can do much to provide a sound administrative base for the College they lead, and perhaps also – in Delors' case at least – for the presidential leadership they wish to provide.

Other services

Like the Secretariat General, most of the Commission's special services undertake horizontal responsibilities and functions. That is to say, they look after matters that cut across policy areas. Table 6.5 lists these services.

The range and nature of the Commission's special services can be demonstrated by looking at some of the more important of them.

The Legal Service is responsible for ensuring that actions and proposals of the Commission are correct in legal terms. Accordingly, most actions and proposals that are envisaged by the Commission have to be referred to the Legal Service before a final decision on them

Table 6.5   *Special services*[a]

- Common Service for External Relations
- European Anti-Fraud Office
- Humanitarian Aid Office
- Joint Interpreting and Conference Service
- Joint Research Centre
- Legal Service
- Press and Communication Service
- Publications Office
- Secretariat General
- Statistical Office (Eurostat)
- Translation Service

Note: [a] Situation in May 2000.

is taken. So, for example, proposals for legislation – whether they are planned to be referred to a College meeting or to be dealt with by written or delegated procedure – must be examined by the Legal Service to check that they are not outside the EU's and/or the Commission's legal competence, that they are consistent with existing EU law, that the correct legal base has been used, and that the legal meaning is the same in all official EU languages. If the Legal Service objects to any aspect of a text referred to it, the text must either be revised or have an explanatory statement attached to it and be referred to a College meeting for resolution. The Legal Service thus occupies a powerful position within the Commission's decision-making processes and it is very much in the interests of those within the Commission who wish to advance a measure of some kind to ensure that the Legal Service will not put obstacles in their way.

Another important responsibility of the Service is to represent the Commission in any actions in which it is involved in the Court of Justice.

Given the considerable workload that the Legal Service carries, it is difficult not to be sympathetic to the claims of those who work in it that, with around 200 employees, it is seriously understaffed.

The Joint Interpreting and Conference Service is responsible for providing interpreters for Commission meetings as required. In theory, this could mean having to work in 110 language combinations since there are eleven official languages in the EU. In practice, the workload, though considerable, is not as onerous as it might appear to be at first sight. There are two reasons for this. First, most internal Commission business below the level of the Commissioners is conducted in French or, less commonly, English. Second, though the Commission is formally obliged to provide a full translation service for all meetings which involve representatives of the member states, of outside interests, and of other EU institutions, it is common for such meetings to be able to manage with four or five languages. On those occasions where 'core' languages do not suffice – because participants in meetings cannot or will not use a non-native language – then relays are frequently used for less common combinations: so, for example, Portuguese is not usually interpreted directly into Swedish, but into English and from there into Swedish.

The Translation Service sees to the translation of all externally released Commission documents from the language in which they are written into the other ten official languages. In so doing, the Service must ensure that the meaning of documents is the same in all languages – especially where legislation is involved because different linguistic interpretations can, and sometimes do, result in cases being brought before the courts. An illustration of the need for perfect translation was seen in 1994 when the Court of Justice ruled that an £18 million fine on an alleged plastics cartel should be quashed because of discrepancies between the English, French and German versions of the relevant legal texts.

In addition to translating externally released Commission documents, the Service also translates internal documents when requested to do so, although normally this is just done on a restricted basis.

The Translation Service, which employs around 1400 translators and 500 clerical staff, is structured in a somewhat complex manner, with staff grouped not only into language units but also functional units (so that they deal with the same sort of technical jargon on a daily basis) and with their location being split between Brussels and Luxembourg.

The Joint Research Centre (JRC) is a very distinctive service. Most of the EU's Research and Technological Development (R&TD) work consists of sponsoring research undertaken by outside organisations on a shared-cost or contract basis. However, the EU also directly undertakes R&TD work itself and this is the responsibility of the JRC. Much of the administrative work of the JRC is done in Brussels, but the research itself is undertaken in eight institutes located at sites at Ispra in Italy (by far the largest site), Karlsruhe in Germany, Geel in Belgium, Petten in the Netherlands, and Sevillia (Spain). The Centre's research activities are focused in four broad areas: specific research programmes under the EU's Research Framework Programmes; support for the work of Commission services; work under contract for outside bodies; and exploratory research. Prominent amongst the research spheres covered are nuclear energy, advanced materials, system engineering and information technology, remote sensory applications, safety technology and the environment. The JRC employs just over 2000 staff, of whom around 1500 are scientific staff. Over two-thirds of the JRC's staff are on fixed-term contracts.

In addition to the special services that have just been described, other important special services include: the Humanitarian Aid Office (ECHO) which, as its name indicates, deals with humanitarian relief work; the Common Service for External Relations, which handles each year thousands of calls for tender, contracts, and financial transactions in connection with EU aid programmes and schemes; the European Anti-Fraud Office (OLAF), which leads and coordinates the Commission's efforts to minimise fraud, especially in relation to payments made in the frameworks of the CAP and the structural policies; and the Press and Communication Service, which has been strengthened under Prodi and which is responsible for informational flow from the Commission to the media.

When short-term or time-limited issues need attention, temporary special services, often in the form of task forces, are sometimes established. The Enlargement Task Force established under the Delors III Commission to deal with the applications for EU accession from Austria, Finland, Norway and Sweden was just such a temporary task force: it was established in early 1993 to coincide with the opening of accession negotiations; it was headed by an official who was given director general status; it consisted of an assistant to the director general, chief negotiators at director-grade level for each of the four applicant states, and officials from the Legal Service, the Secretariat General, and DGs which had a particular interest or expertise in enlargement issues; it was placed under the responsibility of the Commissioner for External Political Relations, Hans van den Broek; and it was wound up after the negotiations concluded in the spring of 1994. A similar, though larger, task force was established under Santer to deal with the applications from Central and Eastern European countries, and it exists now as the Enlargement DG.

Conflicts within the services

In all organisations the dispersal of staff into sub-divisions inevitably produces a degree of compartmentalisation and fragmentation. In the Commission's case the dispersal has promoted, as Stevens (2000: pp. 196–205) shows, three general sorts of inter-service conflict:

- *Territorial conflict* for influence and control over and within policy areas. With many issues cutting across internal organisational boundaries, with new issues frequently coming onto the EU's agenda, and with Commission staff wishing to at least defend their existing responsibilities and sometimes to expand them, 'turf wars' can occur between DGs. Hooghe (1996a) has described turf wars over cohesion policy in the early 1990s, as the Regional Policy DG fought (successfully) to establish itself as the main coordinating entity for the policy area. Amongst other struggles in recent years have been ones over competition policy (where DGs such as Transport and Energy – which were merged in early 2000 – have attempted to resist 'interference' from the Competition DG), and environmental policy (where DGs such as Internal Market and Taxation and Customs Union have taken a strong interest in proposals from the Environment DG that have market and taxation implications).
- *Ideological conflict* over policy approaches and solutions. Although virtually all Commission staff support 'the European project', there is no consensus about just what this means in policy terms. Significantly different views exist in parts of the services about what the Commission should be doing and how it should be doing it. As Armstrong and Bulmer (1998) have observed, some DGs virtually have their own norms and missions, which can lead to inter-service conflicts such as those that periodically break out between the Environment DG, which is concerned with good environmental practice, and DGs that are more concerned with opening frontier controls and promoting a competitive business environment. This issue of location-based administrative cultures is taken up at some length in Chapter 7.
- *Conflict over resources.* Services compete for both physical and intangible resources. Competition for the most obvious physical resources – staffing and operational budgets – has in the past been constrained by operational rigidities, but the more fluid frameworks being created under the Prodi reform programme are likely

in the future to result in greater transfers of resources between different parts of the services. Competition for intangible resources takes a number of forms, including prioritising policy objectives and enhancing institutional standing. Cini and McGowan show how the Competition DG has been highly active in competing for intangible resources: 'its organisational and policy goals are the creation of both a competitive and integrated European economy and the maintenance of its own high status within the Commission' (1998: 53).

In addition to these general sorts of conflicts there are always, as Chapters 9–11 show, numerous specific inter-service conflicts and disagreements on particular policy matters.

Inter-service coordination

The existence of conflict, coupled with the fact that no parts of the services are completely self-contained, raises the question of how the services reconcile disagreements and coordinate activities. They do so in a number of ways. Since, however, these ways are examined in detail at various points elsewhere in the book, only an overview summary will be given here.

An initial point to be made is that, as was shown in Chapters 3–5 and as is further shown in Chapters 10–11, the services are subject to College-level political coordination. The President, the College, and the *cabinets* all have responsibilities to ensure that not only they but also the services are marching to the same tune.

Political coordination, however, needs to be supported by services-level coordination. Much of this occurs in an informal manner, but established mechanisms also exist. The role of these mechanisms is to provide for the exchange of information and, where necessary and possible, for the resolution of differences. The main mechanisms are:

- The 'horizontal' services, especially the Secretariat General and the Legal Service (see above and Chapter 10).
- The weekly meetings of directors general and of assistants to directors general.
- The requirement in the Commission's Rules of Procedure that all services with a potential interest in an initiative or proposal be given the opportunity to make observations before reference is made upwards to the College (see Chapter 10).

- Inter-service meetings, which may be *ad hoc* and relatively informal, or, especially in policy areas where there is an overlap of responsibilities or where policies have cross-sectoral implications, be based on standing inter-service committees (see Chapters 10 and 11).

A consequence of the existence of so many inter-service mechanisms, and 'above them' of political level mechanisms, results in internal Commission conflicts being resolved and coordination being achieved more through incrementalism than through leadership intervention.

Concluding remarks

The Commission services consist of Directorates General, which have mainly policy-focused responsibilities, and special services, which have mainly horizontal responsibilities.

One of the key purposes of the internal reforms instituted under Romano Prodi's presidency is to strengthen the position of the services as the administrative arm of the Commission. So as to ensure this occurs, new Commission Rules of Procedure adopted in September 1999 drew a sharp distinction between the political role of Commissioners and the implementing role of services (Commission, 1999d).

Strengthening of the services has also involved streamlining structures. This has seen DGs being disbanded, merged and reorganised, and new DGs being created. Overall, the number of Commission departments (DGs plus special services) has been reduced from 42 to (at the time of writing) 34 under Prodi (but the number keeps changing).

Another central feature of the Prodi reform programme is focused on the services' personnel, and it is with them that Chapter 7 is concerned.

Chapter 7
Personnel

Size

The impression that is often given of the Commission, especially by sections of the media, is of a large and grossly over-staffed institution. In fact, the Commission employs far fewer people than do the national governments of even small EU member states. Indeed, many ministries and municipalities within member states have more staff than does the Commission.

At first sight this situation seems to be quite extraordinary. How can it be the Commission employs only a relatively small number of staff given the wide range of its policy responsibilities? The explanation is essentially threefold. First, national governments rather than the EU are mainly responsible for labour-intensive public policies such as education, health, social welfare, and defence. Second, where the EU does have extensive public policy commitments – such as with trade, agriculture, and the environment – the Commission's responsibilities are concerned more with promoting policy development and monitoring policy application than they are with direct service provision. This last task – which is heavily labour-intensive – is primarily the responsibility of national, regional, and local administrative agencies. Third, the EU's budgetary authorities, especially the Council, have always been concerned with maintaining budgetary discipline and accordingly have been reluctant to release the staffing resources the Commission has claimed it needs.

How many people do work for the Commission? This seemingly simple question is not as straightforward to answer as might be anticipated, for the fact is that the Commission is less than transparent with its staffing figures. Different 'returns' usually produce different figures, with some categories of staff being reported in some returns and not in others and with some staff almost invariably being 'hidden' and not reported in any returns.

Table 7.1 provides figures from two different sources on Commission staffing. The first set of figures, which produce a total of 21 703 Commission staff, are taken from the 2000 EU budget appropriations, whilst the second set, which produce a total of 31 013 man/years, are taken from the 1997–99 DECODE screening exercise (see Chapter 2 for an account of the nature of the exercise). The budget figures, which are the figures that are usually reported in official statements and in commentaries on the Commission, can be regarded as minimalist in that certain categories of staff, especially those with non-established posts, are either under-represented or are missing altogether. The DECODE figures, which include all categories of staff identified by those conducting the screening exercise and include also conversions of occasional and part-time staff into equivalent full-time posts, provide the most accurate figures available on the Commission's overall staffing resources.

There is little difference between the budget and DECODE figures on what is by far the largest and most important single element of the Commission's staffing resources, namely administrative staff in established posts. The differences primarily concern non-established staff. These two categories of Commission staff – established and non-established – will now be examined.

Established staff

The Commission employs around three-quarters of all EU staff on establishment. In 2000 the Commission's establishment plan comprised: 16 409 permanent posts, of which 1903 were language service posts, and 678 temporary posts for administrative duties; 3704 posts for research and technological development, of which 2080 were based in the Joint Research Centre; 522 posts for the Office for Official Publications; 194 posts for the European Anti-Fraud Office; and 166 posts, including 36 temporary posts, for two information gathering/research institutes – the European Centre for the Development of Vocational Training and the European Foundation for the Improvement of Living and Working Conditions (see Table 7.1).

Non-established staff

The Commission makes extensive use of non-established staff. It does so because they provide a way of circumventing problems arising from an under-resourcement of established staff and also from an absence – especially in new and developing policy areas – of 'in-house' expertise and experience. Non-established staff have the advantage of not counting in the same way as established staff against budgetary allocations, of being capable of being appointed quickly and easily,

Table 7.1   *Staffing resources*

1   As indicated in 2000 Budget Appropriations

	Permanent posts	Temporary posts	Total
Administration	16 409	678	17 087
Research and technological development[a]	3 704	–	3 704
Office for Official Publications	522		522
European Anti-Fraud Office	194	30	224
European Centre for the Development of Vocational Training	45	36	81
European Foundation for the Improvement of Living and Working Conditions	85	–	85
	Total		21 703

[a] Of which 2080 are assigned to the Joint Research Centre and 1624 to indirect action (indirect actions are research programmes that are financed by the EU budget but are not directly implemented by EU staff).

Source: *Official Journal of the European Communities*, L40, 2 February 2000: 135.

and of being able to bring to the Commission a wide range of different qualifications, backgrounds, and specialised knowledge.

In terms of employment status and conditions there are a number of different types of non-established staff working for the Commission (see Stevens and Maor, 1996; Spence, 1997a: 77–81; Stevens, 2000: 19–23). Two broad types are of particular importance:

Seconded officials, or *detached national experts*   These officials usually come from national public agencies, and more specifically from national civil services. They normally stay with the Commission for a period of between two and three years. Virtually all seconded officials are employed at the policy and managerial A-grade, with the

Table 7.1 cont.

2 As indicated in the DECODE Report

Intramural Staff[a]

(a) Established posts	18 047	of which:	16 527	permanent
			1 520	temporary
(b) Local agents	214	(mainly in Commission Offices in the member states)		
(c) External posts	4235	of which:	1033	auxilliaries
			760	seconded national experts
			606	casual employees
			1836	service providers (in restaurants, creches, etc.)
Sub-total	22 496			

Extramural staff[b]	3765	of which:	863	in technical assistance offices
			947	consultants
			383	man-years for studies
			1572	other man-years

Not covered in DECODE screening	4752	of which:	1834	in Joint Research Centre
			393	in *cabinets*
			2525	in Commission delegation in non member states
Grand total	31 013			

[a] Defined as employees working in the Commission buildings.
[b] Defined as employees working outside the Commission building.

Source: Commission (1999h: 9, 16).

majority being between A4 and A6 (middle-management grades). In recent years between 700 and 800 officials have usually been working in the Commission on a seconded basis at any one time, resulting in them accounting for 11 per cent of all A-grade staff and probably around 25 per cent of A4–A6 staff. The highest proportions are in the Statistical Office (over 25 per cent), and the Environment and the Taxation and Customs Union DGs (over 19 per cent) (Commission, 1999h: 9).

Seconded officials provide a range of benefits for the Commission through their different backgrounds, experiences and expertise. They also, however, provide benefits for member states, with it being extremely useful for governments and other public agencies to have on their staff officials who have worked in the parts of the Commission with which the agencies must deal. For this reason, the salaries of seconded officials are paid by the national employer, with the EU confining itself to paying a living expenses supplement.

Temporary agents   Many people are employed by the Commission for a fixed-term period to undertake a specific task or to work in a specific area. Their duties can range from managing EU programmes to providing technical and administrative support. Many of these people are financed not from Part A – administrative expenditure – of the EU budget, which provides for staffing resources approved by the Council and the EP as the joint budgetary authorities, but rather from 'diverted' Part B – operational expenditure – funds. Although all temporary agents are inevitably in a somewhat vulnerable employment position, staff funded from operational expenditure are especially so since they are not protected by the Staff Regulations covering employment conditions and rights.

Most temporary agents are employed as in-house 'consultants'/ 'experts'/'advisers'. Others are employed through outside agencies known as technical assistance offices (TAOs), which undertake tasks for the Commission in areas where it would not be cost-effective to recruit full-time and permanent Commission officials. TAOs undertake two main types of task: certain labour-intensive activities, such as organising conferences and dealing with enquiries; and activities requiring expensive and specialist staff on an *ad hoc* basis. A report undertaken by the Commission's Inspectorate General in 1996 identified 51 TAOs used by the Commission (almost certainly an underestimate), employing 600 people, working with 14 DGs (*European Report*, 2336, 19 July 1998). The DECODE exercise identified 863 people working in TAOs.

It is not possible to give absolutely precise figures of the number of temporary agents who work in the Commission: they are not all grouped together on a central register; payments made to them are scattered under many different budgetary headings and amongst many different sub-budgets; and attempts are often made to 'hide' them because their numbers, and indeed their very existence, have been criticised by the Court of Auditors, the EP, and – within the Commission – the Personnel and Administration DG.

On the basis of the DECODE figures, around 40 per cent of Commission human resources are temporary agents, broadly defined. Narrowing the term to refer only to those staff who are not covered by the Staff Regulations, the figure falls to nearer 30 per cent (Commission, 1999h: 16–18). These staff tend to be concentrated, as would be expected, in science and technology areas, in new and expanding policy areas, and in areas where specialised research needs to be undertaken and reports need to be quickly compiled. DGs such as Enterprise, Research, and Employment and Social Affairs have as many as one-third of their staff employed on temporary contracts. By contrast, most of the central services that provide horizontal support to the DGs, and DGs dealing with highly sensitive information such as Competition, Budget, and Personnel and Administration, employ no more than a handful of temporary agents.

The number of temporary agents is scheduled to be reduced as part of the Kinnock internal reform programme (see Box 2.1, p. 59).

Stagiaires

Although they are not on staff, mention needs also to be made of *stagiaires*, who provide a useful additional personnel resource for the Commission.

The *stage* scheme was developed in the early years of the Community to give Europe's future professionals a chance to see the Commission (and other European institutions) 'from the inside'. A Commission *stage* involves a five-month placement in the services and can result in the *stagiare* doing almost anything from humdrum clerical duties, to participating in policy work, to representing hard-pressed officials at EP committee meetings.

There are two *stage* rounds each year, with around 750 of the 10 000 or so applicants for each round accepted. Of these 750, 450 are awarded grants whilst the remainder must pay their own way. In practice, the selection and placement processes for *stages* are based on connections as well as on merit.

Distribution of staff

The DECODE screening exercise calculated the average size of a Commission department to be 560 persons (Commission, 1999h: 111). There are, of course, very considerable departures from this average with, generally speaking, the largest departments being those with wide-ranging responsibilities and/or heavy administrative duties and the smallest being those which are highly specialised in their focus and relatively light in their administrative duties. Taking the Commission's

22 496 intramural staff – that is, staff working in Commission buildings – the DECODE exercise showed the largest DGs to be Personnel and Administration (2932 persons), Science, Research and Development (1268), Agriculture (1006) and Industry (988), and the smallest to be Enterprise Policy (212), Financial Control (231) and Fisheries (262). The largest special services were the Translation Service (1902), the Secretariat General (693), the Security Office (685) and the Joint Interpreting and Conference Service (668), and the smallest was the European Supply Agency (23) (Commission, 1999h: 8).

Until recently there was considerable rigidity in the distribution of the Commission's staff amongst the DGs and special services. Although it was commonly acknowledged that some parts of the services were under-resourced and others were over-resourced, rigidities in personnel policy made it difficult to move staff from one part of the Commission to another. A measure of flexibility did begin to creep into the system from the early 1990s when, in response to growing strains on resources, steps were taken to at least marginally increase internal staff mobility, but significant movements of staff occurred only occasionally – when a department was created, abolished, or restructured.

The Prodi Commission has made personnel policy more flexible so as to bring about a more efficient use of staff resources. The extensive restructuring of the services that was effected at the beginning of the Prodi Commission was driven in large part by the Commissioner for Personnel and Administration, Neil Kinnock, who was given responsibility for internal reform and who – working closely with the Commission's Secretary General, Carlo Trojan – sought to use 'the new mood' to move 'surplus' staff to locations where more effective use could be made of them. The biggest casualty in the restructuring was the Information, Communication, Culture and Audiovisual DG, which had long been regarded by many insiders as over-resourced and under-worked. It was divested of many of its responsibilities, greatly slimmed down, restructured, and partly resurrected as the Education and Culture DG.

The staff grading system

The staff grading system used by the Commission is part of a system that is common to all of the EU's main institutions. There are five separate grades:

- *A-grade*. This is, essentially, the policy-making and policy management grade. It is, as such, the grade which is the most important for the purposes of this book and the grade, therefore, with which this chapter is most concerned. The grade is divided into eight points, with the responsibility at each point usually, but not invariably, being as follows: A1 – director general or equivalent; A2 – deputy director general, director, or principal adviser; A3 – head of unit; A4–A5 – principal administrator, or in some cases head of unit; A6–A8 – assistant administrator. In 1999 there was a total of 7068 A-grade officials in the Commission, of which 52 were A1 grade. Just under half of all A-grade staff are at points A4 or A5 on the A-grade scale. In total, permanent A-grade staff constitute 34 per cent of the Commission's establishment.
- *LA-grade*. This grade is for translators and interpreters, all of whom must be able to work in at least two languages in addition to their mother tongue. There are six points within the grade, from LA3 to LA8. In 1999 there were 1903 LA-grade staff, constituting 9 per cent of the Commission's establishment.
- *B-grade*. Officials in this grade usually undertake relatively routine, non-policy-oriented, administrative tasks. Typical responsibilities in the grade include office manager, senior secretary and archivist. There are five points within the grade, from B1 to B5. There were 4473 permanent B-grade officials in 1999, constituting 22 per cent of the Commission's establishment.
- *C-grade*. This is the grade for clerical and secretarial staff. Like the B-grade, the C-grade is divided into five points, from C1 to C5. There were 6491 permanent C-grade staff in 1999, constituting 31 per cent of the Commission's establishment.
- *D-grade*. Employees in this grade undertake service and manual jobs such as porter, postman and cleaner. The grade is divided into four points, from D1 to D4. There were 872 D-grade staff in 1999, constituting 4 per cent of the Commission's establishment.

This grading system was criticised in the Commission's 2000 White Paper on reform (Commission, 2000b) for being over-compartmenta-lised (too difficult to move between grades) and over-rigid (too difficult for talented staff to move up quickly within grades). The Paper proposed that a more linear grading system, providing for more flexible career opportunities, be established. It will be some time before it is so, with a system having to be worked out, agreed with other institutions, and negotiated with staff representatives.

Becoming an established A-grade official

Established A-grade posts in the Commission are much sought after, being well paid, prestigious, and generally challenging and interesting. It is, therefore, extremely difficult to gain entry to the grade. There are, essentially, four entry routes.

The first, and in terms of overall numbers by far the most important, route is recruitment by open competition at A8 and A7 levels. Candidates for entry must possess a good degree, be proficient in at least one EU language other than their mother tongue, and if they wish to be considered for appointment as an A7 have at least two years' working experience. Selection of candidates is via the *concours*, which consists of written and oral tests (see Stevens and Maor 1996, and Stevens 2000, for detailed explanations of how these tests result in a progressive filtering of candidates).

The intensity of competition via this 'standard' entry route is shown by the fact that in 1998 almost 30 000 candidates applied for the 150–200 posts that were likely to be available. In years following EU enlargements, when officials from new member states have to be squeezed in, and in years of restrictive budgets when tight controls are placed on recruitment, the number of A8/A7 vacancies to be filled by open competition may fall to little more than a handful.

Candidates who are successful in the *concours* are not immediately appointed to posts. Rather, they are placed on what is known as the 'reserve list', which is a list of people who have been successful in the *concours* and who are available and eligible for appointment to their first posting. The reserve list remains open for at least one year, though this period is often extended. Moving from the reserve list to a post is by no means automatic. People on the list may be fortunate and be approached by a DG that is looking for someone with their characteristics – the Environment DG, for example, may have a vacancy and may have a preference for appointing a young Nordic with particular knowledge/experience of water pollution problems – but usually those on the reserve list who wish for a posting need to be pro-active. Those who do not seek to make contact with people in the Commission who may be in a position to give them some assistance – by, for example, 'putting in a word' when a vacancy arises – may never be offered a post. This is because when junior vacancies arise those who are responsible for filling positions – heads of unit and directors – are likely to lean towards people on the list of whom they are aware or about whom they have received recommendations and favourable reports.

The second route is direct and competitive entry at middle and senior management levels. Prior to the Kinnock reform programme this really only applied to middle-management levels, and even there only a small number of people entered – mainly because direct entry recruitment is resisted by staff and unions on the grounds that it reduces the number of internal promotions. Most middle-management people entering via this route have been either temporary staff (often on secondment from national governments) who have made a good impression and/or have been targeted because they have a skill or experience that the Commission requires. There used to be a special *concours* for such people, but strong criticisms of it – based partly on its high pass rates – resulted in it being scrapped in 1999.

The direct entry route has been extended, though only on a very restricted basis, to senior A-grade staff as part of the Kinnock reform process. New rules for the appointment of A1 and A2 officials specify that though positions should generally be filled 'from among the management grades in the institution or in other [EU] institutions', where there are situations where a case can be made for recruiting from outside then the posts must be filled only following external advertisement (Commission, 1999g).

The third route is *parachutage*, which involves people from outside the services being parachuted into senior posts – usually at A1–A3 levels. Normally such people come either from national civil services or from the *cabinets* of Commissioners who are resigning or who are not being reappointed. It is customary towards the end of a College's term of office for as many as 15–20 *cabinet* officials to be looking to move into, or back into, the services – at director level or above if they have been a *chef* or a *deputy chef* of a *cabinet*. Their chances of being able to make such a move have in the past usually been quite good if they have been supported by their Commissioner and if appropriate posts have been scheduled to become available – which they may well have been since vacant posts have sometimes been held back and new ones have been created for precisely this purpose as the days of a College have drawn towards their close. It is probable, however, that this form of *parachutage* will be less common in the future, for in addition to the new rules concerning the advertisement of A1 and A2 posts, transfers of non-established *cabinet* staff into the services were made more difficult under other new rules adopted in September 1999 by the Prodi Commission (see Chapter 5, and Commission, 1999b).

The very considerable role that *parachutage* has exercised in Commission recruitment is seen in data compiled by Page (1997: 49–51). Taking *parachutage* as meaning officials who started working for the Commission as senior officials, though not necessarily in their present post, he estimates that in the 1992–93 period 81.8 per cent of A1 grades, 65.7 per cent of A2 grades, and 44.9 per cent of A3 grades were parachutists.

Parachutage has advantages and disadvantages from the viewpoint of the functioning of the Commission. The main advantage is that it provides a way for people with alternative career patterns to those who have always worked in the services to enter Commission management at senior levels. Such entrants can bring new and useful experiences and ideas with them. The main disadvantages are that inappropriately qualified people may be appointed to posts and existing staff may resent what they see as queue-jumping.

The fourth route is when enlargement creates a sudden need for large-scale recruitment from a newly acceding country or, more usually, number of countries. Recruitment targets are set, as for example in 1995 when the following targets were set for the recruitment of Austrian officials: A1 – 2, including 1 *ad personam*; A2 – 5 to 9; A3 – 17 to 22; A4/5 – 11 to 15 (Commission, 1995f). To accommodate the newcomers additional posts are created and inducements are made available – especially at senior levels – to encourage existing staff to take early retirement. The incoming staff are supposed to be recruited by normal procedures and to meet the customary standards, but the large numbers that are involved in a short period inevitably means that there is a 'relaxation' of the rules and also that the Commission relies heavily on advice tendered by national capitals.

Getting promoted

Promotions are formally made by promotions boards, except for A1 and A2 levels where they are made by the College (see pp. 177–8 for details of how A1 and A2 vacancies are filled).

Promotions boards include representatives of the Personnel and Administration DG, the DG in which the official is based, the DG in which the post is based (if this is different), and – for posts up to and including A4 – staff unions. The boards conduct interviews, but their decisions are, in practice, mainly determined by information that is already available to them.

For junior and middle-ranking levels, three types of information are especially important: age; length of service in the post – junior officials can begin to think realistically about promotion after three years or so, whilst middle and senior officials normally have to wait longer; and merit – which is assessed primarily on the basis of the staff reports that are kept on all officials and that include amongst their contents accounts and evaluations drawn up by line managers of work experience and quality of work.

For senior levels – beyond A4, but including A4 and even A5 if a head of unit position is at stake – nationality and political connections are, or at least have been prior to the Kinnock reform programme, also very important. Nationality has been important in that an unofficial quota system has existed for A1–A3 grades, with each member state virtually having an 'entitlement' to a number of positions in approximate relationship to its size. Political connections have been important because the nationality factor has resulted in Commissioners, mainly through their *cabinets*, taking a close interest in senior appointments. Successful candidates for senior positions have needed the support both of 'their' national Commissioner(s) and of the Commissioner responsible for the department where the vacancy has been located. As will be explained below, the significance of nationality and political connections is likely to decline, though not disappear, as the Kinnock reforms take effect.

Rather than waiting to be promoted within his/her DG or special service, an ambitious official, especially at junior and middle-ranking levels where there are more posts than at senior levels, may seek to advance promotion by moving to another part of the Commission. The ability to do this is normally improved if the individual concerned is flexible about what sort of posts are acceptable, for some parts of the Commission – such as the External Relations and Trade DGs – are generally seen as being more attractive, and are therefore more difficult to be appointed to, than are others. Having identified a possible suitable vacancy, an aspirant official must then make contact with key people in the part of the Commission where the vacancy is located – partly to establish that the vacancy has not, in effect, already been assigned, and partly to press the case for being considered. If such 'preliminaries' are not observed, applications are unlikely to be successful.

Promotion processes are, up to a point, thus fluid and manipulable. However, as the section below on reform will show, they are likely to become more 'regularised' in the future.

The multi-national staffing policy

The Commission has long pursued a multi-national staffing policy designed to ensure that there is a balanced representation of nationals from all members states throughout the services. As was noted above, prior to the Kinnock reform programme the policy extended to the existence of an unofficial national quota system at senior levels. Tables 7.2 and 7.3 show the effects of this multi-national policy, with the larger states having the largest proportion of A-grade and A1 posts, but with the smaller states being guaranteed a presence.

Table 7.2   *A-grade staff per member state[a]*

	%
France	15
Germany	12
Italy	12
UK	11
Belgium	11
Spain	10
Netherlands	5
Greece	5
Portugal	4
Sweden	3
Ireland	3
Austria	3
Denmark	3
Finland	2
Luxembourg	1
Total	100

Note: [a] Situation in October 1999.
Source: Europa website.

Table 7.3   *A1 staff per member state*[a]

France	8
Germany	8
United Kingdom	8
Italy	5
Spain	5
Belgium	3
Netherlands	3
Luxembourg	2
Greece	2
Austria	2
Sweden	2
Denmark	1
Ireland	1
Portugal	1
Finland	1
Total	52[b]

Notes: [a] Situation in October 1999.
[b] Of which 28 permanent posts and 24 *ad personam* posts.

Source: drawn from *Europa* website and *Official Journal*.

This multi-national policy has advantages and disadvantages. There are three main advantages:

- The presence of fellow nationals in the Commission helps to promote the confidence and trust of member states in the Commission as an institution. Quite simply, the presence of fellow nationals can result in the Commission being seen as not quite so distant, so remote, or so 'foreign' by those who have to deal with it.
- As well as helping to build general confidence and trust, the existence of a reasonable distribution of nationals from all member states can help Commission-member state relations in more specific ways. It is, for example, common for individuals/ agencies/organisations/firms which wish to make contact with the Commission to use fellow nationals as a route into the system. This is not because it is believed that compatriots will act as representatives, but rather because it is easier – especially at the

first point of contact – to approach someone who speaks the same language and who is likely to have an awareness of, and perhaps some sympathy with, the issue in hand.

- The Commission's understanding of how to deal with policies can be assisted if its officials can feed in information from their own knowledge about the implications at national, regional, and local levels of taking certain courses of action.

Just as there are three main advantages of the national balance principle, so are there three main disadvantages:

- The principle does not sit easily alongside the meritocratic principle. Inefficiencies can arise when national balance is given precedence over merit, with the people who are most qualified for entry or for promotion not necessarily being successful. This has certainly been a problem in the past at senior levels, when a need to 'fit in' nationals of under-represented and new member states has resulted in high-quality people sometimes being blocked and lower-quality people being advanced.
- It can result in rigidities. One type of rigidity that has been seen in the past has been when a much-needed reorganisation of senior posts has been blocked because a member state has been concerned about its 'allocation'. Another type of rigidity commonly seen in the past has been when posts have been left unfilled for a long time because they have been 'flagged' for a particular member state and no suitable person from that state has been identified or been available. Both of these types of rigidity should wither under the Kinnock reforms.
- It is not conducive to high staff morale. People who are doing a good job but who know their promotion prospects are hindered because they are of the 'wrong' nationality inevitably become frustrated and disillusioned. Up to and including A4 level, the best of the Commission's staff can make reasonable career progress irrespective of their nationality, especially if they are prepared to network and move around the Commission system. However, even the highest-calibre staff have found it difficult to make further progress, particularly if they have been from an 'over-represented' state. This problem should also be eased as a result of the Kinnock reforms, but it is difficult to see how senior posts can be completely opened up to the meritocratic principle because there is to be a continuing attachment to geographical balance.

Reforming personnel policy

As was shown in Chapter 2 and as is further shown in Chapter 11, the Commission came under increasing attack in the 1990s for its handling of its executive responsibilities. In seeking to respond to the criticisms, the Santer Commission launched three major reform initiatives to improve executive performance – SEM 200, MAP 2000, and DECODE – all of which had implications for personnel activities and policies. In the event, the reform programme, which was making progress but was far from being completed when the crisis of early 1999 erupted, did not save the Santer Commission, but Santer is justified in the claims he has made since leaving office that he has not been given sufficient credit for tackling internal problems, including personnel problems, that Delors did little about in his ten-year stint as Commission President.

The reform programme of the Prodi Commission is focusing much of its attention on personnel policy. In so doing, it is drawing on and making use of the groundwork undertaken by the Santer Commission. The Prodi Commission is, however, taking a much more radical approach than its predecessor, not least because of the strong criticisms of Commission practices made in the two reports of the Committee of Independent Experts (see Chapters 2 and 11). Structures, practices and attitudes are being shaken up with the aim of sustaining 'an independent, permanent and high quality European civil service that equips the Commission to fulfil its tasks as a world class organisation' (Commission, 2000a: 9).

The reform programme was 'launched' by Prodi even before his College assumed office, with the issuing of new procedures for A1 and A2 appointments. Under the procedures it was specified that: (a) posts should normally be filled 'from among the management grades in the institution or in other institutions' rather than from outside (a blow to *parachutage*); (b) whilst final decisions would, as before, be made by the College, they would make their decisions on the basis of opinions submitted to them by the Consultative Committee on Appointments, and agreed proposals from the President, the Personnel and Administration Commissioner and the member of the Commission responsible for the area concerned in the case of A1 posts, and from the member of the Commission and the director general of the area concerned in the case of A2 posts (a blow to interference by Commissioners and also to the national quota system); (c) all vacancies would be publicised and filled according to clear and transparent assessment criteria (another blow to interference by Commissioners and a blow more generally to the 'fixing' of appointments) (Commission, 1999g).

On being appointed by Prodi as the Commissioner responsible for internal reform, Neil Kinnock set about creating a new framework for personnel policy. Like Prodi, he started with senior appointments, identifying in a speech in September 1999 five operational principles that would now govern such appointments:

- 'Merit and experience' would be 'the critical considerations in making appointments'.
- While the Commission would 'maintain a broad geographical balance', nationality would 'no longer be the determinant in appointing a new occupant to a specific post'. The application of this principle would mean 'an end to the convention of attaching national flags to senior positions'.
- Top officials – directors-general and directors – would be 'required to change posts at reasonable regular intervals'.
- Directors-general 'sharing the same nationality as the Commissioner responsible for the related portfolio' would be 'required to move to other suitable posts'.
- The College would 'take positive action to ensure a higher number of women in senior management positions' (Kinnock, 1999).

The new procedures and principles resulted in immediate personnel changes at senior levels in the Commission. Amongst those affected were: the heads of the Education and Culture DG and of the Common Service for External Relations, who were asked to retire early because 'their skills no longer match the Commission's requirements'; the heads of the Agriculture DG, the Economic and Financial Affairs DG, and the Budget DG, who had all long been in their posts and in the first two cases occupied 'national flag' posts (the Directors General of Agriculture and Economic and Financial Affairs were offered other posts, whilst the Director General of the Budget retired); and the Directors General of the Enlargement DG and the Energy DG who were of the same nationality as their new Commissioners – German in the first case and Spanish in the second – who were moved to other posts.

Beyond senior appointments, other personnel reforms signalled by Kinnock in the closing months of 1999 included: a stronger approach would be taken towards moving staff from over-resourced to under-resourced and from low-priority to high-priority areas; whilst geographical balance would continue to be respected, more emphasis would be given to individual merit; and a more flexible staff grading system would be created. The Kinnock reform programme was elaborated and developed in the January 2000 consultative document and the March 2000 White Paper (see Box 2.1 for a summary of the White Paper's proposals). A central feature of the White Paper was an emphasis on a need for the Commission to become more manage-ment-focused. Specific reforms to achieve this would be: managers at all levels would be required to participate in a systematic programme of management and training; more weight would be given to management abilities by appointments and promotions boards; mechanisms would be established to enhance the capacity of managers to recognise and reward individual abilities and merit; and there would be clearer individual job descriptions with annual performance targets and evaluations.

The reforms to personnel policy will be phased in at different times, but all are scheduled to have at least begun by 2002.

Background characteristics of Commission officials

The background characteristics of the Commission's A-grade officials are in some ways similar and are in some ways different to the background characteristics that are typical of national civil servants.

Commission officials are, like senior national officials, overwhel-mingly male, middle aged, and well educated. Page (1997: 70–80) provides data on these three characteristics: male – only 14 per cent of Commission officials at A3 and above are female, with the figure shrinking to 3 per cent for A1; middle aged – the average age of A1–A3 officials is 54, with A1 officials being, as would be expected, the oldest, at just over 56; well educated – virtually all senior A-grade officials have a university degree – most commonly in law or one of the social sciences – and most have a higher degree.

As for differences with national civil servants, the most obvious is the multi-national character of the Commission's staff. This multi-nationality helps to explain other differences, including linguistic skills – senior Commission officials can, on average, speak four languages including their mother tongue.

Salaries

Just as there is a common grading system for the EU's main institutions, so is there a common salary system. The system rests on a matrix based on grades, points within grades, and steps within points (see Stevens 2000: 47–51 for an analysis of pay and benefits).

How the level of salaries compares with the level of salaries of employees of national governments naturally varies between both member states and grades. In general, however, it is clear that the EU salary levels are high, especially in the A-grade. An indication of the relative level of A-grade salaries is given by Page (1997: 42–3), who suggests that they are generally well above levels paid to domestic civil servants but below levels paid to diplomatic civil servants.

Use of language

The EU has eleven official languages: Danish, Dutch, English, Finnish, French, German, Greek, Italian, Portuguese, Spanish and Swedish. This means that there are 110 possible language combinations.

Clearly it would be totally impractical for the Commission to allow for the possibility of its everyday work to be conducted in all of the official languages. Quite apart from the immense costs this would involve for interpretation and translation, work would be slowed to a snail's pace, with conversations and meetings between officials who did not share the same mother tongue not being possible until interpreters were present, and with internal papers and documents not being circulated until they had been translated into all of the languages.

The way in which the problem has been resolved is for there to be, in effect, two working languages – French and English, with French being the most used. Officials are naturally quite entitled to talk to each other in other languages if they so choose – a meeting of three Spanish officials, for example, is hardly likely to be conducted in anything other than Spanish – but most meetings involving officials with different mother tongues are conducted in French or English. Which of these two languages is used in particular circumstances is usually a matter of agreement between the individuals involved. Reaching such an agreement is not normally a problem – someone simply starts talking in one of the languages and others follow suit or, especially in large meetings, a chairman/chairwoman poses the question 'Does anyone object if we use French (or English) for the purposes of this meeting?'

This virtual dual use of French and English marks a significant departure from the early years of the Commission when French was the dominant language. Two factors account for the undermining of the dominance of French. One is the impact of EC/EU enlargements. The 1973 enlargement was especially important, most obviously because it brought in Ireland and the UK, whose first language is English, and also Denmark, whose officials are much more proficient in English than they are in French, but also because it gave an 'excuse' to officials from existing states, especially Germany, to use English rather than French. The 1995 enlargement further assisted English, because officials from the three countries which joined – Austria, Finland, and Sweden – tend, like the Danes, to know English much better than they know French. The second factor is that the Commission is inevitably influenced by the fact that English is the principal international language.

This advance of English has caused some problems and has been the subject of some resentment within the Commission. In attempts to either stem the incoming English tide or, at least, to make symbolic protests, native French speakers who speak perfectly good English sometimes insist on speaking in French on formal and/or semi-formal occasions even when it would be more convenient for other participants if they spoke in English.

Insofar as there is a language 'problem' in the Commission – and the extent to which there is should not be exaggerated – it does not revolve wholly around the French–English balance. German speakers have most to complain about for German is the most common first language of EU citizens: Germany and Austria – the two German-speaking countries – have a combined population of around 88 million people, as against some 65 million native French speakers (in France, half of Belgium, and Luxembourg), and some 62 million native English speakers (in the UK and Ireland). But though there is some dissatisfaction, and not a little resentment, about the dominant role of French and English, it does not, in practice, have too much effect on the functioning of the Commission. The most important circumstance in which the French–English dominance can create problems is when internal documents have been translated only into

French or English (for reasons of speed/cost/practicality), and non-native speaking French or English officials insist that the technicalities of the documents are such that they can be worked on only when translated into their own language.

Culture and cultures in the services

Much has been written in recent years about the culture, and more especially the sub-cultures, of the Commission (see, for example, Abélès, Bellier and McDonald, 1993; Abélès and Bellier, 1996; Cini, 1996a).

National identities and cultures

The most obvious manifestation of sub-cultures and of cultural complexity within the services stems from the multi-national character of the Commission's staff, which results in national identities, traditions and cultures feeding into the everyday functioning of the Commission. These identities and traditions are, as was noted in Chapter 2, partly combined in a 'cultural compromise', but not completely.

The most obvious way in which national identity affects the functioning of the Commission is that officials naturally often take a particular interest in the likely impact of policy proposals on their own member state. This is not to say that they act as proponents of policies or aspects of policies that are likely to be especially favourable to their country – although this charge is sometimes laid. Rather, it is to say that policy inputs of officials are sometimes influenced by national background. An official may, for example, draw attention to particular administrative difficulties that will be created in his/her member state if a proposal is not amended in a certain way. As was noted earlier in the chapter, such policy inputs can be beneficial for the Commission, both by improving the quality of policy proposals and by heading off possible objections to proposals when they are referred to the Council for decision-making.

Another way in which the nationality of officials influences the functioning of the Commission is in working practices. It is, for example, the case, very broadly speaking, that officials from northern member states subscribe to a more rule-driven way of working than do those from southern states. It is also the case that officials from northern member states, and especially Nordic states, tend to prefer to operate in a more open and transparent way than their Mediterranean counterparts. Differences such as these make for a working environment in which, as McDonald has put it, there are 'different – sometimes competing, sometimes enriching, sometimes contradictory – ideas of what the organisation is and does, and how it does or should work' (1997: 69). As Stevens (2000) shows, attempts began under the Santer presidency to override these national differences, with the SEM 2000 programme being partly devised with this aim in mind. Under the Prodi presidency it is intended that a new code of conduct for officials be introduced, partly so as to try and establish more uniform standards of conduct and behaviour regulation.

National background also influences the functioning of the Commission in that it can both facilitate and hamper internal communications. It can facilitate communications in that shared nationality can help ease the way to the passing on of information and the exchange of ideas. So, for example, an Italian official in the Agriculture DG working on a sensitive land-usage proposal with environmental implications may well be prepared to informally explore options and possibilities with Italians in the Environment DG but be wary about doing so with non-Italians. This is especially likely to be the case if Italians in Environment are already known to the Agriculture official – which they may well be since there are numerous informal national networks in the Commission, many of which are forged and strengthened through off-duty socialising. National background can, however, hamper communications if officials judge the national characteristics of officials with whom they must deal with caution or suspicion. The extent to which officials perceive negative national characteristics of fellow officials to exist must not be exaggerated, but unquestionably such perceptions are held and they can play a part in making it difficult for officials to work effectively with one another.

Locational cultures

Whilst the significance of the nationality factor in the Commission must be recognised, it should not be over-stated for, like people in all walks of life, Commission officials are subject to numerous influences and have many identities and attachments. An especially important identification and attachment for officials is the part of the Commission in which they are located, for this is often associated with particularistic views of what the Commission should be doing and how it should be doing it.

A frequently cited example of contrasting locationally-based cultures is the strongly liberal and anti-interventionist ethos prevailing in the Competition DG and the more interventionist spirit in such DGs as Enterprise and Regional Policy (see, for example, Abélès, Bellier and McDonald, 1993; Cini, 1996a, 1996b, 1997). Another, related, example of location-based cultures is the different positions of the Transport DG and the Employment and Social Affairs DG on the use of state aid to assist national airlines. The former has increasingly adopted a 'be lean and mean' view, whilst the latter has often supported subsidies to protect employment.

The most important consequence of the existence of location-based cultures in the Commission is a fragmentation that can lead to inter-service tensions, disputes and competition.

Unity within diversity

Cultural fragmentation is clearly an important feature of the Commission. Factors militating against internal cultural homogeneity include the constant organisational evolution of the Commission, the recruitment of staff with diverse backgrounds, and the Commission's operating interdependence with outside actors. The fact is, as Hooghe (1999a: 5–7) has argued, the Commission is not sufficiently insulated from the outside world to prevail upon or to expect its employees to be culturally homogeneous. 'Fifty years after its creation, the Commission still does not have powerful mechanisms for selective recruitment, socialization or cognitive association that may produce a more unitary "mindset"' (Hooghe, 1999b: 365).

But important though the cultural fragmentation is, its extent and consequences should not be exaggerated. It does not make for wholesale friction and division. A key reason why it does not do so is that the sub-cultures are framed in a broader, albeit rather loose, Commission-wide culture. At the heart of this culture is a desire on the part of most services' staff to see the Commission be successful as an institution. Staff are bonded, too, by performing similar tasks and by being subject to similar conditions of service, operating practices and working environments. Such shared outlooks and experiences have produced, as Shore has noted (2000a and 2000b), a reasonably well-developed *esprit de corps*, which is seen in the way staff frequently speak with loyalty and affection of 'the House' (as the Commission is commonly referred to by insiders).

It used to be the case that Commission culture was also characterised by widespread and firm support for the European project and for strengthening the European institutions. Such 'Europeanness' is still a feature of Commission culture (see Abélès, Bellier and McDonald, 1993; Edwards, 1997; Page, 1997; Hooghe, 1999b), but not as much as in the formative years when many of the first generation of Commission officials were European idealists (Coombes, 1970; Wessels, 1985). Personal careerism is a greater concern today.

Concluding remarks

The Commission's personnel do not constitute the vast and underworked 'Eurocracy' of popular imagination. On the contrary, they are relatively few in number and are, for the most part, fully stretched and hard-working.

There have, however, been problems with personnel organisation and working practices, which has contributed to the under-performance the Commission has displayed in some aspects of its work. The Kinnock reform programme is tackling many of these staffing weaknesses. It will be some years before these reforms work their way fully through, but they should increasingly provide for a more modern and efficient institution.

Chapter 8

The Commission's Relations With Other EU Actors

This chapter examines the Commission's relations with the EU's other main actors. Its purpose is to present an overview, which is important both in itself and also to provide a foundation for Chapters 9–12 which include considerations of more specific aspects of these relations.

The chapter does not attempt to examine the EU's other actors as such. Dinan (1999) and Nugent (1999) do this in a general manner, whilst detailed studies include Hayes-Renshaw and Wallace (1997) and Westlake (1999) on the Council of Ministers, Corbett, Jacobs and Shackleton (2000) and Westlake (1994, 1997a) on the EP, Dehousse (1998) on the Court of Justice, and Greenwood (1997) on interests.

The European Council

The European Council brings together the Heads of State or Government of the member states and the President of the Commission. According to Article 4 of the TEU they are assisted by Foreign Ministers and a member of the Commission, though in practice Economic and Finance (Ecofin) Ministers are also increasingly involved. The European Council meets twice a year in normal session, usually for a couple of days on each occasion, and generally also holds one or two special sessions.

The role of the European Council is analogous to that of a board of directors: determining the general direction of the EU, making strategic decisions, and keeping a general overview of the situation. Virtually all matters of major importance pass through its hands, either by way of it indicating courses of action to other EU institutions, pronouncing on initiatives that have originated elsewhere, or taking final decisions – the latter usually not being legal decisions but often being political decisions to which other institutions must give legal effect. Just about every major EU initiative of recent years has been discussed, and frequently negotiated, in the

European Council. The European Council is thus the EU's peak political forum.

But though it is the peak political forum, it is institutionally weak in the sense that it meets only infrequently and when it does meet it is hampered by internal divisions – of both a national and an ideological kind. This institutional weakness makes it difficult for the European Council to act in a dynamic, innovative, and independent manner. It means that it is necessarily heavily dependent on ideas and proposals being presented to it. This presents agenda-shaping and agenda-setting opportunities for the Commission which, alongside various parts of the Council of Ministers machinery, is actively involved in helping to prepare European Council meetings. The preparations commonly include the Commission preparing reports, which can include ready-made initiatives/decisions on pressing issues. Over half of the twenty or so documents that are presented to normal European Council sessions are usually from the Commission, some of which are presented at the request of earlier summits and others of which are on the Commission's own initiative.

Amongst the policy areas where the Commission has been able to take advantage of the European Council's institutional weaknesses so as to inject a significant influence of its own are the SEM programme, budgetary reform, CAP and Structural Funds reform, policies for growth and job creation, and the enlargement process. Just how the Commission has done this is explored in Chapter 9.

The Council of Ministers

The Council of Ministers is the principal meeting place of national governmental representatives in the EU system. The work of the Council is carried out within an essentially three-level hierarchical structure: at the lowest level national government officials meet in working parties to undertake detailed examination of issues – including Commission legislative proposals; at the middle level national Permanent Representatives and their deputies meet in the Committee of Permanent Representatives (COREPER) to prepare the ground for ministerial meetings (Permanent Representatives head the Permanent Representations of the member states in Brussels, which act in the manner of embassies to the EU); at the most senior level ministers meet to take final decisions.

Like the European Council, the Council of Ministers is essentially a negotiating forum between representatives of the governments of the member states. The responsibility of its most senior members – ministers – is both to take decisions on proposed policies and laws and also to protect national interests. This latter responsibility tends to make the Council better at reacting to proposals that are presented to it than striking out with bold and innovative initiatives of its own. Other institutional limitations of the Council include the following: because it meets in different policy formations – limited to a maximum of fifteen since the 1999 Helsinki summit – it is difficult for the Council to give an overall sense of direction and purpose to EU affairs; insofar as the Council can be said to have a central focus it is in its presidency, but this rotates on a six-monthly basis, so time is not usually available during a single presidency for proposals to be seen through from initiation to final decision; where legislation is envisaged, the Council is prevented by treaty from initiating a proposal, though it can request the Commission to present a proposal to it; and whilst the institutional capacity of the Council has been greatly improved since the mid-1980s by an increased ability and willingness to take decisions by QMV, there are still many treaty articles – covering mostly sensitive and politically charged issues – where unanimity is required.

These factors combine to make the Council highly dependent on the Commission for ideas, initiatives, guidance, specific proposals, and brokerage. Just how extensive is the dependence, and what use the Commission is able to make of it, varies according to a number of factors. In broad terms, however, it can be said that the Commission is most successful in its dealings with the Council when: matters fall under the first pillar rather than the second or third pillars; deliberations are about technical rather than political matters (though the Council still relies on the Commission to draft political compromises); the governments of the member states are all committed to a policy initiative; the governments are looking to the Commission to drive an initiative forward; no member state, and especially no large member state, is strongly opposed to a proposed course of action; the Council presidency is weak (variations in the drive and competency of presidencies can occur both between states and between sectoral Councils during the same presidency); and QMV rules apply and the member states are willing to use them – for then not all Council members must agree with the Commission for its proposals to be approved.

The European Parliament

Long thought of as little more than a special sort of advisory body, the EP has acquired increasing influence and powers over the years, to the extent that it is now an extremely important actor in EU decision-making processes. As this has occurred, the EP has become less the 'supportive ally' of the Commission 'against' the Council that it was inclined to be and has become more the third side of an institutional triangle.

As with national parliaments, the role and influence of the EP is exercised in three main ways: through participation in the legislative and budgetary processes and through the exercise of control over the executive.

Participation in the legislative process

EU law is made via four main procedures, which are described in Chapter 10. Each of the procedures brings the EP into close contact with the Commission, not least via an array of formal and informal interactions which have as their purpose the resolution of differences regarding what are considered to be desirable and undesirable, and acceptable and unacceptable, features of legislative proposals. The precise nature of these interactions depends on the procedure applying, but most commonly they take the form of the EP seeking to persuade, pressurise, or oblige the Commission to accept amendments to legislative proposals – the Commission being able to amend a text at any point during first and second legislative reading stages. Because EP amendments are more likely to be incorporated into EU legislation if they are accepted by the Commission – the Council being able to amend a text against the Commission's wishes only by unanimity – the EP often delays legislative progress when the Commission is deemed to be insufficiently sympathetic to its amendments. It does this by, especially at first reading (when tight legislative timetables do not apply), referring proposals back to EP committees rather than issuing the formal opinions that are necessary before proposals can be considered by the Council. The impact of such EP activity is considered in Chapter 10.

Participation in the budgetary process

The EP is a co-decision-maker with the Council on the annual budget and its approval is necessary for the budget to be passed. However, in practice, the EP's influence on the contents of the budget is limited. There are three main reasons for this. First, since 1988 budgets have been set within the framework of multi-annual financial perspectives, to which the EP is a party but which are essentially negotiated between the governments of the member states on the basis of information and recommendations from the Commission. The financial perspectives allow for only limited manoeuvring within budget headings and thus provide little opportunity for the EP to increase or decrease expenditure to any significant extent. Second, the EP is prevented by treaty from being able to do much about what is known as compulsory or obligatory expenditure, which is mainly used for agriculture and accounts for just under half of the budget. And third, the Commission begins, and sets the framework of, the budgetary decision-making cycle when it issues, several months before a budget is scheduled to take effect (in January), what is known as the preliminary draft budget (PDB). (On the budget and budgetary decision-making, see Laffan, 1997a; Nugent, 1999.)

Despite these weaknesses, the EP does what it can to influence the contents of the budget. So, for example, before the Commission issues the PDB there are informal 'pre-proposal' exchanges between leading members of EP committees and relevant Commission officials. At subsequent stages of the budgetary process the two institutions liaise closely, primarily through the chairperson, *rapporteur* and leading members of the Budgets Committee on the EP side and through the Commissioner for Budget and officials of the Budget DG on the Commission side. A key feature of the budgetary process is that the Commission does not 'own' the budget in the way that it may be said to 'own' legislative proposals, so it is obliged to incorporate EP (and Council) amendments into post-PDB drafts, provided they do not breach budgetary rules. As with so much EU decision-making, final agreement on the contents of the budget is reached via a Council-EP 'deal' which the Commission usually does much to help bring about.

The exercise of control over the executive

The EP's ability to control the executive is hampered by several weaknesses, many of which are associated with the fact that executive authority in the EU is dispersed – with broad controlling and supervisory responsibilities being shared, in an overlapping and somewhat blurred manner, between the Commission, the Council of Ministers and the European Council, and with day-to-day 'front line' policy implementation being partly the responsibility of the Commission but mainly the responsibility of agencies in the member states. The ability of the EP to call these institutions and agencies to account varies, but is mostly very strictly limited except in relation to the Commission. There are five main types of 'control' over the Commission.

First, MEPs can ask written and oral questions. In 1999 a total of 3187 questions were asked, of which 2606 were written, 58 were oral with debate, and 523 were during question time (Commission, 2000f: 400).

Second, the EP can conduct investigations into, and produce reports on, matters that, directly or indirectly, involve the way in which the Commission exercises its responsibilities. It is a capacity that has acquired a greater potential in recent years. An important reason why it has done so is that the Maastricht Treaty empowered the EP to establish temporary committees of enquiry 'to investigate . . . alleged contraventions or maladministration in the implementation of Community law' (Article 193, ex-138c, TEC). The second enquiry to be conducted under the post-Maastricht rules, which was in 1996–97 on the crisis in the beef industry caused by BSE, led both to a highly critical report on the way the Commission had handled matters and to the EP indicating in its resolution on the report that if specified reforms were not carried through by November 1997 a motion of censure on the Commission would be tabled (see Westlake, 1997b). This had the desired effect and the Commission quickly made organisational changes to the way it handles food hygiene. As Shackleton has observed, the EP's threat of censure 'concentrated minds in the Commission and showed how the right of enquiry can be exercised in conjunction with the other powers that the Parliament has to bring about changes that the Commission might well not otherwise have conceded' (1998: 125).

Third, under Article 276 TEC, the EP, acting on a recommendation of the Council, grants discharge – that is, approval – to the Commission for the implementation of the EU's budget. It does so after examining the accounts of the previous year relating to implementation, the annual report of the Court of Auditors, and replies from the Commission and other institutions to observations of the

Court. This rather dry-sounding duty of the EP came to be used with some effect in the 1990s, with the EP delaying discharge until it was assured that implementation weaknesses were being addressed. Such an occasion occured in March 1998, when discharge was postponed on the 1996 budget because of concerns over alleged mismanagement and fraud. When the matter came back to the EP, at its December plenary, discharge was again refused, despite a recommendation from the Parliament's Budgetary Control Committee that it be granted. The reasons for the refusal were a perceived inadequate response by the Commission to the concerns expressed by the EP in March, and a knowledge that the Court of Auditors had recently issued its report for 1997 and that this was also critical of the Commission. This decision of the EP produced an angry response from Jacques Santer who called on Parliament to back or sack the College. This ill-judged call set in motion the sequence of events described in Chapter 2 that led to the Commission's eventual resignation in March 2000.

Fourth, the EP has, as was shown in Chapters 3 and 4, a role in the appointment of the College, with confirmatory powers on both the person nominated by the member states to be Commission President and on the College as a whole. The confirmatory processes are gruelling, but they have significantly bolstered the Commission's position in the EU system by giving it some claim to have a democratic, or at least quasi-democratic, base and mandate. It may be a weak claim – the Prodi Commission that was confirmed in September 1999 had a Centre-Left majority even though the EP elections of only three months previously had produced a Centre-Right majority in the Parliament – but it gives the College some protection from accusations that it is wholly divorced from demo-cratic requirements and procedures. Confirmation by the EP thus helps to underpin the Commission's legitimacy and authority.

Fifth, the EP has the power to dismiss the whole of the College, though not individual Commissioners. This power is set out in Article 201 (ex-144) TEC which specifies that the College must resign if a motion of censure is carried by a two-thirds majority representing a majority of MEPs. No such motion has ever been passed, though, as was shown in Chapter 2, criticisms of Commission performance coupled with circulating, though at the time unsubstantiated, criti-cisms of the behaviour of a few Commissioners, resulted in strong support for a censure motion in January 1999. The only factor to save the College was the appointment of the Committee of Independent Experts charged with establishing the facts. When the Committee produced its highly critical report in March, the Santer College resigned – in advance of the censure motion that almost certainly would have been passed on it.

Though the EP's formal powers are, for the most part, weaker than those of national parliaments, in practice it exercises considerable influence in the EU system. Indeed, a good case can be made to the effect that it is a much more significant institution than its counterparts in some member states. As the power and independence of the EP have grown so has the Commission had to strengthen its organisational capacity for managing relations between the two institutions. The main features of the Commission's arrangements for dealing with the EP are as follows: one of the Commission's two Vice-Presidents has a specific responsibility for relations with the EP; all Commissioners are expected to liaise with, and appear before, EP committees and plenary sessions in respect of their particular responsibilities; all Commissioners' *cabinets* have a member who has liaison with the EP amongst his/her responsibilities; all DGs have a unit or an official who is responsible for coordinating relations with the EP; there is a special directorate in the Secretariat General which has a general responsibility for ensuring that the Commission's relations with the EP are handled in an efficient and expeditious manner; the *Groupe des Affaires Parlementaires* (GAP), which is a committee serviced by the Secretariat General and composed mainly of the EP liaison members of the *cabinets,* has as its main responsibility preparing for the next EP plenary session by, amongst other things, reviewing the responses the Commission will give to oral questions, deciding on Commission statements, and noting which Commissioners will be present for debates; and the Coordinators Group, which is chaired by the Secretariat General and composed of the parliamentary coordinators from the DGs, prepares business for EP committees and plenaries and acts as a forum for exchanging information and coordinating activities.

The European Court of Justice

The European Court of Justice (ECJ), to which is attached a Court of First Instance (CFI), has two main functions. First, in certain types of cases it has direct responsibility for applying the law. Such cases include various aspects of competition policy and all cases that pitch an EU institution against a member state or against another EU institution. The Commission brings many such direct actions before the Court each year. Under, for example, Article 226 TEC, which obliges the Commission to act if it believes a member state has failed to fulfil an obligation under the Treaty, 40–50 annual references by the Commission to the Court are commonly made. Second, the Court has a general responsibility for ensuring that EU law is interpreted in a clear, consistent and uniform manner. This second responsibility is exercised via a range of cases that are brought before the Court, including through the many references that are made to it by national courts for 'preliminary rulings' to be given on the relevance and applicability of EU law in particular circumstances.

Because EU law is still developing and is less than precise in many respects, Court judgements sometimes set important precedents for the functioning of the EU and its institutions. Six examples will be taken here to show the implications Court judgements can have for the Commission:

- The renowned 1979 *Cassis de Dijon* judgement (C-120/78) greatly reduced the need for detailed harmonisation market legislation, by establishing the principle of mutual recognition – whereby a product that is lawfully produced and marketed in one member state must be accepted onto the markets of other member states. This judgement was crucial in enabling the Commission to open up the market via broad framework legislation.
- In its 1986 *Nouvelles Frontières* judgement (joined cases 209–213/84), the Court ruled that competition law applied to airlines. The Commission used this judgement to initiate infringement proceedings against national airlines for breaching competition rules and to indicate to member states that it would use its powers under Article 90 (now 86) of the EEC (now EC) Treaty to directly issue liberalising directives if the member states did not approve competition-promoting legislation. Such legislation was forthcoming from the late 1980s.
- In 1987, in its *Philip Morris* judgement (joined cases 142/84–156/84), the Court ruled that that agreements resulting in mergers between companies could be regarded as restrictive agreements under Article 85 (now 81), and therefore subject to Commission scrutiny. As a result of the ruling, companies began referring mergers to the Commission for clearance and both the Commission and companies pressed the Council for legislation that would

clarify legal uncertainties that now existed – concerning, not least, the Commission's powers. These pressures led to the 1989 Merger Control Regulation which, as is shown in Chapter 11, gave the Commission power of authorisation over large mergers.

- In 1992, in *Spain, Belgium and* Italy v. *Commission* (C-271, 281, 289/90), the Court ruled that under the EEC Treaty the Commission's powers in relation to monopolies were not limited to applying Council legislation but extended to taking a pro-active role to breaking monopolies. Like the *Nouvelles Frontières* ruling, this judgement, along with others, boosted the Commission's capacity to take direct action to promote competition.

- In 1994, the Court disappointed the Commission when, in Opinion 1/94, it ruled that the negotiation of external agreements on services and intellectual property was not, like negotiations on trade in goods, an exclusive Community competence (where the Commission negotiates on behalf of the member states) but rather was a shared competence (where the Commission negotiates together with the member states).

- In 1998, in *UK* v. *Commission* (C-106/96), the Court placed tight restrictions on the Commission's ability to take independent decisions on spending programmes by ruling that if no appropriate instrument of secondary legislation had been adopted the Commission could charge only minor measures to the EU budget. The short-term effect of this was the suspension of certain Commission programmes and the longer-term effect was to oblige the Commission to ensure that all relevant programmes were authorised during the annual budgetary process.

As these examples illustrate, though some Court rulings are unhelpful to the Commission some are extremely helpful in that they increase the Commission's powers and/or provide opportunities for it to take advantage of judgements. Sometimes judgement are not even necessary for the Court to be helpful, but rather just indications from the Commission that if certain actions are not taken then legal action may follow. Member states, for example, are sometimes prodded into action because a reference to the Court will mean loss of control over decision-making and an uncertain decisional outcome. Susanne Schmidt, who has provided solid empirical examples of the Commission successfully using 'threats' of legal action against member states to advance de-regulatory policies in the 1990s (1997a, 1997b, 1998), is clear that '[b]y credibly threatening judicial policy-making from the

Court, the Commission may compel the Council to take action' (1997b: 32). Putting this another way, she observes that '[b]y following up on existing or by initiating new Court rulings the Commission can deliberately set incentives for the adoption [by the Council] of its legislative proposals' (Schmidt, 2000: 39).

The governments of the Member States

In addition to the dealings that the Commission has with the governments of the member states in the collective settings of the European Council and the Council of Ministers it also has an array of direct dealings with them. This is so in respect of virtually all of the tasks it performs, from the initiation of broad policy programmes to the detailed implementation of EU law.

The governments of the member states, and in certain respects also sub-national governments within the member states, need to be and wish to be in close touch with the Commission for a variety of reasons. These include pressing preferences on legislative proposals, ensuring grant applications are properly presented, seeking flexibility on the application of EU laws that are causing difficulties, and soliciting advance information on Commission thinking. The Commission is more than willing to respond to this wish for close relations, not least because it has reasons of its own for needing and wanting relations to be close. One of these reasons is that national governments are the voting units in the European Council and Council of Ministers, so the Commission needs their support if its initiative and proposals are to make progress. Other reasons include the role of national and sub-national governments as key policy implementers and their position as repositories of detailed information on all sorts of matters that are of interest to the Commission.

There are many channels via which Commission–member state government relations are conducted. At the most senior level they include direct meetings between the President of the Commission and Heads of Government and between Commissioners and national ministers – meetings that may be either specially convened to discuss a particular issue or which may occur spontaneously on the margins of European Council and Council of Ministers meetings. At more junior levels all known means of communications – post, e-mails, faxes, the telephone, meetings, etc. – are in constant use to channel information and views between Commission officials on the one hand

and national officials based in national ministries and the Permanent Representations on the other.

The Commission's relations with the governments of the member states highlight one of the Commission's central institutional features, namely that it is not only an administrative institution but is also a highly political one. On significant and potentially difficult issues the Commission cannot afford to 'go its own way' but must always be sensitive to the positions of the national governments. If a government indicates that a matter is extremely important to it the Commission must attempt to seek at least some accommodation with the government's position, whether or not it thinks the position is based on genuine policy grounds or is occasioned by 'non-valid' domestic political circumstances. If the Commission does not display sensitivity when a government indicates it has serious difficulties with an issue it risks displeasing the Council, which does not normally wish to see any of its members becoming aggrieved, and it risks also alienating the national government in question, which may then become uncooperative with the Commission and 'awkward' in the Council on other issues.

In consequence of this need to be sensitive to the positions of national governments, the Commission frequently moderates, or retreats from, positions it would like to take and sometimes from decisions that legally it ought to take were it to be acting in a wholly mechanical way. Examples of the Commission so allowing itself to be influenced by the individual positions of national governments can be found in all policy areas, but none more notoriously than in the sphere of competition policy where national governments have frequently been successful in persuading the Commission to, for example, allow state subsidies that are questionable under the treaties and impose only modest requirements in respect of company mergers which though borderline in strictly legal terms may be of great economic importance. Three decisions taken at a College meeting on 24 June 1998 illustrate the strong political tinge that is often attached to the Commission's actions in the competition sphere. In all three cases officials in the Competition DG had long argued that legal action was warranted and desirable, but the national governments concerned were known to have lobbied hard against such action being taken and they were known also to have attempted to lean on 'their' Commissioner(s). In the first case the College (again) postponed plans to take the French Government before the ECJ over its 1991 *Loi Evin*, which restricts television coverage of sports events where alcohol adverts are featured. In the second case the College decided not to initiate legal action against Greece for its 1994 ban on television adverts on children's toys (which, the toy manufacturers of other member states claimed, discriminated in favour of Greek manufacturers). In the third case the College decided to postpone action against German recycling quotas on drinks containers until after the country's parliamentary election which was to be held in September (non-German manufacturers were complaining that the 72 per cent quota favoured local manufacturers) (*European Voice*, 25 June–1 July 1998).

Non-governmental interests

The range and importance of EU policy activities means that many non-governmental interests cluster around EU institutions and decision-makers. These interests are of three main types: private and public companies; national interest groups; and Eurogroups – that is, groups that draw their membership from several countries (usually via the affiliation of national groups) and which seek to represent the views of their sector or cause at the EU level.

It is not possible to be precise as regards the numbers of interests that focus attention on the EU since they are not all centrally registered, they do not all have offices in Brussels, and for most of them EU-watching and lobbying constitutes only part of what they do. Some indication of the size of the 'hard core' of the interest lobby can, however, be gained from a 1992 Commission study of the subject, which estimated that there were around 3000 interest groups in Brussels seeking to influence the EU in some way and there were around 10 000 lobbyists involved in EU interest representation (Commission, 1992d).

Business is by far the best represented and best resourced element of EU-focused interests. Of the 700 or so Eurogroups, about 65 per cent represent business, about 20 per cent are public interest groups, about 10 per cent represent the professions, and about 5 per cent represent trade unions, consumers, environmentalists and other interests (Greenwood, 1997: 58–9). In addition to the business Eurogroups, over 200 business firms – most of them multinational corporations – have EU lobbying/liaison offices in Brussels.

The Commission is naturally the main target for most interests wishing to influence EU policy activity. This is because of its many important policy responsibilities in regard to both policy areas covered and tasks undertaken. The wide range of these responsibilities means that interests look to the Commission for many different purposes. For example: to provide advance information about forthcoming policy developments; to initiate new legislative proposals and to amend existing legislation; to influence nascent legislation; to adjust the way laws are applied; and to assist with applications to funding programmes. The parts of the Commission that are most targeted are naturally those that operate in policy areas where EU competencies are strong. So, for example: Enterprise and Internal Market are amongst a number of DGs that are heavily lobbied by industry; the Environment DG, because of its important regulatory powers, is vigorously lobbied not only by environmental groups but also by business; and the Agriculture DG has long received the attentions of the farming lobby.

But not only do interests wish to gain access to the Commission but the Commission often seeks contact with them. It does so for four main reasons. First, interests often have access to information which the Commission needs if it is to be able to exercise its responsibilities efficiently. In respect of possible legislation, for example, the Commission cannot itself know, especially in specialised and technical areas, what is required, what will work, and what will create implementation difficulties. Second, the Commission's negotiating hand with the Council of Ministers is strengthened if it can demonstrate that its proposals are supported by influential interests – as, for instance, with many of its attempts to approximate European standards, which often are not only supported by multinational corporations but stem from them. Third, if the Commission does not try to satisfy interests and brings forward proposals to which influential interests are opposed, it is likely to meet with resistance in the Council of Ministers and the EP – especially when proposals have potentially damaging implications for one or more member states. Fourth, where Eurogroups come forward with broadly united and coherent positions, they can greatly assist the Commission by allowing it to deal with aggregated sectional views.

The Commission is thus in an ongoing, and for the most part mutually beneficial, dialogue with a host of non-governmental interests. It is so via a variety of formal and informal channels. The main formal channels are the 500 or so advisory committees that the Commission uses for soliciting specialist information and for gauging the views of interested parties in particular policy areas (see

Chapter 10). Drawing usually at least some of their members from interests (most commonly from Eurogroups) advisory committees range across the policy spectrum, from the Joint Committee on Shipping to the Advisory Committee on Arable Crops. The main informal channels are direct meetings, which are normally held on a case-by-case basis, between Commission officials, or occasionally Commissioners or *cabinet* members, on the one hand, and interest representatives on the other.

Some interests have such good access to the Commission that they acquire insider status and become part of one or more of the various types of policy networks that are based in Brussels. Richardson has noted (1996: 20), that these networks are 'more usually the loose, more dynamic issue-networks on the US model . . . rather than the policy community model', but whatever sort they are membership of them tends to result in influence by interests being exercised not only via traditional lobbying tactics but also in more subtle ways. As Greenwood has observed, policy networks 'are not simply vehicles for private interests to table their own needs, but are fora in which public policies arise between two parties with a common set of perceptions, with socialising affects on the parties involved, reinforcing the ways in which issues are defined and responded to and common interests are identified' (1997: 40). (On EU policy networks see also Peterson, 1995c; Peterson and Bomberg, 1999.)

Interests sometimes get so close to DGs or parts of DGs as to appear virtually to capture them. So, for example, Mazey and Richardson (1999: 122) have noted how, at a general policy level, business interests have contributed to the capturing of many sectoral debates across the Commission in a pro-competitiveness policy frame. That is to say, business has helped to create a policy frame in which policy debates are structured around an assumption that there is an overriding need not to damage the competitiveness of European industry. At more specific policy levels, opportunities for agency capture are presented by the reliance of the Commission on outside interests for advice and information. The Commission can sometimes be so weak in terms of its in-house expertise that interests virtually produce policy papers for it – either directly or, as can happen, via consultancy firms that win Commission contracts put out to tender.

But the extent of agency capture should not be exaggerated. After all, the Commission is open to all sorts of interests, with the consequence that it is very difficult for any one interest to dominate or control input into the Commission over a long period. So, business interests may be strong, but in recent years they have not been able to prevent a number of significant policy advances supported by women's groups, environmentalists, consumers, and trade unions. Furthermore, many important issues are not treated holistically, but rather are broken down into specific issues and problems that require technical and specialist inputs from different interests. Rather then than a model of 'agency capture' applying to Commission–interest relations, it is usually much more the case that the Commission is, as Mazey and Richardson have put it (1997: 180), a *bourse* where problems, policies and interests are traded in an extremely complex and varied network of relationships involving EU institutions, member states, and interests. In these relationships, the Commission may seek to act as a 'broker of interests' in favour of policy change (Mazey and Richardson, 1997: 181).

The activities and influence of interests are further discussed in Chapter 10.

Concluding remarks

The EU is a multi-actor system, with many different sorts of actors involved, or attempting to be involved, in its activities and processes. The treaties lay down a framework for the nature of some inter-actor relations, but only in very formal terms. There have thus been opportunities, and indeed requirements, for actors to develop, clarify, and cultivate their relations with one another. Given its position at the heart of the EU system, these processes have involved the Commission more than any other EU actor.

Specific aspects of the Commission's relations with other actors are further explored in the chapters that follow.

Chapter 9

The Provision of Leadership

The leadership problem in the EU

The Commission exists within the framework of a unique system of governance. One of the most important characteristics of this system is its considerable dispersal of political power and its associated lack of direct accountability between the governing and the governed. In the member states of the EU there is an identifiable, usually reasonably coherent, and democratically elected source of authority – the central feature of which is a government supported by a majority in parliament. This source of authority has political and policy orientations which draw on ideological perspectives, and these orientations and perspectives guide the general shape and direction of public decision-making. So, for example, a national election in Germany or in Spain is likely to result in a Centre-Right or Centre-Left party or coalition of parties with a majority in parliament and this majority is then likely to pursue and apply policies which, though affected by the evolution of circumstances and events, reflect the ideologies of the parties and the commitments they have made in manifestoes and programmes. To put this another way, in the member states there is an institutional structure which is capable of being used by political movements and actors to provide a basis for political power and authority. This, in turn, can be used to provide political leadership.

In the EU there is no comparable focus of power and authority. The governing structure, as set out in treaties and as clarified by political practice, results in political power and authority being divided and shared between several institutions. Of these institutions, the Commission, along with the Court of Justice, might be thought to be the most inappropriate and unsuited institution to provide leadership and drive for the EU. It is, after all, an appointed body with no popular base or mandate and its formal decision-making powers are relatively weak. The European Council and Council of Ministers, by contrast, bring together the most senior political representatives of the governments of the member states, and both have extensive decision-making powers at their disposal – powers that stem partly from the treaties and partly from the political status of the members. As for the EP, it brings together the directly elected representatives of the people and its powers are now considerable as a result of reforms contained in the SEA and the Maastricht and Amsterdam treaties.

In practice, however, the European Council, the Council of Ministers and the EP – the institutions which have the formal power to take most important EU decisions and the institutions with some claim to democratic legitimacy – are constrained in what they can do by way of providing leadership and impetus for the EU. The European Council and the Council of Ministers are constrained by, amongst other factors, their internal divisions, their very nature as rolling series of international negotiations, and the short term of office – six months – of their presidency. The EP is constrained by the size and heterogeneity of its membership and also by the nature of its powers which favour it being a reactive rather than a pro-active body.

There is then, if not a complete lack of democratically-based political leadership in the EU, at least a shortfall. Most crucially, there is no EU counterpart to national governments. In consequence, the Commission is not subject to the same degree of political direction as national administrative agencies. This has presented opportunities for the Commission to exercise not just the advisory and administrative roles that are the normal business of national civil servants and international secretariats, but also leadership roles in relation to the shaping and management of political and policy agendas.

One key leadership role is prescribed for the Commission by the EU's treaties. This is formal agenda-setting, which requires the Commission to bring forward policy and legislative proposals that will serve the interests of EU members. The right to propose policies is not exclusive to the Commission, but the right to propose legislation is. Beyond this formally-assigned leadership role, other leadership opportunities are less obvious and in some respects are more subtle but they are nonetheless of considerable importance. Adapting from Sandholtz (1993a: 250), these more informal leadership roles include: *suggesting* – pointing out to potential collaborators areas where collective action would be mutually beneficial; *mobilising* – bringing potential collaborators together; *informal agenda-setting* – defining issues and identifying frameworks of possible action; *building consensus* – promoting common understandings of the nature of problems and of how they might be tackled; and *brokering compromises* – identifying potential spheres of agreement where disagreements exist.

The commitment to leadership

Most senior Commission staff – Commissioners, *cabinet* members, high-ranking officials – believe, albeit with varying degrees of intensity, that the Commission has a duty to provide leadership for the EU. Most also believe that the leadership so provided should foster the process of European integration. If the Commission does not assume such a pioneering role and act as the motor force of integration then who, it is asked, will? Other EU political actors are seen as being able to make important contributions in this regard, but their heterogeneous memberships, their organisational structures, and the nature of their powers make it extremely difficult for them to be able to initiate and drive ahead with integrative developments on a consistent basis.

The origins of the view that the Commission has special responsibilities in promoting integration go back to the way in which the European Community was founded in the 1950s, and more particularly to the vision of Jean Monnet. As was shown in Chapter 2, Monnet had been the originator and head of the Planning Commission which was established in France at the end of the Second World War to guide the reconstruction of the national economy. Monnet's experiences at the Planning Commission had convinced him of the merits of economic planning by enlightened officials and also of the need for much of such planning to be conducted at a European rather than at a national level. Accordingly, when he helped devise the ECSC in the early 1950s Monnet sought to ensure that at the heart of the institutional arrangements was an appointed body of senior officials whose responsibilities included strategic planning. It is perhaps not a complete coincidence that the modern Commission was at its most adventurous, its most ambitious, and its most forward-looking during the period of the Delors' presidencies – for Delors had long been inspired by thinking and ideas which were in many respects similar to those of Monnet and in the 1960s Delors had spent several years as a prominent figure in the French Planning Commission.

Delors' presidencies may in time come to be seen as the high point of Commission activism and drive. They should not, however, be seen as aberrations in terms of the Commission wanting to assert itself. The desire to be doing something useful and important is an ongoing characteristic of the Commission. Whilst the idealistic, almost pioneering, vision of many of the early employees of the Commission has necessarily been replaced by more pragmatic attitudes as the institution has become more bureaucratised (see Hooghe, 1999a, 1999b), the notion that it is the duty of the Commission to be pushing ahead with integration is still widely held. As Ludlow has commented, 'the function of *animateur* permeates the whole structure and ethos of the institution' (1991: 97).

Problems in providing leadership

Like the other main EU institutions, the Commission's leadership potential is hampered by weaknesses. Prominent amongst these weaknesses are:

- The Commission's most prominent members – Commissioners are not chosen first and foremost on the basis of what would be best for the Commission. What national governments have in mind when they nominate 'their' Commissioner(s) varies, but at least some attention is given to the likely willingness and capability of the nominee(s) to keep an eye on the national interest (as that is defined by the dominant party(ies) in government).
- Even at its highest level – the College – the Commission is an appointed rather than an elected body, and so legitimacy is a problem if it tries to be too bold. This weakness has been partially offset by the requirement that incoming Colleges must receive a vote of confidence in the EP before formally taking up office, but this still leaves the Commission a long way short of being able to claim that it has popular endorsement, let alone a popular mandate.
- Although the Commission can, and indeed is expected to, come forward with policy initiatives, it does not have the power to carry such initiatives into action. For that it is dependent on other institutions giving their approval – European Council political approval normally being necessary for major policy issues, and Council of Ministers approval, and where the co-decision procedure applies also EP approval, being necessary when legislation is envisaged.

- The Commission is in many respects not the cohesive force it is popularly perceived as being. On the contrary, it is highly pluralistic, with a diversity of preferences, styles and cultures at both College and services levels. With Commissioners and many of the DGs enjoying a considerable degree of independence in the exercise of their duties, this diversity can make political and policy dynamism, and overall coherence, difficult to achieve.

Notwithstanding such weaknesses, however, the Commission is still well placed to be able to exercise a leadership role, and is in possession of resources to enable it to do so.

Leadership resources

Treaty powers

The Commission's treaty powers are potentially considerable. Article 211 TEC is the key article in regard to the Commission seeking to provide general leadership:

> In order to ensure the proper functioning and development of the common market, the Commission shall:
>
> - ensure that the provisions of this Treaty and the measures taken by the institutions pursuant thereto are applied;
> - formulate recommendations or deliver opinions on matters dealt with in this Treaty, if it expressly so provides or if the Commission considers it necessary;
> - have its own power of decision and participate in the shaping of measures taken by the Council and by the European Parliament in the manner provided for in this Treaty;
> - exercise the powers conferred on it by the Council for the implementation of the rules laid down by the latter.

Article 211 gives to the Commission a considerable potential for launching new initiatives and shaping the terms of the ongoing debate about EU policies and structures. It does so by virtue of the vagueness of some of its provisions as to what the Commission should be doing, and by virtue of its references to the need to ensure that 'this Treaty' is properly applied and developed. The significance of this is that there are few policy areas, other than those that are covered by the CFSP and JHA pillars of the TEU, which are completely excluded from the EC Treaty's remit. Article 211 thus permits the Commission to move on a broad front if it so wishes – by, for example, issuing position or discussion papers which are designed to set or shape the agenda. If the ideas expressed in such papers are then endorsed by other institutions, especially by the European Council and/or the Council of Ministers, or if they lead to requests for the Commission to develop its thinking further, perhaps in the form of a White Paper, they can then become a source of legitimacy and a framework in which more specific proposals are advanced. Such, for example, has been the pattern in the sphere of the social dimension, where the Commission's 1989 *Community Charter of Fundamental Social Rights for Workers* (the so-called Social Charter), which was endorsed by the December 1989 Strasbourg European Council meeting, served in the 1990s as a reference point and a legitimiser for a stream of specific legislative proposals.

At more modest leadership levels, that is to say at those levels where leadership is concerned with the advancement of specific proposals rather than with the broad sweep and direction of policy and institutional development, the Commission is also strongly placed constitutionally. It is so in two particular ways. First, it enjoys the sole right to propose and draft legislation and also enjoys a considerable control over proposals as they make their way through legislative processes. It can be requested by the Council and the EP to submit appropriate proposals and it functions in a context wherein it is subject to a constant barrage of representations from all sorts of outside interests on the need for EU legislation. The Commission alone, however, decides just how and when to proceed, albeit sometimes under pressure, and no other institution or outside interest is in a position to issue instructions to the Commission concerning the substantive content or timetable of its proposals. This legislative role of the Commission is considered at length in Chapter 10. Second, the TEC is less than precise in many respects. This has created opportunities for the Commission to take action and to advance proposals where it has felt it to be necessary and appropriate to do so. For example, it has taken advantage of TEC Articles 81–89 (ex-85–94), which deal with competition policy, to be highly pro-active in seeking to ensure that restrictive and protectionist practices in the internal market are minimised. Article 308 (ex-235) of the Treaty is also useful for the Commission because it allows it to make a proposal if 'action by the Community should prove necessary to attain, in the cause of the operation of the common market, one of the objectives of the Community and this Treaty has not provided the necessary powers . . .'. Illustration of the use of this Article is seen in the way it was frequently invoked prior to the SEA to enable the Commission to begin to develop a Community environmental policy. Significantly, and this can be seen in other policy areas too, once environmental policy began to become established as a legitimate Community goal, it was incorporated into the Treaty. Incorporation of a policy area into the Treaty has the effect of further increasing the Commission's powers because the appropriateness of the EU being involved in the area cannot then be questioned.

Political resources

Political resources of different kinds are utilised and mobilised by the Commission.

The background of Commissioners is one such resource, with the College being composed of former national politicians, most of whom have held senior office in their countries (see Chapter 4, and MacMullen, 1997). Commissioners, in other words, are people who are used to exercising power and influence, and they usually come to Brussels with the idea of wishing to continue to exercise such powers and influence both in respect of the portfolio they are assigned and the College as a whole. The extent to which, in practice, they succeed in their aims naturally varies, but virtually all, and especially those who take up major portfolios, have a political standing and experience that is extremely useful in assisting them to make a mark – by launching new initiatives, dealing with intractable issues, and generally moving the agenda forward.

The increasing visibility and status of the position of President of the Commission is another political resource that has helped to raise the Commission's profile and influence. As has been shown in earlier chapters, several factors account for this enhanced position of the President, of which the most prominent are the growing significance of the EU itself, the increased powers given to the President by the Maastricht and Amsterdam treaties, the need of the media to focus on an individual, and the presence of the President at important and media-swamped gatherings of national leaders If he so chooses and if he has the ability, a forceful President can do much to enhance the Commission's position and standing and to make the Commission a highly pro-activist institutional actor.

At all policy-making levels the Commission has acquired a wide range of political skills and these have served as another valuable political resource that it has been able to use to its advantage. One such skill has been an ability to play a part in focusing political discourse on the merits of policy actions at the EU level rather than at national levels. In policy areas such as the SEM, EMU and the social dimension the Commission has virtually run public relations campaigns and Commission representatives – especially Commissioners – have actively engaged in public debate. A related discourse has seen the Commission citing successes in existing policy areas to justify the development of other policy areas – what Matláry (1997a) has called 'agenda building through linkages'. An example of this sort of discourse is the relating of benefits that are claimed to have accrued from the SEM programme to the benefits it is suggested will also accrue if and when public utilities are opened up to more competition.

Another political skill has been an ability to take advantage of windows of opportunity and of seemingly innocuous policy instruments to promote significant expansions of the EU's policy agenda. As Cram has observed (1994: 199), the Commission has acted as a 'purposeful opportunist' – that is, as 'an organisation which has a notion of its overall objectives and aims but is quite flexible as to the means of achieving them' (1994: 214). In acting as a purposeful opportunist to expand the scope of Union competence (and in so doing its own scope for action, too) the Commission has employed a variety of techniques that are designed to make proposed policies and laws acceptable.

One of these techniques is to use of 'soft law', which is non-binding legislation in the form of such instruments as declarations, recommendations and communications. Soft law instruments do not need to be approved by the Council or the EP, so they give the Commission more manoeuvrability than it normally has when it is proposing and devising hard law. They can be used to help bring issues onto the agenda or to suggest new policy approaches in existing issue areas. Moreover, as Snyder has observed (1994: 214), once soft law is elaborated it is sometimes transformed into hard law, usually via an ECJ decision or by legislation. Cram (1994, 1995) has demonstrated the use of soft law in the social policy sphere.

Another technique, as Majone (1996b) has shown, has been to prioritise the promotion of regulatory policies. Such policies tend to be less problematical for the Commission, and more broadly for the EU, than distributional policies. They are so for two main reasons:

they do not make heavy demands on tight EU budgetary resources since the costs of implementation fall on public authorities and private firms in the member states rather than directly on the EU; and the effects of regulatory policies are not usually so clear as are the effects of distributional policies, so they are less likely to be contested by national governments.

Technical knowledge

Officials in the Commission's services develop an understanding and knowledge of their respective policy spheres. When the necessary expertise is not to be found amongst the Commission's permanent staff, outside help is frequently called in – usually by contracting consultants of some kind or by making use of the extensive advisory committee system that is clustered around the Commission. But whether the knowledge is directly or indirectly acquired, the Commission has an extensive technical expertise and a fund of information about the content and impact of EU policies. Such expertise and information are key power resources: little that is sensible or workable can be done in any policy area without an understanding of highly complex issues and without access to a mass of what are often almost impenetrable facts and figures. All EU actors develop some such understanding and access, but not usually to the same extent as the Commission, which results in the Commission being advantageously placed to make itself indispensable to most initiatives and developments.

Neutrality and independence

The Commission has, in theory at least, a quality that is absent from the European Council, the Council of Ministers and the EP: neutrality and independence *vis à vis* national and other interests. Since the Commission is staffed by nationals of the member states, there are naturally sometimes suspicions that a particular Commissioner or official has used his/her position to look sympathetically at a matter concerning his/her country, but this is not common. For the most part, the impartiality that all Commission employees are expected to display in the exercise of their duties is respected, and is generally seen to be so. This impartiality means that when the Commission launches initiatives, be they of a general directional or of a specific policy kind, or when it tries to promote a consensus on a contentious issue, it tends to be viewed with less suspicion than other institutions and actors when they seek to do something similar.

This is not, of course, to suggest that Commission initiatives and actions are necessarily liked or accepted, or even that they are not viewed by some as evidence of an unwanted Commission bias. The most notable instance of perceived bias in recent times is the way in which the Eurosceptic Conservative UK governments of the 1980s and 1990s looked on the Commission as being too pro-integrationist in its leanings. Generally speaking, however, the Commission is seen to be trying to act in the interests of the EU as a whole. For many, it is, and must be, the conscience of the Union – because it is the only body with the potential to so be.

The importance of operational contexts

The extent to which the Commission is able to use its resources in such a way as to provide the EU with effective leadership depends in large part on the contexts in which it is operating. Three contexts are especially important: perceptions by the member states of the need for, and desirability of, activity at the EU level; perceptions by the member states of the role of the Commission; and the decision-making framework.

Perceptions by the member states of the need for, and desirability of, activity at EU level

Clearly, the Commission's prospects of advancing the policy agenda and bringing forward policy proposals that will be received favourably are considerably enhanced when those who make the final decisions – which means particularly the representatives of the member states – are convinced of the need for, and the desirability of, policy activity at EU level.

That this is so is no more clearly seen than in the background to the launching of the SEM programme in 1985. The many studies that have been undertaken on the reasons for the launching of the programme have focused on several claimed causational factors –

ranging from pressure by European business groupings to political entrepreneurship by the Commission – but virtually all have agreed that little progress could have been made had not a consensus emerged between the member states on the need to integrate the still fractured internal market (see, for example, Sandholtz and Zysman, 1989; Moravcsik, 1991; Cameron, 1992).

A consensus similarly emerged in the 1980s that the EU should be active in the closely related policy areas of information technology, telecommunications, and research development. This was because of a growing recognition of the inadequacy of national policies in these areas and fears about European competitiveness in an increasingly high-tech world. The Commission both stoked and used these changing attitudes to establish itself as an important agenda-setter in these areas (see, for example, Sandholtz, 1992a and b; Fuchs, 1994, 1995; Schneider, Dang-Nguyen and Werle, 1994; Peterson and Sharp, 1998).

Just as the existence of a favourable consensus helps explain Commission success with the SEM programme and technology policy, so does its absence help explain Commission difficulties in opening up gas and electricity networks. As Schmidt (1997a, 1998) has shown, member states, and in particular France, have not been convinced that wholesale liberalisation of gas and electricity is in their interests and consequently have been resistant to being led too far by the Commission in this direction. A key reason for them not being convinced is the diverse character of national gas and electricity markets and structures.

Perceptions by the member states of the role of the Commission

Whilst increased perceptions by the member states that there should be policy activity at EU level normally enhances the Commission's leadership capacities, this is not always so. There are circumstances in which member states may have doubts about, and may even be opposed to, allowing further EU activity to automatically result in a greater leadership role for the Commission. Usually such doubts and opposition are part of a broader concern about the increasingly supranational tilt of the EU. This was, for example, the case in the 1991 IGC negotiations on the institutional implications of expanding the EU's policy remit, when the decision to establish the CFSP and JHA pillars outside the EC Treaty was motivated by concerns not just to keep the Commission's powers at bay but also by a more general concern to retain the pre-eminence of national governmental power in these spheres.

It is, however, not only general perceptions and political orientations that influence the attitudes of member states regarding their expectations of the Commission and the sort of leadership it ought to be offering. Other factors play a role, too, of which perhaps the most important is whether or not the Commission is seen to be 'doing a good job'. At the individual member state level, what is deemed to constitute doing a good job varies considerably according to national interests and priorities – Italy, for example, which is generally supportive of Commission leadership, has resisted such leadership in the context of Commission proposals for restructuring the EU steel industry because they are judged to be too damaging to Italian interests. At the overall EU level, it is more difficult to say what is deemed to constitute 'doing a good job' because it involves general notions of competence, efficiency, fairness, etc. Certainly, however, there can be little doubt that one of the reasons why the Commission's leadership lost some of its effectiveness in the closing period of Delors' presidency was that the Commission as a whole was just not seen as being as competent as it had been previously: the open conflicts between some Commissioners were seen as being damaging and the Commission was blamed for having contributed to the climate of opinion which brought about the June 1992 Danish referendum result by having been too integrationist in its rhetoric in the weeks preceding the vote.

The decision-making framework

The decision-making framework in which the Commission finds itself naturally has many implications for the leadership it is expected and is able to provide. It is a framework that is in almost constant evolution in response to political and constitutional changes, with consequences that are sometimes helpful and are sometimes unhelpful from the viewpoint of the Commission's being able to offer and provide leadership. Three areas of framework evolution that have had particularly significant implications for the leadership potential of the Commission will be cited here.

First, the expansion of the policy areas included in the TEC has strengthened the Commission's ability to act as an agenda-setter in these areas. By the same token, the Commission's hand is not so strong in policy areas that have been placed in the intergovernmental second and third pillars of the TEU or in areas that have no explicit treaty base at all.

Second, the greater use of QMV in the Council of Ministers since the mid-1980s and the expansion of the policy areas in which QMV is permissible has meant that the Commission has been able to be bolder with many of its policy ideas and proposals. Where QMV applies, the Commission need not be unduly inhibited about floating an idea or bringing forward a proposal if there is opposition in just one or two states, and need not necessarily water down its preferences in the hope that potential minority opposition will be withdrawn or removed.

Third, the emergence of the European Council as the place where major political decisions concerning the direction of the EU are taken has also assisted the Commission's agenda-setting and policy-proposing capacities. It might be thought that this involvement of the European Council in the 'grand issues' would undermine the Commission's leadership capacities, and indeed it would do so if the national leaders were able to agree on principles designed to provide a reference framework for future action to which the Commission was opposed. However, much of the discussion at summits is on the basis of papers that have been drawn up by the Commission – either on its own initiative, or at the request of an earlier summit, or on the basis of ideas that have been originally floated by the Commission and on which a summit has then requested further information or a more detailed report. Once a decision, Commission inspired or otherwise, has been taken by the European Council, subsequent Commission action to give effect to the decision is underpinned with considerable political authority and legitimacy. As Lord Cockfield, the Internal Market Commissioner in the first Delors Commission, has written of the European Council's approval of the SEM programme:

> the public endorsement by the European Council on this and indeed on subsequent occasions was not only valuable in public relations terms but of utmost value in dealing with the Council of Ministers. It enabled me in particular to argue that the principle had already been decided by their Heads of Government and their concern was not to debate the principle but to deal with the legislation which implemented the principle. (Cockfield, 1994: 100)

Linkages between resources and operational contexts

The Commission's resources and its operational contexts are closely linked. An obvious instance of linkage at a general level is the way in which several of the resources – most notably those of treaty powers, expectations that the Commission should act as the engine of integration, and the special position of the President – were capable of being used with much greater potency prior to the 1992 Danish referendum than they were after it. The change was brought about because two of the operating contexts – the perceived need for policy activity at the EU level and the perceived need for the Commission to be centrally involved in that policy activity – suddenly became less favourable.

It is thus very much in the Commission's interests to use its resources to make its operating contexts as favourable as possible. Three different sorts of examples will be taken to illustrate how it has sought to do this.

(1) Prior to and during rounds of treaty reform the Commission has 'talked up' the need for institutional change. There have been calls for both direct changes in its own position (with, for example, consistent calls for increased powers for the President) and for other changes that would be to its institutional advantage (such as streamlining decision-making procedures and extending QMV in the Council). The establishment in September 1999 by President Prodi of a committee to examine 'the institutional implications in view of the forthcoming Intergovernmental Conference', recommendations from that committee that the IGC should 'aim at a comprehensive approach to institutional reform' (Weizsäcker, Dehaene and Simon, 1999: 15), and broad endorsement by the College of the committee's recommendations in the opinion it presented to the IGC (Commission 2000e), is but the latest instance of the Commission's consistent pro-integrationist approach to treaty reform.

(2) When a Commission initiative is, or is likely to be, resisted by the governments of at least some member states, then the Commission often makes use of appropriate resources to attempt to reduce that resistance. For example, Schmidt (1997b), has shown how, in its attempts to open up such sectors as

telecommunications, postal services and air transport, the Commission has drawn on a number of resources and employed a number of devices to make national governments, and so in turn the Council, receptive to its proposals. One approach has been to pursue a 'divide and conquer' strategy, which has involved the Commission taking or threatening to take actions that may 'soften' at least some national positions in the Council. Such actions include examinations of national practices and initiation of infringement proceedings in the ECJ. Another approach has been a 'prevent worse' strategy, which has involved the Commission threatening to take a matter to the ECJ – where, as was shown in Chapter 8, a 'harder' decision may be taken – if a measure is not adopted by the Council.

(3)   Where there has been little success, and there is little prospect of success, of persuading national governments to act in policy areas in which the Commission believes action is desirable, then the Commission sometimes tries to persuade other key actors to its way of thinking, and through them to persuade national governments. Such, for example, was the case with information technology in the 1980s: as Peterson has noted 'the Commission helped engineer an industrial consensus for new collaborative schemes, was supported by industry in urging the transfer of authority over technology policy to the EC level, and was ultimately able to convince governments to launch the Esprit programme in 1983' (Peterson, 1991: 276).

There are, therefore, dynamic interactions between resources and operational contexts, with each capable of assisting, but also of harming, the other in terms of their implications for the Commission's leadership capacity. Crucially, the interactions are not wholly independent from the Commission's own actions but are capable of being influenced, for better or worse, by them. From the Commission's viewpoint, its successful attempts since the mid-1980s to use such resources as its expertise and its neutrality to make member states more accommodating to the view that the SEM initiative must be ever wider in scope is an example of interactions being influenced for the better. By contrast, the use of much the same resources in 1991–92 to press the case for faster integration, which resulted in the governments of several member states concluding that the Commission was over-reaching itself, is an example of interactions being influenced for the worse.

The Commission, leadership and the integration process

Different forms of leadership

It was noted earlier in the chapter that leadership can take different forms. Agenda-setting, mobilising, building consensus, and brokering compromises were identified as being amongst the ways in which leadership can be exercised.

The Commission has sought to exercise all of these possible forms of leadership. It has, for instance, sought to shape the agenda through such devices as the issuing of discussion papers (an increasingly common practice) and Commissioners publicly advocating courses of action – as when, for example, Neil Kinnock, Transport Commissioner in the Santer College, pressed the governments of the member states to be less protectionist on air transport policy issues. It has sought to focus debate and frame decisions through major policy papers, such as the 1997 document, *Agenda 2000* (Commission, 1997b) which set out proposals on future enlargement strategy, on the reform of existing expenditure policies, and on the financial framework for the years 2000–06. And it has sought to drive, persuade, mobilise and assist the other EU institutions and policy actors to act – as in 1992 and 1993 when it cajoled and helped to persuade the member states to accept the trade deals negotiated within the context of the General Agreement on Tariffs and Trade (GATT) Uruguay Round.

Difficulties in establishing the exercise of leadership

Though the leadership roles that the Commission has *attempted* to exercise can be identified, it is more difficult to identify those that it actually *has* exercised. To take, for example, agenda-setting, which is the leadership function most commonly associated with the Commission, member states and groups of member states, several EU institutions, and numerous national and transnational sectional interests are part of ongoing, interconnected and overlapping discussions and negotiations about what the EU should be doing. Given this situation, it is frequently virtually impossible in particular instances to disentangle contributions and determine with precision which institution(s) and actor(s) did what, and in so far as they did do something the extent to which they did it on their own volition and in an autonomous manner.

The academic debate

The difficulties just mentioned provide the foundations of a long-standing debate between scholars on the nature of the EU as an organisation and on the nature of the integration process. The debate is pertinent to the consideration being given here to the Commission and the provision of leadership because it is much taken up with the extent to which, and the ways in which, the Commission is an independent driving force in the EU system and in the integration process.

Those who subscribe to a broadly intergovernmentalist perspective focus very much on the motivations of nation states and how the EU serves national interests. These national interests are seen as taking a number of different forms, with commentators varying in the importance which they ascribe to them. Amongst the interests most frequently identified are the political advantages that accrue to states from being able to continue to assert themselves via regularised and effective inter-state bargaining in an increasingly interdependent world, and the economic advantages which flow from market, and increasingly also broader economic, integration. In the intergovernmental perspective integrationist advance is heavily dependent on these advantages coming to be seen in a similar way by national governments, so that national preferences converge.

This emphasis by intergovernmentalists on the calculations made by states as to whether integration serves national interests is linked to how decision-making processes are viewed. States are seen as generally being concerned to protect their decision-making powers, particularly where constitutional, financial, and security issues are concerned. A consequence of this is that they are also seen as being reluctant to cede much in the way of an independent role to non-governmental institutions – of which, of course, the Commission is one. This means that the Commission is not, and cannot be, the independent supranational institution it is portrayed by some as being. For Andrew Moravcsik, who in recent years has been the foremost proponent of what might broadly be described as the intergovernmentalist perspective, the Commission is mainly concerned with assisting and facilitating inter-state bargaining and with seeing to the enforcement of decisions which come out of that bargaining (1991, 1993, 1995, 1998). There is, Moravcsik concedes, some room for independent manoeuvre available to the Commission in relation to agenda-setting, but it is generally from a subservient and servicing position: 'As a reliable source of independent proposals, the Commission assures that technical information necessary for decision is available. More importantly, as a neutral arbiter, it provides an authoritative means of reducing the number of proposals to be considered' (Moravcsik, 1993).

By contrast with this intergovernmentalist emphasis on the role of states in the integration process, those who take a supranational perspective argue that a prominent place needs to be given also to the role of non-state-based and non-state-focused actors. That states would not be members of the EU and would not support the development of the EU if it did not serve national interests is not denied. Nor is it disputed that states are key EU actors, with the individual and collective importance of national governments acknowledged. What must also be recognised, however, it is argued, is the important and independent role of non-governmental actors. The Commission is generally seen as being the most prominent of these non-governmental actors (see, for example, Matláry, 1997b; Stone Sweet and Sandholtz, 1997; Sandholtz and Stone Sweet, 1998; Schmidt, 2000).

A point that is often stressed by those who wish to emphasise the importance of the Commission as a policy actor is that intergovernmentalists tend to focus rather too much on decision-*taking* and not enough on the whole process of decision-*making*. The representatives of member states may indeed be the main formal players at the decision-taking stage, but what they do at this stage is largely conditioned and shaped by what has happened at earlier stages of the decision-making process: stages in which the Commission is prominent in shaping the policy agenda and in formulating and drafting policy proposals (see, for example, George, 1994; Wincott, 1995).

A related point that is also frequently emphasised by those who argue that the Commission exercises an autonomous, or at least semi-autonomous, influence in EU decision-making is that few of the policy preferences of the governments of the member states are a consequence of decisions independently taken in national capitals. Arguably, national governmental preferences on a few very big issues – such as whether or not to be part of the single currency or of the Schengen System removing border controls – are made in this way, but there are few such issues, or at least there are few such issues that are not broken down into smaller and more specific issues. In undertaking much of the preparatory work on smaller and more specific issues – through such means as consultation, issuing position papers, floating ideas, and indicating possible courses of action – the Commission is not normally faced with principled and immovable national opposition. Rather, national preferences are rarely completely fixed, so by being pro-active the Commission is potentially capable of shaping, or even altering, them. Indeed, it can sometimes push member states into defining their preferences partly in relation to its own preferences, as Smyrl (1998) has shown in a detailed study of national preference formation in the 1980s.

Illustrations of Commission leadership

It is perhaps not surprising, given the focus of this book on the Commission, that the position taken here is closer to the supranational than to the intergovernmental stance. It is readily acknowledged that many initiatives and proposals issuing from the Commission find their origins in preferences and wishes first expressed elsewhere, not least by member states on an individual and/or collective basis. It is further acknowledged that there are methodological difficulties in establishing that the Commission has acted independently for, as Pollack (1997a: 117) has put it, Commission activity is not in itself evidence of Commission independence. These acknowledgements having been made, however, the fact is that there is an abundance of empirical evidence which suggests that in launching initiatives and framing proposals the Commission is frequently doing more than simply responding in an automatic manner to external pressures. Rather, it is often offering an independent lead itself. Moreover, no matter where the original idea for initiatives or proposals may stem from, once the Commission begins working on them it can do much to frame the terms in which they are considered, when they are considered, by whom they are considered, and with what receptivity they are considered.

Documented illustrations of the Commission providing leadership in different ways and through the utilisation of different resources, strategies and tactics, are to be found in many important areas of EU policy activity. Indeed, as Marks, Hooghe and Blank (1996: 365) have pointed out, whilst much of the recent theoretical literature on European integration has stressed the intergovernmental character of the EU, most of the empirical literature has in fact emphasised the influence of the Commission. Examples of this empirical literature include:

- In the telecommunications sector, Fuchs has shown how the Commission has 'become a centrally located and powerful actor' and 'has achieved this without a clear constitutional or policy mandate and against the open resistance of some member states' (1994: 179). He identifies the key role of the ECJ in backing the Commission's expanding regulatory competence in the sphere of telecommunications, and emphasises also how the Commission has 'cleverly exploited the situation of insecurity and change dominant in this field on the national level' (1995: 414). Schneider, Dang-Nguyen and Werle broadly confirm these views of Fuchs and emphasise how in the telecommunications sphere 'the Commission has succeeded in transforming an initially national issue into a European one, pushing the Member States towards harmonisation of their policies and, moreover, setting the pace for a constant and convergent development of their legislation into the direction defined by the Commission itself' (1994: 1994). A crucially important means by which the Commission has been able to do this, according to Schneider and his colleagues, has been by mobilising a network of supporters at the European and national levels amongst large users, computer firms anxious to enter the telecommunications market, standardisation bodies, and 'friendly' governments (1994: 454).
- Lawton (1997) has charted the Commission's advancement of industrial policy since the late 1970s. Utilising an advocacy coalition – based on a Commission–big business partnership – that it itself fashioned, and constantly citing the need for a collective European response to the competitive challenge from the US and Asia, the Commission has cajoled often reluctant governments to permit industrial policy instruments to be developed at the EU level. This reluctance of governments has resulted in the Commission pursuing its agenda 'more by stealth than by candour' (p. 142). As part of this strategy of 'integration by stealth', industrial policy as such was barely explicitly mentioned by the Commission until it produced a communication on the subject in 1990 (Commission, 1990). Rather, until then, the strategy was to focus on the creation of the internal market and on specific policies such as competition, trade, research and technological development and a few sectoral policies. The 1990 communication was something of a turning point for it 'served, in effect, to establish a *de jure* industrial policy, albeit one of a somewhat general and ambiguous nature' (Lawton, 1997: 136). It did so by

setting out broad objectives and principles, most of which were placed within the general framework of greater competitiveness. Since the 1990 communication, industrial policy has featured openly and prominently on the policy agenda and the Commission has been highly active in advocating and promoting policy developments.

- In the sphere of social policy a number of studies have shown the Commission using an array of devices to advance the debate at EU level and to make governments more receptive to EU-level activity. Cram (1993), for example, has demonstrated how the Commission sometimes prepares the ground for future action through the use of 'soft law' (non-binding legislation) and 'process law' (establishing institutions, rules and procedures) from which may later be developed substantive law. She also emphasises how the Commission has been careful to concentrate on social law of a regulatory rather than of a spending kind – thus allowing it to assume the role of 'calling the tune without paying the piper' (p. 136). Wendon (1998), in similarly showing the Commission advancing EU social policy in an incrementalist manner, suggests that a dual approach has characterised the Commission's strategic approach in recent years. On the one hand, it has assisted the development of new institutional arrangements in order to create a stronger EU policy-making framework (Cram's 'process law'). As part of this strengthening of the framework, the Commission has encouraged the social partners (the two sides of industry) to become more active in policy formulation while it 'has found new roles in helping, funding, researching and nurturing' (p. 35). On the other hand, the Commission has directed the image and rhetoric of EU social policy away from its former emphasis on social rights and protection towards a new, and more politically acceptable, emphasis on how social measures contribute to productiveness, competitiveness, and new technology and training.
- Matláry (1997a) has demonstrated how the Commission has been active in promoting and developing energy policy through such tactics as mobilising supportive networks of industrial users, linking energy policy to other policy developments (especially the SEM and environmental policy) and the forceful use of the competition powers allocated to it by the TEC.
- In the area of equal opportunities, Mazey (1995, 1998) has shown the importance of the Commission's policy-promotional activities, and has stressed particularly its role in steering incrementalist

policy advances. Despite a weak treaty base in the area, the Commission played a significant role in pioneering legislation and action programmes in the 1980s and 1990s, and more recently – as the policy environment has become less conducive to legislation that may increase employers' costs – has made some progress in 'mainstreaming' equal opportunities as an issue within other economic and social policies. Devices used by the Commission in this policy area have included taking advantage of favourable ECJ rulings and promoting the growth of a supportive and monitoring transnational women's lobby.

- The creation of EMU, which is generally seen as being essentially a consequence of intergovernmental bargaining and structural economic trends, is revealed by Jabko (1999) to have been at least partly driven by a political strategy of the Commission. From the late 1980s the Commission constantly made the case for EMU and in the 1990s played a central role in mobilising support behind the project. 'Commission officials . . . performed a pivotal part as recruiting agents for the cause of EMU. Building upon timely perceptions of the Single Market's desirable nature and shape, they induced key actors to reframe their preferences in terms of EMU . . . they fostered solid political momentum behind an originally lukewarm and unfocused demand for monetary integration' (p. 476).

A very different illustration of Commission leadership is seen in the way it seeks to use its annual work programme to help frame the overall nature of the EU's policy activities. The programme indicates the priorities and objectives for the coming year and gives an indication of the actions the Commission intends to take, or hopes other institutions will take, in pursuit of the priorities and objectives.

Apart from years in which a new College assumes office, the programme is issued in the autumn of the year before which it is to take effect. It invariably has been some months in the making. The process begins with the establishment of general priorities and objectives by Commissioners. The Secretariat General then works with the services to establish what steps will be necessary to achieve the priorities and objectives. Working in conjunction with the *cabinet* of the President, the Secretariat General drafts the programme. After the draft has been considered by all Commissioners' *cabinets* and has been approved (if possible) by a meeting of the *chefs de cabinet* it is referred to the College for formal approval.

The ability of the Commission to use its annual programme to frame the EU's policy agenda and working schedule should not be exaggerated. Much of what the programme contains is, in effect, virtually pre-determined by ongoing and unavoidable commitments. Furthermore, Council presidencies present their own work programmes on assuming office, so in drawing up its programme the Commission has to at least liaise with the governments of incoming presidential states (as, indeed, they have to liaise with the Commission on their programmes). Notwithstanding these limitations, however, the Commission does have some manoeuvrability in devising the programme and it can attempt to use this manoeuvrability to prioritise and to bring forward new initiatives and give impetus to existing ones.

The *Commission's Work Programme for 2000*, the first annual programme of the Prodi Commission, demonstrates how the programme helps to provide a framework and tone for EU activities in the forthcoming year (Commission, 2000d). Set within the framework of four strategic objectives for the 2000–05 period that were laid out by the Commission in a communication issued on the same day as the work programme (Commission, 2000c), the programme identified the first steps that would be taken to transform the strategic objectives into reality. The objectives are now set out, along with illustrations of how they were to be pursued in 2000:

- *Promoting new forms of European governance*   As part of this, specific actions in 2000 would include the publication of a White Paper on reform of the Commission, the introduction of activity-based budgeting (ABB) 'as a means to ensure greater coherence in the allocation of operational appropriations and human resources', a number of measures to further develop the Commission's approach to transparency, dialogue and openness, and a full contribution to the 2000 IGC.
- *A stable Europe with a stronger voice in the world*   As part of this, in 2000 the Commission would propose a new human rights strategy, would develop distinctive strategic partnerships with neighbouring countries and regions as part of the preparations for enlargement of the EU, and would attempt to eliminate disputes in trans-Atlantic trade.
- *A new economic and social agenda*   As part of this, in 2000 the monitoring and coordination of the economic and monetary policies of the member states would be strengthened, a new social

action programme would be presented, and a communication would be issued setting out a new strategy for enterprise and competitiveness.

• *A better quality of life for all*   As part of this, in 2000 a Sixth Environmental Action Programme would be developed, a Green Paper examining the role of public transport and of private cars in cities would be issued, and the Commission would work with the member states to continue the development of a European Charter of Fundamental Rights.

The 2000 programme was operationalised via an accompanying 'Indicative List of Actions Foreseen', which set out 257 legislative proposals (most of them of a relatively routine kind), 176 non-legislative projects (such as White Papers, communications, and reports), and 70 autonomous acts (primarily Commission legislation). Box 9.1 illustrates the nature of the 2000 programme, by reproducing one of the 13 pages of envisaged legislative proposals (the whole list of Actions Foreseen ran to 23 pages).

Variations in the provision of leadership

The illustrations given above of the Commission being an innovative and independent EU actor must not disguise the fact that the Commission also has policy failures. Examples of high-profile failures in recent times include the non-adoption by the Council of the Commission's long-advanced proposals for a European Company Statute and for a carbon energy tax, the lack of much progress in establishing a more harmonised – and employment-promoting – EU taxation system, and the rejection by the December 1999 Helsinki summit of Commission calls for the 2000 IGC to have a bold and broad agenda.

Putting these and other Commission failures alongside the successes shows that the Commission is not able to be an innovative and independent actor on a consistent and across-the-board basis. Rather, there are variations in the leadership it provides, as regards both time periods and policy areas.

Variations between time periods   In very general terms it can be said that years of relatively high independent Commission activism have been 1958–65 and 1985–92, whilst years of relatively low independent

Box 9.1 Commission Work Programme for 2000: Legislative Proposals

Prog. No.	Area(s) of activity	Title	Lead service(s)
Energy/Environment			
2000/056	Energy/Environment	Proposal for a Regulation on a Community energy efficiency labelling programme for office and communication technology equipment	TREN
Energy/Research/External affairs			
2000/057	Energy/Research/ External affairs	Agreement on nuclear co-operation between Euratom and Ukraine (conclusion)	TREN/ RTD
Energy/Transport			
2000/058	Energy/Transport	Proposals for amendments to Decisions 1254/96 and 1692/96 on trans-European networks for energy and transport, accompanied by a communication	TREN
Enterprise			
2000/059	Enterprise	Agreement between the EU and the Republic of Cyprus establishing co-operation in the field of SMEs within the framework of the third multiannual programme for SMEs in the EU (1997 to 2000) (conclusion)	ENTR
2000/060	Enterprise	Proposal for a Directive on starting materials used in the manufacture of medicinal products	ENTR
2000/061	Enterprise	Proposal for a Decision on a multiannual programme for enterprise and entrepreneurship (2001–2006)	ENTR
2000/062	Enterprise	Proposal for a Decision on standardisation, including the information and communications technologies (ICT) field	ENTR
2000/063	Enterprise	Proposal for recasting Directive 98/37/EC relating to machinery	ENTR
2000/064	Enterprise	Proposal for a Directive evaluating and reviewing Community marketing authorisation procedures for medicinal products and evaluating the functions of the European Medicine Evaluation Agency	ENTR

Extracts from Indicative List of Actions Foreseen –

Procedure for adoption by the Commission	Date estimated for adoption by the Commission	Type of action	Treaty legal basis envisaged at this stage*	Probable adoption procedure in Parliament
written procedure	28/01/2000	regulation	Art. 95	codecision (COD)
written procedure	3rd quarter	Council decision for the conclusion of an agreement with third countries	Art. 101 Euratom	—
oral procedure	June	decision	Art. 156	codecision (COD)
written procedure	February	Council decision for the conclusion of an agreement with third countries	Art. 300(3)	—
written procedure	February	directive	Art. 95	codecision (COD)
oral procedure	08/03/2000	decision	Art. 157	consultation (CNS)
oral procedure	September	decision	Art. 157(3)	consultation (CNS)
written procedure	November	directive	Art. 95	codecision (COD)
written procedure	December	directive	Art. 95 or 308	codecision (COD)

→

Box 9.1 continued

Prog. No.	Area(s) of activity	Title	Lead service(s)
Enterprise/Agriculture and rural development/Audit/Budget/External trade/Customs/			
2000/065	Enterprise/Agriculture and rural development/Audit/Budget/External trade/Customs/External affairs	Proposal for a Decision in the form of an exchange of letters on conclusion of protocol 3 (regarding the processed agricultural components) of the European Economic Area (EEA)	ENTR
2000/066	Enterprise/Agriculture and rural development/Audit/Budget/External trade/Customs/External affairs	Proposal for a Decision in the form of an exchange of letters on the adaptation of protocol 2 (regarding the processed agricultural products) to the free trade agreement with Switzerland	ENTR
2000/067	Enterprise/Agriculture and rural development/Audit/Budget/External trade/Customs/External affairs	Proposal for a Decision in form of exchange of letters on the adaptation of protocol 2 (regarding the processed agricultural products) to the Free Trade Agreement with Norway	ENTR
2000/068	Enterprise/Agriculture and rural development/Audit/Budget/External trade/Customs/External affairs	Proposal for a Decision adjusting protocols 2 and 3 of the European agreements with the following countries: Poland, Hungary, Czech Republic, Slovak Republic, Romania, Bulgaria, Slovenia, Estonia, Latvia and Lithuania	ENTR
Enterprise/Agriculture and rural development/Customs			
2000/069	Enterprise/Agriculture and rural development/Customs	Proposals for a modification of Regulation 3448/93 laying down the trade arrangements applicable to certain goods resulting from the processing of agricultural products	ENTR
Enterprise/Environment/Internal market			
2000/070	Enterprise/Environment/Internal market	Proposal for a modification of Directive 70/220/EEC on measures to be taken against air pollution by emissions from motor vehicles (LPG; NG; OBD)	ENTR
2000/071	Enterprise/Environment/Internal market	Proposal for a modification of the Directive 94/25/EC on recreational craft	ENTR

Procedure for adoption by the Commission	Date estimated for adoption by the Commission	Type of action	Treaty legal basis envisaged at this stage*	Probable adoption procedure in Parliament
External affairs				
written procedure	February	Council decision for the conclusion of an agreement with third countries	Art. 300(3)	—
written procedure	February	Council decision for the conclusion of an agreement with third countries	Art. 300(3)	—
written procedure	February	Council decision for the conclusion of an agreement with third countries	Art. 300(3)	—
written procedure	May	Council decision for the conclusion of an agreement with third countries	Art. 300(3)	—
written procedure	April	regulation	Art.37, 133	consultation (CNS)
written procedure	February	directive	Art. 95	codecision (COD)
written procedure	June	directive	Art. 95	codecision (COD)

→

Box 9.1 continued

Prog. No.	Area(s) of activity	Title	Lead service(s)
Enterprise/Environment/Internal Market *continued*			
2000/072	Enterprise/Environment/Internal market	Proposal for a modification of the Directive 97/24/EC on certain components and characteristics of two or three-wheel motor vehicles (pollutant emissions limit values)	ENTR
2000/073	Enterprise/Environment/Internal market	Proposal for a modification of Directive 88/77/EEC on measures to be taken against the emission of gaseous pollutants from diesel engines for use in vehicles	ENTR
Enterprises/Internal market			
2000/074	Enterprise/Internal market	Proposal for a Directive on car construction requirements to reduce pedestrian injuries	ENTR
2000/075	Enterprise/Internal market	Proposal for a modification of Directive 74/150/EEC on the type-approval of wheeled agricultural or forestry tractors (extension of scope)	ENTR

Key:
ENTR Enterprise DG.
TREN Energy and Transport DG.
R&D   Research DG.

Source: Commission (2000d, Annex: p. 4)

activism have been 1966 to the early 1980s and 1992 to the mid-1990s. Several factors combine to explain why there has been this history of phases, the most important of which were considered above in the section on operational contexts. So, for example, to take perceptions of the desirability of EU-level policy activity, a growing recognition by the member states of the damaging consequences of the continuing fragmentation of the European market resulted in them looking increasingly to the Commission for a lead in the mid-1980s, just as a realisation in the wake of the 1992 Danish referendum on the Maastricht Treaty that elite opinion was getting too far in advance of public opinion resulted in them signalling to the Commission that policy brakes should be applied.

Procedure for adoption by the Commission	Date estimated for adoption by the Commission	Type of action	Treaty legal basis envisaged at this stage*	Probable adoption procedure in Parliament
written procedure	June	directive	Art. 95	codecision (COD)
written procedure	December	directive	Art. 95	codecision (COD)
written procedure	April	directive	Art. 95	codecision (COD)
written procedure	April	directive	Art. 95	codecision (COD)

* The legal basis mentioned is that envisaged at this stage by the lead service; it will be determined by the Commission in the light of the aim and exact content of the act, as yet undetermined at this stage in the planning.

Variations between policy areas The Commission tends to have, as Pollack (1997b, 1999) has pointed out, more opportunity for independent action when it has clear and strong powers, when it does not have to be too concerned about minority member state views (because QMV rules apply in the Council), when there is uncertainty of information, and when there is the possibility of exploiting differences between member states (and the Commission may be aware not only of national preferences but also of the intensity of preferences). There is less opportunity for independent action when the Commission's treaty powers are not strong or clear, when 'the Community method' is not used, when unanimity rules apply in the Council, and when tight controlling mechanisms are in place.

Enlargement is an example of an issue where the Commission has exercised strong and independent leadership. It has increasingly taken the lead since the early 1990s in directing and managing the enlargement of the EU to Central and Eastern European countries (CEECs), initially through the issuing of policy papers and subsequently, as the process has become more formalised, through making recommendations on when, with whom, and how accession negotiations should be opened, and shaping and participating in those negotiations when they have opened. The firm direction provided by the Commission is illustrated by its recommendations to the December 1999 Helsinki summit that accession negotiations should be broadened from their existing '5 + 1' character (five CEECs plus Cyprus) to a '10 + 2' character (the remaining five CEECs and Malta), that Turkey's status should be elevated to that of a candidate country, and that the EU should be prepared to take decisions on accession dates by 2002 (Commission, 1999j). The first two of these recommendations were accepted at Helsinki, though the third was weakened. The Commission has been able to exercise an independent leadership role on enlargement ('independent' in the sense that the member states have not interfered too much in its work and have not instructed it as regards what policy recommendations it should make) because although the factors identified in the previous paragraph as being favourable for the exercise of independent action have not wholly applied, they have done so to a sufficient extent. Taking them in turn: the Commission does not have strong treaty powers to manage EU enlargements, but the European Council delegates to it responsibility to produce opinions on applications, to conduct negotiations, and since 1998 has required it to produce annual progress reports on applicant states; unanimity rules apply for Council decisions, which is a potentially weakening factor, though it does not appear to have resulted in the Commission adjusting its preferences because of anticipated reactions; there is uncertainty of information – about, for example, how prepared the CEECs are for accession; and there are differences between the member states – on, for example, how fast the enlargement process should proceed, how rigorously the EU's accession criteria should be applied, and what position should be taken on the two highly problematic applications of Cyprus and Turkey. (The Commission's role in the enlargement process is considered further in Chapter 12.)

An example of a policy sphere where there has not been much independent policy leadership is Justice and Home Affairs (JHA).

Emek Uçarer (1999a, 1999b) has shown that in the mid-to-late 1990s the Commission felt unable to launch the bold initiatives which many who were working in this policy sphere would have liked. Rather, it took a 'soft' approach, focusing on agenda-shaping and confidence-building with the Council through the issuing of non-legislative documents in the form of communications. The main constraints on the Commission were treaty-based – it had only a shared right of legislative initiative rather than the exclusive right it had under pillar one, the unanimity rule applied in the Council, and policy tools were only vaguely identified – but there were other constraints, too. Amongst these other constraints were: the JHA Commissioner in the Santer College, Anita Gradin, was cautious by nature, preferred a low-key approach, and was slow to follow through on policy pronouncements; Gradin's *cabinet* members were almost exclusively fellow Swedes, who because Sweden was a new member state had few connections with Commission networks and little experience of how the EU worked; Santer assigned services-level responsibility for JHA to a task force rather than creating a DG (Prodi created a JHA DG in 1999); and the JHA Task Force was quickly overworked and under-staffed (Uçarer, 1999).

The examples of enlargement and JHA thus demonstrate that the Commission's ability to exercise independent leadership in particular policy spheres is contingent on a number of factors. As Pollack (1999: 218) has stated, 'Supranational autonomy and influence . . . is not a simple binary matter of "obedient servants" or "runaway Eurocracies", but rather varies along a continuum between the two points'. This links to an important point made by Schmidt (1997a) regarding the theoretical controversy amongst scholars about the nature of the integration process, which includes the intense debate about whether the Commission exercises independent powers or is but an agent of the member states: the controversies are a consequence not only of the strengths of the theoretical models employed but also of the choice of empirical evidence used.

Concluding remarks

The view taken in this chapter has been that the EU's leadership deficit provides opportunities for the Commission. Using an array of resources the Commission seeks to take advantage of these opportunities and in so doing is able to exercise leadership of various sorts. It is often a contested and disputed leadership, and at some times and in some circumstances it is very difficult for it to be exercised effectively, but it a significant leadership nonetheless.

Those who take an intergovernmental view of the integration process frequently portray the role of the Commission in principal–agent terms, with the member states as the principal and the Commission as their agent. The Commission cannot, it is argued, break free of the control of its principal, especially when the principal has clear and set positions on issues. Breaking free in such circumstances is indeed difficult, and sometimes impossible, but the fact is that on many important issues member states do not have clear and set positions, especially on a collective basis. Moreover, when the Commission is given instructions from the member states, via the European Council or the Council of Ministers, it is often in the form of only general directions.

The Commission is thus well placed to take the lead in initiating and shaping policy deliberations. It is also, as Chapter 10 will show, advantageously positioned to mobilise and mediate between policy actors so as to facilitate and guide decision-making.

The Making of EU Legislation

Types of legislation

EU legislation is issued in three main forms:

- *Directives* are binding in the result to be achieved, but it is left to each member state to decide the most appropriate form and method of incorporating directives into national law.
- *Regulations* are binding in their entirety and are directly applicable in all member states.
- *Decisions* are also binding in their entirety and directly applicable, but whereas regulations are general and are addressed to all member states, decisions are specific to those to whom they are addressed – which may be one or more member states, corporate actors, or even individuals.

In terms of their content there is not a rigid distinction between these three types of legislation, but usually regulations and decisions are concerned with the detailed application of EU law whereas directives are more concerned with the laying down of policy principles that member states must seek to achieve. To put this another way, regulations and decisions usually – although not always – take the form of administrative and implementing legislation, whereas directives tend to be more political in character. In 1999 the EU issued 986 regulations, 655 decisions, and 99 directives (Commission, 2000). This figure represents a considerable fall-off from the 7000–8000 legislative instruments the EU used to issue in an average year. The figure has declined because of legislative streamlining, the importance that is now attached to the subsidiarity principle, and the virtual completion of the SEM legislative programme.

The vast majority of administrative/implementing legislation – that is to say most regulations and decisions – is issued in the name of the Commission, acting on the basis of delegated rule-making powers. The ways in which the Commission uses its administrative legislative powers are examined in Chapter 11.

Most policy legislation, by contrast – that is to say, many directives and a few regulations and decisions – is issued in the name either of the Council (with the consultation and cooperation decision-making procedures applying) or of the EP and the Council (with the co-decision or assent procedures applying). It is with policy-making legislation that this chapter is primarily concerned.

The origins of legislation

As is shown later in the chapter, the EU has four main legislative procedures. Under all four procedures the Commission has the exclusive power under the TEC to formally propose and draft legislation (apart from the JHA policies that were transferred by the Amsterdam Treaty from pillar three of the TEU to pillar one, where there is a five-year transitional period in which the power to propose is shared with the member states). The EP and the Council each have the power to 'request' that the Commission submit proposals on matters they deem to be appropriate, but they cannot insist upon it.

In an immediate sense EU legislation can thus be said to originate with the Commission. More particularly, it can be said to originate with its annual work programme and with the legislative programme that is part of it (see Chapter 9). In a broader sense, however, the origins of EU legislation are many and various. The Commission may be the only body that can formally propose laws (apart from the JHA exception just noted) but in undertaking this proposing function it does not act wholly on the basis of its own ideas and preferences. For far from operating in a vacuum in which in some detached and distanced sense it decides what proposals need to be brought forward in the general EU interest, the Commission operates rather in an environment that results in much of what it does being heavily constrained. More often than not legislative proposals emanate from the Commission not because it has itself identified needs or problems that require tackling but rather because it is honouring treaty or international obligations, it is adjusting or developing already established policy commitments, or it is responding to suggestions and requests of others.

Insofar as numerical assessments can be made of the origins of ideas for legislative proposals, Commission sources always attach a figure of well under 20 per cent to the Commission. For example, John Fitzmaurice, a Commission official, has estimated that '[u]nder

10 per cent of legislation in both 1991 and 1992 arose from spontaneous and independent Commission initiatives' (1994: 186). David Williamson (1995), a former Commission Secretary-General, has estimated that around 15 per cent of legislative proposals 'start out' as Commission initiatives. A Commission analysis of 535 of its proposals in 1991 concluded that only 30 had been its own ideas, though the 30 did include controversial proposals on maternity leave, working time, and the liberalisation of electricity markets (Grant, 1994: 220). And data collected by Santer's *cabinet* put the figure of pure 'spontaneous' Commission initiatives at between 5 and 10 per cent (Peterson, 1999b: 59).

Even allowing for the many questions that can be posed against such numerical assessments, it is thus clear that the Commission is not the 'initial mover' of most EU legislation. Rather the 'real' origins of legislation normally lie elsewhere. Three of these origins will now be examined.

The policy inheritance

Most EU legislation necessarily takes the form of developing, adjusting, and updating existing and ongoing policy commitments. As has been shown in previous chapters, the Commission plays an important role in devising and formulating these commitments, but final decisions on their contents are taken by the Council or by the EP and the Council. Moreover, once commitments are established on the EU policy agenda, they are discussed in Council and EP forums, so the Commission usually has a reasonably clear idea on what legislative measures the EP and the Council wish to have brought forward and what will be acceptable.

The *new* legislative initiatives contained in The Commission's 'Work Programme For 1998' illustrate how much of the Commission's legislative proposing function takes the form of following-up on existing programmes and priorities (Commission, 1998b). Of the 31 new proposals, 14 consisted of measures designed to give legislative effect to the July 1997 *Agenda 2000* document (Commission, 1997b), with most of these 14 consisting of amendments and/or revisions to the CAP and the Structural Funds. Of the other 17 new proposals, several fell within the broad framework of the still continuing SEM programme (including proposals covering financial services, VAT rates, and late payments in commercial transactions), three were set within the priorities of the Fifth Environmental Action Programme (national emission ceilings, air quality, and electronic waste), and a number of others built on existing commitments (including developing the social sector and extending the scope of the Working Time Directive).

Other EU institutions

Several EU institutions other than the Commission wish to be involved in the process of legislative proposing. The most important of these institutions are the European Council, the Council of Ministers and the EP, but in their (more limited) spheres of reference, the Economic and Social Committee (ESC) and the Committee of the Regions (CoR) also attempt to exercise influence.

The Commission's *Agenda 2000* document (Commission, 1997b) illustrates how these other EU institutions can signal their legislative wishes and preferences to the Commission. The document itself was framed very much in the knowledge of the preferences of the other EU institutions on the issues under consideration – notably future EU financing and reform of the CAP and the Structural Funds. Once it was published, and prior to the issuing of legislative proposals designed to give it legislative effect, *Agenda 2000* was considered at length by the Council, the EP, the ESC and the CoR. The Commission, as is customary, was represented at all relevant meetings of these bodies (albeit in some cases only by junior officials) and had several resolutions/declarations/statements submitted to it. So, to take the Agriculture Council by way of example, the agricultural and rural implications of *Agenda 2000* were considered at four ministerial level meetings (in July, September, October and November 1997) and at several meetings of both COREPER and the Special Committee on Agriculture (SCA – the senior Council agriculture preparatory/advisory body). The November ministerial meeting issued a five-page 'outcome of proceedings' that set out, in broad terms, the ministers' reactions to the *Agenda 2000* document and called on the Commission 'to frame, at the earliest opportunity, its formal proposals on the basis of the above agreed approach and in the light of the detailed positions already stated by Member States both in the SCA . . . and in the Agriculture Council' (Council Press Release, 17–19 November 1997: 8). Somewhat unusually, this ministerial document was attached in an approving manner to the Conclusions of the December 1997 meeting of the Luxembourg European Council, and was thus given added force.

It was given added force because although the European Council has no treaty-based power to issue instructions or requests to the Commission, the fact is that its political standing means that the Commission has little option but to comply with any instructions or requests the European Council issues to it. Normally, such instructions or requests are not problematical for the Commission, since many of the deliberations at European Council meetings are based to at least some degree on Commission documents. So, for example, at the June 1997 Amsterdam European Council a discussion on the internal market was focused on the Commission's *Action Plan for the Single Market* that had just been published (Commission, 1997i). The summit welcomed the Action Plan, endorsed its overall objective, and opened the door to legislative proposals:

> The European Council requests the Commission to examine ways and means of guaranteeing in an effective manner the free movement of goods. It requests the Commission to submit relevant proposals before its next meeting in December 1997 . . .
> It further invites the Council [of Ministers] to take the necessary steps, where appropriate on the basis of further proposals by the Commission, to reach the widest possible agreement by early 1999 on the other key areas of the internal market. (European Council, 1997a: 13)

Such 'invitations' by the European Council strengthen the Commission's hand when it brings forward proposals. For precisely this reason they are sometimes positively sought.

By contrast with the European Council, the Council of Ministers and the EP do have the treaty power to request the Commission to submit proposals. They do not, however, have the formal power to specify the contents of the proposals or to lay down a timetable for their submission, although they can, of course, let their views be known. The power of request has been more used by the Council than by the EP, and with greater effect. An example of a Council request, which as is frequently the case was made in the context of an ongoing dialogue with the Commission, is that made by the Environment Council in June 1999: the Council asked the Commission to continue negotiations with car manufacturers aimed at the conclusion of environmental agreements committing the manufacturers to reducing CO_2 emissions, but should the negotiations fail the Commission should 'submit to Council for its October meeting a detailed assessment of alternative measures envisaged, including possible legislation' (Council Press Release, 9406/99).

The EP has been hampered in its use of the power to request by a requirement that an absolute majority of MEPs must support the request (absolute majorities are difficult to achieve in the EP, even on the most important of issues), and by the Commission tending to be less responsive to the EP than to the Council. Since the EP was given the power to request by the Maastricht Treaty, only a handful of requests have been made – six up to March 2000 – on such subjects as car insurance, fire safety, and environmental liability. The Commission has responded to these EP requests in various ways – including taking little action at all, issuing consultation papers, and producing one legislative proposal on car insurance in 1997. In its March 2000 resolution on the Commission's annual legislative programme the EP expressed its regret that the Commission had so far shown so little response to Parliament's calls for specific legislative proposals (*Session News: The Week*, 13–17 March 2000).

Over and above direction that is provided to the Commission through collective and formal actions by the Council and the EP, individual members of these two institutions attempt to exert influence through informal contacts with Commissioners and Commission officials. As is evident throughout this book, the Commission is involved in a very wide range of cooperative relationships with the Council and the EP, so representatives of these institutions are in frequent contact with one another in all sorts of ways. There are, therefore, countless informal settings and occasions – on the way to meetings, in dining rooms, in social gatherings and so on – when something might be suggested or said by Council and EP representatives that the Commission notes and acts upon.

Running alongside Commission–Council contacts are countless contacts between the Commission and representatives of the member states. An important way in which national governments seek to develop and maintain close contacts with the Commission is through officials in their Permanent Representations in Brussels cultivating close links with their Commission counterparts. Often such contacts spill over into close personal relations, especially between fellow nationals.

In addition to the EU institutions that wish to be involved in originating legislative proposals, there is an institution that may not consciously wish to be involved but sometimes is so – the ECJ. Rulings by the Court can significantly affect policy contexts and understandings and can prompt – sometimes reluctantly, but frequently willingly – the Commission into legislative action, often in difficult policy areas. A proposal brought forward in 1996 to amend a 1986 directive on equal treatment for men and women in occupational social security schemes provides an example of the Commission being so prompted. The 1986 directive contained derogations so as to satisfy national governments which wished to see pensionable age and survivors' pensions excluded from its scope. However, a number of Court judgements, commencing with the 1990 *Barber* v. *Guardian Royal Exchange* judgement (C-262/88), ruled that the derogations were invalid, so with its 1996 proposal the Commission was seeking to bring legislation into line with ECJ case law.

Interests

A description of the large number and wide range of interests that wish to have access to the Commission was given in Chapter 8. It was emphasised there that such wishes are often accommodated, with the Commission making itself available to, and consulting with, interests via a variety of formal and informal channels. A central reason why interests and the Commission interact so much is that they are in a classic situation of resource interdependency. On the one hand, interests wish for access to the Commission because it undertakes functions that directly affect them. On the other hand, the Commission wishes for relationships with interests because they often are sources of information and support which the Commission needs or can use.

The extent to which the Commission is swayed by interests in its policy and legislative thinking and actions does, of course, depend on many factors, not the least of which are the constraints of the policy inheritance and the influence that is being exerted by other EU institutions and by Commission advisory committees. In general, however, it can be said that the more influential interests are those that have at least some of the following characteristics: control of information and expertise that the Commission needs or would like; the ability, when necessary, to provide that information and expertise quickly and concisely; resources sufficient to permit well organised lobbying; economic and political weight; convincing representational claims; internal cohesion and associated clear and consistent views; and access to relevant Commission representatives (Nugent, 1999: 313–15).

The European Round Table of Industrialists (ERT) – which brings together, on an invitation-only basis, 50 or so chief executives of large multi-national companies – is an example of an umbrella interest grouping (it is not an interest group as traditionally defined) that has been able to promote the interests of members through legislative action. Formed, with the support of the Commission, in the early 1980s as a forum for promoting improvements in the European business environment, it did much to set the agenda for the SEM programme and once that programme was under way it kept a close monitoring and lobbying watch on its contents and progress (Green Cowles, 1995). In terms of sectoral areas, the ERT has taken a particular interest in information technology (IT), and according to Collins (1993) has done much to influence the contents of Commission IT policy.

The preparation of legislative proposals

The responsibility for preparing a legislative proposal lies with the DG under whose policy remit the proposal falls. When a proposal crosses the remits of more than one DG then a decision has to be made as to which is to be the lead DG, or *chef de file*. Usually this is a reasonably straightforward matter, with the balance of the policy content of the proposal clearly being tipped in a particular direction. Occasionally, however, the right to be the lead DG may be disputed. If in such circumstances the DGs concerned cannot agree on which of them is to take the lead, the Secretariat General may have to arbitrate.

Within the lead DG a senior to middle-ranking official – usually between A3 and A5 grade, and normally a head of unit or an official with an appropriate expertise – assumes responsibility for what is known as the *dossier* (file) on the proposal. This involves preparing the proposal and shepherding it through its decision-making stages. In working on the drafting of the proposal this official – known as the *rapporteur* – has an absolutely crucial task since the legislation that is eventually adopted is likely to contain most of what is in the Commission's draft (though see the discussion later in the chapter on this point).

The manoeuvrability and flexibility available to *rapporteurs* – and the line managers who watch over and authorise their actions – varies according to circumstances. As regards working methods, there are usually some margins of choice in respect of such matters as whether draft proposals should be preceded by background position papers, the nature and extent of consultation with external interests, and the stage at which the Commissioner's *cabinet* is made aware of and is asked to comment on developments. As regards the contents of proposals, there is normally more manoeuvrability for new proposals in expanding policy areas than for proposals that consist essentially of measures designed to give effect to policy guidelines laid down in existing framework legislation.

No matter what, however, the discretion available to *rapporteurs* may be, the drafting process is patterned and constraints are imposed in that a number of requirements and features invariably apply. Prominent amongst these requirements and features are the following.

Lead DGs consult with other DGs where interests overlap

Precisely how, and to what extent, consultation occurs depends very much on the circumstances applying. If there is very little overlap consultation may consist of little more than circulating potentially interested DGs with the *dossier*, keeping them informed of developments, and proceeding if no objections are raised. If, however, there is considerable overlap, if other DGs wish to take a close interest in a proposal, or if objections are raised, there may be extensive informal exchanges between officials and the convening of one or more inter-service meetings. Such meetings may be *ad hoc* in nature or based on one of the many permanent inter-service groups that exist in parts of the Commission. Inter-service meetings, which are normally chaired from the lead DG, often start off as information-sharing occasions but spill over into consensus-building exercises.

In cases of doubt or of dispute the Secretariat General decides which services must be consulted on proposals. It also keeps an overall check on coordination procedures and ensures that unresolved differences between DGs are noted and explained in *dossiers* as they make their way through the Commission system.

Advisory Committees are consulted

Over 500 advisory committees are clustered around the Commission. These committees vary enormously in terms of their powers, their functions, their sizes, the nature of their composition, the regularity of their meetings, and their ways of operating. (A list of the committees is published each year in the *General Budget of the EU*, which appears in the *Official Journal* in January or February.)

Notwithstanding the variations between them, most committees have at least some potential to feed ideas into the Commission which can affect its thinking both in respect of the initiation, and more especially the drafting, of legislation. Even those committees that are designed not so much to offer policy and legislative advice but rather to assist with the implementation of EU programmes and/or to enable the national governments to oversee and control the way in which the Commission uses its delegated administrative powers can exercise an influence on the Commission's legislative thinking and actions. This is partly because the Commission's policy and legislation-making re-sponsibilities overlap with its implementation responsibilities. It is partly also because the Commission is generally only too willing to be given good advice, especially if it is from those who can be useful to it by, perhaps, providing it with much-needed information or by assisting it with the passage and implementation of legislation.

The point having been made that even implementing and over-seeing committees can exercise an influence on the Commission in respect of its legislative deliberations, attention here is now focused on what are normally called advisory committees. (Implementing and overseeing committees are examined in Chapter 11.) Advisory com-mittees are of two main types, with hybrids ranged in between. The following account of these committees draws on Nugent (1999: 121–3).

- *Expert committees* consist of national officials and experts. Although nominated by national governments the members are not normally viewed as official governmental spokesmen so it is usually possible for the committees to conduct their affairs on an informal basis. Many of these committees are well established, meet on a fairly regular basis, and have a more or less fixed membership; others are *ad hoc* – often set up to discuss an early draft of a Commission legislative proposal – and can hardly be even described as committees in that they may only ever meet once or twice. As for their interests and concerns, some of the committees are broad and wide-ranging, such as the Advisory Committee on Restrictive Practices and Dominant Positions and the Advisory Committee on Media, while others are more specialised and technical, such as the Advisory Committee on

Unfair Pricing Practices in Maritime Transport and the Committee on the Export of Cultural Goods.

- *Consultative committees* are composed of representatives of sectional interests and are organised and funded by the Commission without reference to the national governments. Members are normally appointed by the Commission from nominations made by representative EU-level organisations: either umbrella groups such as the Union of Industrial and Employers' Confederations of Europe (UNICE), the European Trade Union Confederation (ETUC), and the Committee of Agricultural Organisations in the European Union (COPA), or more specialised sectoral organisations and liaison groups such as the European Association of Consumer Electronics Manufacturers (EACEM), the European Biotechnology Coordinating Group (EBCG), and the Committee of Transport Unions in the Community (ITF–ICFTU). The effect of this appointments policy is that the consultative committees are made up overwhelmingly of full-time employees of associations and groups.

The advisory committees are usually chaired and serviced by the Commission. A few are serviced by the Council and are, technically, Council committees, but the Commission is entitled to observer status on these so the distinction between the two types of committees is of little significance in terms of their ability to advise the Commission.

The extent to which policy sectors are covered by advisory committees varies. One factor making for variation is the importance of policy within the EU's policy framework – it is hardly surprising, for example, that there are many more agricultural advisory committees than there are educational advisory committees. Another factor is the dependence of the Commission in particular policy areas on outside expertise and technical knowledge. And a third factor is the preferences of DGs – some incline towards the establishment of committees to provide them with advice while others prefer to do their listening in less structured ways.

The influence exercised by advisory committees varies enormously. In general, the committees of national experts are better placed than the consultative committees. There are a number of reasons for this. First, Commission consultation with expert committees is usually compulsory in the procedure for drafting legislation, whereas it is usually optional with the consultative committees. Second, expert committees can often go beyond offering the Commission technical advice to alerting it to probable governmental reactions to a proposal and, therefore, to possible problems that may arise at a future decision-making stage if certain views are not incorporated. Indeed, members of expert committees are often also members of the working parties that examine Commission proposals when they are passed to the Council. Third, expert committees tend to meet more regularly than consultative committees – often convening as and when it is deemed to be useful rather than being restricted, as most consultative committees are, to no more than two or three meetings a year. Usually, consultative committees are at their most influential when they have high-ranking figures amongst their membership, when they are given the opportunity to discuss policy at an early stage of development, when the timetable for the enactment of a proposal is flexible, and when the matter under consideration is not too constrained by existing legislation.

External policy actors are consulted

An array of external policy actors were shown earlier in the chapter to exercise influence over the origins of legislative proposals. So, too, can they exercise influence over the drafting of proposals.

External policy actors that are well networked and/or which are regarded by the Commission as being important are often invited to make an input at the policy-drafting stage by being given early warning of proposals. Other policy actors may be invited to make a contribution because they are in possession of information or have an expertise that the Commission itself does not have. These actors may include consultancies and research institutes from whom reports may be contracted.

Four factors are especially important in determining the impact external actors can have on the content of legislative proposals:

- The stage at which consultation occurs. Broadly speaking, the more advanced a draft is the more difficult it is to change: hence the thirst of external actors for advance information on Commission thinking.
- The extent to which outsiders are in possession of knowledge and expertise that the Commission does not itself have, or of which it can make use.

- The potential for outsiders to create difficulties for the Commission at a later stage of the legislative process if their views are not accommodated. For example, lobbyists' views may return to the legislative process via the EP or the Council.
- The preferred way of working of Commission officials. Whilst the Commission as an institution leans towards openness and transparency, individual officials can vary in the extent to which they are receptive to views and ideas from outside.

The legal base is important

When proposing legislation an extremely important consideration for the Commission is the treaty article or articles on which the proposed legislation is to be based. The importance of this is that the treaty base determines which legislative procedure applies, which in turn determines the formal powers of the institutions involved in the legislative process and also the means by which they can exercise their powers. Usually the choice of legal base is straightforward and uncontroversial, but sometimes it is queried – by, for example, the EP claiming that the treaty base is incorrect and that another base, involving a procedure that gives it more power, should have been selected. Legal challenges to the treaty base can result in appeals to the ECJ, so the Commission – through its Legal Service – has to be extremely careful when specifying the treaty base in cases where legislation does not fall easily and readily under one single treaty article.

Financial considerations are weighed and considered

New proposals must have a financial statement attached to them and must be referred to the Personnel and Administration DG and the Budget DG for their observations. All proposals with resource implications need to be developed in close cooperation with these DGs.

Subsidiarity and proportionality must be respected

The principles of subsidiarity and proportionality have been accorded considerable importance by the EU since the early 1990s.

At the 1992 Edinburgh European Council the Commission undertook to include in the explanatory memorandum that accompanies all legislative proposals a justification in terms of the subsidiarity principle (European Council, 1992) and in 1993 an interinstitutional agreement to this effect was concluded between the Commission, the Council and the EP. Just precisely what subsidiarity involves has been much debated in EU circles, but it is generally taken to mean that the EU should take action only if objectives cannot be sufficiently achieved through member states acting by themselves.

The related principle of proportionality means that EU action should not exceed what is necessary to achieve agreed objectives.

Legislation should be accessible

Accompanying the attention that has been accorded to subsidiarity and proportionality, greater attention has been given since the mid-1990s to the quality of EU legislation. More particularly, there has been a keen interest in ensuring that EU legislation is as simple, comprehensible, transparent and accessible as possible.

One means of improving the quality of EU legislation has been to consolidate existing legislation, often by incorporating streamlined versions of a number of laws into one framework law. So, between 1995 and 1998 some 435 consolidations were completed, allowing 3000 or so legal instruments to be merged (*European Report*, 2365, 5 December 1998). An example of such a consolidation is a 1998 directive on the approximation of member states' legislation relating to machinery, which superseded several existing directives.

Another means of improving the quality of legislation has been to ensure that new legislation is free from jargon. With this in mind, the Council in June 1993 issued a resolution containing guidelines against which Council texts should be checked as they were drafted (Council, 1993). Jacques Delors endorsed the guidelines in a written answer given to the EP in November 1993 and stated that the Commission would take the necessary action to implement them (*Official Journal*, C226/35, 16/8/1994). The importance of the quality of legislation was further reaffirmed by the national governments in 1997 when they attached a declaration on the subject to the Amsterdam Treaty which called for the EP, the Council and the Commission to establish guidelines on the quality of the drafting of Community legislation (Treaty of Amsterdam, Declaration 3a). The guidelines were subsequently set down in an EP–Council–Commission interinstitutional agreement of December 1998 (*Interinstitutional Agreement*, 1999). The thrust of the agreement, which covered much the same ground as the Council's 1993 resolution, is illustrated by Article 4: 'Provisions of acts shall be as homogeneous as possible. Overly long articles and sentences, unnecessarily convoluted wording and excessive use of abbreviations should be avoided.' The agreement also called for all three institutions to take appropriate measures – such as creating drafting units and providing training in legal drafting for officials – to ensure the guidelines would be properly applied.

A more specific initiative designed to promote legislative clarity and accessibility is *Simpler Legislation for the Internal Market* (SLIM) which was launched by the Commission in 1996. Aimed at ensuring that internal market legislation is as simple and transparent as possible, SLIM was initially limited to four specific market areas on a trial basis, but it has progressively been extended and now covers such important areas as value added tax and banking.

The impact on business must be considered

Since 1986 the Commission has operated a business impact assessment system for new legislative proposals. This involves attaching to proposals a *fiche d'impact* that specifies who will be affected by the legislation, what companies will have to do to comply, what the economic effects are likely to be, and the implications for small and medium-sized enterprises (SMEs).

For the first few years of the scheme all new legislative proposals required business impact assessments, which in the peak years of the single market legislative programme meant that upwards of 300 assessments had to be undertaken. This strained resources, with the consequence that assessments usually did not exceed one page, were drawn up at the last minute, and were generally ineffective (*Business Europe*, 29 January 1997). The format has now been changed, so that assessments are much more thorough but are undertaken only on legislation with significant implications for business.

The impact on the environment must be considered

The Commission is committed to ensuring that environmental concerns are integrated into other EU policy areas as appropriate. As part of this commitment, legislative proposals that have significant environmental implications must be subject to environmental impact assessments and to evaluations of the environmental costs and benefits.

The progression of legislative proposals within the Commission

Allowing for differences arising from the importance, controversiality and policy nature of proposals, and allowing too for the fact that the sequence of events is by no means fixed, legislative drafts typically proceed through the Commission system in the following manner:

- The early drafting work is undertaken mainly by the *rapporteur* in the lead DG. This drafting process proceeds on the basis of extensive internal and external consultation.
- Heads of unit keep their directors informed about progress, and the latter may suggest changes to drafts.
- Directors general and/or deputy directors general in lead DGs have a look at advanced drafts, but are unlikely to be much interested in details unless proposals are controversial.
- The 'board of management' – often called the policy group – of the lead DG is kept in touch with developments, and can become involved at any stage of the drafting process. The composition of this management body varies between DGs. In the Environment DG, for example, it consists of the director general and an assistant, the deputy director general, and the six directors. This Environment Policy Group meets weekly to review, amongst other things, progress on the DG's various draft proposals (McCormick, 2000).
- When there is controversy, proposals may be discussed by directors general and/or deputy directors general of DGs that have an interest. These discussions may be held on a bi-lateral basis or possibly in one of the weekly meetings of directors general and their deputies.
- All draft proposals must be referred to the Legal Service for an opinion on their legality. The point in the process at which the Legal Service is brought in depends very much on whether there are thought to be legal problems and whether the lead DG has its own legal unit. Favourable opinions from the Legal Service do not prevent it from suggesting drafting amendments.
- Before moving towards formal adoption by the College, drafts require the approval of the lead Commissioner. At what stage the Commission, via his/her *cabinet*, becomes involved with a draft depends on a number of factors. Early reference to the Commissioner's *cabinet* – usually through the person in the

cabinet who is responsible for the policy area in question – is most common when a proposal is deemed to be particularly important and/or controversial and when easy relations exist between officials and *cabinet* members. Sometimes, if circumstances appear to warrant it, the *cabinets* of other interested Commissioners are also contacted and sounded out for their views. Inputs from *cabinets* tend to be focused on political rather than on technical considerations: does the proposal chime with the Commissioner's policy preferences?; is there a powerful interest in the Commissioner's home state which will be damaged by the proposal?; and is it worth softening/hardening/adjusting the proposal to head off opposition from other Commissioners or from, at a later decision-making stage, a member state or states?

- Once a draft has been approved by the lead Commissioner, the Registry within the Secretariat General – commonly known as the *greffe* – checks that all formal procedures and requirements have been met. Assuming they have been, the proposal can be formally adopted by the College in the name of the Commission.

- As was explained in Chapter 4, the College can formally adopt measures by three means: *habilitation* (delegated powers to the Commissioner), written procedure, and decision by the College at its weekly meeting. Legislative proposals that are not of a very routine and administrative kind are normally adopted by the third of these means. Where proposals are uncontroversial and there are no outstanding differences between Commissioners or DGs then the meeting of *chefs de cabinets*, which prepares College meetings, lists them as A-points and they are approved by the College without discussion. Where, however, there is controversy and there are differences, attempts are made by *cabinets* to resolve differences before the College meets. This may involve referring proposals back to *rapporteurs* for re-drafting. If problems cannot be resolved at *cabinet* level they are likely to be eventually referred to the College, where the main possible outcomes are: reference back down the system, with suggestions perhaps attached as to where agreement might be found; agreement on outstanding issues; disagreement on outstanding issues, and no vote is taken – perhaps because powerful Commissioners are closely involved with the proposal, or because it is clear that the proposal in its existing form will be strongly resisted by important member states; and disagreement on outstanding issues, and a vote is taken.

*   *   *

As this and the previous section of this chapter have shown, the processes within the Commission for preparing EU legislation are complex. They are often also extremely protracted. Although some stages of the process have timetables attached to them, others do not. So, for example, DGs that are asked by lead DGs whether they wish to take an interest in a proposal must respond within ten working days, but there is no overall obligation on the Commission to act quickly if it chooses not to develop or formally adopt a proposal until it is assured of having sufficient support amongst the governments of member states. It is not uncommon for several years to pass between a *rapporteur* starting work on an initial draft and the College formally adopting a proposal.

The Commission's attempts to develop legislation regulating media ownership can be taken to illustrate how and why the preparation of legislative proposals can be so drawn out. As Arribas (1997) has shown, this issue was on the Commission's agenda from 1984, but it was seriously taken up only in 1992 when the then DG III (Internal Market and Industrial Affairs) issued a consultative Green Paper on the subject (Commission, 1992e). The Green Paper prompted opposition amongst both national governments and affected interests, with several of the former arguing that controls on media ownership were a national rather than an EU concern, and with media companies and advertising agencies arguing that EU controls would limit market expansion. Taking a contrary position, the EP passed a resolution calling for harmonisation of national media regulations and the protection of pluralism. Responding to such views, the DG to which responsibility for the media was transferred in 1993 – the reconstructed DG XV (Internal Market and Financial Services) – issued a follow-up Green Paper in 1994 (Commission, 1994b) in which it extolled the merits of EU-level regulation and suggested a further two-year consultation process. During this consultation process, a draft directive on media concentration was prepared and was submitted to the College by the Internal Market Commissioner, Mario Monti, in mid-1996. The College held a policy debate on the proposal in September 1996, but though Commissioners were able to agree on the general objectives of the proposal they could not agree on how they should be achieved. Reflecting the views of 'their' DGs, Commissioners differed over whether legislation or exhortation was the best approach to the problem, and if there was to be legislation where the balance should be between intervention and liberalism on the one hand and between compulsion and recommendation on the other (for further details see Arribas, 1997: 8–9). The lack of agreement between Commissioners resulted in Commissioner Monti being asked to undertake further work on the proposal in the light of the opinions expressed, and to bring the proposal back to the College when he felt Commissioners might be able to reach a consensus on its contents.

The Commission and the EU's legislative processes

Powers, responsibilities and potential influence

Once legislative proposals have been adopted by the College they are referred to the Council and the EP. They are also referred to the ESC and the CoR when the contents of proposals fall within the remits of these institutions. The ESC and the CoR have only advisory powers, but the Council and the EP have decision-making powers. The nature of these decision-making powers vary according to which legislative procedure applies (see below).

However, whatever procedure applies, the Commission always exercises important powers and responsibilities. There are three main reasons for this:

- As the drafter of proposals the Commission is in command of expert and technical information that the EP and the Council may not have. In consequence, reference is frequently made in EP and Council forums to the Commission for advice and guidance.
- The Commision has treaty powers that can be used in ways that significantly affect the prospects and nature of proposals as they make their way through the legislative process. These powers are outlined below. Some of the powers are reinforced by EP/Council/Commission interinstitutional agreements, such as one in 1999 on the co-decision procedure (*Joint Declaration*, 1999)
- The Commission is represented at all formal stages of legislative procedures: in EP committees and plenary sessions; in Council meetings at all levels (working parties, COREPER, ministerial); and at interinstitutional meetings. It thus has excellent knowledge of what the EP and the Council want and may settle for. This knowledge can be used, often in an informal manner, to promote and broker compromises and settlements on difficult points.

The Commission is thus extremely well placed to be an important actor during EU legislative decision-making processes. In particular, it has the potential to promote proposals and to facilitate their progress. The extent to which, and the ways in which, the Commission in practice is able to play these roles in respect of particular proposals depends on four main factors.

First, do the EP and the Council really want a proposal to be approved, and if so are they prepared to reach accommodations on its contents in the event of disagreements? If the answer to both of these questions is yes, the Commission's ability to help prod a proposal forward is greatly enhanced.

Second, how skilful is/are the Commission representative(s) who are seeking to usher a proposal through the Council and the EP? (Who these representatives are depends mainly on the level of seniority of the forum, whether or not the proposal is controversial, and who is available. So, for example, when a relatively routine proposal is being considered by Council working parties and EP committees the Commission is normally represented by the proposal's *rapporteur* and by an official from the Secretariat General.)

Third, what is the nature of the relations between the Commission's representatives who are involved with a proposal and their counterparts in the EP and the Council? Personal relations can count for a lot in EU policy processes, with the consequence that the Commission's ability to influence the contents and progress of a proposal once it has left the College is enhanced if, for example, its *rapporteur* is able to work closely with the *EP's rapporteur* and with officials from the Council Presidency and Secretariat.

Fourth, what legislative procedure applies? As the next section shows, the Commission's position is not the same under all procedures.

The legislative procedures

The EU has four main legislative procedures: consultation, cooperation, co-decision and assent. An outline now follows of the principal features of these procedures and of the different positions of the Commission within them. (The nature of these procedures is examined at greater length in Nugent, 1999: 360–74.)

Consultation   This is a single reading procedure in which the Council is the sole final decision-maker. However, it cannot take final decisions until it has received the opinion of the EP. On some proposals it must also await the opinions of the ESC and the CoR.

The Commission has two main formal powers under this procedure – powers that it also has available under the cooperation procedure and at the first two stages of the co-decision procedure. First, the Council can make amendments to which the Commission is opposed only by acting unanimously. This rarely occurs, since if the Commission wishes to dig in on a particular point there is always likely to be at least one member state which supports its position. Second, the Commission can change, and *in extremis* can even withdraw, a proposal at any time prior to Council adoption. This latter eventuality is extremely unusual once a proposal is well advanced in the process, but occasionally it has occurred when the Commission has felt that either the Council has emasculated the original purpose of the proposal or has come to believe that events and circumstances have overtaken the rationale or contents of the proposal.

Until the SEA came into effect in 1987 the consultation procedure was the only legislative procedure. It has subsequently been joined by the three other procedures described below, so the policy areas to which it applies have naturally been reduced. Following the Amsterdam Treaty, the main areas to which the consultation procedure applies are agriculture and those justice and home affairs issues that are located within the TEC.

Cooperation This is different from the consultation procedure in that there are two readings and it is much more difficult for the Council to ignore the wishes of the EP.

On receipt of the EP's opinion and, where appropriate, also of the opinions of the ESC and CoR, the Council at its first reading adopts, by qualified majority if necessary, a 'common position'. The Council must provide the EP with an explanation of the common position, and the Commission must explain its own position – especially in respect of EP first-reading amendments that it has not accepted.

At its second reading the EP can approve, amend, reject, or take no action on, the common position. If the first or last of these options is exercised the Council can adopt the common position as a legislative act. If, however, common positions are amended or rejected by an absolute majority of all MEPs, the EP is in a powerful position. It is so because: rejections can be adopted by the Council only by unanimity; amendments that are accepted by the Commission can be adopted by qualified majority but can be amended only by unanimity; amendments that are not accepted by the Commission can be accepted only by unanimity.

This procedure naturally encourages the EP, the Council and the Commission to engage in extensive interinstitutional bargaining. Such bargaining is seen not least at EP second reading stage, when the Commission is obliged to inform MEPs before they formally vote of what its attitude is to their proposed amendments.

The cooperation procedure was first introduced by the SEA and its remit was extended by the Maastricht Treaty. Most of the policy areas falling within its remit were, however, 'upgraded' to the co-decision procedure by the Amsterdam Treaty and its use is now confined to four aspects of EMU.

Co-decision   This procedure, which was created by the Maastricht Treaty, is similar to the cooperation procedure in its early stages, though with two important differences: a text can be adopted at first reading if the Council and the EP are in agreement; the Council is obliged to adopt some common positions by unanimity rather than by qualified majority.

Co-decision extends cooperation in that if the Council at second reading is unable to accept the EP's position, the proposal enters what is virtually a third reading. It does so by being referred to a conciliation committee composed of an equal number of representatives of the Council and the EP. If the committee agrees on a joint text, the proposal is referred back to the Council and the EP for final adoption, with the former acting by QMV and the latter by a majority of the votes cast. Failure by the Council and the EP to agree on a text means that the proposal cannot be adopted.

The Commission's position under conciliation is theoretically weaker than it is during the first two stages of the procedure. This is because it cannot withdraw proposals and amendments to which it is opposed do not require unanimous approval in the Council to be carried. However, the Commission still has a key role, with the TEC article laying down the provisions of the procedure – Article 251 – specifying that the Commission 'shall take part' in the conciliation proceedings and 'shall take all the necessary initiatives with a view to reconciling the positions of the EP and the Council'. This reconciling role is exercised in a number of forums, since much of the business of conciliation is conducted not in formal Council–EP bargaining sessions but in separate meetings of the Council and EP delegations, which the Commission attends, and in trialogue meetings between the heads of the two delegations and the most senior Commission official present. At these meetings the Commission is often invited to contribute to the discussion and to suggest a way forward. One way in which it may do so is by issuing modified proposals.

Following the Amsterdam Treaty, most EU legislation is subject to the co-decision procedure.

Assent   This is the simplest of the four procedures in that it is a single stage procedure and there is no provision for the EP to amend Commission proposals. Assent requires unanimity in the Council, whilst in the EP a simple majority suffices for some measures but an absolute majority is required for others.

The assent procedure is not used for what might be thought of as 'normal' legislation, but rather is reserved for special circumstances. These include international agreements of certain kinds, enlargements, the framework of the Structural Funds, and – a provision introduced by the Amsterdam Treaty – sanctions in the event of a serious and persistent breach of fundamental rights by a member state.

Because many assent issues are thus high-profile and 'macro' in nature, the Commission works very closely with the Council when drafting proposals. Indeed, some proposals involve little more than putting Council political agreements into legal form.

Legislative processes and legislative outcomes

What is the eventual outcome of Commission legislative proposals? There are two aspects to this.

The proportion of Commission proposals that become EU law   It used to be the case – when the Commission was launching scores of proposals each year and when QMV was not generally available – that proposals commonly became bogged down in the Council and never became law. This is now not so acute a problem following the reduction in the number of Commission proposals, the widespread availability of QMV, and the application of timetables to the later stages of the cooperation and co-decision procedures. Nonetheless there still are problems: in November 1998 there were 205 legislative proposals on which the EP had issued an opinion that had been awaiting a Council decision for at least nine months, of which 68 had been waiting since before December 1994 (*Official Journal*, C297/63, 15 October, 1999).

The EP has in the past had neither the powers nor the inclination to be as obstructive as the Council. The powers have increased under treaty reforms, but it is still relatively unusual for the EP to wish to block, as opposed to amend, legislative proposals. Up to the end of 1999 only three proposals had been formally blocked by the EP using its co-decision veto power: in 1994 when it rejected a Council confirmation of its common position on a directive concerning the applicability of open network provision (prior to the Amsterdam Treaty the Council could try to impose its common position in the event of non-agreement in the conciliation committee); in 1995 when it rejected an agreement reached in conciliation committee on a biotechnology directive; and in 1998 when no agreement could be reached in conciliation committee on a directive on investment levies.

Jo Shaw (1995b) has provided an interesting case study of a proposal that the EP played a major part in blocking, though not through the formal exercise of a veto. The proposal was for a Council directive on the liability of suppliers of services (Com (90) 482), which was initially published in 1990. In retrospect, the draft can be seen as having been over-ambitious and as not chiming with the climate of the times in that its approach was based on 'old-style' internal market harmonisation rather than on 'new-style' approximation and subsidiarity. The proposal quickly ran into stiff and almost universal opposition from organisations representing service suppliers. This opposition was not counterbalanced by support from consumer organisations, who were at best only lukewarm in their support – especially after the Commission watered down the proposal in an attempt to placate critics. Opposition within the ESC and, more importantly, the EP, was similarly fierce, with the Legal Affairs Committee of the latter expressing considerable dissatisfaction, especially after the Commission suggested amending the legal base in such a way as would have been to the Parliament's disadvantage. In June 1994 the proposal was formally withdrawn by the Commission, although in effect it had been virtually dead for two years. The Commission gave the reasons for the withdrawal as being opposition to the proposal and the new emphasis on subsidiarity. It indicated that it would explore alternative avenues for progress.

Alternative avenues are commonly used by the Commission when it suffers 'defeats', with measures often brought forward again in either an amended or softer form at a later date. Such an instance occurred in 1996 when the Commission withdrew a proposal on pension funds following resistance in the Council, but then subsequently refloated some of the proposal's ideas in a Green Paper (*European Voice*, 28 November–4 December 1996: 6).

The proportion of Commission proposals that are amended   It is not possible to be precise about how responsive the Commission is to the Council and the EP in terms of incorporating their views into legislative proposals. One reason for this is because views are often communicated off the record – in, for instance, discussions between Commission officials on the one hand and the Council Presidency or the EP *rapporteur* on the other – rather than through formal amendments. A second reason is because the Commission often goes some way to accepting the spirit of amendments but does not accept the way they are constructed or phrased. A third reason is because numerical estimates of the success of amendments do not indicate whether the most significant parts of proposals remain or have been removed. And a fourth reason is because information on Council amendments is not available on a systematic basis.

Bearing in mind these reservations, 'crude figures' indicate a high degree of Commission responsiveness to EP amendments Under the co-decision procedure, at first reading the Commission accepts on average over 50 per cent of EP amendments (the Council accepts over 40 per cent); at second reading – when many EP amendments are in effect rejected first reading amendments – the Commission accepts over 60 per cent (the Council accepts over 45 per cent); at conciliation stage the Council and the EP are usually able to agree joint compromise texts, which may well incorporate further changes to the Commission's original proposal (European Parliament, 1999d: 39–40).

Kreppel (1999) has analysed the Commission's response to particular types of EP amendments under the (since Amsterdam now largely defunct) cooperation procedure. She shows the Commission (and also the Council) to be most receptive to amendments that are largely technical or aimed at clarification, but also accepting a substantial number of 'extension' amendments (expanding the domain of a proposal) and 'policy' amendments (adding a new policy arena).

As regards the proportion of the Commission's draft that remains in proposals that are finally accepted, Hull (1993: 80) estimates that, on average, 80 per cent does so. This is as useful a figure as any in giving a general impression of what occurs but, like the figures just given on EP amendments, it needs to be treated with caution.

Many documented case studies show how extensive variations in the fortunes of Commission proposals can be (see, for example, Peterson and Bomberg, 1999, for a very useful collection of such case studies). Two case studies will be cited here to illustrate this point about variations.

Hooghe (1996c) illustrates considerable Commission success in her analysis of how decisions were made on the reform of the Structural Funds in 1988 and 1992. Her conclusion is that whilst the size of the Funds – what she calls the 'budgetary envelope' – was very much a Council decision, the principles and rules governing the operation of the Funds were determined by the Commission, were contained in the Commission's original legislative proposals, and were little changed by the Council. The Commission, she suggests, 'emerges as the pivotal actor in designing the regulations' (p. 14). A key reason for this was that the Commission 'approached the reform with a distinctly political strategy designed to realise the maximum of its preferences, and by insulating the drafting process to minimise the impact of state preferences' (p. 14).

By contrast, Golub (1996) shows how the policy goals and proposals set out by the Commission in its draft proposal for what became the 1994 Packaging Waste Directive were largely removed by the Council during the legislative process. The Directive, he asserts, 'represented the lowest common denominator because the Commission was forced to capitulate to a qualified majority in the Council' (p. 326).

Concluding remarks

The changes that have been made to the EU's legislative decision-making procedures since the SEA have been focused primarily on the powers of the EP and the decision-making capacity of the Council. However, though the Commission has not been the direct focus of the changes it has been much affected by them. It has been so in three particular respects. First, the increased powers of the EP have meant that the Commission has had to become much more sensitive to the desires and concerns of MEPs at all legislative stages. Second, the increased use of QMV in the Council has meant that the Commission has come to feel that it is not always necessary for it to attempt to accommodate the positions of all member states in its proposals. Third, the changes have increased the need for the Commission to exercise facilitating and brokering skills as law-making has come to based on a triangular interinstitutional relationship.

The Commission's influence over legislation is most obvious in the early stages of law-making, when decisions are made about which of the many policy ideas that are being aired in EU circles ought to be formulated into legislative proposals and when the initial drafting of proposals – over which the Commission has exclusive power – is undertaken. Once drafts have been approved by the College and become formal Commission proposals the Council and the EP become the main policy actors in so far as they are the formal decision-takers. However, the Commission is centrally involved in helping to shepherd proposals through the Council and the EP, which results in it exercising a powerful influence over both the extent to which proposals are amended and their prospects of eventual passage.

Chapter 11

Executive Functions

Introduction

This chapter examines the many executive functions undertaken by the Commission. It does so with three particular questions in mind: what is the nature of the functions?; what are the Commission's powers and capabilities in respect of the functions?; and how are the functions exercised?

The EU-level/national-level balance

Although the Commission carries extensive executive responsibilities, it is restricted in what it can and cannot do because it is heavily reliant on the member states for many aspects of its executive work. For example, it needs member states' approval for much of the administrative legislation it produces and it is dependent on agencies in the member states for the bulk of direct 'day-to-day' implementation of EU policies and laws.

The restrictions that are placed on the Commission are a consequence of the member states' desire to retain in national hands as much executive responsibility as is compatible with the existence of acceptable levels of mutual trust and policy efficiency. A number of overlapping factors combine to explain this preference for administering via national authorities wherever possible:

- In all member states, but in some more strongly than others, retention of executive powers is part of a desire to retain as much national independence as possible.
- In the many policy areas where EU and national policies sit side-by-side – for example, environmental, regional and consumer protection policies – it would create administrative confusion, duplication and inefficiency to have two different sets of officials –

262

one EU and one national – seeking to implement different aspects of an interwoven policy framework.

- Some policies benefit from allowing national officials to make executive decisions on the basis of local knowledge and circumstances. Uniform conformity to the law is not always wholly compatible with the maximisation of efficiency.
- Member states sometimes wish for manoeuvrability and adaptability in policy execution so as to be able to delay or even avoid implementing policies that are seen as being unsuitable and/or undesirable.
- Most significant expansions in the Commission's executive responsibilities have budgetary implications, and there has never been any prospect of member states being willing to increase the EU's budget to anything like the size that would be necessary if the Commission was to start assuming administrative responsibilities of the sort and on the scale of national administrative authorities.
- Policy execution at the national level helps to promote the principle of subsidiarity – a principle that has featured prominently amongst the EU's goals since the early 1990s.

These factors have combined to produce a spectrum of EU policy implementation, at one end of which the Commission carries the main implementing responsibility and at the other end of which national agencies do.

Only a few policy areas fall at the end of the spectrum where implementation is undertaken primarily by the Commission. Some aspects of ECSC, Euratom, and development assistance policies are of this type, as increasingly has become parts of competition policy.

In the middle of the spectrum, where responsibilities are divided between the Commission and national agencies, the precise nature of the balance between the Commission and the national level, and the respective responsibilities and duties of the two, differs considerably according to the policy concerned. In general terms, however, it can be said that the Commission concentrates, as appropriate, on developing, specifying, and adjusting implementing regulations and ground rules, on allocating global (as opposed to detailed and specific) budgetary amounts to spending programmes, on coordinating policy activities, and on monitoring the implementing activities of the national agencies. For their part, the national agencies undertake most of the detailed, ground-level implementation of policy. Policy areas of this type include the Common Commercial Policy (CCP) (which is examined in detail in Chapter 12), the Common Agricultural Policy (CAP), and the Structural Funds.

At the end of the spectrum where the Commission's implementing responsibilities are limited, policies tend to be essentially technical and regulatory in character, and are usually in spheres of activity where European standards have been laid down in EU legislation and/ or via European standards organisations. Examples of the sort of standards which exist are technical standards applying to marketed industrial products, hygiene standards applying to marketed food products, and health and safety standards applying to conditions in the workplace. Once such standards have been set it is the responsibility of national agencies to ensure that they are fully and properly applied on a day-to day basis. Amongst national agencies exercising these responsibilities are industry and trade ministries, factory inspectorates, and health and safety departments. The Commission tries to monitor the diligence and effectiveness of these national agencies and receives reports from them.

This outline of the varying extent of Commission executive responsibilities has, in passing, noted also the varying nature of the involvement. It is with the different aspects of this varying nature that most of the rest of this chapter is concerned.

Rule-maker

By far the greatest quantity of EU legislation is issued in the name of the Commission. Of the 1500–2000 legislative instruments that are issued by the EU each year (a figure that marks a considerable drop from the 6000–7000 that used to be issued), all but 500 or so take the form of Commission legislation. This legislation consists of around 800 regulations, 600 decisions, and 50 directives. In addition, the Commission issues a handful of other instruments – mainly recommendations and opinions – which are designed to be primarily exhortative and advisory in nature, but which have sometimes been interpreted by the ECJ as having legal effect.

The Commission thus appears to be an extremely important legislator. The appearance, however, does not fully reflect reality, for Commission legislation is mostly of a 'second-order' nature and is made via procedures under which the Commission is normally subject to Council scrutiny and, if necessary, control.

The nature of Commission legislation

Commission legislation tends to be highly specific and technical in character and does not normally involve issues that raise questions of political principle and/or judgement. Most Commission legislation is formulated within the framework of enabling Council or EP and Council legislation and has as its purpose adjusting that enabling legislation to changed circumstances and conditions. The adjustment is usually of a virtually automatic kind – with the largest single component of Commission legislation consisting of alterations to agricultural prices and market support measures that have been triggered by changes on world and EU markets. Commission legislation is thus very much implementing or administrative legislation. It is legislation that is vital for quick and effective policy implementation in certain policy areas, but it is precisely because it is administrative rather than political that it is delegated to the Commission. Table 11.1 illustrates the nature of Commission legislation, by listing Commission legislative acts published in a typical issue of the *Official Journal*.

Of course, there is a grey area where administrative law overlaps with policy law and this does give some opportunities to the Commission to use its legislative powers to do more than implement in a purely automatic manner. One such set of opportunities exists in the context of the CCP, where the Commission has powers to apply preventative measures – most notably in the form of anti-dumping duties – to protect the EU market from unfair competition by third countries. Another set of opportunities exists under Article 86 (ex-90) TEC, which gives the Commission powers to directly apply competition rules to a range of public undertakings, including key utilities such as electricity, gas, water, transport and telecommunications. Prior to the launch of the SEM programme in the mid-1980s the Commission did not make much use of this article, but since then it has used it, albeit cautiously and in conjunction with other competition policy instruments, to drive forward liberalisation in most of the major utility sectors. (For detailed analyses of the Commission's use of Article 86, see Cini and McGowan, 1998; Schmidt, 1998.)

A final point that ought to be made on the nature of Commission legislation is that not all of the administrative rules that are necessary to implement EU law are made by the Commission. Most importantly, many rules that are designed to give detailed effect to EU law relating to the internal market are made by European standards

Table 11.1   *Examples of Commission legislation*[†]

I *Acts whose publication is obligatory*

Commission Regulation (EC) No 2557/1999 3 December 1999 establishing the standard import values for determing the entry price of certain fruit and vegetables

* Commission Regulation (EC) No 2558/1999 of 2 December 1999 derogating temporarily from certain provisions on the issuing of export licences with advance fixing of the refund for agricultural products

* Commission Regulation (EC) No 2559/1999 of 3 December 1999 prohibiting fishing for salmon by vessels flying the flag of Sweden

* Commission Regulation (EC) No 2560/1999 of 3 December 1999 prohibiting fishing for herring by vessels flying the flag of Denmark

* Commission Regulation (EC) No 2561/1999 of 3 December 1999 laying down the marketing standard for peas

* Commission Regulation (EC) No 2562/1999 of 3 December 1999 linking the authorisation of certain additives belonging to the group of antibiotics in feeding-stuffs to persons responsible for putting them into circulation ([1])

* Commission Regulation (EC) No 2563/1999 of 3 December 1999 imposing a provisional anti-dumping duty on imports of compact disc boxes originating in the People's Republic of China

Commission Regulation (EC) No 2564/1999 of 3 December 1999 fixing the maximum export refund on wholly milled long grain rice in connection with the invitation to tender issued in Regulation (EC) No 2176/1999

Commission Regulation (EC) No 2565/1999 of 3 December 1999 fixing the maximum export refund on wholly milled round grain rice in connection with the invitation to tender issued in Regulation (EC) No 2180/1999

Commission Regulation (EC) No 2566/1999 of 3 December 1999 fixing the maximum export refund on wholly milled round grain, medium grain and long grain A rice in connection with the invitation to tender issued in Regulation (EC) No 2179/1999

Commission Regulation (EC) No 2567/1999 of 3 December 1999 fixing the maximum export refund on wholly milled medium grain and long grain A rice in connection with the invitation to tender issued in Regulation (EC) No 2178/1999

Commission Regulation (EC) No 2568/1999 of 3 December 1999 correcting Regulation (EC) No 2528/1999 fixing Community producer and import prices for carnations and roses with a view to the application of the arrangements governing imports of certain floricultural products originating in Cyprus, Israel, Jordan, Morocco and the West Bank and Gaza Strip

Commission Regulation (EC) No 2569/1999 of 3 December 1999 repealing Regulation (EC) No 2529/1999 suspending the preferential customs duty and re-establishing the Common Customs Tariff duty on imports of multiflorous (spray) carnations originating in Morocco

Commission Regulation (EC) No 2570/1999 of 3 December 1999 on the sale by tender of beef held by certain intervention agencies and repealing Regulation (EC) No 1616/1999

* **Commission Directive 1999/91/EC of 23 November 1999 amending Directive 90/128/EEC relating to plastic materials and articles intended to come into contact with foodstuffs ([1])**

II *Acts whose publication is not obligatory*

Commission

199/787/EC:

* **Commission Decision of 28 July 1999 on state aid granted by the Federal Republic of Germany to Everts Erfurt GmbH ([1]) *(notified under document number C(1999) 3024)***

1999/788/EC:

* **Commission Decision of 3 December 1999 on protective measures with regard to contamination by dioxins of certain products of porcine and poultry origin intended for human or animal consumption ([1]) *notified under document number C(1999) 4220)***

1999/789/EC:

* **Commission Decision of 3 December 1999 concerning certain protection measures relating to African swine fever in Portugal ([1]) *(notified under document number C(1999) 4224)***

([1]) Text with EEA relevance.

[†] This table lists all Commission legislation published on one 'typical' working day.

Acts whose titles are printed in light type are those relating to day-to-day management of agricultural matters, and are generally valid for a limited period. The titles of all other acts are printed in bold type and preceded by an asterisk.

Source: Official Journal, L310 (4 December 1999).

bodies, especially the *Comité Européen de Normalisation* (CEN). Standards bodies, which are wholly independent of the Commission and which are staffed mostly by 'technical experts' from national administrations and business organisations (many from non-EU member states), spend much of their time operationalising the 'essential requirements' that are set by the EU in 'parent' legislation. So, for example, the 1994 Packaging and Packaging Waste Directive stipulated that all packaging must be 'reusable' and 'recoverable' by 1998, but it was left to the CEN to draft detailed definitions of these terms and set thresholds.

Controls on the making of Commission legislation

Most of the Commission's legislative powers are subject to controls by the Council. Even for relatively straightforward administrative matters the governments of the member states have been reluctant to completely relinquish control, with the consequence that instead of delegating full rule-making powers to the Commission they have created a complex web of monitoring and safeguard mechanisms designed to ensure that the Commission does not have too free a hand. These mechanisms take a number of different forms, but are centred on over 500 committees (more if sub-committees are counted) – known collectively as comitology committees – with which the Commission must work and to which it must submit proposals. The committees are chaired by the Commission and are generally composed of between one and three officials from appropriate national ministries in each member state.

Comitology has long been the subject of controversy, with the Commission complaining that it is not given enough manoeuvrability or independence by the Council. Partly because of these complaints, but partly too because there was felt to be a need to tidy up administrative law-making procedures, a Council decision of July 1987 (87/373 EEC, *Official Journal* L197, 18 July 1987) regularised the nature of Council control mechanisms by dividing them into four broad types. The Commission subsequently continued to complain about aspects of, and the Council's use of, these mechanisms but when, in June 1999, the Council replaced the July 1987 decision – with *Council Decision of 28 June 1999 Laying Down the Procedures for the Exercise of Implementing Powers Conferred on the Commission* (1999/468/EC, *Official Journal*, L184, 17 July 1999) – the four central mechanisms remained in place, albeit in streamlined form. The mechanisms are as follows:

Advisory committees The Commission must take 'the utmost account' of the opinions delivered by these committees, but it is not bound by them. The committees may adopt their opinions by a simple majority vote.

Advisory committees are found in many policy areas and vary considerably in character and remit. Examples include the Advisory Committee on Medical Devices, the Advisory Committee on the Free Movement of Workers, and the Banking Advisory Committee. (See pp. 243–6 for a further description of advisory committees.)

Management committees The Commission does not need the approval of these committees to be able to adopt measures, but if there is a qualified majority in committee against a measure it must be referred to the Council and the Commission may defer application of the measure for a time period not exceeding three months. During the three-month period, the Council may take a different decision by QMV.

Management committees are most commonly, but not exclusively, associated with the CAP. There are over thirty CAP management committees dealing with specific product regimes and with more general agricultural administrative issues. Amongst the busiest of these committees – meeting at least once a fortnight and often once a week – are those dealing with sugar, cereals, wine, beef, and milk and milk products. The work undertaken by agricultural management committees naturally varies according to the nature and requirements of their subject area, but commonly includes such matters as discussing and voting on adjustments to product regime rules, discussing and voting on the release of export subsidies (where EU prices are lower than world prices exporters tender for subventions for exports to third countries), reviewing the general operation of their subject area, and exchanging information on shared interests and problems.

Regulatory committees The Commission needs the support of a qualified majority in these committees to be able to adopt measures. Where no such majorities exist, measures are referred to the Council which may take decisions by QMV within a period not exceeding three months. Measures cannot be adopted pending decisions by the

Council, but if the Council has not acted by the end of the three-month period then measures can be adopted.

Regulatory committees tend to be mainly concerned with harmonisation measures. Some of these committees have broad briefs, such as the Standing Committee on Foodstuffs and the Committee on General Customs Rules, whilst others are highly specialised, such as the committees on Adaptation to Technical and Scientific Progress of Directives which include committees on Dangerous Substances and Preparations, Quality of Water Intended for Human Consumption, and Fertilisers.

Safeguard measures   Rule-making powers involving safeguard measures are not channelled via committees, but in some cases the Commission must consult with member states before adopting such measures and in all cases must notify member states of measures taken. States may then ask for the measure to be referred to the Council which, acting by QMV, may confirm, amend, or revoke the Commission's decision. If the Council takes no decision within a specified time period the Commission's decision is – under one variant of the safeguard measure rules – revoked.

Safeguard measures apply mainly to trade-related policy issues.

The control mechanism that applies in particular cases is specified in the enabling legislation. Given the varying powers of the Commission and the Council under the different mechanisms – with the Commission's powers being greatest under the advisory committee procedure and weakest under the regulatory committee procedure – there are sometimes differences between the Commission and the Council when the mechanism that is to apply is being decided. These differences have been sharpened by what the Commission believes to be insufficient use of the advisory committee procedure: in 1999, for example, implementing powers conferred by the Council on the Commission involved advisory committees in 10 cases, management committees in nearly 90 cases, and regulatory committees in 50 or so cases (Commission, 2000: 378).

The comitology system clearly restricts the Commission's implementing powers and manoeuvrability. Whilst the Commission only rarely suffers defeats in the committees (Falke, 1996) – and some of the busier management committees issue over 100 opinions each year – Commission officials readily acknowledge that they are obliged to anticipate reactions in the committees to measures they are considering proposing. If this anticipation suggests that reactions will be unfavourable, then a measure may not be pursued.

Such problems notwithstanding, however, the Commission is strongly placed within the committees, most especially through its policy expertise and the onus that is placed on opponents of proposed measures to construct negative majorities. Commission officials who are doing a good job and who are sensitive to the views of the member states can normally steer measures through committees without too much difficulty.

As a final point on comitology, it should be emphasised that comitology committees can be very useful to the Commission for a variety of informational and policy purposes. For example, assessments in committees of market situations and discussions of how legislation is working can help provide ideas for future implementing, and even broader legislative, measures. (For further information on, and analysis of, the comitology system see van Schelendelen, 1998; Joerges and Vos, 1999; Franchino, 2000).

Direct implementer

The most important policy area where the Commission undertakes direct implementation is competition policy. The main reason for its role in this area is that the smooth and efficient functioning of the internal market is highly dependent on governments and business firms believing there is a reasonably level playing field as regards the application of competition rules, so it is best to give the responsibility for applying the rules to an independent body.

The Commission's strong and relatively autonomous competition powers derive originally from the treaties, especially Articles 81–89 (ex-85–94) of the TEC which deal with such matters as restrictive practices (Article 81, ex-85), abuse of dominant undertakings (Article 82, ex-86), public undertakings (Article 86, ex-90), and state aid (Articles 87–89, ex-92–94). The adoption by the Council in 1962 of what is known as Regulation 17 gave the Commission considerable executive powers in relation to Articles 85–94 – by, for example, obliging enterprises to provide it with information and enabling it to conduct investigations at the premises of enterprises – but for some years difficulties of various kinds made the Commission reluctant to act with much vigour other than under Article 85. Since the mid-1980s, however, a number of factors have combined to make the

Competition DG much more pro-active in pursuing the implementation of the principles set out in the Treaty. Particularly important amongst these factors have been: the momentum provided by the SEM programme; a number of helpful rulings by the ECJ; the development of a greater self-assuredness and a clearer policy 'mission' on the part of Competition DG officials; the appointment of a series of very effective Commissioners; and the granting of full and exclusive powers under the 1989 Merger Control Regulation in respect of certain types of mergers between companies. (For a fuller consideration of these factors, see McGowan, 1997: 49–52.)

But the increasing pro-activism of the Competition DG has been at a price in that it is not able to deal with all the cases that are referred to it or which it would like to investigate. The main reason for this is that the DG just does not have the resources to deal with what can be highly complex cases requiring long and detailed examinations by investigatory teams comprised of lawyers, economists and accountants. Amongst the 'remedies' the DG has adopted have been: national competition authorities and courts have been urged to deal with more cases; there has been a greater prioritisation of cases; more use has been made of informal settlements; and there has been a greater use of block exemptions for types of cases.

A general point to be emphasised about the Commission's implementing powers in the sphere of competition policy is that they often give it broad discretion and enable it to be an important decision-maker in its own right. This is illustrated, for instance, with state aid, which is permissible only after the Commission has made a decision on its compatibility with generally phrased internal market rules. The Commission has used its state aid powers to build up a solid bank of precedent and consolidated practice, which it uses in its dealings with donors and recipients and which also acts as the base for Council deliberations on state aid matters.

Another general point that ought to be made about the Commission's competition powers is that they are sometimes used as cover by national governments for decisions they wish to take but which they know are unpopular. This happens particularly with state aid, where governments may wish to be seen to be sympathetic to appeals for injections of public money whilst privately being hostile. In such circumstances it can be advantageous to invoke the Commission as the barrier to releasing funds and to use it 'to generate political leverage to attain desired objectives or to diminish the risks of achievable but politically costly policies' (M. P. Smith, 1997a: 172).

An illustration of direct implementation: the Merger Control Regulation

Under the 1989 Merger Control Regulation (Council Regulation 4064/89) the Commission is empowered to decide on the permissibility of mergers between companies whose turnover exceeds specified thresholds – 5 billion euro for world turnover and 250 million euro for EU turnover. The Commission has pressed for these thresholds to be lowered, but with only limited success: the Council has resisted a general lowering of the thresholds, but in 1997 did agree that lower thresholds – of 2.5 billion euro for worldwide turnover and 100 million euro for turnover in at least three EU states – could be applied where proposed mergers would require multiple notification to different national competition authorities.

Proposed mergers that fall within the scope of the Regulation must be notified by the companies concerned to the Merger Task Force (MTF) within the Competition DG. Failure to do so can result in financial penalties being imposed. The first occasion penalties were so imposed was in 1998 when Samsung, the South Korean electronics manufacturer, was fined 33 000 euro for failure to notify the Commission of its takeover of the US computer manufacturer AST Research Incorporated and for carrying out the merger without the Commission's clearance (*European Voice*, 2–8 July 1998). Two features of the Samsung case particularly merit comment. First, neither of the companies involved was European, but their merger was deemed to be subject to Commission authorisation because of the business they conducted in Europe. Second, the fine was relatively small because the Commission decided that the merger had no damaging implications for competition in the computer market: in other words, clearance would have been given had proper notification been made.

The MTF is quite open to, and indeed welcomes, companies that are proposing to merge contacting it informally before a formal notification is made. The MTF has no wish to become embroiled in long, complex and confrontational cases. If, therefore, it can signal its thinking to companies and indicate the sort of conditions that a proposed merger would have to meet to be authorised, then so much the better.

The MTF consists of a relatively small number of officials – about 40 permanent A-grade officials, most of whom are lawyers and economists, plus 15–20 seconded specialists from member states. Each case has an MTF official assigned to it as *rapporteur*, whose duty is, in collaboration with a small team of colleagues, to lead the analysis of the case and prepare a draft decision. In considering the desirability or otherwise of proposed mergers, officials are charged only to consider whether they may impede competition in the internal market. They are not empowered to examine commercial, business or industrial strategies that may be behind mergers.

All draft decisions must be referred to at least five other officials in the DG, the Competition Commission's *cabinet*, and the Commission's Legal Service for observations (McGowan, 1997: 156). On receipt of these observations the *rapporteur* prepares a final recommendation which is referred – for approval or otherwise – up to the Commissioner's *cabinet* and to *chefs de cabinet* and College meetings.

So as not to damage valid business developments or to create market uncertainty, the timetable for dealing with cases is tight. (In contrast to Articles 81 and 82 cases, where the average length of cases is between two and three years.) On receipt of all relevant information, the Commission must decide within one month whether it intends to approve a proposed merger on the grounds that competition will not be harmed or whether it wishes to 'open proceedings'. If it wishes to open proceedings – and it does so in less than 10 per cent of cases – it has four months to carry out an investigation, during which time it is entitled to enter the premises of firms and be granted access to all relevant documentation. Any firm that supplies false information during the course of an enquiry or goes ahead with a merger or takeover without being granted clearance from the Commission is liable to be fined up to 10 per cent of its annual sales.

On the completion of investigations the Commission has one of three options available: approval, disapproval, or approval subject to conditions. Approvals are the most common outcome. Disapprovals are not common, with usually no more than two or three a year. Up to March 2000 only twelve proposed mergers had been officially blocked since the Merger Control Regulation came into effect, though a number of others had in effect been blocked but were not entered in official statistics because the companies concerned, anticipating an unfavourable outcome, withdrew their notification before the Commission publicly announced its decision. (See *European Voice*, 23–29 March 2000, for a list of the mergers officially blocked). Approvals subject to conditions are reasonably common, with firms intending to merge being required, for example, to divest themselves of parts of their activities or to reduce parts of their market share. Such requirements can become the subject of intense discussions, amounting at times almost to negotiations, between, on the one hand, MTF officials and sometimes the Commissioner, and on the other representatives of companies concerned and occasionally national governmental officials and politicians. An example of a case in which MTF requirements led to intense and high-level 'negotiations' occurred in 1997 when the Commission laid down conditions in respect of the merger between the US airline manufacturers Boeing and McDonnell Douglas – a merger that had already been approved without conditions by the US Federal Trade Commission (FTC). Amidst suspicions that the Commission was seeking to protect the European airbus business, both the US Secretary of State, Madeleine Albright, and President Clinton raised the issue with EU counterparts. The merger was eventually cleared when, shortly before a College meeting that seemed likely to vote to block the merger was held, the Commission secured a number of guarantees from the US companies – including Boeing agreeing to drop exclusivity clauses in long-term supply arrangements with three US airlines and agreeing also to make available to competitors patents and licenses obtained via McDonnell's US government defence contracts.

As the Boeing/McDonnell Douglas case shows, the Competition DG and the Competition Commissioner can become, as indeed they can become in all spheres of competition policy implementation, subject to intense pressures in undertaking their Merger Control implementation duties. From within the Commission, representations and pressures commonly come from DGs that are more *dirigiste* in spirit than the liberal-leaning Competition DG and from Commissioners who for policy or national interest reasons see advantages in allowing a proposed merger which does not quite meet the competition criteria to proceed. From outside the Commission, pressures can come from firms that are the subject of investigations (hints and threats of reduced investment in Europe if a merger is not permitted are by no means unknown), from firms that would be affected by a merger, and from the governments of countries where firms directly involved in proposed mergers are located.

Under Romano Prodi mechanisms have been put in place to limit intra-Commission negotiations, and more especially to discourage 'special pleading' and lobbying by Commissioners. For example, Commissioners are now obliged to fully explain to College meetings any objections they may have to MTF recommendations, rather than – as was previously possible – being able to 'hide behind' *cabinet* members acting on their behalf.

Supervision of front-line implementation

As stated above, agencies in the member states undertake most of the front-line implementation of EU policies. So, for example: national customs authorities collect the duties that are imposed on goods entering the EU from third countries; national agricultural officials deal with farmers and traders on matters such as milk quotas, the quality of foodstuffs, and payments for produce and set-aside; and national/regional/local officials of various sorts, working usually via monitoring committees whose membership has been approved by the Commission, consider applications for financial assistance from the Structural Funds. So as to ensure that the policies are applied in an acceptably common manner, the Commission attempts to supervise and monitor the national agencies.

Difficulties for the Commission

The Commission is faced with many difficulties in attempting to carry out its supervisory and monitoring tasks, three of which are especially important.

The first is that the Commission has very limited resources. It just does not have enough staff to watch over the activities of national administrative agencies as closely as is ideally desirable. The Commission therefore depends heavily on the good faith and willing cooperation of the agencies. However, even in those policy spheres where it is in almost constant communication with national officials, the Commission cannot know everything that is going on. And with respect to those areas where contacts and flows of communication between Brussels and national agencies are irregular and not well ordered, it is almost impossible for Commission officials to have a very accurate idea of what is happening 'at the front'.

The second difficulty is that national implementing agencies do not always wish to see EU law fully applied. Environmental policy and state aid policy are examples of policy areas where this is sometimes the case. Reluctance to apply environmental law often arises from the heavy capital investment that is required to meet EU standards on, for example, air and water quality. Reluctance to apply state aid policy usually stems from a desire on the part of national or sub-national administrations to protect or promote national and local economic activity, especially where large numbers of jobs are involved.

The third difficulty is that even where national implementing agencies are willing to cooperate fully, they are not always capable of implementing policies in a manner that the Commission would wish. There are a number of reasons for this:

- Some EU policies are, by their very nature, difficult to administer. The rules may be complicated and/or the activity itself may be difficult to track. The Common Fisheries Policy (CFP) is an example of such a policy area, requiring as it does rules on fishing zones, total allowable catches and conservation measures, and with its implementing mechanisms requiring obligatory and properly entered logbooks, port inspections, and aerial surveillance.
- There are enormous differences between member states in terms of the types of administrative agencies they use for implementation purposes. The extent of these differences has increased over the years as member states have created new, or have made increasing use of existing, sub-national layers of government, and as there has been a general hiving off of many governmental administrative responsibilities to private, quasi-private, and quasi-public agencies. This increasing decentralisation, fragmentation, and agencification of national administrative systems has, as Guy Peters (1997) has noted, tended to diminish the hierarchical control of the governments of the EU's member states. Given that national governments thus have problems with the effectiveness of their implementation agencies, it is clear that the Commission, which is so reliant on the agencies but must deal with them at one stage further removed, is in an even more difficult position.
- National governments are not always willing to pay for the number of inspectors/controllers/administrators that a policy area requires. Fishing may be cited again, with the number of inspectors varying considerably between member states. This means, amongst other things, that there are variations in member states' capacities to check on unofficial landing places and on officially landed fish (as opposed to the fish that are recorded in logbooks).
- There are considerable differences between member states regarding the sanctions that can be applied against transgressors of EU law. To stay with the example of the CFP: a few member states regard breaches of fishing laws as criminal acts which can be subject to imprisonment, fines, forfeit of catch or tackle, or withdrawal of fishing licences; Finland and Denmark regard such breaches as civil offences which are liable to fines only; and some

member states regard such breaches as a matter for administrative penalties only. Clearly these widely different legal positions is a factor fishermen who are considering breaching CFP laws are likely to weigh in their calculations.

- National officials are not always sufficiently trained, experienced, or competent to deal with complex and often rapidly changing EU rules. It does, for example, require a high degree of proficiency to be able to fully understand and accurately administer the maze of complicated regulations that apply to import tariffs or export refunds.

Means and mechanisms used by the Commission to supervise front-line implementation

Given the many problems it faces, how does the Commission supervise front-line implementation? The short answer is that it uses whatever means it judges to be appropriate and it can resource.

An important aspect of the Commission's supervisory function is checking that all member states have the correct legal framework in place. As part of ensuring that this is so, member states must, within specified time periods, notify the Commission of the steps they have taken to incorporate EU directives into national law. When incorporation has not occurred by the date specified within the directive, or has occurred in an incorrect or only partial manner, the Commission follows this up with the member state(s) concerned and if remedial action does not follow may refer the matter to the ECJ. Another way in which the Commission checks that the correct legal framework is in place is via an obligation placed on member states to notify the Commission about all national draft regulations and standards concerning the technical specifications of marketed goods. The purpose of this process of self-notification is to enable the Commission to check that new national legal requirements do not undermine EU legal requirements and so cause barriers to trade within the internal market.

Having the correct legal framework in place is one thing, applying it is quite another. From its offices in Brussels, it is clearly much easier for the Commission to supervise the former than it is the latter. Given its lack of physical presence 'at the front', the Commission uses a number of mechanisms – which vary in their extent, usefulness and effectiveness between policy areas – to assist it in keeping watch on how national officials are applying EU law.

The provision and checking of information is the most important supervisory mechanism used by the Commission, with member states being required to provide it with reports of various kinds on policy application. The Commission also undertakes a limited amount of on-the-spot checking and supervision in the member states.

Paralleling and supplementing the checking and the supervision, the Commission engages in a constant two-way flow of communications with implementing agencies and issues countless explanatory memoranda, codes and notices which provide guidance as to how particular rules should be applied.

Dealing with irregularities

The approach of the Commission to irregularities in front-line policy implementation is considered below in the section on guardian of EU law. Suffice it to note here that an informal approach is usually initially taken – in the form, for example, of discussing problems with relevant management figures in offending member states, holding briefing seminars for senior national officials, and issuing clarificatory letters and tighter guidelines. In the event of such approaches not producing the desired effect, stiffer approaches – involving ultimately reference to the ECJ – may follow.

A case study of implementation supervision

As part of reforms to the CAP, an increasing emphasis has been placed on the promotion of environmentally-friendly farming. An important EU law in this context is Council Regulation 2078/92, which provides financial inducements to farmers to farm in ways that are compatible with environmental protection. The financial inducements take the form of subsidies to compensate farmers for the income losses and extra workload costs incurred by adopting environmentally-sensitive farming methods.

The implementing arrangements for the Regulation are set out in another Regulation – 746/96. This implementing regulation assigns most of the responsibility for the day-to-day management of the scheme to national authorities. In exercising their responsibilities, the national authorities have considerable latitude over such matters as the farming practices falling within the scope of the legislation that they choose to support, the level of subsidies that are to be paid within the ceilings set out in the legislation, and the length of time to which farmers participating in the scheme must commit themselves. Member states must, however, submit their implementation programmes to the Agriculture DG for approval.

At the Commission end of the implementation structure, the Agriculture DG, working in close association with the Environment DG, carries the responsibility for overseeing the implementation undertaken by the national authorities. (The Agriculture DG takes 'precedence' over the Environment DG because it was the lead DG in the drafting of the Regulation and because the subsidies to farmers are drawn from the Guarantee Section of the European Agricultural Guidance and Guarantee Fund.) The responsibility is exercised in three main ways:

- National implementing authorities submit regular monitoring and evaluation reports to the Agri-Environmental Unit in the Agriculture DG. There is also regular financial monitoring.
- Control visits are made by Agriculture DG officials to the member states. These officials are not the same as those who deal with the monitoring and evaluation reports, but are drawn from a unit which deals with many different types of CAP control visits.
- There are frequent contacts between officials in the member states and officials in the Agriculture and, to a lesser extent, the Environment, DGs. These contacts can range in character from exchanges of information on the telephone to formal meetings in Brussels.

Where implementation problems with the Regulation are perceived by the Commission to exist, its approach is to move in stages: make sure that relevant officials in member states are aware of their responsibilities and duties under the Regulation; encourage them to act; harry and assert some pressure; and move to legal action only as a last resort.

Guardian of EU law

Though it is not quite a normal executive task, the Commission's role as guardian of EU law is best treated here since it very much overlaps and intermingles with the role of supervisor of policy implementation that has just been examined. Essentially, the legal guardian role requires the Commission to act as a watchdog, doing what it can to ensure that EU law is applied and respected throughout the Union.

This, in turn, requires it to be on guard for possible breaches and transgressions in EU law, to conduct investigations into such possible breaches and transgressions when appropriate, and to take remediative and/or punitive action when necessary.

Investigating cases

The Commission may become aware of possible legal breaches and transgressions in many different ways. Three examples will serve to illustrate this point. In respect of non- or incorrect transposition of directives into national law, that is relatively straightforward for, as was noted above, member states are obliged to notify the Commission of the steps they have taken to give effect to incorporation. In respect of budgetary funds not being used for the purposes for which they were allocated, that is most likely to come to the Commission's attention during audits or on-site spot checks by Commission officials. And in respect of irregularities under the competition policy rules, the Commission is often made aware of possible problems by 'whistle blowing' by individuals, business firms, or governments who believe their interests are being damaged by the alleged illegal actions of another. Whistle blowing that uncovers business cartels is positively encouraged through financial inducements, with the Commission reducing fines on companies that reveal cartels of which they are members and/or which cooperate with Commission enquiries.

The Commission is not in a position to investigate all possible and suspected cases of infringements of EU law. The DGs that are most likely to have to deal with infringements – such as Competition and Environment – are simply not adequately resourced to be able to do this. As Michelle Cini observes of the Competition DG, 'Its work, therefore, is as much about defining how firms and governments ought to behave – that is, establishing the "rules of the game" – as it is about chasing up and prioritising breaches of those rules' (1997: 83).

When it is decided to pursue a case – perhaps because it is especially important, it is high-profile, it could be used to send out a warning signal to other possible transgressors, or it just looks as though it will be relatively straightforward to investigate – the Commission does not rush to judgement. For it to be seen as a fair and impartial guardian of EU law and, more broadly, if its institutional standing in the EU system is to remain high, it must be reasonably sure of its ground before taking formal action. Furthermore, it is just not in the

Commission's interests to unnecessarily antagonise EU actors with which it must work and on which it is, especially in the case of national governments, highly dependent. The general approach of the Commission when investigating possible irregularities is, therefore, to proceed cautiously. Its precise way of proceeding varies between policy areas – with some policies, for example, requiring more covert operations than others – but most types of cases proceed along the following lines:

- Relevant information is gathered.
- In the first instance, a fairly gentle approach is usually taken with possible offending parties. Encouragement to 'fall in line' and/or to reach an agreement with the Commission is normally preferred to heavy-handed formal action. This use of informal proceedings and settlements acts as a sort of enforcement shortcut.
- Whenever possible, cases are pushed back 'down the line' to national governments and other national implementing agencies.
- Matters are investigated fully before final decisions are reached on whether to initiate formal action. Such investigations may involve 'site visits', though the Commission's investigating powers 'on site' vary considerably between policy areas – the powers being greatest in respect of competition policy where, in so-called 'dawn raids', Commission officials can insist on access to premises and all relevant documentation. An example of a 'dawn raid' based on competition powers occurred in July 1999 when Commission officials entered, unannounced, the premises of Coca-Cola plants and bottlers in four European countries as part of an investigation into claims that the drinks company was abusing its dominant market position by offering retailers unlawful incentives.
- If the evidence indicates that an infringement has occurred and informal processes do not rectify the situation to the Commission's satisfaction, then formal procedures – which are described in the two following sections – are initiated.

Actions against member states

Infringement proceedings are initiated against member states for not notifying the Commission of measures taken to incorporate directives into national law, for non-incorporation or incorrect incorporation of directives, and for non-application or incorrect application of EU law – most commonly in connection with the internal market and industrial affairs, indirect taxation, agriculture, trade, and environmental and consumer protection.

Before any action is taken against a state it is informed by the Commission in a letter of formal notice that it is in possible breach of its legal obligations. It is then usually given a final opportunity to rectify the suspected infringement. If it does not do so, the Commission carries out an investigation and if the breach is confirmed and continued a procedure comes into force, under Article 226 of the TEC, whereby the Commission 'shall deliver a reasoned opinion on the matter after giving the State concerned the opportunity to submit its observations. If the State concerned does not comply with the opinion within the period laid down by the Commission, the latter may bring the matter before the Court of Justice'. Since most infringements have implications for the functioning of the market, the Commission usually seeks to ensure that these procedures operate according to a tight timetable: normally about two months for the state to present its observations and a similar period for it to comply with the reasoned opinion. Most cases are settled at an early stage with, in an average year, the Commission issuing over 1000 letters of formal notice, delivering around 300 reasoned opinions, and making 50–100 references to the ECJ. (Precise figures for each year are set out in the Commission-produced *Annual Report on Monitoring the Application of Community Law* which is published, usually in August, in the *Official Journal*.) One reason for so many early settlements is that most infringements occur not as a result of intentional avoidance of EU law but rather because of genuine differences over interpretation or because national administrative and legislative procedures have occasioned delay. Although there are differences between member states in their enthusiasm for aspects of EU law, they do not usually wish to engage in open confrontation with EU institutions. If states do not wish to submit to an EU law it is, therefore, more customary for them to drag their feet rather than be openly obstructive. Delay can, however, be a form of obstruction in that states know it can be months before the Commission, and years before the ECJ, conclude actions against them.

What sanctions can be imposed against member states for not fulfilling their legal obligations? Prior to the entry into force of the Maastricht Treaty, the Commission had no power to call for or to impose financial penalties against member states deemed to be in breach of EU law. It could do little more than hope that states would recognise its authority as expressed in reasoned opinions, and if they did not do so to proceed to refer cases to the ECJ – though it, too, could not impose financial penalties and, like the Commission, depended on states appreciating that continued avoidance or ignoral of unfavourable judgements could endanger the whole EU legal system. This clearly unsatisfactory position was rectified when the Maastricht Treaty gave the Commission the power, when referring states back to the Court for refusing to comply with an ECJ judgement, to 'specify the amount of the lump sum or penalty payment to be paid by the Member State concerned which it considers appropriate in the circumstances' (Article 228, ex-171, TEC). The final decision on the imposition of a lump sum or penalty payment is left to the Court.

When the Maastricht Treaty entered into force in 1993 the Commission did not rush to use its new powers to ask the Court to impose financial penalties on member states. One reason for this was legal and technical uncertainties as to the size and type of financial penalties that should be imposed. It was not until January 1997 that a sliding scale of penalties was agreed, based on the seriousness of the repercussions of the member state's refusal to apply the Court's judgement, the length of time the ruling had been ignored, and the member state's relative importance in the Union and ability to pay. A second reason why the Commission delayed, and why it is still very cautious about using its power to urge the fining of member states, is the political sensitivities involved. The first application for penalty payments to be heard by the Court was in June 1999 in *Commission v. Greece* (C-387/97), which concerned Greece's failure to observe a judgement concerning the implementation of waste disposal directives. The Commission asked for penalty payments of 24 600 euro per day, but the Advocate General (who looks at the case on behalf of the Court and gives an opinion to it) recommended in September 1999 that the fine should be 15 375 euro per day from the date of notification of the final judgement. (The judgement is awaited at the time of writing.)

Actions against companies

The Commission may have only recently acquired the power to exercise financial sanctions on the governments of member states for unlawful actions, but it has long had the power to exercise such sanctions against public and private sector business firms. It is a power it has been increasingly willing to use, most particularly in respect of the existence of restrictive practices, the abuse of dominant trading positions, and the receipt of unauthorised and illegal state aid.

Restrictive practices and abuse of dominant trading positions can result in the imposition of fines on the companies concerned. Such figures, as with all Commission competition decisions and sanctions, are subject to appeal to the ECJ. Appeals rarely lead to changes of decision, but do sometimes result in reductions in financial penalties. The largest fine to have been imposed to date was 248 million ecu in December 1994 on 33 cement producers, eight associations of under-takings, and the European Cement Association for participating in a market-sharing agreement. The largest fine on a single company, 102 million ecu, was imposed on Volkswagen in January 1998 for preventing cross-border customers from taking advantage of cheaper car prices in some member states.

Unauthorised and illegal state aid cases can result in the Commission instructing the governments of member states concerned to abolish or alter the aid, and can also result in recipient firms being required to repay some or all of the aid. Amongst the most celebrated of many high-profile Commission actions against state aid was the Renault case of the late 1980s: in March 1988 the Commission approved French government aid to Renault subject to certain conditions; the approval was revoked in November 1989 on the grounds that the conditions had not been met; protracted exchanges then followed between the Commission and the French Government on the amount of aid which should be repaid, with an agreement eventually being struck under which Renault was obliged to pay back half of the money it had received. The Renault case has had the effect of encouraging governments and business companies to, in effect, seek to negotiate with the Commission on the amounts and terms of state aid. Such negotiations occurred in 1995, when the Spanish Government announced that it wished to inject 130 billion pesetas of investment aid into the state-owned airline, Iberia. The Commission duly conducted an investigation, led by the Transport Commissioner, Neil Kinnock, and the Transport DG, in close association with the Competition Commissioner, Karel van Miert, and the Competition DG. During the investigation there was an almost constant dialogue between the Commission, the Spanish Government, and Iberia's management, with Kinnock meeting the Spanish Industry Minister no fewer than six times. The final decision, which was announced in January 1996, was to permit 87 billion pesetas of aid, subject to a number of conditions on restructuring and divestment of loss-making holdings. (On the Iberia case, see *European Voice*, 15–21 February 1996: 29; M. P. Smith, 1997a.) Interestingly, and significantly in terms of how the Commission's powers are viewed, the troubled Italian airline, Alitalia, announced shortly after the Iberia decision that it had no wish to follow Iberia's example if it could avoid doing so. According to Alitalia's Commercial Director: 'If we have to go to Brussels, they will force us to cut capacity, limit our aggressive pricing strategy and make us sell assets . . . we absolutely want to avoid that' (*European Voice*, 15–21 February 1996: 29).

Political considerations

Political considerations impinge on many aspects of the Commission's executive work. They do so in a particularly sharp way in respect of its legal guardianship role, especially in competition cases where overstrict and zealous Commission action may be seen by national governments as threatening investment, employment, growth, and general economic well-being. Since the Commission has no wish to upset or politically embarrass national governments, nor any wish to cause economic damage by, for example, taking actions that results in companies transferring their activities outside the EU, it is incumbent upon the Commission to carefully weigh all relevant considerations when taking decisions.

For the most part, the Commission's competition decisions do display political sensitivity. To take, for example, the imposition of financial penalties, fines are often more symbolic than punitive in character, instructed repayments of state aid often constitute only a small proportion of the aid actually received, and decision-making processes leading to the issuing of penalties often incorporate what amount to negotiations between the Commission and offending parties.

Manager of EU finances

The Commission undertakes a number of tasks in connection with the management of EU finances. Most, though not all, of EU finances are channelled through the annual budget and it is on these that attention is primarily focused here. (For accounts of all the Commission's financial tasks and for detailed analyses of the EU's budget and budgetary processes, see Laffan, 1997a; Nugent, 1999.)

As a preliminary point it is worth emphasising that the EU's budget is relatively small in size, amounting – at 93 281 billion euro in commitment payments for 2000 – to just over 1 per cent of total EU GNP. The reason for the budget being so modest is that virtually all policies that weigh heavily on the public purse – including welfare, education, health and defence – are controlled and financed by the member states. The EU has some important expenditure responsibilities – notably in respect of the CAP and the Structural Funds – but most EU policies are essentially regulatory in character. Regulatory policies do have expenditure implications, but mainly for public and private bodies in the member states rather than for the EU itself.

Managing revenue

There are three main sources of EU budgetary revenue: a payment by each member state that is related to the Gross National Product (GNP); a proportion of the Value Added Tax (VAT) that is collected in each member state; and duties and levies that are collected in respect of trade with non-member states.

The Commission oversees the collection of this budgetary revenue. In so doing it has a number of responsibilities which, in practice, interrelate and overlap with one another:

- It specifies what monies national agencies should be collecting on behalf of the EU. Where the monies to be collected are subject to changing rates – as with customs duties and CAP levies – the Commission has to issue updating administrative legislation as required.
- It monitors the activities of national collecting agencies – which are mostly customs, excise, and VAT authorities – to ensure as best it can that they are collecting what they are supposed to collect.
- It explains to national agencies the often highly complex and detailed rules which apply. Amongst the devices commonly used for this purpose are explanatory communications and information exchange seminars.
- It calculates the GNP-based payments which member states make to the budget. This is essentially a technical exercise, but it is sometimes given a political edge by member states challenging the assumptions and figures on which the calculations are made.

Managing expenditure

The extent and nature of the Commission's involvement in managing expenditure varies in relation to both management stage and management approach.

Variations according to management stage   There are, as Levy has noted (1997: 210–15), four management stages in budgetary expenditure:

- *Authorisation*: the processing of requests for funds and the taking of decisions on particular programmes and projects.
- *Allocation and administration*: the operational management of programmes.
- *Audit*: this mainly involves checking that expenditure has been used for its intended purpose, but it overlaps with:
- *Review and evaluation*: consideration of outputs and of the extent to which goals have been achieved.

The Commission is heavily and directly involved at the authorisation, audit, and review and evaluation stages, but is usually less so at the allocation and administration stage where its role is mainly one of monitoring the work of national agencies. One reason for this less active involvement in the allocation and administration stage is the Commission's customary problem of having only limited staffing available – this being the stage that is most demanding on staffing resources. Another reason is that the application of the subsidiarity principle is seen as being appropriate for this stage. And a third reason is that certain principles applying to the implementation of the budget have less of a management impact at the allocation and administration stage. There are four main such principles: expenditure must have a clear base in EU law; expenditure must be provided for in the annual budget that is approved by the Council and the EP; expenditure must be subject to proper financial control mechanisms; and – the most difficult principle to operationalise – expenditure must be aimed at achieving value for money in programme delivery.

The administrative application of the first two of these principles occurs primarily at the authorisation stage. Two bodies give consideration to whether funding applications meet the principles: the member state agencies which draw up and forward applications; and the spending DGs which examine funding applications (for example, the Agriculture DG for CAP funding). (There used to be a third authorising authority body in the form of the Financial Control DG, but this was abolished as part of the reform programme announced in the March 2000 White Paper – see below and Box 2.1.)

The administrative application of the third and fourth principles occurs mainly at the audit and review and evaluation stages. The conduct of these stages is shared with outside bodies rather more than is the authorisation stage. National government and local agencies, the Court of Auditors, and the EP (mainly through its Budgetary Control Committee) are all involved in various ways in the complex and overlapping processes of audit and of review and evaluation. The Commission is obliged to work closely with these outside bodies, not least because: national agencies often have much more detailed information available to them than has the Commission about what is happening 'at the front'; the Court of Auditors is charged with issuing an annual report on the implementation of the budget – a report which has in recent years been very critical of aspects of the ways in which the Commission undertakes its implementation responsibilities; and the EP – acting on the basis of information received from various sources, including the Court of Auditors' annual report – has the responsibility of granting annual discharge to the Commission for the implementation of the budget.

Within the Commission, auditing and review and evaluation functions are undertaken by units in the spending DGs, who are monitored by central auditing bodies (see below and Box 2.1).

Variations according to the management approach applying Strasser (1992) and Levy (1997) have shown that the processes by which the EU implements its expenditure programmes can be grouped into three broad categories of management approach: direct, decentralised, and shared.

- Direct management covers those parts of budgetary expenditure that are managed by the Commission without the assistance of national agencies. Apart from its own administrative expenditure, the most notable types of expenditure in this category are certain external aid programmes and operational research expenditure. The former are often channelled through technical assistance offices (see Chapter 7) whilst the largest single component of the latter is used to fund activities of the Joint Research Centre (JRC).

- Decentralised management takes the form of the Commission establishing the administrative frameworks and rules, national agencies undertaking the front-line implementation, and the Commission overseeing, checking, and evaluating the work of the national agencies. The decentralisation thus occurs primarily, though not exclusively, at the allocation and administration stage of the implementation cycle. Examples of policy areas that are administered in this way are the CAP, the collection of EU revenues, and some development aid programmes. This management approach contains considerable variations in the extent to which national agencies have discretion as to what they can do and how they can operate.

- Shared management also embodies a division of responsibility between the Commission on the one hand and national agencies on the other, with the responsibilities of the latter again being greatest at the allocation and administration stage of implementation. However, whereas under decentralised management the national authorities are essentially agents of the Commission, under shared management they are partners. The main reason why they are partners is that the shared management approach usually applies to programmes and projects which the EU is only partially funding: the rest of the funding is provided most commonly either by member states (as with the Structural Funds), by third countries (as with certain development aid programmes), or by research institutes (as with some R&TD programmes). The most important practical effect of the emphasis on partnership is that national agencies – which often take the form of programme committees of some sort – have real decision-making powers in regard to the local operation of programmes and projects. As under decentralised management, the Commission monitors and reviews the activities of national agencies where shared management applies.

Financial management problems and the reform programme

It became increasingly apparent in the 1990s that all was not well with the Commission's financial management processes and practices. Criticisms were increasingly heard, not least from the Court of Auditors, that between 5 and 10 per cent of the EU budget could not be accounted for and that the Commission's control mechanisms were focusing too much on whether procedures were being followed and not enough on whether spending was achieving its intended results. Whilst the Court and others readily acknowledged that member states – who execute some 80 per cent of the budget – carried much of the responsibility for poor financial management, the Commission was strongly criticised for, amongst other things, unrealistic financial planning, insufficient monitoring, non-implementation of control mechanisms, and failures to make proper checks before making payments.

The criticisms led to the Commission adapting some of its financial practices. In regard, for example, to the Structural Funds, which account for over one-third of budgetary expenditure, the increasing importance of the partnership principle was twinned with greater 'regulatory centralisation and system standardisation' (Levy, 1997: 223). More broadly, the SEM 2000 programme of financial management reform which was launched in 1995 included measures to improve the procedures for verifying expenditure, to strengthen auditing arrangements, and to make all EU legislation as fraud-proof as possible.

Such reforms, however, still left major problems with financial management. These problems became swept up in the crisis which enveloped the Commission from late 1998 with, as was shown in Chapter 2, a major triggering factor in the crisis being strong criticisms of the Commission by the Court of Auditors in its reports on the 1996 and 1997 financial years and the decision by the EP in December 1998 not to grant discharge to the Commission in respect of its implementation of the 1996 budget. The crisis resulted in the establishment of the Committee of Independent Experts (CIE), which produced two reports – in March and September 1999 – that logged numerous weaknesses in the Commission's management of EU finances. For example, regarding the practice of contracting work out, the Committee noted in its second report: 'Generally, there are grounds for believing that the Commission's current difficulties are due not only to a lack of human resources but also to a lack of management tools and the inadequacy of the contracting system, which have made it difficult to contract work out to reliable partners (CIE, 1999b: 31). A theme of both CIE reports was that the Commission had long been aware of system deficiencies, but had been slow to tackle them.

The second CIE report made ninety recommendations for reform, some of which were already under consideration in the Commission or even beginning to be implemented as a result of the earlier SEM 2000, MAP 2000 and DECODE programmes (see Chapter 2, and Stevens 2000). Most of the CIE's proposals were subsequently incorporated in the March 2000 White Paper on the reform of the Commission (Commission, 2000b; see Box 2.1 for a summary of the White Paper's key points). Fundamental reforms to the ways in which the Commission undertakes its financial management tasks are to come into effect as the White Paper proposals are implemented. The key financial management reforms proposals of the Paper are:

- the adoption of activity-based management and budgeting, which will provide for improved financial planning and bring political priorities and the allocation of resources into better alignment;
- accountability within the Commission to be enhanced, notably by assigning greater financial independence to officers who authorise programmes and projects;
- responsibility within the Commission for approving and auditing expenditure to be decentralised to DGs (responsibility for both functions had hitherto lain with the Financial Control DG, but with less than 250 staff, it had become overwhelmed with the increasing volume of transactions – in 1999 it was able to check on only 10 per cent of the approximately 600 000 transactions that needed its approval, and it was able to undertake only 284 audits, CIE, 1999b: 137);
- in parallel with the decentralisation of the approval and auditing functions, a sharper separation to be made between them. This to be achieved by: (a) the abolition of the Financial Control DG; (b) the creation of new central 'help desks' – a Central Financial Service and an Internal Audit Service – to oversee and advise on the exercise of the functions; (c) the establishment of an Audit Progress Committee to monitor all audit work and to ensure audit recommendations are followed-through;
- less contracting out of services;
- a strengthening of the resources and powers of OLAF – the Anti-Fraud Office.

It is hoped and expected that as the reform programme becomes operational, the Commission's exercise of its financial management responsibilities will become much more efficient.

Concluding remarks: the management and implementation challenge

Increasing attention has been focused in recent years on the Commission's executive responsibilities. This has been partly because, with the SEM legislative programme now largely in place and subsidiarity a guiding principle for new EU policy activity, the Commission's focus has necessarily had to shift somewhat from policy development to policy application. It has been partly, too, because of high-profile criticisms of the Commission's management of EU finances.

The criticisms of the Commission's management of EU finances reflect wider concerns about the Commission's executive capacities and abilities, with it long having been commonplace to observe that the Commission is more suited to, and is better at, pre-decisional phases of policy-making than it is at post-decisional. As Ludlow (1991: 107) has observed 'Senior Commission staff are, for the most part, better at drafting directives than they are at implementing them, stronger at planning programs than they are at administering them'.

A much-cited explanation as to why this might be so was put forward many years ago by David Coombes when he suggested that the tasks of formulation and implementation require different types of institutional structure (Coombes, 1970). Formulation, he suggested, requires an *organic* organisation in which tasks are not broken into compartments, in which there is no strong hierarchical command structure, and in which control is not externally imposed on the members of the organisation but is internally generated from a commitment to the enterprise. Such an organisation requires dynamic leadership to hold it together, is adaptive to changing circumstances, is good at generating ideas, but is not particularly efficient in matters of routine administration. Implementation, by contrast, Coombes suggested, requires a *mechanistic* organisation resembling Weber's classical bureaucracy. Such an organisation is marked by a high degree of internal specialisation and fragmentation of tasks, by a clear definition of the rights and obligations of each section and of each individual, and by a rigidly hierarchical system of control, authority and communication. Such an organisation is unsuited to innovative tasks, but is well adapted to the efficient performance of routine administration.

There are limitations with Coombes' thesis in providing an explanation for the Commission's difficulties with policy implementation, not least since the Commission is far from being a model organic organisation. But several commentators have recently echoed Coombes' argument that an organisation that was designed primarily to exercise innovative functions might have difficulty in effectively performing executive functions. One such commentator is Metcalfe (1992, 1996), who has argued that there is a 'management deficit' in the EU that is accounted for in no small part by weak coordination within the Commission and, more especially, by inadequate coordination between the Commission on the one hand and national and subnational levels of government undertaking EU implementing responsibilities on the other. One way of tackling this management deficit problem, according to Metcalfe, would be for the Commission to act more as a manager of European political and administrative networks. The increasing interdependence of government makes it impossible for the Commission to undertake the many tasks which were assigned to it in the treaties, but make it increasingly possible – indeed, increasingly necessary and desirable – for it to function as a network organisation prompting the development of organisational capacities and coordination at different decision-making and management levels. In Metcalfe's view, the effective management of EU policies is not achieved by the Commission acquiring increasing capacities for managing EU policies itself and exercising increasing centralised control, but rather through collaborative advantage. This 'means creating conditions in which the organizations responsible for managing particular policies are able to work together effectively . . . In broad terms the development of collaborative advantage requires the Commission to develop expertise in ensuring the coherence and reliability of European management networks' (1996: 5). Crucially, 'the Commission should develop core competences in constructing decentralized management regimes, designing administrative partnerships and developing coordination capacities for managing European policies' (1996: 8).

The sort of ideas being advanced by Metcalfe have already been partly taken up by the Commission in some policy areas, including several spending programmes where the principles of administrative partnership, shared management, and decentralisation are well established. These principles, which constitute part of the new management thinking that has so influenced reforms in European civil services in recent years, are increasingly being extended to other policy areas as the Commission attempts to respond to feelings that power in the EU is too concentrated and searches for more efficient ways to cope with its ever-increasing executive responsibilities.

One option that has been widely canvassed to improve the quality of policy execution is the creation of independent regulatory agencies (see, for example, Vibert, 1995). These are seen as being useful in relieving an over-burdened Commission of some of its responsibilities and desirable in that they can both utilise relevant technical expertise and be insulated from political pressures. There has already been a limited movement at EU level in this direction, with the creation – mostly in the early 1990s – of ten semi-autonomous agencies These agencies are, for the most part, expected to act, as Dehousse (1997: 246) puts it, 'as network coordinators, rather than as central regulators'. However, three of them do have non-exclusive regulatory powers (exercised in parallel with national regulatory authorities) relating to marketed goods in the internal market: the Office for Harmonisation in the Internal Market (Trade Marks and Designs) registers Community trade marks; the European Agency for the Evaluation of Medicinal Products can approve medicines; and the Community Plant Variety Office can grant property rights for new plant varieties. These three agencies may prove in time to be the forerunners of a wider and stronger 'agencification' of Commission regulatory powers, though it has to be said this does not appear to be an immediate prospect. The idea, for example, that has been floated, not least by the German Government, of transferring most of the implementing powers of the Competition DG to an independent European Cartel Office has run up against a series of key questions that national governments answer in different ways: would the Office be completely removed from political control?; would it be guided solely by competition criteria or could it allow for other EU policy objectives?; to whom would it report?; and would it deal with all types of competition cases, including those that are politically charged? (On the ten European agencies, see Kreher, 1997; Dehousse, 1997; Majone, 1997.)

But though a fundamental uprooting of the arrangements by which the EU exercises its executive responsibilities – through, for example, a hiving-off of key functions – may be unlikely in the foreseeable future, important adapting reforms are under way. Some of these reforms have been considered in this chapter and others were considered in Chapter 7. The purpose of the reforms is to give the Commission an enhanced management capability and a sharper focus and edge in relation to its executive responsibilities. Whether the reforms will have all of their desired effect remains to be seen, but it is clear they mark a very significant attempt to meet the challenge of unsatisfactory executive performance.

Chapter 12

External Relations

The Commission undertakes many external relations tasks. This chapter begins with an outline of the nature of these tasks and an explanation of why they have so increased in recent years. There is then a description of the Commission's organisational arrangements for undertaking the tasks and an analysis of why they have been so problematical and subject to frequent change. The chapter then looks at four of the tasks in some detail – trade negotiator, trade implementer, manager of enlargement, and external representative. The chapter ends with some general conclusions.

Increasing responsibilities

The external relations functions of the Commission have increased enormously over the years. From a somewhat limited Founding Treaty base, in which its external relations responsibilities were largely confined to acting as the EC's external negotiator with third countries on trade matters, the Commission now exercises a wide range of external relations responsibilities across a broad policy spectrum. Prominent amongst these responsibilities are:

- It is the main, and usually the sole, negotiator for the EU in bilateral and multilateral trade negotiations with non-member states under the Common Commercial Policy (CCP).
- It is the main negotiator for the EU when broadly-based cooperation and association agreements, going beyond trade, are negotiated with non-member states.
- It deals and negotiates, sometimes by itself and sometimes alongside the Council Presidency and/or member states' representatives, with non-member states in respect of the many internal EU policies – including environment, transport and energy – that have external aspects and dimensions.
- It is associated with the EU's Common Foreign and Security Policy (CFSP) and seeks to play important policy proposing and coordinating roles therein.

- It advises the Council on EU accession negotiations and it negotiates terms of entry with prospective new members.
- It undertakes a wide variety of tasks within the framework of the EU's policies towards developing countries.
- It is the main coordinator of EU humanitarian and emergency aid.
- It participates in the work of international organisations such as the United Nations (UN) and its specialised agencies, the Council of Europe, the Organisation for Economic Cooperation and Development (OECD), and the International Energy Agency (IEA).
- It staffs and runs over 130 offices in non-member states, and it liaises closely with over 160 missions to the EU that non-member states have established in Brussels.

The Commission is thus a very significant external policy actor. How has it come to assume such a range of competences and expand so considerably its external powers, authority and profile?

A key factor has been the increased importance of international commercial relations that has followed upon the globalisation of the world economy. This has been very much to the institutional advantage of the Commission because it is precisely in this sphere of policy activity that its legal powers to act as the EU's external representative are at their strongest (see Macleod, Hendry and Hyett, 1996).

Globalisation has been useful to the Commission in another way, too, in that it has helped to break down some of the barriers between internal and external policies. This has provided opportunities for the Commission to extend its well established, treaty-based, responsibilities and powers for internal policies to the external dimensions of these policies. Environmental policy, energy policy and competition policy are examples of policy areas where the Commission has taken advantage of this situation by, for example, taking a lead in promoting and negotiating international treaties of various kinds.

The Commission's ability to act as the EU's external representative on internal policies has been strengthened, as it has also in some other external policy spheres, by ECJ rulings (see Macleod, Henry and Hyett, 1996). Of particular importance has been the increasingly expansive interpretation given by the Court to the principle of parallelism, whereby the existence of internal policy competences is assumed to be paralleled by the existence of external powers.

The increasingly prominent place of foreign policy cooperation on the EU agenda has also contributed to the Commission's growing role as an external relations actor, even though this policy area is still largely based on intergovernmental principles. Since the SEA the Commission has been 'fully associated' with Community/Union foreign policy, and under the TEU it is, along with the Council, given a particular responsibility to ensure 'the consistency of [the Union's] external activities as a whole in the context of its external relations, security, economic and development policies' (Article 3, ex-C).

A final important factor is that since the mid-1980s the Commission has acted in a pro-active manner so as to establish influential powers and authority for itself in as many spheres of external policy as it can. On a 'routine' basis, such pro-activism has included launching external initiatives and taking external actions in respect of internal policies, submitting policy and position papers to the Council on CFSP issues, and establishing links between CFSP issues and CCP issues. On a necessarily more occasional basis, pro-activism has included seeking greater external powers via treaty reform: in, for example, its submission to the 1996–97 IGC, the Commission called, in effect, for the operation of much of the CFSP to be based on a Council Presidency-Commission tandem (Commission, 1996b: 15–17) – a call that was, in the event, rejected.

Organisational structure

How is the Commission structured to undertake the many external policy responsibilities it now exercises? This question is best answered by examining arrangements at College level and services level separately.

College level

At College level, the organisation of external policy portfolios has, in recent times, been altered every time a new College has assumed office. Table 12.1, which lists the main external policy portfolios at the beginning of the Delors I, Santer and Prodi Colleges, shows three very different sets of arrangements just a few years apart. Striking features of the portfolio allocations in the Santer College as opposed to those in the Delors I College are the formal assumption of tasks by the President, the much more detailed and regionally focused specification of responsibilities, and the increased number of external

Table 12.1   *Principal external policy portfolios of Commissioners in the Delors I, Santer and Prodi Colleges*

Delors I College (1985)

Jacques Delors (President)	No specific portfolio allocated, but an informally understood external 'representative' role on major occasions.
Willy de Clerq	External relations and trade policy.
Claude Cheysson	Mediterranean policy. North–South relations.
Lorenzo Natali	Cooperation and development.

Santer College (1995)

Jacques Santer (President)	CFSP and human rights (with Hans van den Broek).
Hans van den Broek	External relations with the countries of Central and Eastern Europe, the former Soviet Union, Mongolia, Turkey, Cyprus, Malta and other European countries. CFSP and human rights (in agreement with Jacques Santer). External missions.
Sir Leon Brittan	External relations with North America, Australia, New Zealand, Japan, China, Korea, Hong Kong, Macao and Taiwan. Common commercial policy. Relations with OECD and WTO.
Manuel Marin	External relations with southern Mediterranean countries, the Middle East, Latin America and Asia (except Japan, China, Korea, Hong Kong, Macao and Taiwan), including development aid.
Joao de Deus Pinheiro	External relations with ACP countries and South Africa, including development aid. The Lomé Convention.
Emma Bonino	European Community Humanitarian Office (ECHO).

Prodi College (1999)

Chris Patten	External Relations
Günter Verheugen	Enlargement
Poul Nielson	Development and Humanitarian Aid
Pascal Lamy	Trade

portfolios. An indication of how widely spread external policy responsibilities at College level became under Santer is seen in the fact that it was common for General Affairs (Foreign Ministers) Councils to be attended by at least five of the six External Relations Commissioners – the so-called RELEX Commissioners (after the French *relations extérieurs*), plus occasionally also by other Commissioners when an agenda item required it. In the interests of rationalising the division of responsibilities at College level, President Prodi assumed no explicit external relations responsibility himself and simplified the portfolios of the RELEX Commissioners – most importantly by placing them on a functional basis and removing geographical responsibilities. Prodi also sought to promote coordination between the RELEX Commissioners by giving one of them – Chris Patten – a coordinating brief in addition to his CFSP portfolio. As part of his coordinating brief, Patten was to chair the Standing Commissioners' Group on External Relations which was to consist of, in addition to himself, the three other RELEX Commissioners and the Commissioner for Economic and Monetary Affairs.

Services level

At services level, most external policy responsibilities were managed for many years by two DGs – DG I (External Relations) and DG VIII (Development) – plus, as needs arose, special, and usually temporary, units in the Secretariat General. In 1993, following a division of the external policy portfolio in the College between external economic policy and foreign policy, DG I was split into two DGs – DG I (External Economic Relations) and DG IA (External Political Relations). This arrangement was short-lived and in 1995 there was a further reorganisation, again designed to reflect changes in the distribution of external policy portfolios in the College where the emphasis was shifted from functionally focused to regionally focused responsibilities. The 1995 reorganisation saw DGs I and IA re-vamped and a new DG IB created. Under this arrangement there were thus, as Table 12.2 shows, four external relations – RELEX – DGs.

As with Commissioners' portfolios, Prodi simplified the policy remits of the RELEX DGs by placing them on a functional basis. This resulted in the regional focus that had been established in 1995 disappearing and the RELEX DGs now consisting of Trade, External Relations (largely foreign policy), Development, and Enlargement – the last being created to deal with the increasingly heavy workload

Table 12.2   *External relations DGs and services*

Santer College (1995)

DGs

- DG I (External Relations: Commercial Policy and Relations with North America, the Far East, Australia and New Zealand)
- DG IA (External Relations: Europe and the Newly Independent States, Common Foreign and Security Policy and External Missions)
- DG IB (External Relations: Southern Mediterranean, Middle East, Latin America, South and South-East Asia and North–South Cooperation)
- DG VIII (Development: External Relations and Development Cooperation with the ACP countries; Lomé Convention)

Other Services

- European Community Humanitarian Office

Prodi College (1999)

DGs

- External Relations
- Trade
- Development
- Enlargement

Other Services

- Humanitarian Aid Office
- Common Service for External Relations

---

involved with the enlargement problem, which previously had been handled by a special task force.

In addition to the RELEX DGs, two other services also deal with external relations issues. One is the Humanitarian Aid Office (ECHO). Established initially, in 1992, to deal primarily with the needs of humanitarian assistance in the former Yugoslavia, ECHO's operations now stretch throughout the world. It works very closely with, and on a contractual basis channels most of its funds through, a wide assortment of non-governmental organisations (NGOs) and UN agencies. Although it is a directorate rather than a DG, ECHO is commonly regarded as being part of the group of RELEX DGs. The other service is the Common Service for External Relations. This was established in 1998 to deal with the thousands of contracts the Commission signs and oversees as part of its development and assistance policies throughout the world. Jacques Santer informed the EP in February 1999 that the annual workload of the Common Service was estimated at 2000 calls for tender, 10 000 contracts, and 50 000 financial transactions (*Official Journal*, C207: 153, 21 July 1999). The thinking behind the establishment of the Common Service was that policy planning would be clearer and policy implementation would be more efficient if these tasks were separated.

In addition to the RELEX DGs and services, several other parts of the Commission – including the Economic and Financial Affairs, the Agriculture and the Energy and Transport DGs – also have important external relations functions. This is because of the international nature of some of the policy issues in their remit.

The reasons behind the frequent organisational changes

What explains the almost constant chopping and changing of the Commission's external policy organisational arrangements in recent years? A combination of four, overlapping and interlinking, factors do so.

The most obvious of these factors is that the Commission has had to accommodate itself to increased external policy responsibilities. Whether it is the EU's leading external policy actor (as in important respects it is in commercial and many commercial-related policy areas) or is a supporting actor (as it is on CFSP matters), it has had to cover its increased responsibilities with appropriate portfolio allocations in the College and policy designations in the services.

The second factor is that external policy is not only a developing area for the Commission but it is also a highly complex area, with many different, yet interconnected, aspects and dimensions. This means that in policy-process terms it is an area in which there are, as Smith has noted (1997: 264–5), 'boundary' problems: between domestic and external policies; between commercial, foreign, and security and defence policies; and between the responsibilities of many actors – most notably the Commission, the Council and the member states. These boundary problems mean that there is no one clear, obvious, and uncontentious way of organising responsibilities. Rather, there are many possibilities.

The third factor stems from the fact that in undertaking its external policy responsibilities the Commission is concerned not only to be efficient, but also to be creating, and taking advantage of, opportunities which enable it to establish strong positions for itself across the spectrum of external policies. These concerns are not necessarily wholly complementary in organisational terms and shifts in emphasis between the two can suggest different organisational arrangements. Such shifts provide much of the explanation for why the distribution of the external policy portfolios and the structure of the external policy DGs were subject to three major reorganisations in the 1990s. In the 1993 reorganisation, a major motivating factor behind the move to a more functional focus was a belief that this would give the Commission a stronger organisational base from which it could seek to play an influential role in the arrangements made in the TEU for the CFSP. The 1995 reorganisation was stimulated in no small part by widely held beliefs that the essentially horizontal division embodied in the 1993 reorganisation between external economic and external political policy did not allow sufficiently for the intermingling of these policies and prevented policies from being dealt with on holistic regional bases. The 1999 reorganisation was driven largely by beliefs that the 1995 reorganisation had been unsuccessful in that it had produced too complex a division of internal responsibilities, had made it very difficult for there to be overall coherence on horizontal issues, and had produced confusion on 'who speaks for the Commission'. The 1993 reorganisation may thus be said to have been motivated primarily by institutional opportunism, whilst the 1995 and 1999 reorganisations gave rather more – though by no means exclusive – attention to policy efficiency.

The fourth factor is that the division and allocation of responsibilities between Commissioners and within the services is partly a consequence of political jostling, especially at College level where most incoming Commissioners want, and in some cases expect to be given, important and high-profile portfolios. The increased number of Commissioners that has followed upon EC/EU enlargements has made it ever more difficult for all Commissioners to be satisfied with the portfolios they are assigned, so the creation of several jobs in the prestigious and high-profile field of external policy is one way of smoothing potentially ruffled feathers. The creation and redefining of these jobs has necessarily resulted in external policy DG structures having also to be reconsidered and, when necessary, changed.

Trade negotiator

Negotiating resources and formal powers

The strength and nature of the EU market combine to make the EU an extremely powerful influence and force in the world economy. The *strength* of the market manifests itself in several ways: the combined Gross Domestic Product (GDP) of the EU countries accounts for around 22 per cent of world GDP, as compared with around 25 per cent for the US; EU exports account for around 20 per cent of world exports and EU imports account for around 19 per cent of world imports, as compared with figures of 16 per cent and 20 per cent respectively for the US; and the population of the EU market is 370 million, as compared with 250 million in the US. The key features of the *nature* of the EU market are that it is increasingly integrated and that it conducts most of its external trade relations as a single body. This latter behaviour and capacity stems from the EEC Treaty which, in laying the foundations for a common market, made provisions for a Common External Tariff (CET) and an associated Common Commercial Policy (CCP).

These features of the EU market mean that those who speak and act on its behalf in international trading forums are necessarily themselves important international trading actors. The Commission is the main actor which so speaks and acts on behalf of the EU market. It does so because it is identified in the TEC as the body which conducts CCP negotiations on behalf of the Community, though it does so within the framework of such directives as may be given to it by the Council and with the outcome of negotiations subject to Council approval.

The key TEC article is Article 133, (ex-113), which includes the following:

1   The common commercial policy shall be based on uniform principles, particularly in regard to changes in tariff rates, the conclusion of tariff and trade agreements, the achievement of uniformity in measures of liberalisation, export policy and measures to protect trade such as those to be taken in the event of dumping or subsidies.
2   The Commission shall submit proposals to the Council for implementing the common commercial policy.

3   Where agreements with one or more States or international organisations need to be negotiated, the Commission shall make recommendations to the Council, which shall authorize the Commission to open the necessary negotiations.

The Commission shall conduct these negotiations in consultation with a special committee appointed by the Council to assist the Commission in this task and within the framework of such directives as the Council may issue to it.

The relevant provisions of Article 300 shall apply.

4   In exercising the powers conferred upon it by this Article, the Council shall act by a qualified majority.

Article 300, which is referred to in paragraph 3 of Article 133, sets out the procedures that apply in respect of external agreements. Several possible procedures are so set out, and which one applies in particular circumstances depends on the provisions of the Treaty article(s) on which the substantive content of agreements are based. To put this another way, all external agreements made within the framework of the TEC are based on at least two Treaty articles: one (or more than one) provides Treaty underpinning/justification for making agreements in particular policy areas, whilst Article 300 specifies the procedures which apply to the making of agreements, with some variations occurring according to their policy content.

The reasonably detailed contents of Article 133 result in Article 300 having little to add about the Commission's responsibilities and powers in respect of trade agreements. The Treaty is, however, far from being the sole determiner of how trade policy processes operate in practice. Rather, it lays down important parameters for what the Commission and other policy actors must do, cannot do and may attempt to do, but within the parameters there is ample room for political, economic, legal, personnel and other factors to produce variations, as the following two sections will show.

Decision-making processes

In a formal sense, decision-making begins with the Commission making a recommendation to the General Affairs Council (Foreign Ministers, but with trade ministers sometimes attending) that the EU should seek to conclude or update a trade agreement with a third country, group of countries, or international trading organisation. Behind such a recommendation, however, lies a range of less formal activities and processes in which the Commission is constantly engaged: it monitors and assesses the effects of existing trade agreements and possible future trade agreements on EU trade flows and economic performance; it exchanges information and discusses – in both bilateral and multilateral forms – matters of mutual interest with trading partners; and it floats ideas before, and it receives ideas from, all sorts of policy actors – most notably the Council via the Article 133 Committee (see below on this Committee).

When the Commission makes a recommendation to open negotiations on a trade agreement the matter is discussed by the Article 133 Committee and the Committee of Permanent Representatives (COREPER) and is then placed on the agenda of the General Affairs Council with a view to a decision being made as to whether negotiations should formally be opened. If they are to be opened, the Council not only gives permission to the Commission to proceed with negotiations but also a mandate in the form of negotiating directives and guidelines. The Commission tries to ensure that the mandate is as broad and unrestrictive as possible, but often it is tightly drawn because it represents a compromise between the interests of different member states and/or between the views of those governments which favour liberalisation and those which favour retaining a measure of protectionism. The Council can take its decisions about the opening of negotiations and the specifications of mandates by QMV, but this is not usually necessary and the mandate is usually in practice agreed upon by COREPER.

The actual conduct of trade negotiations is the responsibility of the Commission, acting on behalf of all EU member states (though see below for complications in respect of mixed agreements). The Commission's negotiating team depends on the nature and importance of the issues to be considered, but typically it consists of an appropriate head of division who is assisted by two or three relevant specialised officials. The tight negotiating mandates which the Council often issues, coupled with the need not to disturb the compromises on which the mandates are usually based and which may have been agreed only with difficulty, mean that the Commission's room for manoeuvre in negotiations can be limited. The extent of the limitations should not, however, be overstated, for Commission officials acknowledge privately that the mandates are often less of a dead weight than is commonly supposed. Moreover, it is possible for the mandates even to be used to advantage, with the Commission gaining negotiating ground by pronouncing in response to unwanted proposals from those with whom it is negotiating that 'the Council would never agree to that'. During particularly difficult or important negotiations the Commission may ask the Council for clarification of the mandate or for an amended mandate which might break a deadlock.

Throughout the period during which negotiations are being conducted, the Commission has the Council looking over its shoulder and monitoring its actions. The main channel of communications between the two institutions is the Council's Article 133 Committee, to which the Commission reports on the progress of negotiations. The Committee meets at two levels. Full members, who are normally senior officials from the national ministries responsible for trade plus the Director General of the Trade DG, gather once a month to consider general policy issues. There can be up to eighty people in these meetings, with members bringing a couple of experts from national ministries and an official from the Permanent Representation with them. Deputies, who are not quite so senior officials, usually meet three times a month plus as and when it is necessary to deal with specific rather than general policy issues. Peterson and Bomberg (1999: 112) have suggested that the Commission found the Article 133 Committee becoming more vigilant and confrontational in the 1990s, but overall it appears to be the case that, as Hayes-Renshaw and Wallace (1997: 90) have observed, the Committee works with, rather than against, the Commission, indicating to the latter what is and what is not likely to be accepted by the ministers and what should be referred back to the Council for reconsideration and perhaps for new or modified negotiating mandates. Hayes-Renshaw and Wallace have further observed that the usefulness of the Committee to the Commission may be gauged from the fact that although it is under no treaty obligation to do so, the Commission has frequently agreed to the creation of similar committees to assist it in international negotiations that are not based on Article 133 (1997: 90).

At the (apparent) conclusion of negotiations, the Commission can initial negotiated settlements, but Council approval, by QMV if necessary, is required for agreements to be formally authorised and signed.

Procedural problems

Such is the importance of external trade as a policy issue, and such are the powers of, and the relations between and within, the EU's institutions in connection with the CCP, that tensions of different sorts are by no means uncommon. Four areas cause particular difficulties for the Commission.

First, the respective roles of, and the power balance between, the Commission and the Council can be a source of tensions. A not uncommon problem in this context is representation at negotiations, with the Commission having its much-treasured and defended position to be the sole EU trade negotiator challenged on the grounds that the issues covered in the negotiations are not an exclusive Community competence and/or do not fall wholly under Article 133. When such differences of view on representation cannot be resolved by political accommodation – involving, perhaps, the Council Presidency or a particularly interested member state being 'permitted' by the Commission to be present in some unofficial, non-speaking, capacity at negotiations – then they may be referred to the ECJ for adjudication. Contrary to the widely held view that the Court normally takes a pro-integrationist line when handing down its judgements, it has tended to be very cautious when dealing with Council-Commission institutional trade-related disputes. As Shaw (1995a: 92) has commented in respect of the important opinion issued by the Court in 1994 on the agreement establishing the World Trade Organisation (WTO) – a case in which the Commission was unsuccessful in its attempt to have exclusive powers granted to it by the Court to negotiate on services and intellectual property – the Court failed 'either to push at the limits of Community external competence or clarify uncertainties about the notion of exclusive competence'. The Commission subsequently pressed in the 1996–97 IGC to be given exclusive competences in respect of services and intellectual property, but without success.

The nature of negotiating mandates to be given to the Commission can also create difficulties concerning the roles of, and the power balance between, the Commission and the Council. Usually, the essence of the problem is that the Council wants a tight mandate so as to ensure that the Commission remains under its control, whilst the Commission wants a loose mandate so that it has enough manoeuvrability to enable it to be an effective negotiator. Sometimes problems along these lines can be solved with a bit of give and take, but if it is so minded the Council may simply impose much tighter negotiating terms than the Commission thinks is either necessary or desirable.

Direct and open clashes between the Commission and the Council are relatively unusual since the former is well aware of views in the latter on key issues, so does not bring forward proposals that are likely to result in confrontation and eventual rejection. A clash did, however, occur in December 1999 when, in an attempt to further progress in the troubled WTO talks in Seattle on the remit of the proposed new round of world trade negotiations, the Commission indicated that it might be prepared to discuss biotechnology issues in a WTO working group. EU trade ministers, who were also present in Seattle, strongly supported by EU environment ministers, quickly rejected the Commission's initiative. They did so because they suspected a WTO working group would threaten the successful conclusion of separate and ongoing negotiations on a bio-safety protocol to the United Nations biodiversity convention (*Financial Times*, 3 December 1999).

Second, the different national interests and preferences of the member states can create difficulties in the Council and for the Commission. A graphic instance of this was seen in the high-profile campaign of resistance led by France to what it saw to be the excessively liberal agreement negotiated by the Commission with the US in November 1992 on agricultural trade aspects of the GATT Uruguay Round. In 1993 France mobilised support in the Council – most crucially from Germany – for there to be what amounted to a renegotiation of parts of the agreement. The Commission was strongly opposed to this, but the Trade Commissioner, Sir Leon Brittan, was despatched to the US to seek better terms. Morever, he was despatched with a firm negotiating mandate, even though he had argued that he was 'big enough' to negotiate without one (Webber, 1998: 588).

Third, problems can arise when Commissioners and DGs other than the Trade Commissioner and DG have, or claim they have, an interest in particular external trade policies and agreements. In such circumstances – which are not uncommon given the complex linkages which exist between many policy areas – the Commission's negotiating credibility and effectiveness can be undermined if it becomes known that, for instance, the Competition DG or the Energy DG have clashed with the Trade DG. Internal coordinating mechanisms are thus an extremely important part of the Commission's trade relations decision-making apparatus and, indeed, of external relations policies more generally. The main coordination mechanisms are:

- the weekly meeting of the College and the *cabinet*-level meetings that prepare it;
- the Commissioners' Standing Group on External Relations (which the Secretary General attends and which may also be attended by non-RELEX Commissioners as and when agenda items cover matters within their portfolio);
- bi-lateral meetings between relevant Commissioners;
- bi-lateral meetings between relevant *cabinet* members;
- meetings of RELEX directors general – which are held at least once every month, including before all meetings of the Commissioners' Standing Group;
- meetings of RELEX deputy directors general and assistants to directors general;
- bi-lateral meetings between relevant directors general and/or other senior DG officials;
- the numerous inter-service groupings and meetings that exist and are held in the external policy area: most of these are *ad hoc* and informal in that they are convened as and when they are necessary so as to bring relevant people together on particular issues, but others – including those on the US, Japan, and the WTO – are formalised and established in the sense that they meet regularly (every two months or so), are based on a fairly stable membership (which can range in size from as few as half a dozen officials to over forty), and have a permanent chairperson (normally the most appropriate director or head of unit).

Fourth, Members of the European Parliament (MEPs) have long been dissatisfied that the Parliament has no automatic right to be consulted, let alone to insist that its views be considered, in connection with Article 133 agreements. In practice, the EP is notified about agreements, and the Commission, and to a lesser extent the Council, do discuss external trade matters with the EP – primarily in the forum of the Parliament's External Economic Relations Committee – but it is clear that Parliament's influence is usually limited. Or, at least, it has been so in the past, but it is now increasing. An important reason why it is so is that the EP has constantly pressed its dissatisfaction and has done what it can to maximise its influence, not least by incorporating into its Rules of Procedure a range of measures requesting the Council, and thereby the Commission, to take note of the EP when opening, negotiating and concluding trade agreements.

Implementation of trade policies

The Commission's trade implementation roles and responsibilities take a number of different forms.

The most visible form is the 1000 plus trade-related regulations that are issued each year in the name of the Commission. Many of these regulations have the purpose of adjusting EU tariffs and levies to changes in world prices, especially agricultural prices. The regulations are triggered in a semi-automatic manner and are very much administrative/technical in character. They do not involve the Commission making political or policy judgements. Committees made up of representatives of the member states monitor these implementing regulations, but they seldom challenge their content.

As with most other spheres of EU policy and law, the actual front-line implementation of trade policies is undertaken by appropriate agencies in the member states. The Commission's role is primarily to ensure that the agencies are fully familiar with, and properly apply, the prevailing EU laws. This it does via constant two-way flows of information with the national agencies and, when it is deemed to be appropriate, occasional on-the-spot checking. It is a role in which many DGs are involved. To take, by way of example, the collection of customs tariffs and levies, DGs with a direct involvement are: Trade, Agriculture, Budget, and Taxation and Customs Union. No matter how many DGs are involved in a particular activity, however, limited resources mean that the Commission's monitoring and checking capacities are not as comprehensive or as effective as is ideally desirable. Where this results in policy implementation defects, the EU is thereby damaged. So when, for instance, national customs authorities deal with imports from third countries in different ways – as they inevitably can do given the great volume and complexity of customs regulations and given, too, variations in national working procedures and practices – at least two problems arise. First, the functioning of the internal market is distorted, because one of the foundations on which the market rests is that goods entering the market are subject to the same entry requirements no matter where their point of entry. Second, the income to the EU budget is affected, because tariffs and levies constitute just under one-fifth of budgetary revenue (although this proportion is declining as the reduced tariffs that were negotiated in the Uruguay Round come into force).

The Commission also has important executive tasks to perform when a trading partner breaches, or is suspected of breaching, trading rules and agreements. When a breach is alleged the Commission may decide to conduct an investigation. If the investigation shows that a breach does indeed seem to have occurred – relating perhaps to infringement of rules of origin or to the payment of 'unfair' government subsidies designed to assist a product to gain market share – then the Commission has three broad, though by no means mutually exclusive, courses of action available:

- It can seek to resolve the matter through direct dialogue with the trading partner concerned. Such dialogue may well involve using a mixture of sticks and carrots to seek an accord that is mutually acceptable. So, for example, an agreement was reached in 1992 with Japanese manufacturers of dynamic random access memory chips (DRAMS) and erasable programmable read-only memory (EPROMS) that was based on the EC agreeing to suspend anti-dumping duties in exchange for the manufacturers agreeing not to sell their products in the EC below a certain floor, or reference, price.
- It can seek Council authorisation to refer the matter to the WTO dispute settlement process. So, in October 1996 the Foreign Ministers agreed that the Commission should request a WTO panel to consider the EU's case against the US Helms-Burton and D'Amato Acts. (These Acts provided for financial penalties to be imposed on non US citizens and firms who conducted trade with, respectively, Cuba and with Iran or Libya. The EU objected to the Acts on the grounds that they were an attempt to impose US law outside US territory.)
- It can authorise, or can recommend to the Council, that the EU takes retaliatory action. The most common type of such action is anti-dumping measures. The countries which have been most subject to such measures are Japan, China, South Korea, and Turkey.

There are four main stages to anti-dumping procedures. First, an action normally begins with an EU-based company or group of companies, who must represent at least 25 per cent of the industry, complaining to the Commission that foreign imports are being dumped (that is, are being sold on the European market more cheaply than on the domestic market). Second, if the Commission accepts that the complaint may be justified it conducts an investigation into whether: (a) there is dumping; (b) domestic producers are suffering; (c) the suffering is a direct result of dumping; (d) there are wider 'Community interests' beyond those of importers – most notably, consumer interests. Investigations, which are undertaken by small teams including at least one accountant and one lawyer, normally involve sending long questionnaires to all those, or to a representative sample of those, who are concerned with or may be affected by the alleged dumping. On-the-spot investigations may also be undertaken. Third, after consulting an advisory committee made up of national representatives, the Commission may or may not decide to impose provisional anti-dumping duties for a period of up to nine months. Before the duties are imposed, exporters can give an 'undertaking' to increase prices, which the Commission can accept as an alternative to duties. Fourth, if provisional duties are to be made 'definitive' (which normally means for five years), the Council must give its approval – on the basis of a simple majority if necessary.

To give an example of a specific anti-dumping case: following complaints from European-based industry that South Korean car radios were being sold on the European market at a price that was significantly lower than the cost of producing them, the Commission carried out a preliminary investigation and imposed duties early in 1992; the Commission then undertook a more comprehensive, six-month-long, investigation into the production and marketing practices of South Korean firms that had been exporting car radios to the European market; in August 1992 the anti-dumping duties that had been imposed earlier in the year were confirmed by the Council, but the 'standard' duty of 34.4 per cent was reduced for 18 companies which had cooperated with the Commission's investigation (*Financial Times*, 11 August 1992).

Taking retaliatory action can, of course, give rise to resentment in those countries which are the targets of such action. So as to try and ensure that this does not cause long-term damage to the Commission's relations with third countries, retaliatory actions are normally distanced from the relevant geographical directorates and divisions within the Commission. This is particularly so with anti-dumping cases, which are dealt with by a separate directorate in the Trade DG. The anti-dumping directorate keeps relevant geographical directorates and divisions informed about the progress of anti-dumping cases within their domain, but does not openly associate them with the cases. This separate treatment of anti-dumping cases enables geographical directorates and divisions to profess ignorance and say it is not their responsibility when they receive anti-dumping enquiries and criticisms from 'client countries'. In this way, good relations are more easily established and maintained.

Manager of enlargement

Enlargement has featured prominently and almost permanently on the EC/EU agenda. Since the first UK application to join the EC was made in 1961, there have always been states which have been interested in becoming members.

Handling such interest has caused immense difficulties for EC/EU decision-makers, not least since most formal membership applications have arrived in waves shortly after previous enlargement rounds have been completed. This has meant that the EC/EU has had to deal with new applications at the same time as it has been attempting to assimilate new members. So, for example, the wave of applications from Central and Eastern European countries (CEECs) in the mid-1990s began – with applications from Hungary and Poland in 1994 – even before the EFTA countries that had agreed and ratified entry terms (Austria, Finland and Sweden) formally acceded in 1995.

The precise form and timescale of enlargements varies considerably. The most important factors determining the course and pace of events are the political and economic circumstances of applicants, the implications of enlargement for the existing member states, and the extent to which the EU has to make adjustments to accommodate newcomers. Where these factors raise major problems and require significant developments and/or changes, then the enlargement process is normally difficult and protracted. Such is the case with the CEECs. Where, however, no major problems arise and no significant developments or changes are required, then enlargement can proceed fairly smoothly and quickly. This happened with the EFTA states, all of which benefited from having well established liberal democratic political systems, prosperous market-based economies, laws and regulations that were already well adjusted to the internal market, and relatively small populations. Their position was also greatly helped by many issues having already been thrashed out in negotiations between them and the EC in the early 1990s to establish a European Economic Area (EEA). The EFTA applications are the quickest wave to have been processed to date, and Finland is the quickest country to have been processed – it delivered its application in March 1992, negotiations were opened in February 1993 and concluded in March 1994, and Finland became an EU member in January 1995.

But though there are important variations in the precise form and timetable of enlargement processes, all enlargements entail, as Dinan

(1997c) has shown, five stages. The Commission is involved, to a greater or lesser extent, in each of these stages:

The pre-application stage is the period during which it becomes clear that an application is probable.

Prior to the EFTAn enlargement the Commission did not do much at this stage, other than to establish preliminary and unofficial estimates of the implications of enlargement and give consideration to how the application process should be managed. The EFTAn enlargement was rather different, however, because the Commission was concerned that a further widening might threaten deepening, so much time and effort was spent pioneering and negotiating what became the EEA in the ultimately unsuccessful hope that this might head off applications.

The unsuccessful strategy towards the EFTAns played an important part in shaping strategy towards the CEECs. As it became obvious in 1991–92 that membership applications from CEECs would be forthcoming, the Commission, working through and with the European Council and the Council of Ministers (Foreign Ministers), began to develop a medium to long-term strategy designed to enable CEECs to meet the conditions of Union membership. The development of this strategy can be monitored through the many reports the Commission prepared for the European Council and the Council of Ministers on the subject in the early-to-mid-1990s. In broad terms the strategy developed from the identification of general operational principles, such as were set out in the Commission's report *Towards a New Association with the Countries of Central and Eastern Europe* (Commission, 1992a) which was considered at the 1992 Edinburgh and 1993 Copenhagen European Council meetings, to the development of assistance and adjustment programmes and the specification and monitoring of transitional requirements and progress, such as were provided for in the Commission's White Paper *Preparation of the Associated Countries of Central and Eastern Europe for Integration into the Internal Market of the Union* which was considered at the 1995 Cannes European Council (Commission, 1995b).

The application stage is the period between the receipt of a membership application and the opening of accession negotiations.

During this period the Commission draws up an opinion (*avis*) for the European Council on the application. This evaluates the suitability of the applicant state for membership and sets out the likely implications for the EU of accepting the application. Drawing up opinions is a major logistical exercise, with vast amounts of information to be considered and virtually all of the Commission's DGs involved to at least some extent.

The ten membership applications lodged by CEECs in the 1990s naturally resulted in much time and effort on the part of the Commission in preparing opinions. As part of the preparation, in April 1996 the Enlargement Task Force, which was based in DGIA, sent a 165-page questionnaire – dealing with a range of essentially technical matters – to all ten applicants. Apart from minor variations designed to cater for special national conditions, all questionnaires were the same and covered questions such as 'Does your anti-trust law contain horizontal and vertical provisions?', and 'What are your investment needs in the energy sub-sectors?' The CEECs were given three months to respond, and when they did so the Commission was faced with the task of digesting and evaluating some 2000–3000 pages of information from each applicant state. With some of the responses being too vague and theoretical, the Commission also had to embark on a clarification and verification exercise with the governments of applicant states (*European Voice*, 21–27 November 1996).

The Commission produced its opinions on the CEEC applications in June 1997, as part of its *Agenda 2000* report. It recommended that negotiations should be opened with five of the ten CEEC applicants (Hungary, Poland, the Czech Republic, Estonia and Slovenia) plus Cyprus (which had been given a favourable opinion in 1993), but should be delayed with the other five (Bulgaria, Romania, Slovakia, Latvia and Lithuania) until their economic (and in the case of Slovakia, political) transitions were more advanced (Commission, 1997c). In October 1999, as part of the annual progress and monitoring reports the Commission was now producing on all thirteen applicants to the EU (the ten CEECs, Cyprus, Malta and Turkey), it was recommended that negotiations should be opened in 2000 with the five 'second-wave' CEECs plus Malta (Commission, 1999j). (Malta had withdrawn its application in 1996, but renewed it in 1999.)

The member states are not obliged to accept the recommendations that are contained in Commission opinions, but they almost invariably do. The only occasion on which they have taken a different view was in the mid-1970s with the Greek application: the Commission stated that Greece was not economically ready to become an EC member and proposed a pre-accession strategy of an unspecified duration, but the member states chose to give a higher priority to

Greece's arguments that membership would help to underpin Greek democracy and consolidate Greece's Western European and Western Alliance bonds.

In addition to the preparation of opinions, the application stage also involves the Commission continuing with, and developing, preparations for enlargement which are already under way. This has been most particularly so with the CEECs, for the prospective accession of these countries has involved a much more conscious and developed pre-accession strategy than has been the case with earlier applicants. The cornerstone of this strategy have been Association Agreements (called Europe Agreements) and Accession Partnerships, which the Commission has played a central role in developing, which it keeps constantly under review, and which require it to engage, with the Council, in constant ongoing exchanges, deliberations and negotiations with politicians and officials in the applicant states.

The negotiation stage   sees the Council taking the formal lead in conducting negotiations on behalf of the EU, but the Commission in practice dealing with most of the detailed and technical aspects. So, for example, when negotiations officially opened with the five 'first-wave' CEECs and Cyprus in March 1998, the Commission was immediately obliged to handle what is known as the 'screening process', which involves examining information from applicants on the extent to which they both comply with the EU *acquis* and need to take further measures.

The Commission is also responsible for many vital supporting services at the negotiating stage. These services include sifting and filing the enormous volume of often highly complex documentation that is necessary for an EU accession, answering queries by applicant states, producing progress reports, liaising with member state and applicant state representatives with a view to identifying compromises and possible areas of agreement where there are difficulties, and helping to draft treaties and acts of accession.

The ratification stage   is essentially for the existing member states, the applicant states and the EP. The Commission's responsibilities are limited and do not extend much beyond providing information that is requested by the participants in the ratification processes. Occasionally, however, the Commission may itself become a participant, albeit a somewhat indirect one. An example of Commission participation was seen in 1994 when President-designate Jacques Santer sought to encourage reluctant Norwegians to vote affirmatively in the ratification referendum by attempting to allay their long-held concerns about the impact on Norway of the Common Fisheries Policy (CFP). The method he used was to assign the fisheries portfolio in the College which was due to assume office in January 1995 to the Norwegian Commissioner-designate, Thorval Stoltenberg. The intervention seemingly had little effect and the Norwegian people voted not to approve accession.

The implementation stage   involves accession treaties being put into effect by new member states and EU institutions.

For a new member state, putting its accession treaty into effect means adjusting to the many and varied aspects of the EU regime. The Commission, acting in its capacities as implementer of EU laws and guardian of the legal framework, assists with and watches over this adjustment process.

For EU institutions, putting an accession treaty into effect means incorporating new member state representatives into existing structures and procedures, and learning to deal with new member state working styles and practices. The Commission has had difficulties with these incorporation and learning requirements at both College and services levels.

At College level, the treaty stipulation that all member states have at least one Commissioner has resulted in incorporations producing a College which most observers think has reached, or even exceeded, its optimum size in relation to the number of significant portfolios that are available. The 1996–97 IGC identified a partial solution to this problem by laying the basis for an agreement in the 2000 IGC by which the number of Commissioners in future Colleges will be restricted to one per member state (see Chapter 4). At services level, incorporations have been accompanied by some – though not proportionate – increases in staffing, in the 'ring fencing' of certain vacancies, in encouragement being given to the early retirement of senior officials, and in a reshuffling of some posts and responsibilities.

As for learning requirements, serving Commissioners and officials have had to accommodate themselves to, or at least have had to find a way of dealing with, the different customs and norms that Commissioners and officials from acceding states have brought with them. So, for example, the accession of Sweden in 1995 brought into the Commission people who were used to working in a decision-making system that was more open than that currently prevailing. It can be anticipated that the enlargement to CEECs will require even greater 'cultural adaptation'.

The Commission is thus involved in the enlargement process from beginning to end, and within the process exercises a range of important formal and informal roles and functions.

External representative

The Commission carries the main responsibility for providing EU representation in non-member states and a few international organisations.

There is a Commission office of some kind in most countries of the world. Most of these are called 'external delegations', though a handful are representations, offices, or resident advisers. Some small, geographically proximate, countries are grouped together for representation purposes. For example, the external delegation in India is responsible also for Bhutan, Sri Lanka, the Maldives and Nepal.

In total, the number of staff working in the delegations is around 3000. Of these, less than half – about 1200 – are Commission *fonctionnaires* and over half – about 1800 – are local agents. Of the *fonctionnaires*, around 450 are A-grade staff. Of the local agents, just over 100 are categorised as being engaged in 'conceptual work', around 140 in administrative work, around 700 in secretarial work, and approaching 800 in other work – such as chauffeuring and security (Commission, 1995d).

The delegations function, as Bruter (1999) has shown, virtually as EU embassies. Their main responsibilities are as follows:

- To explain the nature of the EU and its activities to elites, opinion formers and the general public. This is done in a number of ways, ranging from the cultivation of contacts throughout the public and private sectors to the mounting of public information exhibitions.
- To promote the interests of the EU. Just what these interests are does, of course, vary. It can vary between host countries with, for example, some host countries being producers of raw materials on which EU member states are dependent and some being countries on which the EU has issued CFSP common positions. It can vary, too, between member states, especially if they are engaged in trade

competition in the host country. When this latter situation applies, member state embassies and trade missions are likely to be active, so the Commission must take great care not to display any national bias and to confine itself largely to the role of general facilitator.

- To encourage and facilitate cooperation and, where possible, coordination between the policies and activities of the member states in host countries. With varying degrees of success, activities include exchanging and pooling political and economic information, coordinating development aid activities, and cooperating on consular matters. In host countries the heads of the diplomatic missions of the member states and of the Commission delegation meet regularly.

- To assist with the implementation of EU policies. Which policies are relevant to and apply in host countries naturally depends on many circumstances. In Hungary, for example, the delegation is involved with the host country's movement towards EU accession, which means that, amongst other things, it helps to organise and monitor technological development and investment, facilitates scientific cooperation, and arranges training programmes for officials in such subjects as management techniques and quality evaluation. In Sudan, by contrast, the focus of the delegation is very much on the EU's development aid programmes, which involves working with host country politicians and officials to establish policy priorities and plan projects, monitoring the activities of the consulting agencies that are normally contracted to run projects, and acting as an intermediary between the Development DG on the one hand and local representatives and field workers on the other.

The responsibilities and roles of the Commission's delegations to international organisations depend very much on the nature and functions of the organisations to which they are attached, the internal and external powers of the Commission in the policy spheres covered by the organisations, and the interests which EU member states have in the activities of the organisations. So, for example, the Commission is able to play an active and influential policy role in the UN's Food and Agricultural Organisation (FAO) in Rome, but it is confined more to coordinating and liaising roles, and often has to play second fiddle to the Council Presidency, in respect of CFSP issues in the UN's headquarters in New York.

Concluding remarks

This chapter has demonstrated that the Commission exercises a range of important functions and responsibilities in different spheres of external relations. These functions and responsibilities have extended in scope over the years, pressed forward by such factors as the logic of issue linkages, the indispensability and usefulness of the Commission in so many decision-making situations, and the natural gravitation of external actors towards the Commission as a fixed point when they wish to deal with the EU.

In exercising its functions and responsibilities the Commission has inevitably become a prominent and influential international actor. This is seen most obviously in the many, often high-profile, representative roles exercised by Commissioners in forums ranging from G7 meetings to important international trade talks. It is seen, too, in the way in which Commission officials − especially in the external relations DGs and in external delegations − are in frequent contact with their counterparts in third countries and can often more easily gain access to senior people in the governments of third countries than can officials in the external policy departments and embassies of EU member states.

Crucial, however, though the Commission is to the conduct of many aspects of external relations, it is not usually capable of acting with full and unfettered authority. Even in the field of external trade relations, where the treaties give the Commission a clear right to act as the representative of the EU as a whole, it has to negotiate on mandates agreed by the member states in the Council of Ministers, and it has always to keep an eye on what is likely to be acceptable to the member states for they have to ratify final agreements. The fact is that when the Commission is negotiating on issues that have potentially important economic and political implications for member states, the states are very reluctant to accept that the Commission should have too many powers and they are very anxious that such powers as it does have are monitored and are subject to control.

The varying relationships that exist between the Commission and the member states are but the most obvious of the many variations that exist in external relations policy processes. The different dimensions of the EU's external relations place the Commission in a host of different policy-making situations. Between each of the dimensions there are differences in respect of the parts of the Commission that are brought into play, the formal and informal powers and opportunities that are available to the Commission, the procedures to which the Commission is subject, the external policy actors with which the Commission comes into contact, and the policy styles which apply within the Commission and in the broader EU setting. The Commission, in short, functions within numerous and varied external relations policy arenas.

Looking to the future, the 1999 reorganisation of the management of the Commission's external relations functions should help to at least partly overcome the compartmentalisation that has rather characterised thinking on external policies in the past. This certainly is highly desirable for it seems reasonable to suppose that the EU will continue to develop an increasing, and increasingly complex, range of contacts and relationships with the outside world. Past experience suggests that if the Commission uses its powers to the full and with adeptness, if it makes itself useful in situations where its formal status is uncertain, and if it does not overplay its hand, then its position across a range of external relations activities and functions will be further consolidated and may even be expanded.

Chapter 13

Conclusions

This book has covered much ground in its examination of the development, nature, operation, and functions of the Commission. As was signalled in the Introduction, four themes have underlain much of the analysis. This chapter returns to these themes.

Between independence and dependence

As was shown in Chapter 9, there is a long-standing academic debate on the extent and the nature of Commission influence in the EU system. The view taken in this book has tended towards the supranational perspective, though couched in qualified terms. A somewhat cautious approach has been taken because the multi-actor, multi-process nature of most EU decision-making, in which policy activity is often based on complex and shifting policy networks of various kinds, means that it can be very difficult to identify which policy actors are the 'first movers' and the 'real shapers' of initiatives and proposals. It is clear who are the main final decision-takers – they are, according to the type of decision concerned, the European Council, the Council of Ministers and the European Parliament – but it is often far from clear who has exercised what influence in the pre decision-taking stages of decision-making. It is indisputable, however, that the Commission is almost invariably an active participant in all of these stages and that there are few policy spheres in which the nature of the debate and framework in which decisions are taken is not at least strongly shaped by the Commission.

But though the Commission can do much to usher decision-takers towards decisions, it cannot make them take decisions to which they are resistant. That they cannot be pushed against their will is demonstrated by the Council's failure to adopt, or its dilution of, Commission recommendations and proposals on such matters as the protection of the ozone layer, harmonising certain forms of taxation, and treaty reform. Much Commission time is therefore necessarily taken up with trying to create a permissive consensus amongst decision-takers and brokering agreements on proposals and actions.

The unwillingness of the Council to act upon everything the Commission presents to it is but one aspect of the very considerable degree of control member states exercise over the Commission. As Pollack (1997a and 1997b) and others have pointed out, the extent and the effectiveness of the control varies according to context, but the fact is that the member states appoint all the members of the College (with the EP having confirmatory power), determine the Commission's formal powers when they hold IGCs, and through the comitology system and other mechanisms are able to keep a close check on most Commission activities.

When the new College headed by Romano Prodi assumed office in September 1999, the dependence of the Commission on other EU institutions appeared in some respects to be greater than at any time in the Commission's history: the EP had just forced the Santer College to resign – the first time a College had ever failed to complete its term of office; the European Council was seemingly requiring an increasing number of decisions to be channelled via its meetings; 'regular' decision-making processes were now only infrequently based on the former prevailing Commission–Council axis and were now usually based on a Commission–Council–EP triangle; although the Amsterdam Treaty had supposedly given the President-designate a veto power over the nomination of Commissioners, it was clear that in practice Prodi was able to exercise only a limited influence over who were to be his new colleagues; and in the period leading up to the confirmatory vote by MEPs on the Prodi College, Prodi was pressed into making a series of far-reaching promises about how he and his fellow Commissioners would make themselves available to the EP and would do all they reasonably could to take note of Parliament's policy preferences and views about the Commission's performance.

These developments might be seen as marking an important shift in the balance between independence and dependence that has long characterised the Commission's position in the EU. In so doing they might further be seen as weakening the Commission's ability to be a central policy player in its own right. The case should not, however, be overstated, for there have been other developments in recent years that have been to the Commission's institutional advantage. Prominent amongst these developments are the increased use of QMV in the Council (which makes it less likely that Commission legislative proposals will be blocked), the heavy reliance of the European

Council on Commission steering when taking many of its major policy decisions (such as with the 2000–06 financial perspective and the accession of CEECs), and the increased capacity of the Commission to pursue strong and consistent policies (via the strengthening of the position of the President in the Amsterdam Treaty and via new working practices instigated by Prodi).

Recent and ongoing developments thus present the Commission with both challenges and opportunities. The opportunities are perhaps not on the scale of those that were available in the mid-1980s when the Commission played a central role in the 're-launching' of the integration process, but they are nonetheless considerable. There is, furthermore, a project to hand – enlargement to the CEECs – which, if it does not quite match the 'big idea' of the internal market that did so much to underpin the dynamism of the Commission in the late 1980s and early 1990s, most certainly does provide a major issue on which the Commission can be seen to be leading the EU

A political and administrative hybrid

The Commission is a political and administrative hybrid in respect of both its organisational structure and the roles it undertakes in the EU system of governance. This hyrid character is a strength in so far as it means that the Commission is involved in virtually all aspects of EU activities. It is, however, a weakness in that it creates organisational difficulties and it gives rise to uncertainties, and sometimes disputes, amongst external actors regarding Commission activities.

The programme of Commission reform being carried out under Romano Prodi has sought to address some of the organisational difficulties arising from the Commission's mixed political/administrative character. This is being done in a number of ways. For example, a new Code of Conduct provides for close working relationships between the political and administrative arms but also specifies the distinctions between their respective responsibilities. The general principle is that 'Commissioners shall assume full political responsibility. Directors General shall be answerable to their Commissioner for the sound implementation of the policy guidelines laid down by the Commission and the Commissioner' (Commission, 1999c). Amongst the intended consequences of the Code is that less will be heard in the future of political 'interference' by *cabinets* in the work of the services. Another way in which organisational difficulties arising from the mixed political/administrative character of the Commission is being tackled is by de-politicising personnel policy as far as possible. Whilst the national balance principle is not being completely removed from appointments and promotions criteria, it is being downgraded in parallel with an upgrading of the meritocratic principle.

As for the Commission's mixture of political and administrative roles, an important reason for the crisis that erupted around the Santer Commission in 1999 was that too much concentration on the political roles had resulted in the performance of the administrative roles coming to be somewhat neglected. This situation is now being tackled. It was beginning to be so under Santer as, with the SEM legislative programme largely in place, there was a developing awareness of the importance of that law being fully and properly implemented. An important reason for this developing awareness was a succession of Court of Auditors Reports that was strongly critical of EU law evasion and of inadequate Commission control over EU programmes, especially spending programmes. The Prodi reform programme is much concerned with improving the Commission's management and administrative capacities.

Change within a framework of stability

Some of the core features of the Commission have been relatively unchanged over the years. For example, the division into political and administrative arms, the compartmentalisation of the services into DGs, and the mix of political and administrative roles are features that were forged in the early days of the Commission.

Within, however, this framework of stability the Commission has changed in many ways. It has done so in large part because it has been forced to adapt to changes in its operating environments. This can be illustrated by taking three of the major changes to which the Commission has had to accommodate itself in recent years:

- EU policy responsibilities have expanded considerably since the mid-1980s. They have done so both in terms of breadth – with policy areas such as defence and health finding at least some place on the agenda – and depth – with matters such as competition rules and product standards increasingly being determined at EU level. This expansion has seen the Commission having to broaden its policy expertise and take on an increasing workload in respect of, for example, policy monitoring and implementation.

- The new and the amended decision-making processes brought about by treaty reforms have obliged the Commission to alter and refine aspects of its dealings with other EU institutions. For example, as the EP has assumed real legislative powers so has the Commission had to become much more sensitive to the EP's views and be not just a channel between the EP and the Council but also, wherever possible, a broker and a conciliator between them.

- The greater emphasis given by the EU since the early 1990s to the principles of subsidiarity and transparency has seen the Commission having to adjust its behaviour in a number of ways. Regarding subsidiarity, the Commission now weighs more carefully than it used to do whether new legislation should be proposed, and if it is proposed an explicit justification in terms of subsidiarity is given. Regarding transparency, steps taken by the Commission include creating better public access to information (via, for example, the improvement of databases), giving greater advance warning of likely policy developments (via, for example, publicising work programmes and legislative programmes), and improving opportunities for interested parties to examine and comment upon Commission thinking at formative policy stages (via, for example, making greater use of Green and White Papers).

As well as changing because it has been obliged to do so as a result of changes in its operating environments, the Commission has also changed because it has sometimes sought to pro-actively advance its institutional position and/or improve its operational effectiveness. This has, for example, been the case with the CFSP, where the Commission is given only limited powers under the TEU. Devices used by the Commission to try and inject itself into a strong position in this increasingly important policy area include major organisational changes at College and services levels under the Delors, Santer and Prodi presidencies, the frequent feeding of position papers and communications into the Council, and attempts to link 'pure' foreign policy issues (where the Commission's powers are weak) to trade and development issues (where the Commission's powers are much stronger).

However, the extent to which the Commission has used change to further its own institutional interests should not be exaggerated. The Commission may be a 'purposeful opportunist' (Cram, 1993), but only up to a point. One reason why the Commission's pursual of institutional interests should not be overstated is that even at the highest levels most Commission staff spend most of their time in reactive rather than pro-active mode. As Ross has observed of his experience as a participant observer in the Delors' *cabinet*, 'the Commission lived constantly with the pressure of urgent deadlines and the necessity of responding rapidly to unforeseen events' (1955: 75). Another reason for not exaggerating the Commission's pursual of institutional interests is that, as Hooghe (1999a, 1999b) has shown, Commission officials are not so enthused about pressing an integrationist or supranational agenda as is often supposed. And a third reason is that the Commission is far from being a unified body, with a clear and coherent set of institutional goals which all staff support.

Organisational problems

The Commission has been shown to be an institution with considerable organisational problems. Four of these problems have impacted particularly on its effectiveness and efficiency.

First, there has been an internal leadership problem, with neither of the 'contenders' for leadership – the presidency and the College – being able to fully assert themselves. The presidency has been hampered by weak powers and by the appointment to the office of several less than dynamic figures. The College has been hampered by the nature of its composition, which is a consequence largely of the balance of national political forces at the time of the College's appointment rather than a consequence of careful construction designed to create a cohesive and balanced team.

Second, there has been structural fragmentation, most obviously with the division between the political and administrative arms, but also with divisions within the arms. In the political arm policy responsibilities have been fairly rigidly divided between Commissioners, whilst in the administrative arm they have been similarly divided between DGs. In the opinion of many observers, these divisions have made for excessive compartmentalisation and at times almost insuperable difficulties in the way of achieving optimum coordination.

Third, the existence of micro-cultures within the Commission, focused mainly around nationality and locational identity, have resulted in attachments that have sometimes made working relationships difficult. Some DGs, for example, have developed 'missions' that have clashed with one another on important policy issues.

Fourth, there have been serious staffing shortages in some parts of the Commission. The increased number of tasks falling to the Commission have not been matched by corresponding staffing increases – mainly because the Council of Ministers has wished to keep a tight control on the EU budget. The Commission has sought to compensate for this restriction on recruitment by making extensive use of temporary personnel and outside consultants, but this has not been as satisfactory as being fully and properly staffed by permanent employees.

There has been no shortage of ideas as to how the Commission's organisational problems might be tackled. Regarding, for example, lack of political leadership, suggestions that have frequently been made over the years have included stronger powers for the President, a smaller College, and the appointment of 'senior' and 'junior' Commissioners. A problem with these and many other suggestions, however, has been that they have raised political sensitivities that the member states – which control those reforms of the Commission that require treaty amendments – have not been willing or able to tackle.

Some progress was, however, made in the Amsterdam Treaty, with the position of the President being enhanced by a new provision stipulating that the Commission should work under his 'political guidance' and with the nature of a future deal in which the size of the Commission will be capped being outlined. Considerable progress has been made, too, in introducing reforms that do not need to be treaty-based, with Romano Prodi taking advantage of the circumstances that resulted in him being appointed Commission President in 1999 to initiate a major internal reform programme. Features of the programme have included streamlining Commissioners' portfolios, re-organising parts of the services, enhancing coordination mechanisms, making personnel policy more flexible, and updating and strengthening managerial practices.

All large organisations do, of course, evolve, but that such major organisational changes should be made in the Commission in so short a time is testimony to how it continues very much to be a developing institution. It is still in the process of building its structures, its working practices and its culture. One reason why it continues to develop is that its responsibilities keep expanding as the European integration process moves forward in ever-deepening and widening directions. Another reason is that tensions between its political/ bureaucratic and innovative/administrative roles give rise to different views as to how the Commission is best organised in the interests of effectiveness and efficiency. And a third reason is that the national, and hence also the cultural, composition of the Commission's personnel keeps changing every few years in response to periodic rounds of EU enlargement. The newcomers find that there is still 'much to play for' in respect of organisational arrangements and working procedures and practices. It is likely that within a few years there will, with the CEECs, be many more such newcomers.

Bibliography

Abélès, M. and Bellier, I. (1996) 'La Commission Européenne: Du Compromis Culturel à la Culture Politique du Compromis', *Revue Française de Science Politique*, vol. 46, no. 3, pp. 431–56.

Abélès, M., Bellier, I. and McDonald, M. (1993) *Approche Anthropologique de la Commission Européenne*, unpublished report for the Commission.

Acharya, R. (1996) *Making Trade Policy in the EU*, Discussion Paper no. 61. London, Royal Institute of International Affairs.

Allen, D. and Smith, M. (1996) 'External Policy Developments', in Nugent (1996), pp. 63–84.

Andersen, S. S. and Eliassen, K. A. (eds) (1996) *The European Union: How Democratic Is It?*. London, Sage.

Armstrong, K. and Bulmer, S. (1998) *The Governance of the Single European Market*. Manchester, Manchester University Press.

Arribas, E. (1997) 'How do Policy Problems Emerge in the EU Policy-Making Process? The Case of the Commission's Proposals on Media Ownership', *Current Issues in Europe*, vol. 1, no. 1, Department of European Studies, University of Bradford.

Bellier, I. (1994) 'La Commission Européenne: Hauts Fonctionnaires et "Culture du Management"', *Revue Française d'Administration Publique*, no. 70, pp. 253–62.

Bellier, I. (1995) 'Une Culture de la Commission Européenne? De la Rencontre des Cultures et du Multilinguisme des Fonctionnaires', in Mény, Muller and Quermonne (1995), pp. 49–60.

Bellier, I (1997) 'The Commission as an Actor: An Anthropologist's View', in Wallace and Young (1997).

Berlin, D. (1987) 'Organisation et Fonctionnement de la Commission des Communautés Européennes', in Cassese (1987b), pp. 21–442.

Bourtembourg, C. (1987) 'Les Fonctionnaires de la Commission des Communautés Européennes', in Cassese (1987b), pp. 497–522.

Bruter, M. (1999) 'Diplomacy Without a State: The External Delegations of the European Commission', *Journal of European Public Policy*, vol. 6, no. 2, pp. 183–205.

Buitendijk, G. J. and Van Schendelen, M. P. C. M. (1995) 'Brussels Advisory Committees: A Channel for Influence?', *European Law Review*, vol. 20, no. 1, pp. 37–56.

Bulmer, S. (1994a) 'The Governance of the European Union: A New Institutionalist Approach', *Journal of Public Policy*, vol. 13, no. 4, pp. 351–80.

Bulmer, S. (1994b) 'Institutions and Policy Change in the European Communities: The Case of Merger Control', *Public Administration*, vol. 72, Autumn, pp. 423–44.

Business Europe. London, Economist Intelligence Unit, weekly.

Cafruny, A. and Rosenthal, G. (eds) (1993) *The State of the European Community. Volume 2: The Maastricht Debates and Beyond*. Boulder, Lynne Rienner.

Cameron, D. (1992) 'The 1992 Initiative: Causes and Consequences', in Sbragia (1992), pp. 23–74.

Cassese, S. (1987a) 'Divided Powers: European Administration and National Administrations, in Cassesse (1987b), pp. 5–19.

Cassese, S. (ed.) (1987b) *The European Administration/L'Administration Européenne*. Maastricht: European Institute of Public Administration.

Cassese, S. and della Cananea, G. (1992) 'The Commission of the European Economic Community: The Administrative Ramifications of its Political Development', in Heyen (1992), pp. 75–94.

Christiansen, T. (1996) 'A Maturing Bureaucracy? The Role of the Commission in the Policy Process', in Richardson (1996), pp. 77–95.

Christiansen, T. (1997a) 'Reconstructing Space: From Territorial Politics to European Multilevel Governance', in Jørgensen (1997).

Christiansen, T. (1997b) 'Tensions of European Governance: Politicized Bureaucracy and Multiple Accountability in the European Commission', *Journal of European Public Policy*, vol. 4, no. 1, pp. 73–90.

Christoph, J. B. (1993) 'The Effects of Britons in Brussels, The European Community and the Culture of Whitehall', *Governance*, vol. 6, no. 4, pp. 518–37.

CIE (1999a and b), *see* Committee of Independent Experts.

Cini, M. (1996a) 'La Commission Européenne: Lieu d'Emergence de Cultures Administratives. L'Example de la DGIV et de la DGXI, *Revue Française de Science Politique*, vol. 46, no. 3, pp. 457–72.

Cini, M. (1996b) *The European Commission: Leadership, Organisation and Culture in the EU Administration*. Manchester, Manchester University Press.

Cini, M. (1997) 'Administrative Culture in the European Commission: The Cases of Competition and Environment', in Nugent (1997a), pp. 71–88.

Cini, M. and McGowan, L. (1998) *Competition Policy in the European Union*. Basingstoke, Macmillan.

Clark, J. R. A. and Jones, A. (1999) 'From Policy Insider to Policy Outcast? Comité des Organisations Professionales Agricoles, EU Policymaking, and the EU's "Agri-environment" Regulation', *Environment and Planning C: Government and Policy*, vol. 17.

Clergerie, J.-L. (1995) 'L'Improbable Censure de la Commission Européenne', *Revue du Droit Public et de la Science Politique en France et à L'Étranger*, no. 1, pp. 201–20.

Cockfield, Lord (1994) *The European Union: Creating the Single Market.* Chichester, Wiley Chancery.

Coleman, W. D. and Tangermann, S. (1999) 'The 1992 CAP Reform, the Uruguay Round and the Commission', *Journal of Common Market Studies*, vol. 37, no. 3, pp. 385–405.

Collins, M. (1993) *A Complete Guide to European Research, Technology and Consultancy Funds*, 2nd edn. London, Kogan Page.

Commission (1985) *Completing the Internal Market: White Paper From the Commission to the European Council*, Com (85) 310 final. Brussels.

Commission (1988) *Research and Technological Development Policy*, periodical 2/88. Luxembourg, Office for Official Publications of the European Communities.

Commission (1990) *Industrial Policy in An Open and Competitive Environment*, Communication of the Commission to the Council and to the European Parliament, Com (90) 556 final. Brussels.

Commission (1991a) *One Market, One Money: An Evaluation of the Potential Benefits and Costs of Forming an Economic and Monetary Union.* Luxembourg, Office for Official Publications of the European Communities.

Commission (1991b) *The European Electronics and Information Technology Industry: State of Play, Issues at Stake, and Proposals for Action*, SEC (91) 565 final. Brussels.

Commission (1991c) *European Industrial Policy for the 1990's*, in *Bulletin of the European Communities*, Supplement 3/91. Luxembourg, Office for Official Publications of the European Communities.

Commission (1992a) *Towards a New Association with the Countries of Central and Eastern Europe*, SEC (92) 2301 final. Brussels.

Commission (1992b) *Development Co-operation Policy in the Run-up to 2000. The Community's Relations with the Developing Countries Viewed in the Context of Political Union. The Consequences of the Maastricht Treaty*, Communication from the Commission to Council, SEC (92) 915 final (16 September). Brussels.

Commission (1992c) *From the Single Act to Maastricht and Beyond: The Means to Match Our Ambitions*, Com (92) 2000 final. Brussels.

Commission (1992d) *An Open and Structured Dialogue Between the Commission and Special Interest Groups*, SEC (92) 272 final. Brussels.

Commission (1992e) *Green Paper on Pluralism and Media Concentration in the Internal Market*, Com (92) 480 final. Brussels.

Commission (1993) *Growth, Competitiveness, Employment. The Challenges and Way Forward into the 21st Century*, Com (93) 700 final. Brussels.

Commission (1994a) *An Industrial Competitiveness Policy for the European Union*, Communication from the Commission to the Council, Com (94) 319 final. Brussels.

Commission (1994b) *Green Paper on Follow up to the Consultation Process Relating to the Green Paper on Pluralism and Media Concentration in the Internal Market – An Assessment of the Need for Community Action*, Com (94) 353 final. Brussels.

Commission (1995a) *The European Commission 1995–2000*. Brussels, European Commission.

Commission (1995b) *White Paper: Preparation of the Associated Countries of Central and Eastern Europe for Integration in the Internal Market of the Union*, Com (95) 163 final (3 May). Brussels.

Commission (1995c) *Contribution to the Reflection Group*. Luxembourg, Office for Official Publications of the European Communities.

Commission (1995d) *Report from the Commission on the Functioning of the Commission's External Delegations*, Com (95) 68 final (8 March). Brussels.

Commission (1995e) *Annual Report – Cohesion Financial Instrument 1993/ 94*, Com (95) 1 (final) (17 January). Brussels.

Commission (1995f) *Enlargement: Objectives and Practical Arrangements at Administrative Level*, SEC (95) 230 final. Brussels.

Commission (1996a) *General Report on the Activities of the European Union 1995*. Luxembourg, Office for Official Publications of the European Communities.

Commission (1996b) *Intergovernmental Conference 1996. Commission Opinion: Reinforcing Political Union and Preparing for Enlargement*. Luxembourg, Office for Official Publications of the European Communities.

Commission (1997a) *General Report on the Activities of the European Union: 1996*. Luxembourg, Office for Official Publications of the European Communities.

Commission (1997b) *Agenda 2000 – For a Stronger and Wider Union*, Com (97) 2000 final (15 July). Brussels. Also available in *Bulletin of the European Union*, Supplement 5/97. Luxembourg, Office for Official Publications of the European Communities.

Commission (1997c) *Commission opinion on (Hungary's/Poland's/Romania's/Slovakia's/Latvia's/Estonia's/Estonia's/Lithuania's/Bulgaria's/Czech Republic's/Slovenia's) application for membership of the European Union*, Com (97) 2001–10 final (15 July). Brussels. Also available in *Bulletin of the European Union*, Supplements 6–15. Luxembourg, Office for Official Publications of the European Communities.

Commission (1997d) *Better Lawmaking 1997. Commission Report to the European Council*, Com (1997) 626 final (26 November). Brussels.

Commission (1997e) *White Paper on Sectors and Activities Excluded From the Working Time Directive*, Com (97) 334 final (15 July). Brussels.

Commission (1997f) *Promoting Innovation Through Patents. Green Paper on the Community Patent and the Patent System in Europe*, Com (97) 314 final (24 June). Brussels.

Commission (1997g) *Communication. Towards Tax Co-ordination in the European Union. A Package to Tackle Harmful Tax Competition*, Com (97) 495 final (10 October). Brussels.

Commission (1997h) *Green Paper on Vertical Restraints in EC Competition Policy*, Com (96) 721 final (22 January). Brussels.

Commission (1997i) *Action Plan for the Single Market. Communication of the Commission to the European Council*, SEC 1 (final) 4 (June 1997). Brussels.

Commission (1998a) *General Report on the Activities of the European Union: 1997. Luxembourg,* Office for Official Publications of the European Communities.

Commission (1998b) *The Commission's Work Programme for 1998* < http://europa.eu.int/en/comm/co98pr/en/com517.html >.

Commission (1999a) *General Report on the Activities of the European Union: 1998.* Luxembourg, Office for Official Publications of the European Communities.

Commission (1999b) *The Formation of the New Commission: 1 Code of Conduct for Commissioners.* Brussels, European Commission.

Commission (1999c) *The Formation of the New Commission: 2 Code of Conduct for Commissioners and Departments.* Brussels, European Commission.

Commission (1999d) *Rules of Procedure of the Commission*, in *Official Journal of the European Communities*, L252 (25 September), pp. 41–6.

Commission (1999e) *The Operation of the Commission: 2 Groups of Commissioners. Brussels,* European Commission.

Commission (1999f) *The Operation of the Commission: 3 Internal Coordination. Brussels,* European Commission.

Commission (1999g) *The Operation of the Commission: 4 Procedures for Appointments in Grades A1 and A2.* Brussels, European Commission.

Commission (1999h) *Designing Tomorrow's Commission: A Review of the Commission's Organisation and Operation.* Brussels, European Commission.

Commission (1999i) *Guide to Candidates Taking the Entry Competition.* Brussels, European Commission.

Commission (1999j) *Regular Report From the Commission on Progress Towards Accession by Each of the Candidate Countries: Composite Paper and Country Reports.* Brussels, European Commission.

Commission (2000a) *Reforming the Commission: Consultative Document,* CG3 (2000) 1/17 (18 January). Brussels, European Commission.

Commission (2000b) *Reforming the Commission – A White Paper* (1 March). Brussels, European Commission.

Commission (2000c) *Communication from the Commission . . . Strategic Objectives 2000–20005 – 'Shaping the New Europe'*, Com (2000) 154 final (9 February). Brussels.

Commission (2000d) *Communication from the Commission . . . The Commission's Work Programme for 2000*, Com (2000) 155 final (9 February). Brussels.

Commission (2000e) *Adapting the Institutions to Make a Success of Enlargement: Commission Opinion . . . on the Calling of a Conference of Representatives of the Governments of the Member States to Amend the Treaties*, Com (2000) 34 (26 January). Brussels.

Commission (2000f) *General Report on the Activities of the European Union: 1999*. Luxembourg, Office for Official Publications of the European Communities.

Committee of Independent Experts (1999a) *First Report on Allegations Regarding Fraud, Mismanagement and Nepotism in the European Commission*. Brussels, European Parliament (15 March).

Committee of Independent Experts (1999b) *Second Report on Reform of the Commission: Analysis of Current Practice and Proposals for Tackling Mismanagement, Irregularities and Fraud* (2 vols). Brussels, European Parliament (10 September).

Committee of Three (1979) *Report on European Institutions: Presented by the Committee of Three to the European Council*. Luxembourg, Office for Official Publications of the European Communities.

Connolly, B. (1995) *The Rotten Heart of Europe. The Dirty War for Europe's Money*. London, Faber & Faber.

Conrad, Y. (1989) *Jean Monnet et les Debuts de la Fonction Publique Européenne: La Haute Autorité de la CECA 1952–53*. Louvain, Ciaco.

Coombes, D. (1970) *Politics and Bureaucracy in the EC. A Portrait of the Commission of the EEC*. London, George Allen & Unwin.

Corbett, R., Jacobs, F. and Shackleton, M. (2000) *The European Parliament*, 4th edn. London, Cartermill.

Council (1993) *Council Resolution on the Quality of Drafting of Community Legislation*, in *Official Journal of the European Communities*, C 166/1 (17 June).

Council Press Releases. Brussels, General Secretariat of the Council of the European Union (issued after ministerial meetings).

Cram, L. (1993) 'Calling the Tune Without Paying the Piper? Social Policy Regulation: The Role of the Commission in European Community Social Policy', *Policy and Politics*, vol. 21, no. 2, pp. 135–46.

Cram, L. (1994) 'The European Commission as a Multi-Organization: Social Policy and IT Policy in the EU', *Journal of European Public Policy*, vol. 1, no. 2, pp. 195–217.

Cram, L. (1997) *Policy-making in the EU: Conceptual Lenses and the Integration Process*. London, Routledge.

Cram, L. (1999) 'The Commission', in Cram, Dinan and Nugent (1999), pp. 44–61.

Cram, L., Dinan, D. and Nugent, N. (eds) (1999) *Developments in the European Union*. Basingstoke, Macmillan.

Curtin, D. and Heukeb, T. (eds) (1994) *Institutional Dynamics of European Integration: Essays in Honour of Henry G. Schermers*. Dordrecht, Martinus Nijhoff.

Dehousse, R. (1997) 'Regulation by Networks in the European Community: The Role of European Agencies', *Journal of European Public Policy*, vol. 4, no. 2, pp. 246–61.

Dehousse, R. (1998) *The European Court of Justice*. Basingstoke, Macmillan.

Dinan, D. (1995) 'The Commission, Enlargement and the IGC', *ECSA Newsletter*, vol. viii, no. 2, pp. 13–16.

Dinan, D. (1997a) 'The Commission and the Intergovernmental Conferences', in Nugent (1997a), pp. 245–64.

Dinan, D. (1997b) 'The Commission and the Reform Process', in Edwards and Pijpers (1997), pp. 188–211.

Dinan, D. (1997c) 'The Commission and Enlargement', in Redmond and Rosenthal (1997), pp. 17–40.

Dinan, D. (1999a) 'Governance and Institutions: A Transitional Year', in Edwards and Wiessala (1999), pp. 37–61.

Dinan, D. (1999b) *Ever Closer Union? An Introduction to the European Union*, 2nd edn. London, Macmillan.

Docksey, C. and Williams, K. (1994) 'The Commission and the Execution of Community Policy', in Edwards and Spence (1997b), pp. 125–54.

Donnelly, M. (1993) 'The Structure of the European Commission and the Policy Formation Process', in Mazey and Richardson (1993a), pp. 74–81.

Donnelly, M. and Ritchie, E. (1997) 'The College of Commissioners and their Cabinets', in Edwards and Spence (1997b), pp. 33–67.

Drake, H. (1995) 'Political Leadership and European Integration; The Case of Jacques Delors', *West European Politics*, vol. 18, no. 1, pp. 140–60.

Drake, H. (1996) 'The Legitimisation of Authority in the European Union. A Study of the European Commission with Special Reference to the Commission Presidency of Jacques Delors, 1985–1995', PhD thesis. Aston University.

Drake, H. (1997) 'The European Commission and the Politics of Legitimacy in the European Union', in Nugent (1997a), pp. 226–44.

Duchêne, F. (1994) *Jean Monnet: The First Statesman of Interdependence*. New York, W.W. Norton.

Duff, A. (ed.) (1993) *Subsidiarity Within the EC*. London, Federal Trust.

Duff, A. (1994) 'The Main Reforms', in Duff, Pinder and Price (1994), pp. 19–35.

Duff, A., Pinder, J. and Pryce, R. (1994) *Maastricht and Beyond: Building the European Union*. London, Routledge.

Dyson, K. (1994) *Elusive Union. The Process of Economic and Monetary Union in Europe*. London, Longman.

Earnshaw, D. and Judge, D. (1995) 'Early Days: The European Parliament, Co-decision and the European Union Legislative Process Post-Maastricht', *Journal of European Public Policy*, vol. 2, no. 4, pp. 624–49.

Edwards, G. and Pijpers, A. (eds) (1997) *The Politics of European Treaty Reform: The 1996 Intergovernmental Conference and Beyond*. London, Pinter.

Edwards, G. and Spence, D. (1997a) 'The Commission in Perspective', in Edwards and Spence (1997b), pp. 1–32.

Edwards, G. and Spence, D. (eds) (1997b) *The European Commission*, 2nd edn. London, Cartermill.

Edwards, G. and Wiessala, G. (1999) *The European Union: Annual Review 1998/1999*. Oxford, Blackwell.

Egeberg, M. (1996) 'Organization and Nationality in the European Commission Services', *Public Administration*, vol. 74, no. 4, pp. 721–35.

Ehlermann, C.-D. (1994) 'State Aids Under European Community Competition Law', *Fordham International Law Journal*, vol. 18, December, pp. 410–36.

Ehlermann, C.-D. (1995) 'The European Administration and the Public Administration of Member States With Regard to Competition Law', *European Competition Law Review*, vol. 16, September, pp. 454–60.

Endo, K (1999) *The Presidency of the European Commission Under Jacques Delors: The Politics of Shared Leadership*. Basingstoke, Macmillan.

Eurobarometer: Public Opinion in the European Community (two issues each year). Brussels, Office for Official Publications of the European Communities.

Europa website (main website of the EU) < http://europa.eu.int > .

European Council (1992) *Conclusions of the Presidency* (Edinburgh, 11–12 December). Brussels, General Secretariat of the Council.

European Council (1993) *Conclusions of the Presidency* (Copenhagen, 21–22 June). Brussels, General Secretariat of the Council.

European Council (1995) *Presidency Conclusions* (Madrid, 15–16 December). Brussels, General Secretariat of the Council.

European Council (1997a) *Presidency Conclusions* (Amsterdam, 16–17 June). Brussels, General Secretariat of the Council.

European Council (1997b) *Presidency Conclusions* (Luxembourg, 12–13 December). Brussels, General Secretariat of the Council.

European Council (1999a) *Presidency Conclusions* (Berlin, 24–25 March). Brussels, General Secretariat of the Council.

European Council (1999b) *Presidency Conclusions* (Helsinki, 10–11 December). Brussels, General Secretariat of the Council.

European Parliament, Council, Commission Interinstitutional Agreement of 29 October 1993 on Budgetary Discipline and Improvement of the Budgetary Procedure (1993a) in *Official Journal* C331 (7 December), pp. 1–10.

European Parliament (1993) *Rules of Procedure*, 8th edn. Luxembourg, European Parliament.

European Parliament (1999a) *Rules of Procedure*, 14th edn. Luxembourg, European Parliament.

European Parliament (1999b) *Questions for the Hearings with Nominee Commissioners* (questions for, and answers of, all Commissioners-designate entered) on *Europa* website < http://europa.eu.int > (20 September).

European Parliament (1999c) *Hearings with Nominee Commissioners* (all Commissioners-designate hearings entered) on *Europa* website < http://europa.eu.int > (20 September).

European Parliament (1999d) *(Co-)Governing after Maastricht: The European Parliament's Institutional Performance 1994–1999*. Political Series, 10/99. Luxembourg, European Parliament's Directorate General for Research.

European Report (twice weekly). Brussels, European Information Service.

European Voice (weekly). Brussels, The Economist Group.

Fitzmaurice, J. (1994) 'The European Commission', in Duff, Pinder and Price (1994), pp. 179–89.

Franchino, F. (2000) 'Control of the Commission's Executive Functions: Uncertainty, Conflict and Decision Rules', *European Union Politics*, vol. 1, no. 1, pp. 63– 92.

Frontier Free Europe, monthly newsletter issued by DGX. Luxembourg, Office for Official Publications of the European Communities.

Fuchs, G. (1994) 'Policy-Making in a System of Multi-Level Governance – the Commission of the European Community and the Restructuring of the Telecommunications Sector', *Journal of European Public Policy*, vol. 1, no. 2, pp. 177–94.

Fuchs, G. (1995) 'The European Commission as Corporate Actor? European Telecommunications Policy After Maastricht', in Rhodes and Mazey (1995), pp. 413–29.

Garrett, G. (1992) 'International Cooperation and Institutional Choice: The EC's Internal Market', *International Organization*, vol. 46, Spring, pp. 533–60.

Garrett, G. (1995) 'The Politics of Legal Integration in the European Union', *International Organization*, vol. 49, Winter, pp. 171–81.

Garrett, G. and Tsebelis, G. (1996) 'An Institutional Critique of Intergovernmentalism', *International Organization*, vol. 50, no. 2, pp. 269–99.

George, S. (1994) 'Supranational Actors and Domestic Politics: Integration Theory Reconsidered in the Light of the Single European Act and Maastricht', *Sheffield Papers in International Studies*, 22; also available in Nugent (1997b), pp. 387–408.

Gerus, V. (1991) 'Comitology within the European Community's Policy-Making Process: A Mechanism of Political Control in the Inter-Institutional Relations of the Council of Ministers and the Commission', unpublished manuscript. Harvard University (September).

Giustinio, D. de (1996) *A Reader in European Integration*. London, Longman.

Golub, J. (1996) 'State Power and Institutional Influence in European Integration: Lessons from the Packaging Waste Directive', *Journal of Common Market Studies*, vol. 34, no. 3, pp. 313–39.

Grant, C. (1994) *Delors: Inside the House That Jacques Built*. London, Nicholas Brealey Publishing.

Grant, W. (1997) *The Common Agricultural Policy*. Basingstoke, Macmillan.

Graupner, F. (1973) 'Commission Decision Making in Competition Questions', *Common Market Law Review*, vol. 10, August, pp. 291–305.

Green Cowles, M. (1995) 'Setting the Agenda for a New Europe: The ERT and EC 1992', *Journal of Common Market Studies*, vol. 33, no. 4, pp. 501–26.

Greenwood, J. (1997) *Representing Interests in the European Union*. Basingstoke, Macmillan.

Groeben, H. Von der (1987) *The European Community: The Formative Years*. Luxembourg, Office for Official Publications of the European Communities.

Haas, E. (1958) *The Uniting of Europe: Political, Social, and Economic Forces, 1950–57*. Stanford, Stanford University Press.

Hall, M. (1992) 'Behind the European Works Council Directive: The European Commission's Legislative Strategy', *British Journal of Industrial Relations*, vol. 30, no. 4, pp. 547–66.

Hallstein, W. (1962) *United Europe: Challenge and Opportunity*. Cambridge, Mass, Harvard University Press.

Hallstein, W. (1972) *Europe in the Making*. London, George Allen & Unwin.

Hancher, L. (1996) 'The Regulatory Role of the European Union', in Kassim and Menon (1996).

Harryvan, A. G. and Hart, J. van der (1997) *Documents on European Union*. Basingstoke, Macmillan.

Hay, R. (1989) *The European Commission and the Administration of the European Community*. Luxembourg, Office for Official Publications of the European Communities.

Hayes, J. P. (1993) *Making Trade Policy in the European Community*. Basingstoke, Macmillan.

Hayes-Renshaw, F. and Wallace, W. (1997) *The Council of Ministers*. Basingstoke, Macmillan.

Hayward, J. E. S. and Page, E. C. (eds) (1995) *Governing the New Europe*. Cambridge, Polity Press.

Héritier, A. (1995) ' "Leaders" and "Laggards", in European Clean Air Policy', in Unger and van Waarden (1995).

Héritier, A. (1996) 'The Accommodation of Diversity in European Policy-Making and Its Outcomes: Regulatory Policy as a Patchwork', *Journal of European Public Policy*, vol. 3, no. 2, pp. 149–67.

Heyen, E. V. (ed.) (1992) *Yearbook of European Administrative History 4: Early European Community Administration*. Baden Baden, Nomos.

Hill, C. (ed.) (1996) *The Actors in Europe's Foreign Policy*. London, Routledge.

Hill & Knowlton (1999) *The European Commission 2000–2005*. Brussels, Hill & Knowlton Communication Consultants.

Hix, S. (1999) *The Political System of the European Union*. Basingstoke, Macmillan.

Hood, C. and Peters, B. G. (eds) (1994) *Rewards at the Top: A Comparative Study of High Public Office*. London, Sage.

Hooghe, L. (ed.) (1996a) *Cohesion Policy and European Integration: Building Multi-Level Governance*. Oxford, Oxford University Press.

Hooghe, L. (1996b) 'Introduction: Reconciling EU-Wide Policy and National Diversity', in Hooghe (1996a), pp. 1–24.

Hooghe, L. (1996c) 'Building a Europe With the Regions: The Changing Role of the European Commission', in Hooghe (1996a), pp. 89–126.

Hooghe, L. (1997) 'A House with Differing Views: The European Commission and Cohesion Policy', in Nugent (1997a), pp. 89–108.

Hooghe, L. (1999a) 'Beyond Supranational Self-Interest: Commission Officials and European Integration', paper prepared for the European Community Studies Association Sixth International Conference. Pittsburgh (2–7 June).

Hooghe, L. (1999b) 'Images of Europe: Orientations to European Integration Among Senior Officials of the Commission', *British Journal of Political Science*, vol. 29, part 2, pp. 345–67.

Hooghe, L. and Keating, M. (1994) 'The Politics of EU Regional Policy', *Journal of European Public Policy*, vol. 1, no. 3, pp. 367–93.

Hosli, M. (1996) 'Coalition and Power: Effects of Qualified Majority Voting on the Council of the European Union', *Journal of Common Market Studies*, vol. 34, no. 2, pp. 255–74.

Hull, R. (1993) 'Lobbying the European Community: A View From Within', in Mazey and Richardson (1993a), pp. 82–92.

Interinstitutional Agreement (of the European Parliament, Council and Commission) of 22 December 1998 on Commission Guidelines for the Quality of Drafting of Community Legislation (1999) in *Official Journal of the European Communities*, C73: 1–3 (17 March).

Ionescou, G. (1982) 'Speaking Notes with Emile Noël on the Administration of Europe', *Government and Opposition*, vol. 17, no. 1, pp. 37–47.

Jabko, N. (1999) 'In the Name of the Market: How the European Commission Paved the Way For Monetary Union', *Journal of European Public Policy*, vol. 6, no. 3, pp. 475–95.

Jachtenfuchs, M. and Kohler-Koch, B. (eds) (1996) *European Integration*. Opladen, Leske u. Budrich.

Jamar, J. and Wessels, W. (eds) (1985) *Community Bureaucracy at the Crossroads/L'Administration Communautaire a l'Heure du Choix.* Bruges, De Tempel.

Jenkins, R. (1989) *European Diary 1977–1981.* London, Collins.

Joerges, C. and Vos, E. (eds) (1999) *EU Committees: Social Regulation, Law and Politics.* Oxford, Hart Publishing.

Joint Declaration (of the European Parliament, Council and Commission) on Practical Arrangements for the New Co-decision Procedure (Article 251 of the Treaty Establishing the European Community (1999) in *Official Journal of the European Communities,* C148: 1–2 (28 May).

Jones, A. and Clark, J. R. A. (1998) 'The Agri-environment Regulation EU 2078/92: The Role of the European Commission in Policy Shaping and Setting', *Environment and Planning C: Government and Policy,* vol.{vs}16, pp. 51–68.

Jørgensen, K. E. (ed.) (1997) *Reflective Approaches to European Governance.* Basingstoke, Macmillan.

Jourdain, L. (1996) 'La Commission Européenne et la Construction d'un Nouveau Modèle d'Intervention Publique. Le Cas de la Politique de Recherche et de Développement Technologique', *Revue Française de Science Politique,* vol. 46, no. 3, pp. 496–520.

Kassim, H. (1994) 'Policy Networks, Networks and European Union Policy Making: A Sceptical View', *West European Politics,* vol. 17, no 4, pp. 15 27.

Kassim, H. and Menon, A. (eds) (1996) *The European Union and National Industrial Policy.* London, Routledge.

Keohane, R. O. and Hoffmann, S. (eds) (1991) *The New European Community: Decisionmaking and Institutional Change.* Oxford, Westview Press.

Kersbergen, K. van and Verbeek, B. (1994) 'The Politics of Subsidiarity in the European Union', *Journal of Common Market Studies,* vol. 32, no. 2, pp. 215–36.

Kinnock, N. (1999) *Press Statement – 29 September 1999.* Brussels, European Commission.

Kreher, A. (1997) 'Agencies in the European Community – A Step Towards Administrative Integration in Europe', *Journal of European Public Policy,* vol. 4, no. 2, pp. 225–45.

Kreppel, A. (1999) 'What Affects the European Parliament's Legislative Influence?', *Journal of Common Market Studies,* vol. 37, no. 2, pp. 521–38.

Laffan, B. (1997a) *The Finances of the European Union.* Basingstoke, Macmillan.

Laffan, B. (1997b) 'From Policy Entrepreneur to Policy Manager: The Challenge Facing the European Commission', *Journal of European Public Policy,* vol. 4, no. 3, pp. 422–38.

Laudati, L. (1996) 'The European Commission as Regulator: The Uncertain Pursuit of the Competitive Market', in Majone (1996a), pp. 229–61.

Laursen, F. (1996) 'The Role of the Commission', in Andersen and Eliassen (1996), pp. 119–41.

Lawton, T. C. (1996) 'Industrial Policy Partners: Explaining the European Level Firm – Commission Interplay for Electronics', *Policy and Politics*, vol. 24, no. 4, pp. 425–36.

Lawton, T. C. (1997) 'Uniting European Industrial Policy: A Commission Agenda for Integration', in Nugent (1997a), pp. 129–44.

Lenaerts, K. (1991) 'Some Reflections on the Separation of Powers in the European Community', *Common Market Law Review*, no. 28, pp. 11–35.

Lequesne, C. (1996) 'La Commission Européenne Entre Autonomie et Dépendance, *Revue Française de Science Politique*, vol. 46, no. 3, pp. 389–408.

Levy, R. (1996) 'Managing Value-for-Money Audit in the European Union: The Challenge of Diversity', *Journal of Common Market Studies*, vol. 34, no. 4, pp. 509–29.

Levy, R. (1997) 'Managing the Managers: The Commission's Role in the Implementation of Spending Programmes', in Nugent (1997a), pp. 203–25.

Liefferink, D. and Lowe, P. (eds) (1993) *European Integration and Environmental Policy*. Scarborough, Belhaven Press.

Lindberg, L. (1963) *The Political Dynamics of European Economic Integration*. Stanford, Stanford University Press.

Lindberg, K. and Scheingold, S. (1970) *Europe's Would-Be Polity: Patterns of Change in the EC*. Englewood Cliffs, NJ, Prentice-Hall.

Loth, W. (1998) 'Hallstein and de Gaulle: The Disastrous Confrontation', in Loth, Wallace and Wessels (1998), pp. 135–50.

Loth, W., Wallace, W. and Wessels, W. (eds) (1998) *Walter Hallstein: The Forgotten European?*. Basingstoke, Macmillan.

Louis, J-V. and Waelbroek, D. (eds) (1989) *La Commission au Coeur du Système Institutionnel des Communautés Européennes*. Brussels, Editions de l'Université de Bruxelles.

Ludlow, P. (1991) 'The European Commission', in Keohane, and Hoffman (1991), pp. 85–132.

McCormick, J. (1999) *Understanding the European Union: A Concise Introduction*. Basingstoke, Macmillan.

McCormick, J. (2000) *The Greening of the European Union*. Basingstoke, Macmillan.

McDonald, M. (1997) 'Identities in the European Commission', in Nugent (1997a), pp. 49–70.

McGowan, F. (1993) *The Struggle for Power in Europe: Competition and Regulation in the Electricity Industry*. London, Royal Institute of International Affairs.

McGowan, L. (1997) 'Safeguarding the Economic Constitution: The Commission and Competition Policy', in Nugent (1997a), pp. 145–66.

McGowan, L. and Wilks, S. (1995) 'The First Supranational Policy in the European Union: Competition Policy', *European Journal of Political Research*, vol. 28, no. 2, pp. 141–69.

Macleod, I., Hendry, I. D. and Hyett, S. (1996) *The External Relations of the European Communities*. Oxford, Clarendon Press.

MacMullen, A. (1996) 'Evaluating Integration Theory: The Appointment of European Commissioners', *Diplomacy and Statecraft*, vol. 7, no. 1, pp. 221–43.

MacMullen, A. (1997) 'European Commissioners 1952–1995: National Routes to a European Elite', in Nugent (1997a), pp. 27–48.

MacMullen, A. (1999) 'Political Responsibility for the Administration of Europe: The Commission's Resignation March 1999', *Parliamentary Affairs* vol. 52, no. 4, pp. 703–18.

Majone, G. (1989) *Evidence, Argument and Persuasion in the Policy Process*. New Haven, Yale University Press.

Majone, G. (1991) 'Cross-National Sources of Regulatory Policymaking in Europe and the United States', *Journal of Public Policy*, vol. 11, no. 1, pp. 79–106.

Majone, G. (1992) 'Regulatory Federalism in the European Community', *Environment and Planning C: Government and Policy*, vol. 10, no. 3, pp. 299–316.

Majone, G. (1994) 'The Rise of the Regulatory State in Europe', *West European Politics*, vol. 17, no. 3, pp. 77–101.

Majone, G. (1995) *The Development of Social Regulation in the European Community*. Florence, European University Institute.

Majone, G. (ed.) (1996a) *Regulating Europe*. London, Routledge.

Majone, G. (1996b) 'The European Commission as Regulator', in Majone (1996a), pp. 61–79.

Majone, G. (1997) 'The New European Agencies: Regulation by Information, *Journal of European Public Policy*, vol. 4, no. 2, pp. 262–75.

March, J. and Olsen, J. P. (1989) *Rediscovering Institutions: The Organizational Basis of Politics*. New York, Free Press.

Marjolin, R. (1989) *Memoirs 1911–1986: Architect of European Unity*. London, Weidenfeld & Nicolson.

Marks, G. (1992) 'Structural Policy in the European Community', in Sbragia (1992), pp. 191–224.

Marks, G. (1993) 'Structural Policy and Multilevel Governance in the EC', in Cafruny and Rosenthal (1993), pp. 391–410.

Marks, G. (1996) 'Decision Making in Cohesion Policy: Describing and Explaining Variation', in Hooghe (1996a).

Marks, G., Hooghe, L. and Blank, K. (1996) 'European Integration From the 1980s: State-Centric v. Multi-Level Governance', *Journal of Common Market Studies*, vol. 34, no. 3, pp. 341–78.

Martin, S. (ed.) (1994) *The Construction of Europe: Essays in Honour of Emile Noël*. Dordrecht, Kluwer Academic Publishers.

Matláry, J. H. (1993) 'Towards Understanding Integration: An Analysis of the Role of the State in EC Energy Policy 1985–1992', PhD thesis. Oslo, Faculty of Social Science, University of Oslo.

Matláry, J. H. (1997a) *Energy Policy in the European Union*. Basingstoke, Macmillan.

Matláry, J. H. (1997b) 'The Role of the Commission: A Theoretical Discussion', in Nugent (1997a), pp. 265–82.

Matláry, J. H. (1997c) 'New Bottles for New Wine', in Jørgensen (1997).

Mayne, R. (1970) *The Recovery of Europe: From Devastation to Unity*. London, Weidenfeld & Nicolson.

Mazey, S. (1992) 'Conception and Evolution of the High Authority's Administrative Services (1952–1956): From Supranational Principles to Multinational Practices', in Heyen (1992), pp. 31–47.

Mazey, S. (1995) 'The Development of EU Equality Policies: Bureaucratic Expansion on Behalf of Women?', *Public Administration*, vol. 73, no. 4, pp. 591–609.

Mazey. S (1998) 'The European Union and Women's Rights: From the Europeanization of National Agendas to the Nationalization of a European Agenda?, *Journal of European Public Policy*, vol. 5, no. 1, pp. 131–52.

Mazey, S. and Richardson, J. (eds) (1993a) *Lobbying in the European Community*. Oxford, Oxford University Press.

Mazey, S. and Richardson, J. (1993b) 'Conclusion: a European Policy Style?', in Mazey and Richardson (1993a), pp. 246–58.

Mazey, S. and Richardson, J. (1993c) 'EC Policy Making: An Emerging Policy Style?', in Liefferink and Lowe (1993), pp. 14–25.

Mazey, S. and Richardson, J. (1994) 'Policy Co-ordination in Brussels, Environmental and Regional Policy', *Regional Politics and Policy*, vol. 4, no. 1, pp. 22–44.

Mazey, S. and Richardson, J. (1995) 'Promiscuous Policymaking: The European Policy Style?', in Rhodes and Mazey (1995), pp. 337–59.

Mazey, S. and Richardson, J. (1996) 'La Commission Européenne: Une Bourse Pour les Idées et les Intérêts, *Revue Française de Science Politique*, vol. 46, no. 3, pp. 409–30.

Mazey, S. and Richardson, J. (1997) 'The Commission and the Lobby', in Edwards and Spence (1997b), pp. 178–212.

Mazey, S. and Richardson, J. (1999) 'Interests', in Cram, Dinan and Nugent (1999), pp. 105–29.

Mendrinou, M. (1992) 'European Community Fraud and Institutional Development', *The European Policy Research Unit*. Manchester, University of Manchester.

Mendrinou, M. (1996) 'Non-Compliance and the European Commission's Role in Integration', *Journal of European Public Policy*, vol. 3, no. 1, pp. 1–22.

Menon, A. (1999) 'Send the Most Stupid', *London Review of Books*, 9 December, pp. 14–15.

Mény, Y., Muller, P. and Quermonne, J. L. (1995) *Politiques Publiques en Europe*. Paris, L'Harmattan.

Merry, H. J. (1955) 'The European Coal and Steel Community – Operation of the High Authority', *The Western Political Quarterly*, vol. 8, no. 2, pp. 166–85.

Metcalfe, L. (1992) 'After 1992: Can the Commission Manage Europe?', *Australian Journal of Public Administration*, vol. 51, no. 1, pp. 117–30.

Metcalfe, L. (1994) 'International Policy Co-ordination and Public Management Reform', *International Review of Administrative Sciences*, vol. 60, pp. 271–90.

Metcalfe, L. (1996) 'Building Capacities for Integration: The Future Role of the Commission', *Eipascope*, no. 1996/2, pp. 2–8.

Meunier, S. and Nicolaidis, K. C. (1999) 'Who Speaks for Europe? The Delegation of Trade Authority in the EU', *Journal of Common Market Studies*, vol. 37, no. 3, pp. 477–501.

Michelmann, H. J. (1978) *Organisational Effectiveness in a Multinational Bureaucracy*. Farnborough, Saxon House.

Middlemas, K. (1995) *Orchestrating Europe: The Informal Politics of the European Union 1973–1995*. London, Fontana.

Milward, A. (1992) *The European Rescue of the Nation State*. London, Routledge.

Monnet, J. (1978) *Memoirs*. London, Collins.

Moravcsik, A. (1991) 'Negotiating the Single European Act: National Interests and Conventional Statecraft in the European Community', *International Organization*, vol. 45, no. 1, pp. 19–56.

Moravcsik, A. (1993) 'Preferences and Power in the European Community: A Liberal Intergovernmentalist Approach', *Journal of Common Market Studies*, vol. 31, no. 4, pp. 473–524.

Moravcsik, A. (1995) 'Liberal Intergovernmentalism and Integration: A Rejoinder', *Journal of Common Market Studies*, vol. 33, no. 4, pp. 611–28.

Moravcsik, A. (1998) *The Choice for Europe: Social Purpose and State Power From Messina to Maastricht*. Ithaca, NY, Cornell University Press.

Morgan, R. (1992) 'Jean Monnet and the ECSC Administration: Challenges, Functions and the Inheritance of Ideas', in Heyen (1992), pp. 1–9.

Narjes, K. H. (1988) 'Europe's Technological Challenge: A View From the European Commission', *Science and Public Policy*, vol. 15, no. 6, pp. 385–402.

Neale, P. (1994) 'Expert Interest Groups and the European Commission: Professional Influence on EC Legislation', *International Journal of Sociology and Social Policy*, vol. 14, nos. 6–7, pp. 1–24.

Nugent, N. (1995a) 'The Leadership Capacity of the European Commission', *Journal of European Public Policy*, vol. 2, no. 4, pp. 603–23.

Nugent, N. (ed.) (1995b) *The European Union 1994: Annual Review of Activities*. Oxford, Blackwell.

Nugent, N. (ed.) (1996) *The European Union 1995: Annual Review of Activities*. Oxford, Blackwell.

Nugent, N. (ed.) (1997a) *At the Heart of the Union: Studies of the European Commission*. Basingstoke, Macmillan.

Nugent, N. (ed.) (1997b) *The European Union. Volume 1: Perspectives and Theoretical Interpretations*. Aldershot, Dartmouth.

Nugent, N. (1997c) *The European Union 1996: Annual* Review *of Activities*. Oxford, Blackwell.

Nugent, N. (1999) *The Government and Politics of the European Union*, 4th edn. Basingstoke, Macmillan.

Nuttall, S. (1996) 'The Commission: The Struggle for Legitimacy?', in Hill (1996), pp. 130–47.

Nuttall, S. (1997) 'The Commission and Foreign Policy-Making', in Edwards and Spence (1997b), pp. 303–20.

Obradovic, D. (1996) 'Policy Legitimacy and the European Union', *Journal of Common Market Studies*, vol. 34, no. 2, pp. 191–221.

Official Journal of the European Communities (issued most working days). Luxembourg, Office for Official Publications of the European Communities.

Oreja, M. (1995) *Written Answers to the Institutional Affairs Committee of the European Parliament*. Brussels.

O'Toole, R. (1988) 'The Decision-making Process within the Commission of the European Communities in the Light of the Single European Act', *Irish Studies in International Affairs*, vol. 2, no. 4, pp. 65–76.

Paemen, H. And Bensch, A. (1995) *From the GATT to the WTO: The European Community in the Uruguay Round*. Leuven, Leuven University Press.

Pag, S. (1987) 'The Relations Between the Commission and National Bureaucracies', in Cassese (1987b), pp. 443–97.

Page, E. C. (1992) *Political Authority and Bureaucratic Power. A Comparative Analysis*, 2nd edn. Brighton, Harvester Wheatsheaf.

Page. E. C. (1997) *People Who Run Europe*. Oxford, Clarendon Press.

Page, E. C. and Wouters, L. (1994a) 'Bureaucratic Politics and Political Leadership in Brussels', *Public Administration*, vol. 72, Autumn, pp. 445–59.

Page, E. C. and Wouters, L. (1994b) 'Paying the Top People in Europe', in Hood and Peters (1994), pp. 201–14.

Page, E. C. and Wouters, L. (1995) 'The Europeanization of National Bureaucracies', in Pierre (1995).

Perrotti. A. L. (1999) *The Politics of EC Decision Making. The Case of State Aid to the Italian Public Sector Steel Industry* (*1988–1994*, D. Phil thesis) Oxford University.

Peters, B. G. (1992) 'Bureaucratic Politics and the Institutions of the European Community', in Sbragia (1992), pp. 75–122.

Peters, B. G. (1994a) 'Agenda-Setting in the European Community', *Journal of European Public Policy*, vol. 1, no. 1, pp. 9–26.

Peters, B. G. (1994b) *The Politics of Bureaucracy*, 4th edn. New York, Longman.

Peters, B. G. (1997) 'The Commission and Implementation in the European Union: Is There an Implementation Deficit and Why?', in Nugent (1997a), pp. 187–202.

Peterson, J. (1991) 'Technology Policy in Europe: Explaining the Framework Programme and Eureka in Theory and Practice', *Journal of Common Market Studies*, vol. 29, no. 3, pp. 269–90.

Peterson, J. (1992) 'The European Technology Community: Policy Networks in a Supranational Setting', in Marsh and Rhodes (1992), pp. 226–48.

Peterson, J. (1995a) 'EU Research Policy: The Politics of Expertise', in Rhodes and Mazey (1995), pp. 391–412.

Peterson, J. (1995b) 'Playing the Transparency Game: Policy-Making and Consultation in the European Commission', *Public Administration*, vol. 73, no. 3, pp. 473–92.

Peterson, J. (1995c) 'Decision-making in the European Union: Towards a Framework for Analysis', *Journal of European Public Policy*, vol. 2, no. 1, pp. 69–93.

Peterson, J. (1999a) 'The Santer Era: The European Commission in Normative, Historical and Theoretical Perpective', *Journal of European Public Policy*, vol. 6, no. 1, pp. 46–65.

Peterson, J. (1999b) 'Jacques Santer: The EU's Gorbachev', *European Community Studies Association Newsletter*, vol. 12, no. 4, pp. 4–6.

Peterson, J. and Bomberg, E. (1999) *Decision-Making in the European Union*. Basingstoke, Macmillan.

Peterson, J. and Sharp, M. (1998) *Technology Policy in the European Union*. Basingstoke, Macmillan.

Piene, H. C. (1996) *The Establishment of the European Commission: The Building of Administrative Structures Within an Organisation of Political Leadership*, PhD thesis. University of Edinburgh.

Pollack, M. (1994) 'Creeping Competence: The Expanding Agenda of the European Community', *Journal of Public Policy*, vol. 14, no. 2, pp. 95–145.

Pollack, M. (1995) 'Regional Actors in an Intergovernmental Play: The Making and Implementation of EC Structural Policy', in Rhodes and Mazey (1995), pp. 361–90.

Pollack, M. (1996) 'The New Institutionalism and EU Governance: The Promise and Limits of Institutional Analysis', *Governance*, vol. 9, pp. 429–58.

Pollack, M. (1997a) 'The Commission as an Agent', in Nugent (1997a), pp. 109–28.

Pollack, M. (1997b) Delegation, Agency and Agenda Setting in the European Community', *International Organization*, vol. 51, no. 1, pp. 99–134.

Pollack, M. (1999) 'The Engines of Integration? Supranational Autonomy and Influence in the European Union', in Sandholtz and Stone Sweet (1998), pp. 217–49.

Prodi, R (1999a) *Speech to the European Parliament* (4 May) < http:// europa.eu. int/comm/commissioners/prodi/speeches/040599_en.htm > .

Prodi, R. (1999b) *Intervention of Mr. Prodi – Cologne European Council* (3 June) < http:/europa.eu.int/comm/commissioners/prodi/speeches/ 030699_en.htm > .

Prodi, R. (1999c) *Speech by Romano Prodi, President-designate of the European Commission, to the European Parliament, 14 September 1999* < http:/europa.eu.int/comm/commissioners/prodi/speeches/designate/ 140999_en.htm > .

Prodi, R. (2000) *Speech on Changes in Senior Staff of the Commission* (3 May) < http://europa.eu.int/rapid/start/cgi > .

Rhodes, C. and Mazey, S. (1995) *The State of the European Union. Vol 3: Building a European Polity*. Harlow, Longman.

Rhodes, R. A. W., Bache, I. and George, S. (1996) 'Policy Networks and Policy-Making in the European Union: A Critical Appraisal', in Hooghe (1996a), pp. 367–87.

Richardson, J. (ed.) (1996) *European Union: Power and Policy Making*. London, Routledge.

Risse-Kappen, T. (1996) 'Exploring the Nature of the Beast: International Relations Theory and Comparative Policy Analysis Meet the European Union', *Journal of Common Market Studies*, vol. 34, no. 1, pp. 53–80.

Ritchie, E. (1992) 'The Model of the French Ministerial *Cabinet* in the Early European Commission', in Heyen (1992), pp. 95–106.

Rometsch, D. and Wessels, W. (1997) 'The Commission and the Council of the Union', in Edwards and Spence (1997b), pp. 213–38.

Ross, G. (1993) 'Sidling into Industrial Policy: Inside the European Commission', *French Politics and Society*, vol. 11, no. 1, pp. 20–43.

Ross, G. (1994) 'Inside the Delors Cabinet', *Journal of Common Market Studies*, vol. 32, no. 4, pp. 499–523.

Ross, G. (1995) *Jacques Delors and European Integration*. Oxford, Polity Press.

Ruimschotel, D. (1994) 'The EC Budget: Ten Per Cent Fraud? A Policy Analysis Approach', *Journal of Common Market Studies*, vol. 32, no. 3, pp. 319–42.

Salmon, T. and Nicoll, W. (1997) *Building European Union: A Documentary History and Analysis*. Manchester, Manchester University Press.

Sandholtz, W. (1992a) 'ESPRIT and the Politics of International Collective Action', *Journal of Common Market Studies*, vol. 30, no. 1, pp. 1–21.

Sandholtz, W. (1992b) *High-Tech Europe: The Politics of International Cooperation*. Berkeley, University of California Press.

Sandholtz, W. (1993a) 'Institutions and Collective Action: The New Telecommunications in Western Europe', *World Politics*, vol. 45, no. 2, pp. 242–70.

Sandholtz, W. (1993b) 'Choosing Union: Monetary Politics and Maastricht', *International Organization*, vol. 47, no. 1, pp. 1–39.

Sandholtz, W. and Stone Sweet, A. (1998) *European Integration and Supranational Governance*. Oxford, Oxford University Press.

Sandholtz, W. and Zysman, J. (1989) '1992: Recasting the European Bargain', *World Politics*, vol. 42, no. 1, pp. 95–128.

Santer, J. (1995a) *Speech by President Santer to the European Parliament* (17 January), *Europa* website page on key speeches by the Commission President < http://europa.eu.int/en/comm/js/ep-f.html/ >.

Santer, J. (1995b) 'The Future of Europe and the Commission's Role – In Praise of the Community Method', Eighteenth Jean Monnet Lecture. Florence, European University Institute.

Sbragia, A. (ed.) (1992) *Euro-Politics: Institutions and Policymaking in the 'New' European Community*. Washington, DC, Brookings Institution.

Sbragia, A. (1993) 'The European Community: A Balancing Act', *Publius*, vol. 23, Summer, pp. 23–38.

Scharpf, F. W. (1988) 'The Joint-Decision Trap: Lessons from German Federalism and European Integration', *Public Administration*, vol. 66, Autumn, pp. 239–78.

Scharpf, F. W. (1994) 'Community and Autonomy: Multi-Level Policy-Making in the European Union', *Journal of European Public Policy*, vol. 1, no. 2, pp. 219–42.

Scheinman, L. (1966) 'Some Preliminary Notes on Bureaucratic Relationships in the European Community', *International Organisation*, vol. 20.

Schmidt, S. K. (1997a) 'Sterile Debate and Dubious Generalisations; European Integration Theory Tested by Telecommunications and Electricity', *Journal of Public Policy*, vol. 16, no. 3, pp. 233–71.

Schmidt, S. K. (1997b) 'Behind the Council's Agenda: The Commission's Impact on Decisions', *MPIfG Discussion Paper*, 97/4 < http://eiop.or.at/erpa/mpi.htm >.

Schmidt, S. K. (1998) 'Commission Activism: Subsuming Telecommunications and Electricity under European Competition Law', *Journal of European Public Policy*, vol. 5, no. 2, pp. 169–84.

Schmidt, S. K. (2000) 'Only an Agenda Setter? The European Commission's Power Over the Council of Ministers', *European Union Politics*, vol. 1, no. 1, pp. 37– 61.

Schneider, G. (1997) 'Choosing Chameleons: National Interests and the Logic of Coalition Building in the Commission of the European Union', paper prepared for the 5th Biennial Conference of the European Community Studies Association. Seattle (28 May–1 June).

Schneider, V., Dang-Nguyen, G. and Werle, R. (1994) 'Corporate Actor Networks in European Policy-Making: Harmonizing Telecommunications Policy', *Journal of Common Market Studies*, vol. 32, no. 4, pp. 473–98.

Session News: The Week (one issue per month). Brussels, European Parliament Directorate for Press and Audiovisual Services.

Shackleton, M. (1998) 'The European Parliament's New Committees of Enquiry: Tiger or Paper Tiger?', *Journal of Common Market Studies*, vol. 36, no. 1, pp. 115–30.

Shaffer, M. R. (1997) 'The Commission's Role in Moulding the Europe Agreements: Can Liberal Intergovernmentalism Capture it?', paper presented to the Fifth Biennial Conference of the European Community Studies Association. Seattle (29 May–1 June).

Shaw, J. (1995a) 'Legal Developments', in Nugent (1995b), pp. 87–102.

Shaw, J, (1995b) 'The Birth, Life and Death of a Proposal: The Ill-fated Services Draft', paper prepared for the Research Conference of the University Association for Contemporary European Studies. Birmingham (18–19 September).

Shaw, J. (1996) 'Legal Developments', in Nugent (1996), pp. 85–101.

Shore, C. (2000a) 'Rethinking European Institutions: Integration Theory and the Organisational Culture of the European Commission', paper presented to the Research Conference of the University Association for Contemporary European Studies. Budapest (6–8 April).

Shore, C. (2000b) *Building Europe: The Cultural Politics of European Integration*. London, Routledge.

Siedentopf, H. and Ziller, J. (eds) (1988) *Making European Policies Work: The Implementation of Community Legislation in the Member States*, 2 vols. London, Sage.

Smith, A. (1995) 'La Commission, le Territoire et l'Innovation: La Mise en Place du Programme Leader', in Mény, Muller and Quermonne (1995), pp. 305–18.

Smith, A. (1996) 'La Commission Européenne et les Funds Stucturels: Vers Un Nouveau Modèle d'Action', *Revue Française de Science Politique*, vol. 46, no. 3, pp. 474–95.

Smith, M. (1996) 'The EU as an International Actor', in Richardson (1996), pp. 247–62.

Smith, M. (1997) 'The Commission and External Relations', in Edwards and Spence (1997b), pp. 264–302.

Smith, M. P. (1996) 'Integration in Small Steps: the European Commission and Member- State Aid to Industry', *West European Politics*, vol. 19, no. 3, pp. 563–82.

Smith, M. P. (1997a) 'The Commission Made Me Do It: The European Commission as a Strategic Asset in Domestic Politics', in Nugent (1997a), pp. 167–86.

Smith, M. P. (1997b) 'Evening the Playing Field: Institution-Building and the Development of the European Commission's State Aids Policy', unpublished paper.

Smith, M. P. (1998) 'Autonomy by the Rules: The European Commission and the Development of State Aid Policy', *Journal of Common Market Studies*, vol. 36, no. 1, pp. 55–78.

Smyrl, M. (1998) 'When (and How) Do the Commission's Preferences Matter?', *Journal of Common Market Studies*, vol. 36, no. 1, pp. 79–99.

Snyder, F. (ed.) (1992) *European Law in Context: A Reader*. London, Dartmouth.

Snyder, F. (1994) 'Soft Law and Institutional Practice in the European Community', in Martin (1994), pp. 197–225.

Spence, D. (1997a) 'Staff and Personnel Policy in the Commission', in Edwards and Spence (1997b), pp. 68–100.

Spence, D. (1997b) 'Structure, Functions and Procedures in the Commission', in Edwards and Spence (1997b), pp. 103–24.

Spence, D. (2000) 'Plus ça Change, Plus c'est la Même Chose? Attempting to Reform the European Commission', *Journal of European Public Policy*. vol. 7, no. 1, pp. 1–25.

Spierenburg, D. (1979) *Proposals for the Reform of the Commission of the European Communities and Its Services*. Brussels, European Commission.

Spierenburg, D. and Poidevin, R. (1994) *The History of the High Authority of the Coal and Steel Community: Supranationality in Operation*. London, Weidenfeld & Nicolson.

Spinelli, A. (1996) *The Eurocrats: Conflict and Crisis in the European Community*. Baltimore, Johns Hopkins Press.

Stevens, A. (2000) Brussels Bureaucrats: *The Administration of the European Union*. Basingstoke, Macmillan.

Stevens, A. and Stevens, H. (1997) 'Le Non-Management de L'Europe', *Review Politiques et Management Public*, vol. 15, no. 1, pp. 33–52.

Stevens, H. and Maor, M. (1996) *Recruitment and Training in the European Commission*, report issued in the series entitled *Converging Administrative Systems*. London, The European Institute, London School of Economics.

Stone Sweet, A. and Sandholtz, W. (1997) 'European Integration and Supranational Governance', *Journal of European Public Policy*, vol. 4, no. 3, pp. 297–317.

Taylor, P. (1991) 'The European Community and the State: Assumptions, Theories and Propositions', *Review of International Studies*, vol. 17, no. 2, pp. 109–25.

Thelen, K. and Steinmo, S. (eds) (1992a) *Structuring Politics: Historical Institutionalism in Comparative Analysis*. Cambridge, Cambridge University Press.

Thelen, K. and Steinmo, S. (eds) (1992b) 'Historical Institutionalism in Comparative Politics', in Thelen and Steinmo, (1992a), pp. 1–32.

The Week in Europe. London, European Commission (weekly newsletter).

Tindemans, L. (1976) *European Union: Report by Mr. Leo Tindemans to the European Council*, Bulletin of the European Communities, Supplement 2/76.

Tomkins, A. (1999) 'Responsibility and Resignation in the European Commission', *The Modern Law Review* (September), pp. 744–65.

Treaties Establishing the European Communities (1978). Luxembourg, Office for Official Publications of the European Communities.

Treaty Establishing the European Community: Consolidated Version (1997) in *Official Journal of the European Communities*, C340 (10 November), Brussels. Also in *European Union Consolidated Treaties*, (1997). Luxembourg, Office for Official Publications of the European Communities.

Treaty of Amsterdam (1997) in *Official Journal of the European Communities*, C340 (10 November).

Treaty on European Union, Together With the Complete Text of the Treaty Establishing the European Community, (1992) in *Official Journal of the European Communities*, C244 (31 August).

Treaty on European Union: Consolidated Version (1997) in *Official Journal of the European Communities*, C340 (10 November), Brussels. Also in *European Union Consolidated Treaties* (1997). Luxembourg, Office for Official Publications of the European Communities.

Tugendhat, C. (1987) *Making Sense of Europe*. Harmondsworth, Penguin.

Tutt, N. (1989) *Europe on the Fiddle: The Common Market Scandal*. London, Helm.

Uçarer, E. (1999a) 'From the Sidelines to Center Stage? The Commission in Post-Amsterdam Justice and Home Affairs', paper prepared for the 6th International Conference of the European Community Studies Association. Pittsburgh (2–5 June).

Uçarer, E. (1999b) 'Cooperation on Justice and Home Affairs Matters', in Cram, Dinan and Nugent (1999), pp. 247–65.

Urwin, D. W. (1995) *The Community of Europe: A History of European Integration Since 1945*, 2nd edn. Harlow, Longman.

Usher, J. (1997) 'The Commission and the Law', in Edwards and Spence (1997b), pp. 155–77.

Vahl, R. (1992/3) 'The European Commission on the Road to European Union: The Consequences of the Treaty on European Union for the Commission's Power Base', *Acta Politica*, vol. 27, no. 3, pp. 297–322.

Vahl, R. (1997) *Leadership in Disguise: The Role of the European Commission in EC Decision-Making on Agriculture in the Uruguay Round.* Aldershot, Ashgate.

van Rijn, T. (1994) 'The Investigative and Supervisory Powers of the Commission', in Curtin and Heukeb (1994), pp. 409–21.

van Schelendelen, M. P. C. M. (ed.) (1998) *EU Committees as Influential Policymakers.* Aldershot, Ashgate.

Vibert, F. (1995) 'What Future for the European Commission?'. Brussels, Philip Morris Institute.

Wallace, H. and Wallace, W. (eds) (1996) *Policy-Making in the European Union.* Oxford, Oxford University Press.

Wallace, H. and Young, A. R. (1997) *Participation and Policy Making in the European Union.* Oxford, Clarendon Press.

Webber, D. (1998) 'High Midnight in Brussels, An Analysis of the September 1993 Council Meeting on the Uruguay Round', *Journal of European Public Policy*, vol. 5, no. 4, pp. 578–94.

Weizsäcker, R. von, Dehaene, J.-L. and Simon, D. (1999) *The Institutional Implications of Enlargement: Report to the European Commission.* Brussels, European Commission.

Wendon, B. (1998) 'The Commission as Image-Venue Entrepreneur in EU Social Policy', *Journal of European Public Policy*, vol. 5, no. 2, pp. 339–53.

Wessels, W. (1985) 'Community Bureaucracy in a Changing Environment: Criticisms, Trends, Questions', in Jamar and Wessels (1985).

Wessels, W. (1998) 'Comitology: Fusion in Action. Politico–Administrative Trends in the EU System', *Journal of European Public Policy*, vol. 5, no. 2, pp. 209–34.

Westlake, M (1994) *The Commission and the Parliament: Partners and Rivals in the European Policy-Making Process.* London, Butterworths.

Westlake, M. (1997a) 'The Commission and the Parliament', in Edwards and D. Spence (1997b), pp. 239–63.

Westlake, M. (1999b) 'Keynote Article: Mad Cows and Englishmen – The Institutional Consequences of the BSE Crisis', in Nugent (1997c), pp. 11–36.

Westlake, M. (1999) *The Council of the European Union*, 2nd edn. London, Cartermill.

Wilks, S. (1992) 'The Metamorphosis of European Competition Policy', in Snyder (1992).

Wilks, S. and McGowan, L. (1995) 'Disarming the Commission: The Debate Over a European Cartel Office', *Journal of Common Market Studies*, vol. 32, no. 2, pp. 259–73.

Williamson, D. (1995) unpublished lecture, delivered to the Twenty-Fifth Anniversary Conference of the *Journal of Common Market Studies*. Edinburgh, University of Edinburgh.

Wincott, D. (1995) 'Institutional Interaction and European Integration: Towards an Everyday Critique of Liberal Intergovernmentalism', *Journal of Common Market Studies*, vol. 33, no. 4, pp. 597–609.

Zito, A. R. (1995) 'Integrating the Environment into the European Union: The History of the Controversial Carbon Tax', in Rhodes, and Mazey, (1995), pp. 431–48.

Zito, A. R. (1999) *Creating Environmental Policy in the European Union*. Basingstoke, Macmillan.

Index